Boomer Days

Also by Gus Russo

Live By the Sword

The Outfit

Gangsters and GoodFellas (w/ Henry Hill)

Supermob

Brothers in Arms (w/ Stephen Molton)

Boomer Days

Gus Russo

Excelsior!
New York Clapper Gap Bivalve Cut N' Shoot Bucksnort

Copyright ©2011 by Gus Russo

To contact the author for interviews, interior decorating advice, or to put him in your will, email: boomerdays@verizon.net

ISBN-13: 978-1461031512

ISBN-10: 1461031516

First U.S. Edition 2011

Contents

	Introduction	i
1.	Happy Days	1
2.	Spreading Wings	18
3.	The End of the Innocence	39
4.	"Something's Happenin' Here"	55
5.	The Real World	72
6.	Henryville	86
7.	Blue Water, Pt. 1	100
8.	333	134
9.	Hot Shots and Sweet Spots	156
10.	A Banner Year	182
11.	A Magical Time in a Magical Place	198
12.	Blue Water, Pt. 2	226
13.	Manhattan Madness	248
14.	Basket Cases	268
15.	This is Your Brain on the Eighties	278
16.	Adventures in Paradise	294
17.	Brain Damage	305
18.	Beginnings and Endings	328
	Epilogue	340
	Acknowledgements	342
	About the Author	344

Introduction

"You begin to meet people who are in the field of your bliss and they open the doors for you. I say follow your bliss and don't be afraid and doors will open where you didn't know they were going to be."
—Joseph Campbell, 1904-1987

ALTHOUGH CAMPBELL'S INSIGHT didn't surface until the posthumous publication of his book *The Power of Myth* (1988), the spirit of bliss-seeking has been alive throughout history, reborn in the youth culture of the late 1950s, when the World War II baby boomers first started surveying the world they had inherited.[1] The concept had been around for a millennia – Indian Sanskrit, the classical language of Hinduism and Buddhism, taught that bliss represented the brink, the jumping-off place into the ocean of transcendence. In Campbell's interpretation, it isn't merely a matter of doing whatever you like; it instead represents identifying that pursuit which you are truly passionate about and attempting to give yourself absolutely to it. In so doing, you will find your fullest potential and serve your community to the greatest possible extent. Freed from the hardships of our early 20th century predecessors, we children of the fifties (at least Caucasian children) were handed the world on a silver platter.

I was one of many Boomers that heeded the call of dreamers such as Siddhartha and Campbell, and though most of us ultimately succumbed to a more conventional and practical existence, a small minority remained hopelessly trapped by the idea that we would be here only once, so why conform? We reveled not only in personal freedom, but also in the ways that freedom could be channeled to understand our world and improve it. Hippies and Peace Corps volunteers alike shared this common credo.

---

[1] The term "Baby Boom" entered the lexicon in 1960 with the publication of Landon Y. Jones' *Great Expectations: America and the Baby Boom Generation*. During the pre-War decade, the US birthrate was below 1.9%, rising to above 2.5% in the 1950s. By the end of the forties, about 32 million babies had been born, compared with 24 million in the 30s. In 1954, annual births topped four million for the first time and did not drop below that figure until 1965, when four out of ten Americans were under the age of twenty. A simultaneous boom was experienced by many nations that had been engaged in World War Two. The American birthrate fell to a record low of 1.4% in the mid-1970s. Since then it has fluctuated from a level just above 1.5%.

"The unexamined life is not worth living."
—Socrates, 469 BC – 399 BC

I was born in 1949, when the average American male's waist measured 34 inches, a typical US home could be bought for $10,000, and a gallon of gas set one back a staggering twenty-five cents, or just over half the hourly minimum wage. The year would later be perceived as pivotal, with *New York* magazine devoting an entire issue to it 25 years later, calling it "A Year of Great Expectations."

On August 30, the day I was born, the Cold War began. I assume that the genesis of the US-USSR brinksmanship had less to do with the coincidence of my appearance on the scene than with the previous day's detonation of the first Soviet nuke. But who really knows? The contemporary American airwaves were filled with the wonderful analog sounds of Frankie Laine, Perry Como, and Freddy Martin. My parents and their pals spent steamy Baltimore summer nights in air-conditioned theaters that unspooled films such as *Mighty Joe Young* and *All the King's Men*. Although this last of the "postwar years" was a time of astounding conformity in America, seeds were being sown far and wide for a cultural revolution soon to come and shake everything up in ways that made the next era, in my opinion, the best time — including future eras — to be alive in the United States. It was a momentary oasis in a history that was preceded by upheaval and followed by self-inflicted entropy. Obviously, I feel fortunate to have been born when I was.

As I was taking my first breaths in Baltimore's Mercy Hospital, my generation's elders were already well on the road to fulfilling their destiny, their lives soon to play large in my own future, and those of millions of others: eight-year-old John Winston Lennon, abandoned by both parents, was being raised by his aunt in working class Liverpool while gravitating to the great solace provided by American R&B music; his future bandmate, James Paul McCartney, was then a seven-year-old growing up in a loving Liverpool family that surrounded him with the great musical standards; in Hawthorne, California, Brian Douglas Wilson, just two days younger than McCartney, was escaping an abusive father, holing up in his room endlessly listening to Gershwin's *Rhapsody in Blue*, while trying to break down its complexities on his Wurlitzer organ; Elvis Aaron Presley, a fourteen-year-old attending Memphis' Humes High School was receiving his first guitar lessons from Jesse Lee Denson, a slightly older family friend; Lee Harvey Oswald, a hollow-eyed ten-year-old, was attending Ft. Worth's Ridglee

West Elementary School (his fifth school in six years), the fatherless victim of the clinically disturbed mother who was raising him – like Wilson and Lennon, he retreated to his room, but regrettably turned to violent political revolution instead of musical revolution for relief from his God-awful plight.

For budding future musicians such as myself, the period was significant for having a continued reverence for melody, harmony, and overall musicianship (if a tad over-amplified). It would be the last time American youth valued such concepts; future generations would become so enamored of celebrity and video representations that actual musical skills were relegated to afterthoughts — a sad end to the rich American Songbook.

Boomers linked by the 1949 birth date included countless other soon-to-be-musicians who, like me, became forever altered by the same characters and events, among them: Bruce Springsteen, Tom Waits, Alan White & Rick Wakeman, Hank Williams, Jr., David Foster, Lindsey Buckingham, Bonnie Raitt, Leon Redbone, Trevor Horn, Daryl Hall, Paul Shaffer, Gene Simmons, Mark Knopfler, Patti Lupone, Nick Lowe, and Billy Joel. Writers included Christopher Hitchens, Martin Amis, Scott Turow, and Ira Flatow. Media moguls Les Moonves, Graydon Carter, Tommy Mottola, Jon Avnet, and Bill O'Reilly all took their first breaths in 1949. Among the thespians making their debuts were Shelly Long, John Belushi, Tom Berenger, Jeff Bridges, Teri Garr, Richard Gere, Jessica Lange, Dave Thomas, Meryl Streep, Whoopi Goldberg, Don Johnson, Andy Kaufman, and (ahem) Linda Lovelace.

My first memories were of being the constant center of attention — as the first-born child after much trying, my parents doted in the extreme. Perhaps this is what gave me the overconfidence that allowed me to take the unconventional path I would choose. And after six decades living it, I have been persuaded that it's time for me to follow Socrates' dictate and examine my own time on the planet. So, here goes. Enjoy the ride.

*   *   *

Chapter One

Happy Days

"It was the best of times— period."

EVERYONE KNOWS THE FEELING. It's 4 a.m., you're dead asleep — way past REM — and cherishing the most lucid dream imaginable. You know the type, the one so vivid that it flirts impossibly close with reality. That's where I was one morning in October 1992, and although I can only guess, it's a good chance that I was having my reoccurring dream of being Elvis Presley, strumming and singing out in front of my grass shack on the beach at Hanauma Bay, while an enthralled gaggle of Hawaiian beauties gushed. (It was a dream I had actually lived — sort of — for a few years in the eighties, but more about that later).

Perhaps I was focusing in on one particular tanned *wahine* who was approaching me with a Plumeria scented lei when it happened.

R-R-R-R-I-I-I-N-N-N-G-G-G-!!!!!!!!!!!

I jumped up to the stark and sad realization that I was not in Honolulu, but in fact in the dark basement of my mother's home in Maryland, where I was temporarily crashing while looking for an apartment and conducting almost non-stop investigative research trips for my new network gig. I had just relocated after sixteen years playing music in upstate New York and Hawaii.

I answered the blaring real-life phone lying on the floor beside my real-life cot as I kicked the imaginary sand from my feet.

"Yeah."

"Gus, is that you?"

"Yeah."

"It's Oliver."

That cleared up the mystery, since I knew only one "Oliver." As that realization sank in, my mother pounded on the door to the basement — she was also aroused from sleep by the phone call from someone she was certain was a dying relative. My mother is a hard-loving Italian woman, who, because of some childhood trauma unknown to me, lives in a constant state of worry— no exaggeration. Some see the glass half full, others half empty— my mom only worries about who will spill it onto the carpet.

"Gus, what's wrong? Is somebody hurt?" she cried out from the top of the stairs.

"No, mom, it's just Oliver Stone."

"Oh, OK," she said as she trundled back up to her bedroom two floors up.

Now one might think that an unworldly, widowed 66-year-old would be just a tad startled to learn that a multiple Academy Award winning director was calling her son at 4 a.m., but during the time that I crashed at her home, she had actually gotten used to taking messages from my eclectic, and usually eccentric, coterie: "Someone named Rachel Porter called — who's she?" (Lee Oswald's daughter); "You have a message here from Vitas" (That would be tennis whiz and dear friend, Vitas Gerulaitis); "Who is this Madeleine Brown who called today?" (LBJ's mistress); "Someone called from Washington, said you wrote him a letter? His name is Ted — I hope I spelled this right — S-h-a-c-k-l-e-y. Who's he?"

"Just a guy I went to high school with, mom." OK, so I lied, but there was no reason to worry her any more than normal by telling her that Ted Shackley was the senior CIA executive most feared by the Left, viewed as the Devil incarnate, and the man who oversaw Operation Phoenix in Vietnam, a "pacification" program that generated thousands of assassinations. Some even believed he was behind the JFK hit in Dallas.

I had been a consultant to Stone during the making of his paranoid fever dream *JFK*, a masterpiece for its craftsmanship and deft use of quasi-political pedagogy. But that gig had ended over a year before, so this call was quite out of the blue — or should I say *Blue Hawaii*? — and I was surprised to hear from him, to say the least.

"Jesus, Oliver, do you know what time it is?" I asked him.

"I don't know. I'm just getting ready to go to lunch."

"Where the Hell are you?"

"Berlin. Why? Oh, Christ, I'm sorry— you're on the East Coast, aren't you?"

Duh. Yeah, Oliver. Stone's absent-mindedness was nothing new. During the time I spent around him in Dallas, LA, and Washington, I came to be familiar with his near genius, near lunatic mental idiosyncrasies; I think that virtually every day I encountered him he appeared as a bleary-eyed madman, seemingly going up or coming down from some of the most exotic hallucinogens known to ancient Mexican shamanism. But he was functional enough to remain one of the most powerful, and talented, filmmakers in history.

"Look, Gus, I'm going to be interviewed today by Dan Rather about this new JAMA article," Stone explained. "I haven't had time to read it and I want you to give me the headlines."

"The good news is that I read it, but the bad news is I'm still asleep," I mumbled.

"Let me get some coffee and call me back in half an hour."

Stone agreed. He had been referring to a recent article in the *Journal of the American Medical Association* (JAMA) that focused on the first in-depth interviews with JFK's autopsists, interviews that completely undercut Stone's conspiracy theory. Unbeknownst to Stone was the fact that for the last eight months I had been living out of a suitcase, criss-crossing the country for PBS's *Frontline* series. Executive Producer Mike Sullivan had been quietly funding research by myself and *Frontline* veteran reporter and Emmy-winner, W. Scott Malone, aiming at creating a massive three-hour special report on the Kennedy assassination to coincide with the 30th anniversary of the crime in November 1993.* Malone and I were in the enviable position of running down every conspiracy theory we thought was worth the effort, racking up massive frequent flier miles in the process.

(L to R) Lydia Sanchez, Oliver Stone, yours truly

Also unknown to Stone was that just the day before, I had been called by an old pal for whom I occasionally consulted at CBS, Steve Glauber, who just happened to be Rather's producer. Glauber, not knowing of my relationship with Stone, had wanted to know what questions Rather should put to *him*!

Thus, when Stone called back at 4:30, I told him what questions he was likely to hear from Rather. When the CBS Evening

---

* I had proposed the idea to Mike over a year earlier through the intercession of my pal Malone. During our preliminary research trips that encompassed a year of non-stop travel, we ran down some of the most explosive conspiracy theories extant.

News aired that night, I watched as Oliver and Dan, both briefed by me, played to a draw. Neither knew I had rehearsed the other. Stone received kudos for his performance, as I am sure Rather did as well.

That's when it hit me that this was just another in a seemingly endless line of Zelig-like moments in my life.[†] After endless prodding from my friends, I gave in to their demands that I chronicle these events, hence the book you now hold. If you enjoy reading it half as much as I did living it, then I enjoyed it twice as much as you – or something like that.

With that — drum roll — welcome to my idiosyncratic path.

* * *

It was before the Electronic Era and its mixed dubious blessings: a time without cell phones, iPhones, iPods, Twitter, Facebook, Myspace, internet, email, cable TV, eBooks, Blackberrys, texting, video games, synthesizers, GPS's, DVDs, CDs, DVRs, Guitar Hero, online pornography, terrorists, accepted mass theft of recorded music, camcorders, Craigslist rapists, credit cards, air conditioning, photocopiers, gangsta rap, or even personal computers — you know, the time before digital heroin rendered most Homo sapiens overweight, nearsighted, partially deaf, and certifiably brain dead.

But if you lived in middle class white America in the 1950s, here's what you *did* have: family dinners, robust little leagues in every neighborhood, music lessons, libraries filled with actual book lovers (and actual books), budding musicians, writers and artists, pick-up baseball games, time to relax and just ponder, homework, civil conversations in English, adventures every time you went "out to play," daily two-mile walks home from school with your pals after you turned twelve, teachers who were allowed to teach, babies with fathers who actually raised them, three or more thriving newspapers in every major city, clean rivers in which to swim, unclogged highways, and monster movies at a voluminous Art Deco movie palace every Saturday afternoon with your gang — oh, did I forget Frank Sinatra and Dean Martin?

Of course, there was one electronic device we did possess: a 15-inch black-and-white television set, which had to have its rabbit ears,

---

[†] In Yiddish, Zelig means "blessed," and so the comparison is apt if only because I know I have had a blessed life.

fine tuner, and horizontal/vertical controls re-adjusted every time someone breathed. This nuisance actually rendered watching the boob tube an aerobic exercise. Understandably, we kids found this far less interesting than the world outside our doors, the exceptions being The Steve Allen Show, any Marx Brothers movie, and local The Buddy Deane Dance Show.‡

Just writing the words overcomes me with nostalgia. Naturally, the memories of my childhood are, like those of most humans, mostly just a blur of images — some hazy-good, some hazy-bad, but a few virtually burnt into the cortex. For me, the most hardened memories are the ones of large Italian multi-family repasts every Sunday afternoon. That's right: *every* Sunday. My parents and their brothers and sisters took turns hosting these carbohydrate and tomato sauce-fueled feasts, which I later realized was the only form of entertainment these first generation Americans could afford. Imagine "My Big Fat Greek Wedding" playing out every Sunday with Cannoli instead of Baklava.

Me at five-years old.

*   *   *

---

‡ Immortalized as the "Corney Collins Show" in John Waters' 1988 film *Hairspray*. Buddy's show was Baltimore's American Bandstand, and he brought many top performers to his small studio at WJZ TV. It was thanks to Buddy that I fell in love with the music of Motown, Stax, and James Brown, who was a regular guest.

Of course, our parents and their siblings were simply making do, but something tells me now that they knew all along that these bashes, usually attended by fifteen to twenty, were more joyful and more valuable in the ways that count than all the country club wine tastings and Hawaiian sunsets they would never see. If nothing else, we grew up knowing all our cousins as if they were our brothers and sisters, giving us a powerful extended support system. The only extravagance we knew was our yearly family week in Atlantic City. In mid July our nuclear family of four piled into one car, and my mother's parents, with whom we lived for a time, in another for the four-hour drive on US Rt. 40 to its eastern terminus at the Jersey Shore. Although "AC" attracted many sub-types of middle-class whites, Italian-

Americans like the Russos were particularly drawn, especially those from Baltimore. A large area of the seaside city, "Ducktown," or Little Italy, was developed by duck-catching Sicilian immigrants who erected a statue of Christopher Columbus on Baltic Avenue to greet new arrivals. Additionally, the connection to Baltimore stems from Atlantic City's determination to mimic Baltimore's post-World War II revitalization by tearing down huge swaths of blighted buildings to give the city a cleaner, more open entrance. But just as with Baltimore, the forced relocation of thousands of underprivileged residents would come back to haunt the city. But that was years away. For a brief window in time, "AC" was the white middle class place to be.

After checking in at the Shoreham Hotel (later swallowed up by the Trump Taj Mahal Casino), one block from the famous Steel Pier, "the showplace of America," we'd pick up fresh Turkish Taffee on the way to the Boardwalk and beach.

Late afternoons were spent on the Pier, where The Jim Crane Steel Pier Dance Show, The Ed Hurst Show, Tony Grant's Stars of Tomorrow,[§] or Dick Clark took turns holding court in the Golden Dome Ballroom. There were three movie theaters, countless carney-type attractions, and the unspeakably cruel Diving Horse Show, where beautiful, but terrified, horses were forced to jump 50 feet into a small Atlantic ocean pool below, four times a day, seven days a week. In actuality, they were the *falling* horses; after being ridden up to the release gate, the hinged floor fell out from under them, forcing them to jump. So violent was the impact that one of the young female riders who rode the horse down opened her eyes at the moment of impact and was completely, permanently, blinded.

In the evenings, my grandparents babysat us while our parents walked down the boardwalk to "The Five," Skinny D'Amato's mob-friendly "500 Club" (now the Trump Plaza) on Missouri Ave. The club was the home away from home for Sinatra, Martin & Lewis, Louis Prima, and Sammy Davis, Jr. It was just another example of my family's economy: if you could only afford one nightclub outing a year, make  certain that the talent was so strong that it would satiate until your next trip to Atlantic City.

But I was drawn like a magnet to the sounds emanating from the pier's Marine Ballroom, where the concerts were held. The Golden Dome dance shows, with lip-syncing pop stars, were OK, but it was the live music that transported me. It was here, presented against a huge velvet curtain and jammed in with three to five thousand others, that I saw my first professional musicians and singers: Bobby Rydell, Fabian, Paul Anka, Frankie Avalon & Annette, The New Christy Minstrels, and even Louis Armstrong singing "Hello Dolly."[**] I was too young to

---

[§] Grant's show was a monumental improvement over the only talent show I knew, Baltimore's "The Collegians," televised on WMAR TV on Saturday mornings throughout the Fifties. Hosted by a lumberyard owner, T. Oliver Hughes, who had the personality of a Librium-addled mortician. Think that's an exaggeration? See: http://www.youtube.com/watch?v=g4kpEW87sSI Literally anyone who wanted to be on the show got on. This quintessential Baltimore program is credited with warping the minds of many a Baltimore youth, e.g. John Waters.

[**] Over the years, the Marine Ballroom would host the likes of Frank Sinatra, Guy Lombardo, Benny Goodman, Jimmy Dorsey, the Three Stooges, Abbott & Costello, Gene Krupa, Duke Ellington, Perry Como, Dinah Shore, The Association, and the Rolling Stones. Right across

imagine myself in these performers' shoes, but the music nonetheless started to simmer in my DNA. After all, I had been exposed to one very talented amateur for years.

It was at those Sunday family get-togethers that I had first learned the real power of song, for it was only when my father, Anthony, was urged to sing *a cappella* after the meal in his thunderous but pitch-perfect spinto-tenor, that the chaotic scene morphed into a kind of reverie. You can imagine how this ritual played on his kids, who always raised a collective eyebrow as if to say "Here we go again." All we craved after dinner was to throw ourselves on the floor in a tryptophan-induced euphoria in time for the national 8 o'clock ritual: *The Ed Sullivan Show.*

But my father's post-meal vocal was a bigger ritual among the Russo clan, and the story that accompanied the voice had achieved the status of family myth. From the time he was a child, and for the next twenty years, my father sang every week at Sunday mass at Baltimore's St. Jude Shrine. His soaring voice so stood out from the choir that he was in much demand for countless private parish ceremonies. He only stopped in his twenties, when the church organist innocently asked how he spent the $5 fee he was earning for each event. It was the first he had heard of such a thing. Now figuring that his accrued $5,000 could aid his cash-strapped family, Anthony went straight to the rectory and asked for his back pay. When his request was denied, Anthony turned on his heels, and, save for a handful of family weddings and baptisms, never went to church again.

He had displayed the same brinksmanship a few years earlier as a high school sophomore at Baltimore's revered Polytechnic Institute. It seems the principal wanted (read: *ordered*) the big boned student to play on the football team, but Anthony was more interested in his singing, and so politely declined. But the principal was insistent, promising that refusal could affect his grades. Anthony held his ground, and when report cards came out, he was given a 69, one point shy of a passing grade, in each of seven subjects. Upon seeing his report, he rose from his desk, walked to the front of the class, and confronted his teacher, who sneered, "So, I suppose you're reconsidering the football team?" He wasn't. With one mighty swing, Anthony decked his teacher, did his heel-turn and never set foot in a school again.

But I only learned these stories many years later, so I had always wondered about the permanent cloud that seemed to hang over

---

the Boardwalk at the Convention Hall, still more magic, especially when the Beatles played there on my birthday in 1964.

my father, a man who was also traumatized and frost-bitten in the Battle of the Bulge[††] (of which he *never* spoke — I only learned of it through his sister), and who, despite a world class voice, returned home only to wallow in service at his father's "stag bar" in downtown Baltimore. And he wallowed there at least twelve hours a day, six days a week until he died. He seemed to come home only to eat and sleep. For reasons then unknown to my two younger brothers and me, he was a broken, and perhaps bitter man. Which brings us back to his singing.

The story goes that when my father was sixteen years old, one of his arias at St. Jude's was witnessed by an executive for New York's Metropolitan Opera House. The man was so stunned by what he heard — literally the rare voice that could approach that of the Met's legendary Mario Lanza — that he approached my father and his parents, Augustino and Rosina, with an offer to come to New York and sing for the Met. It was a life-changing offer that an *American Idol* win can hardly rival.

"You may not go!" dictated Rosina. "It's too dangerous — many hoodlums." First generation Italians knew exactly what she meant: Rosina had arrived from Mafia terrorized Sicily, and knew that many of these same gangsters now

My father (right of Arrow sign) at Russo's Bar

resided in New York. In Sicily, the Russos had a long history in and out of the mob, and were often engaged in bloody turf wars. Rosina was certain that her son would be targeted if his name became famous (Italian immigrants were convinced that even the great Lanza was under the thumb of New York Mafia don from Sicily, Lucky Luciano.) So for the rest of his life he would serve beers in his father's tavern, where at least once a day he would happily grant a request to turn off the juke box and sing like Lanza from behind the bar. That, and the Sunday evening concertos, would be the only venues for his remarkable gift. My father's fate instilled in me a determination that I was not

---

[††] Almost 90,000 American casualties in the one-month campaign.

going to live a life of compromise; I would be his polar opposite, doing everything I wanted to do. I would do everything he never did, even without his gift. Unlike him, I would not find myself on my deathbed asking, as he did, "What if?" Thus, it was the time I spent in Atlantic City's Marine Ballroom and watching my father tame two roomfuls of rowdy Italians that determined the course of much of my life.

Oh, and there was that little thing happened in 1956.

It was shortly after my seventh birthday, and one year after the tragic death of the would-be youth revolution avatar, 24-year-old actor James Dean. During one typical post-concerto viewing of the *Ed Sullivan Show* (September 9, to be exact), everything changed – for me, for music, for society, you name it. Although 21-year-old Elvis Presley had been making national TV appearances all year long, causing pelvic controversy in the process, it was on his Sullivan appearance that most of us caught him for the first time. Small wonder, for Sullivan's juggernaut embodied the idea of a national cathode ray campfire, and on this night a staggering seventy-two million Americans (forty-three percent of the population and 86 percent of the viewing public) was fixated on the Sullivan show, guest-hosted for an ailing Sullivan[‡‡] by actor Charles Laughton. So focused was the nation's attention that the other two networks cried "Uncle!" in advance by canceling their regular shows and instead running old movies — might as well cut costs since no one was going to be watching anyway.

When Presley walked out onstage (actually by remote from a different stage, in LA, where he was shooting his first film) alone in bold plaid jacket, he shyly addressed the zeitgeist he was about to obliterate:

> "Wow. This is probably the greatest honor I've ever had in my life.
>
> There's not much I can say except I hope it makes you feel good. We want to thank you from the bottom of our heart.
>
> And now, 'Don't Be Cruel.'"

[‡‡] Ed Sullivan was hospitalized for five weeks after a head-on collision near his home in Connecticut.

With that, a guitar-slinging Elvis launched into an impeccable, world changing version of Otis Blackwell's "Don't Be Cruel." Backed by the genius vocal arrangement of the Jordanaires and, off-camera, his regular trio, Scotty Moore (guitar), Bill Black (upright bass), and DJ  Fontana (drums), the skinny kid from Tupelo, Mississippi proceeded to alter the known universe in a mere one minute and fifty-two seconds. And no one who viewed it would have been a bit surprised if told that Elvis would go on to sell one billion records, and become directly responsible for the tens of billions sold by the musicians he inspired in that one-hundred-and-twelve-second musical earthquake. Even composer and New York Philharmonic conductor Leonard Bernstein proclaimed, "Elvis Presley is the greatest cultural force in the twentieth century."

James Dean's shoes had been filled, and then some.

For a generation of young boys, Presley seemed to harness the

power of a thousand "A-Bombs" during those nine TV appearances in 1956. From youngsters like little Brucie Springsteen to Bobby Zimmerman (later "Bob Dylan") to John Stewart to Lindsay Buckingham, to yours truly, many thousands responded to the Elvis Presley detonation and decided to be — make that *needed* to be — musicians. The aftershocks were likewise felt by a battalion of boys overseas. "Before Elvis, there was nothing," said John Winston Lennon, who was fifteen when the Elvis Bomb exploded. One year after the Presley debut, Lennon met fifteen-year-old Elvis fan Paul McCartney, and the two teamed up to make musical history.

Even Elvis, humble by nature, could not deny what he possessed. Actress Natalie Wood, who dated Presley for a brief time, recalled what he had told her. "He felt he had been given this gift, this talent, by God," Wood told an interviewer. "He didn't take it for granted. He thought it was something he had to protect. He had to be nice to people. Otherwise, God would take it all back." For the vast majority of those caught up in Presley's vortex, myself included, becoming a "musician" meant becoming a guitarist, just like The King.

At the time, I neither played an instrument nor sang, and my parents could barely afford my Catholic grade school tuition, let alone a guitar and music lessons. But for the next year or so, when we shopped at the local strip mall, Edmondson Village Shopping Center,§§ I'd gaze longingly at the $15 guitar that hung in the window of the Music Mart record store.

Edmondson Village Shopping Center

Then, one Sunday night after the family dinner at Uncle Frank's, I was told that Frank kept a ukulele in the bedroom, where I disappeared for the next hour. When I emerged, or so my father swore, I played a song, or something resembling a song. That did it.

Very soon thereafter, I was the proud owner of my first guitar (the $15 one from Music Mart), likely bought with money from the Atlantic City fund. I remember my parents sternly telling me what an extravagance it was, and that I had better practice with the *Mel Bay*

---

§§ Constructed in 1947, Edmondson Village Shopping Center is believed to be the first planned shopping center in the US.

Teach Yourself Guitar book that came with it. But I didn't have to be told. I played that cheapo every night until my fingers were raw, picking out songs from the book, off of 45rpm records, the radio—anywhere. I was anything but a natural, but my drive more than made up for it; I was going to master it despite my — and the guitar's— shortcomings. That's all there was to it.

Then, two more life-changers presented themselves: a guy who owned a gorgeous Martin guitar that he played beautifully moved to the neighborhood, and, secondly, I discovered the wondrous Central Branch of the Enoch Pratt Library. For some reason I could not fathom, Fred Kreppel, only a couple years older than I, owned the pricey guitar and was an accomplished player to boot. And for some other unknown reason he was happy to give me free lessons, opening my ears to the wonders of Duane Eddy's "Forty Miles of Bad Road," the Ventures' "Walk, Don't Run," and the Kingston Trio's "MTA." Alright! I had found my own Jesse Lee Denson!

At this time, Jesse Lee's former student was now Private Elvis Presley, stationed in Friedberg, Germany, and with the lull in his output, we felt free to try other styles of music. For many of us, the Kingston Trio, a San Francisco-based acoustic act with amazing vocals and sweet Martin guitars, filled the gap. Years later I learned that one of the reasons the Trio had a special vocal sheen was their unique (at the time) recording technique. On their third album, 1959's *At Large*, the Trio became the first recording artists to employ the "double-voicing" technique, using a three-track tape deck to re-record their vocals in unison with themselves. In 1973, Trio producer Voyle Gilmore, who previously produced Sinatra, recalled, "Double-voicing or overdubbing was my secret. I was one of the first to do it. We didn't have a lot of people in the studio watching the sessions because there was so much overdubbing and work, it would've been boring, and besides, we didn't want people to see what was going on."[***] Later, Gilmore's "secret" trick was adopted by the Beach Boys (who also adopted the Trio's striped shirts and song "Sloop John B"), the Beatles, and countless other pop groups.

[***] Credit for inventing the important technique should be given to the Trio's engineer, Peter Abbot. Of course, genius Les Paul invented overdubbing and had his wife, Mary Ford, harmonize with herself. But the Trio may be the first *group* to overdub in unison with itself in the service of fullness, not harmony.

During this period of my life, every spare nickel I had was saved for records, guitar strings, sheet music, and picks. But I was learning songs faster than I could buy records or sheet music. That's when one of my weekend hobbies turned into a musical goldmine. In the age when Baltimore city was safe for teens to walk around alone, I spent countless Saturdays taking the Number 8 trolley (electric!) from the West Side to the center of town, where I liked to lose myself in the cavernous Central Branch of the Enoch Pratt Free Library, still one of the great metropolitan libraries in the US. Built during the Great Depression, this four-story repository (with three lower levels) takes up a square city block.

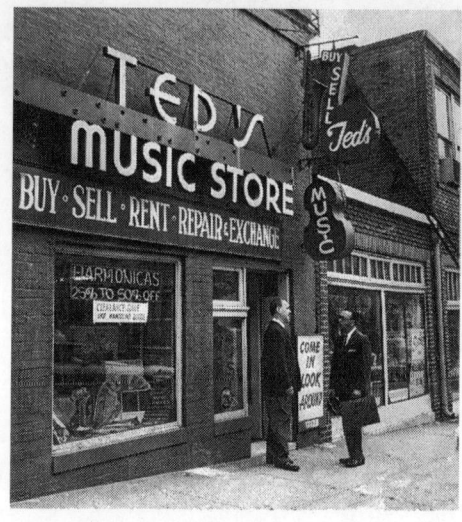

Ted with a customer in 1966

"If you want to get laid, go to college. If you want to learn, go to a library."
—Frank Zappa, another Baltimore-born guitarist.

The imposing grey structure contains countless marbled alcoves crammed with the combined knowledge of 1.2 million books and the staff librarians, who were happy to help an enthralled 12-year-old, full of wide-eyed wonderment. Taming that 275,000 square-foot behemoth would serve me well decades later when I followed my bliss into investigative reporting. Joni Mitchell was right about "The Circle Game."

> We're captive on the carousel of time
> We can't return we can only look behind
> From where we came
> And go round and round and round in the circle game

One of the many cluttered rooms at Ted's

On one such foray, I discovered that the Fine Arts Department on the second floor contained hundreds of music book collections, which could be borrowed for free! There was everything from the folk collections in *Sing Out!* magazine (which I discovered the Kingston Trio often raided to adapt, and adopt, public domain songs) to Show tunes, jazz, and pop. Very little rock, but no matter, I felt like I had hit the number. Two blocks from the library, I searched out the legendary Ted's Music Shop[†††], which catered to struggling musicians and students at the Peabody Conservatory of Music, located just around the corner. Ted Martini, the son of Russian Jewish immigrants (real name Evenchick), had owned a music store in Manhattan around the corner from the Julliard School of Music. When he fell in love with a violinist with the Baltimore Symphony Orchestra, he moved to her town, married her and then opened a store around the corner from Baltimore's Julliard, The Peabody Conservatory.

[†††] Ted's is, amazingly, still in existence (11 E. Centre St.,) and counts actor Johnny Depp as a customer when in town – some of his purchases can be seen in the John Waters film *Cry Baby*. When Ted died in 1989, his widow shrunk the store, with most of the contents loaded into three tractor-trailers and sold at auction for the lump sum of $30,000.

Ted's in 2009

Ted was an amazingly friendly man who would let teenage musicians, almost never there with a parent, try any of the thousands of used, and often bizarre, bargain priced instruments that were hung from the ceiling and piled on the floor in his cluttered, multi-room warehouse; rooms full of guitars, banjos, drums, even exotic instruments like sitars and tablas. Ted's shop, which he had opened in 1931, is where I saw my first — and only — bass banjo, not to mention my first six-pickup electric guitar, bass ukulele, Bolivian armadillo-skin string instrument, Gypsy guitar with an internal resonator, violin made from a shoe, and other musical machines that defy all description.

These musical contraptions were almost all old or used, but most importantly, they were obtainable. As hard as it is to imagine today, Ted would, if his instinct said one was trustworthy, let a teenager rent an instrument for two months for just $10 with no down payment, just proof of where he went to school! This seemingly absurd policy would come in handy very often for this guitarist and countless young B'more musical teens. God bless you, Ted!

(I made a return trip to Ted's in 2009, and fittingly parked outside was a five-ton reminder of those crazy, quirky times. See next page).

Soon, my grandmother pitched in so that I could take weekly private guitar lessons, at $4 per hour, at the Maryland Studio of Music. When I first showed up for an evaluation, the instructor concluded that I could skip the first four years of method books — I had accomplished that much on my own. For the next two years, I read from boring music books for a teacher who, looking back at it, could have been much more involved. But it was better than nothing. Thankfully, I complemented his rote instruction with my — and Fred Kreppel's — continued dissection of pop records. It all seemed to come together in the end.

It was an electric time: swinging young Bostonian John F. Kennedy had just been elected President, teenaged musicians were everywhere, James Bond was protecting us from **S.P.E.C.T.R.E.**[‡‡‡], and

---

[‡‡‡] **SPecial Executive for Counter-intelligence, Terrorism, Revenge and Extortion.**

 we all knew we were on the cusp of something special. My Italian-Catholic family worshipped Irish-Catholic Kennedy, and we hung a portrait (which I still own) of the young, Rat Pack partying President and his beautiful First Lady Jackie Kennedy in our knotty pine-finished club basement. When Kennedy's 1960 campaign swing brought him to the Baltimore's Westview Shopping Center, two miles from our house, my mother trundled me and  my younger brother there to see him. My memories are vague, but I remember shaking the candidate's hand as we followed him off the stage to his waiting limo. But my mother's memory of that day is crystal clear, especially regarding that limo.

It seems that there was a gorgeous brunette sitting with JFK in the backseat, and it certainly wasn't his decidedly plain secretary Evelyn Lincoln, and it definitely wasn't Jackie. We boys didn't recall her, but my mother never stopped talking about the beauty in JFK's car. Fifteen years later, when Kennedy mistress, the striking Judith Campbell Exner, a former Rat Pack babe, surfaced, my mother could finally place a name to the face. And there was no doubt about it. "I never forgot that face," my mother would say. Even Exner, in her autobiography, *My Life*, admitted accompanying her lover Kennedy that summer on the campaign trail while his wife was in Europe vacationing.

I later learned that the press was wise to Kennedy's philandering, but they felt that it was his personal business, and not fit for the public discourse. What a civil time it was, indeed.

Chapter Two

Spreading Wings

"Wisdom is not communicable. The wisdom which a wise man tries to communicate always sounds foolish... Knowledge can be communicated, but not wisdom. One can find it, live it, do wonders through it, but one cannot communicate and teach it."
— Siddhartha

WITH KENNEDY, BOND, and the Rat Pack in control, and no wars to argue over, the world seemed to be at its zenith of hip (having recently progressed from the less-cool descriptive "hep"). Men were at last going into space, on their way to the moon, Mars, and beyond — or so we thought. In fact, men, especially white men, were doing everything it seemed, while women and minorities waited their turn. When James Brown sang, "It's a Man's World," he wasn't whistling "Dixie." To top it off, the International Geophysical Year (IGY) of 1958 was a fresh memory, with its promise of limitless scientific cooperation between the Soviet Union's best white men and the West's best white men. Together we would cure all diseases, conquer space, and design two-way wrist radios that all white men could afford, or so we also thought.

Meanwhile, my favorite group, the Kingston Trio, was providing the soundtrack, with songs such as "The New Frontier,"* and an homage to the Mercury astronauts entitled "These Seven Men." And the admiration was mutual; John Stewart, the Trio member who composed those songs, visited Kennedy in the White House, and happened to be there at the height of the 1962 Cuban Missile Crisis, the official end of any IGY fantasies. Stewart's widow Buffy recalled that JFK had asked Stewart to compose a song that would arouse public support for the US space program and Kennedy's desire for a moon mission. Stewart responded with the song "The New Frontier," released in November 1962, just weeks after Kennedy's "We choose to go to the moon" speech at Rice University. The tune contained the lyrics: "Some to the rivers and some to the sea. Some to the soil that our fathers made

---

* Another great harmony group penned a tribute to Kennedy, not Jack but Jackie – and it became the first of many number one hits for the group, Can you guess? In 1962, Bob Gaudio wrote an upbeat song entitled "Jackie," but at the very last minute before making the recording, his group, The Four Seasons, persuaded him to change the title to "Sherry."

free. Then on to the stars in the heavens for to see. This is the new frontier. This is the new frontier." Stewart's association with the Kennedys would grow ever closer over the years. And hero/astronaut John Glenn would deliver a eulogy at Stewart's funeral four decades later.

Two months after Kennedy's 1961 inauguration, the new President told *Life Magazine* that one of his favorite books was *From Russia With Love*, one of Ian Fleming's "James Bond" potboilers. That sent many a male youth, including myself, to the bookstores to purchase the cheap paperback series. Bond became my generation's Harry Potter, wherein we would devour a new book in one or two sittings. We anxiously awaited the first filmed installment, *Dr. No.*, although I was certain that no actor I had ever seen could embody the Bond character as described by Fleming. I would be proven wrong.

In 1962, one year into the Kennedy administration, I, a mere twelve-year-old, decided it was time to start making my own mark on the world. Perhaps my sense of urgency was amplified by the October 1962 Cuban Missile Crisis, which took the entire planet to the brink. It is impossible to explain to today's youth, so nervous about a terrorist attack that might impact hundreds, or thousands, of victims, how it felt to be at Defcon-2, in the figurative crosshairs of 20,000 thermonuclear weapons. In the immortal words of Spinal Tap's Nigel Tufnel, "It really puts perspective on things, doesn't it?"

Also, understand that for the last year or so, the books I had been borrowing from the Pratt were all from the Male Adventure Section — you know, Mark Twain, Jules Verne, Ian Fleming, and Michener's *Tales of the South Pacific*. Additionally, in Catholic high school, we had a heavy reading load, and the book that most enthralled me was *Siddhartha*, Herman Hesse's 1951 tale of the search for wisdom through experience. I also learned of the other Siddhartha, the founder of Buddhism, the only major religion with which I could find absolutely no faults. The combined influences of my reading list and the super-charged youth revolution gave me a confidence and *joie de vivre* beyond all reason. Although I had no bank account, I truly believed, like Huck Finn, Adam Troy[†], and Siddhartha, that the world was my oyster.

The way I saw it, time was wasting. And the era made it so much easier for a young musician to test the waters than for the youth of today. As inconceivable as it seems to Gen-X'ers, the teenagers of the

---

[†] Main character in the Michener-inspired early-sixties TV show, *Adventures in Paradise*.

1960s had the opportunity to play music (and get paid for it!) at over 500 venues every Friday and Saturday night in Baltimore city alone. There were hundreds more in the county where I resided. This was the result of a robust Catholic Youth Organization (CYO), which held Friday night dances at most of its 200 parish centers, while the city put on dances every Saturday at many of its 500 public school "teen centers." Today, that has tragically all disappeared, but it is where I, and hundreds more, learned to really play music.

By the time I was thirteen, I was the proud owner of a plywood Harmony archtop guitar, a Christmas present valued at around $38, and I was immediately conscripted into providing accompaniment at family get-togethers.

Throughout the period I was rehearsing folk music with various neighbor singers, looking for a duo or trio that clicked. A turning point resulted from a pairing with 14-year-old Mark Regan, then president of our parish CYO, and a fine Irish tenor and guitarist. We started rehearsing, with me learning to sing harmony, setting our sights on the year-end Talent Show. Since I didn't own a "folk" guitar, it made more sense for me to be the requisite banjoist, which was fine, since the Kingston Trio member I most admired was writer-banjo player, John Stewart. There were only two minor problems: I neither owned nor knew how to play a banjo. But then again the astronauts had no idea how to get to the moon, but they did it anyway. Such was the spirit of the times that minor details such as these were only seen as interesting challenges.

My first plan was to use my father's small toolbox (he had built cedar closets in our basement) and information from the Pratt to build a banjo. It seemed a simple prospect: a circular ring of wood, or "pot," attached to a neck, with various parts I would buy, such as the head, strings, and tuning gears. Of course, that calculation, I soon found was drastically naïve.

I got so far as laminating six or more plates of wood, painstakingly hollowing out the center circle, to arrive at a serviceable rim. But the neck threw me completely. I didn't possess the needed equipment to carve a channel for a metal truss rod, the key to keeping the neck from warping. And I know I would have run into problems with the setting the fret heights and distances, so critical for a string instrument to play in tune. Thus, after a few weeks of making a mess in the basement, I surrendered and headed straight for Ted's, where I rented a 5-string, long-neck, Pete Seeger style banjo. A block away, I withdrew a *How-to-Play-Banjo* book at the Pratt. I found that banjo chords were much easier than those on the guitar, and I surprised myself by learning the basic right hand finger rolls pretty quickly. It seemed almost overnight that Mark and I were rehearsing with me on the "long neck." What happened next was worth all the blisters obtained trying to build, and then learn, that darn instrument— and then some.

On the appointed Friday night, Mark and I drowned ourselves in Jade East cologne and took to the St. Joseph's Monastery School stage near the end of the talent show, which was held in a beautiful auditorium, with a stage raised about five feet from the floor that held about 150 seated teens. I don't recall feeling any special jitters before we launched into two rousing songs by the Trio, "A Worried Man" and "MTA." It felt terrific to hear my jangly banjo playing reverberate in the huge space — it actually sounded professional! Before the last note died away, Mark and I started to get an inkling of what Presley felt every day of his life: the crowd rose to its feet in thunderous applause, demanding a encore, which we happily delivered. We won the contest by acclamation.

As CYO president, Mark was accustomed to the spotlight and the affirmation of the kids that had voted him into office repeatedly. But for me, a slightly introverted, bookish kid with glasses, it was so overwhelming that I felt validated for the first time; I was indeed (at last!) a musician, sharing a brotherhood with my heroes.

I can't tell you how often I've reflected about the importance of that talent show to the path of my life, or how often I've wished others could have had a similar confidence boost at such a critical point in their evolution. To this day, the events of that night are a powerful, visceral memory I can call on when needed.

For some, this kind of rush naturally turns into a craving for more attention and celebrity, a powerful addiction to be sure. But for some reason I processed it differently. I believed the accolades of the CYO members weren't directed so much at me, but to the power of the music. Since I was no great banjo player, and certainly not a great singer, it *had* to be something else. What I took away from that night was the magic of the songwriter more than the obvious out-front celebrity. I felt like a vehicle for someone else's genius. I wanted to be *that* genius.

As Mark and I went on to play at parties and hootenannies, I wanted more and more to be the wizard behind the curtain: Burt Bacharach, not Tom Jones; Brian Wilson, not the touring Beach Boys; George Martin, not John Lennon; Tom Jobim, not Stan Getz; Lamont Dozier, not Marvin Gaye, Bob Gaudio, not Frankie Valli. Although I loved being part of the live events, I wanted to be six feet behind the lead singer calling the musical shots. And did I mention that Mr. Bacharach had JFK's good friend Angie Dickenson waiting at home? Not a bad perk, I must say.

America, and the world, was jolted out of its "Happy Days" reverie in the fall of 1962. The stage was unintentionally set in early October with the London premier of Fleming's *Dr. No*, in which a Caribbean-based maniac who was in league with the Soviets to destabilize the US missile program almost incited a nuclear showdown —just a crazy escapist fantasy with no basis in fact. Having read all the Bond books after JFK's endorsement, I made certain I was at Baltimore's New Theater on the first Saturday afternoon of the *Dr. No* US opening. I also had no doubt that the actor chosen to portray Bond would disappoint — I had never seen an actor who approached Fleming's descriptions of Bond — and the director even staged the introduction in a way that ratcheted up the anticipation.[‡]

Bond is first seen from over his shoulder as the camera is focused on the beautiful brunette with whom he is flirting at the baccarat table. When the scene finally reverse-cuts to Bond's face as he coolly lights up his "Morland Special" and we hear his now famous introduction, "Bond, James Bond,"[§] I remember thinking: "They actually did it! Who is this guy?" The guy, of course was relatively unknown Scottish actor Sean Connery. I

[‡] I later learned that the producers' first choice was Cary Grant, after whom Fleming had partially modeled Bond. But Grant declined the offer, believing he was too old (58) to play the part.
[§] It is not widely remembered, but Bond's iconic reverse-name intro actually began as a sarcastic reply to the brunette, who had introduced herself first as "Trench, Sylvia Trench."

wasn't the only one impressed; author Ian Fleming was so stunned that he actually changed his lead character's origins to Scottish in his next six Bond books.

Of course, Bond's appearance was not the main thing I remembered as a 13-year-old, red-blooded boy leaving the New Theater: It was Ursula Andress, as Honeychile Rider, in that bikini! If I hadn't reached manhood when I purchased my ticket, I had by the time I was riding the bus home! So excuse me if I memorialize that quasi-religious experience:

Two weeks after Ursula's — I mean *Dr. No's* — UK premier, life imitated art when a real-life Caribbean-based maniac working with the Russians did the same thing, using real nukes supplied by Mother Russia. But after thirteen days of nuclear terror, President Kennedy, who two years earlier had actually consulted with Fleming about Cuba's Dr. No, Fidel Castro, stared down the suicidal dictator, and we went on with life as usual.

During the summer of 1963, I attended my first concert without my parents — the Kingston Trio of course, at Baltimore's shiny new Civic Center. It still amazes me how that acoustic group held an arena of 8,000 in its palms, especially considering the inadequate sound systems of the day. I kept the program from that show, and it was only three decades later that I got all three of my heroes to sign it.

The concert was a rare break that summer from tackling a large reading list courtesy of my soon-to-be high school.

Aside from the Trio, based in San Francisco, I was becoming interested in the music of another California combo, this one hailing from the southern sector. Although this LA-based group derived some influences from the Bay area's golden boys, that represented only a fraction of the unique, yet elegant, musical mix they concocted. Their first two albums, basic rock fare, had not grabbed me, save for the tone of the lead guitarist's Fender Jaguar guitar. But when I heard the lush harmonies on the third release, *Surfer Girl*, far beyond even what the Kingston Trio attempted, I was hooked for life. It was because of the angelic vocal sounds produced by Brian Wilson's Beach Boys that I first pondered the possibility that music might indeed represent the best evidence of a higher being. I have since found many more musical examples that bolster the hypothesis.

The combination of vibrato-less, Gregorian-like, "sibling harmony" (three Wilson brothers, a cousin and a neighbor), the Kingston Trio's "double voicing" technique, and Brian's great melodic and harmonic sense, all topped off by the best male falsetto in pop history, gave the recording a sheen that was the equivalent of aural honey. Omnipresent also was something that is AWOL in today's pop music: a sense of joyfulness. Incredibly, of the first 86 songs released by the Beach Boys through their eighth LP release, 1965's *Beach Boys Today!*, <u>only one song</u> (1.2% of their output) was in a minor key.**

What all this meant to me was that I now had to add vocal arranging to my list of musical exploration and investigation. I learned that Brian had painstakingly deconstructed the jazz harmonies of the

---

** The song, "We Three Kings," was of course not a Beach Boys composition. Additionally, this song from the *Christmas Album* modulates between minor and major keys, spending at least half its time in major.

Four Freshmen, the vibrato-free jazzers who in the 1950s employed advanced, borderline dissonant, harmony techniques that were light years beyond the Kingston Trio — and me, for that matter. It started with the uncharacteristic placing of the melody on the top of three harmonies that were spaced in such a way as to give the sensation of hearing an extra voice that wasn't there. But it would take years before I started getting insights into what they were doing. It should be noted that in those days, there were no record transcriptions, cassette tapes, audio or video lessons. All young pop musicians learned the same way: we mastered the art of lifting and replacing the needle countless times on a specific musical passage of a vinyl record, then moving on to the next section, destroying the grooves in the process.

The years leading up to my musical epiphanies were fairly placid, and the only dramas that stood out were during a two-year period when I couldn't seem to stop breaking bones: first my right wrist from falling off a bike, then my left arm playing football, and finally a severely dislocated shoulder from another fall. I was in casts so regularly that I can still smell the Plaster of Paris and hear the saw that was used to change the itchy white monstrosities every few weeks.

For years, my group, with me usually in a sling, walked home from school, first passing through the then-bucolic village of Irvington. There I'd stop by the pet store, the candy store, and my grandfather's barbershop to say "Hi," and get a trim every couple of weeks. Pop, as we called him, arrived here from Sicily and got his start in this country cutting hair at a Baltimore reform school for boys called St. Mary's Industrial School.

One of the school's young scamps on whose head Pop learned his craft was a twelve-year resident named George Ruth, later nicknamed "Babe" by baseball fans. Pop would give me a hard-earned 50-cent piece to spend at my next stop, the adjacent Rexall Drug Store, where I'd order a lemon phosphate or soda fountain Coke, heavy on the Coke syrup, thank you.[††] The only

Babe Ruth (top left) at St. Mary's

[††] Little did I realize that a fraction of all the quarters I spent at the drugstore was winding up in the Beverly Hills pockets of Beach Boy Bruce Johnston, the adopted son of Rexall's Vice-President. Bruce, you owe me a coke!

times I skipped the Irvington rites were when I'd race home to watch one of President Kennedy's many mid-afternoon press conferences, which often were a hysterical battle of wits with the press corps.

Pop, my mother's father, was actually named Tony, as was my father, my brother, and a cousin; the remainder of my other male relatives were either named Frank or Vince, and 90% of the women were some variation of Mary or Rose, creating virtual chaos at the family get-togethers. Of all my family, I identified most of all with Pop, who always seemed to have a smile on his face and an absurdist's view of the world.

It was from Pop that I first heard the word "Mafia." When he was a young father, Italian immigrants were being terrorized by "The Black Hand," or extortion notes left on the door. An unwelcome vestige of "the old country," the intrusion of the Black Hand was the reward for working hard and owning a house that would cause the wiseguys to see you as a target. In Pop's case, the choice was simple: change the beneficiary on his fire insurance policy to one of "the boys" and take his family out on a pre-arranged night, or have the house firebombed with no warning. When the house was torched and the arson discovered, my grandfather was charged with insurance fraud and sent to prison, never squealing on the feared Mafiosi who put him up to it.

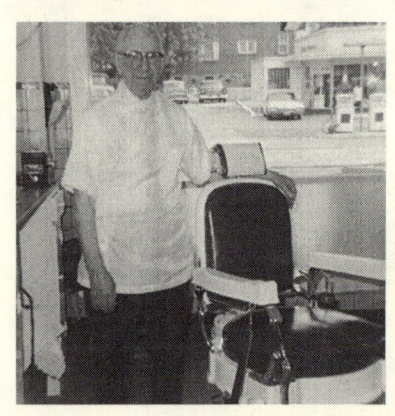

It was he who first told me that, "All politicians are crooks" and "Don't you care what anybody else thinks, live your own life." He always seemed so jovial that I just accepted that he must be right. For my entire life, only Pop cut my hair, and he showed me how to cut it myself. When he died in 1974, I made a secret pledge that, other than myself and Pop, no one else would ever cut my hair. They still haven't.

Pop in his Irvington Shop

When not at the Pratt, Saturdays were occasionally spent at Memorial Stadium watching the amazing Baltimore Orioles baseball team.[‡‡] In those days, for a trolley ride, a ten-cent bus transfer, and $1.50 for a ticket (as a member of the Orioles Junior Advocates) you could sit in the cheap seats with your pals and watch a game. And there

---

[‡‡] Hard to believe now, but in the sixties and seventies, the "Os" were the winning-est team in baseball.

was no great hubbub of planning; usually I'd get a call from a friend at noon, asking, "You wanna go to the game today?" If I said yes and had the cash, off we'd go. That was it.

If I wasn't at a game or at the Pratt, I often met up with a particularly crazy pal named Charlie Price.[§§] We created a great game that we passed on to Mark Regan and others that involved taking the trolley downtown and getting off in the shopping district on Howard Street.

There we'd pick one of the Macy's-like 10-story department stores, usually either Hutzler's or Hochschild-Kohn, go in and flip a coin. Whoever won was given a one-minute head start to go anywhere in the building, the only requirement being he had to keep moving. If the one on the run was found and tagged, he treated the other to lunch. If after thirty minutes he wasn't found, we'd meet back at the starting point and the hunter had to buy. The game was at its most frustrating when the hunter would be going up one escalator, while seeing his prey descending just a yard away. To top it off, the security guards often chased us *both*, alerted by seeing a couple of 13-year-old boys dashing through ladies lingerie or infant apparel. We were escorted out countless times.

The only other weekend activity that had any regularity was the monster movie matinees at one of two great movie palaces within walking distance of my home. There we were enthralled by the classic works from Hammer Films and the mind-boggling creatures created by Ray Harryhausen, of *Jason and the Argonauts* fame. More big-screen thrills came in the form of the PT Barnum-like presentations by William Castle, which often featured an ambulance parked outside the lobby of the Edgewood Theater[***], awaiting the predicted heart

---

[§§] Why "crazy" Charlie? Among his many eccentricities was his penchant for quietly disassembling and reassembling things at his desk during class, *including his desk*. He once wanted to see how few screws it took to hold his desk together, and he found out the hard way when his desk collapsed in a heap during religion class. Walking home from school, Charlie would occasionally take out his house key, and fling it into the woods, just to see how long it took to find it — sometimes hours. Charlie's only big failure was a watch that he took apart. I'll bet he's still working on it somewhere.

[***] The beautiful Art Deco Theater was located just a block from my grade school, St. Bernardine's Catholic School. At the time there was a hit song by Pat Boone about his girlfriend, Bernadine, so

attack victims. At one Castle extravaganza, we had to sign a waiver proffered by the producer's "nurses" before going in, guaranteeing we would not hold this cinematic Barnum liable for any after-effects from the movie. Thanks to these brilliant set-ups, we were already half frightened to death by the time the titles came up.

Although the tickets were cheap, my friends and I went so often that we thought we deserved special consideration. Thus we began doing what movie fan boys were doing everywhere: we'd all pitch in a nickel for one 25-cent ticket. The ticket holder went in, then snuck to the emergency side exit and opened the door for the rest of us (the most we got in on one ticket was eight guys.) Invariably, this would initiate a cat-and-mouse game with the manager who searched in vain for us rogues now scattered in the darkened room, while other kids cheered. It only added to the excitement of a good thriller flick.[†††] Keep in mind, in those days a hit movie (we didn't call them *films*) might run for months, and you had to see it repeatedly, since you might not see it on *The Late Show* for ten years. And the concept of actually *owning* a movie for home viewing was ludicrous.

It was about this time that my interest in playing sports also got serious, first in my neighborhood Norwood Heights Little League, which was headquartered at a field donated by a local millionaire, situated on the sloping edge of his fifty-acre home property. Like almost everything we did in those days, we all walked to the field, for me about six blocks, as my father used our only car to get to work. Although the infield was bumpy, weed-infested, and absurdly undersized, it was the outfield that really took the cake: the left outfield immediately started to incline upward at about a 15° angle, and the right field beyond first base was so steep as to be almost unplayable; we called it "Mount Everest." Therefore, as an infielder backpedaled to catch a pop fly, he had to also negotiate the tilt beneath his feet. Countless little shavers tumbled over and got beaned. Everest was where the hapless last-drafted kids were assigned. But there was an upside: at the end of the season the right fielders were practically certified Sherpas.

And that wasn't the only obstacle — five feet outside the left foul line, for its entire length, was a stand of giant oak trees that prevented us from running down foul balls without getting crunched. But no one complained. It was a dynamic league, with eight teams that

---

for most of my life I pictured the school's namesake as a beautiful woman, when in fact it was a bearded, bald, 14th century man.
[†††] The movies that I recall most fondly are *Jason and the Argonauts, Sinbad, House on Haunted Hill, The Tingler, The Horror of Dracula, The Curse of Frankenstein, Little Shop of Horrors*, and last but not least, *Journey to the Center of the Earth*, which I saw over a dozen times.

took turns using this sad excuse for a field. We had a blast, and I'll bet one non-player did as well: that millionaire, watching from his mansion window as we were falling like Baltimore duckpins, must have had one twisted sense of humor. Looking back, this abominable acreage, aptly named Random Field, was so awful that today's attorneys would never have allowed a pitch to be thrown there.

My experience with the little league only added to my growing self-confidence. The season started with the drafting of over twenty anxious rookies, who scrimmaged over a week or so, then on the last day lined up nervously on the foul line as their names were called by their new team coach. I was chosen first, by the defending champion Yankees, and played first base and relief pitcher. I was tall for my age, and since our field was so small, my sidearm fastball fired from a pitcher's mound about thirty feet from the plate was terrifying. Batters often a foot shorter than I began bailing out of the batter's box as soon as I started my windup. I wasn't a good pitcher, but I knew that the sidearm was a great weapon for the legendary Dizzy Dean, and no matter how accurate was so frightening that right-handed batters would have to take a swing while leaning backwards. Predictably, there were a lot of unintentional bunts when I was on the hill.

One day I nailed a poor kid in the left side, eliciting an awful crying jag. Even though he was a chubby thing with lots of padding, I was so shaken by hurting him that, when he saw my 10-mph pitch to the next batter, my coach ran out to the mound to console *me*. I knew that had I hit that kid in the head I would have killed him (this was when batting helmets were optional, and made of useless cheap plastic.) I asked to be removed from the game, and I don't think I pitched again, happy to stay at first base, guarding the gateway to the Himalayas.

That posting led to another major boost. During the championship game, the local beat reporter for the *Baltimore Sun* showed up to cover the game, and it just so happened that the action photo he took, and that ran the following day, was of me outstretched at first base trying to put out a runner while salvaging an errant throw from the shortstop.

FANCY FOOTWORK—Oriole runner Pete DeMartino, Yank first baseman Gus Russo and umpire Jim McCormick appear to be performing ballet at Random Field. Runner was called safe on a close play. The Norwood Heights Yanks won the league pennant with a 7-1 record.

All this fun without the word "digital" ever mentioned.

There was one other notable occurrence during that blazing B'more summer. One sunny Saturday afternoon I was leaving the backyard on the way to play baseball when I noticed something in the sky that would prove impossible to forget. As mentioned, our house was part of a subdivision that rested on a hillside that had a view of a wooded area about 150 yards away, the beginning of the vast Lancelotta property that also contained our infamous baseball field. An amazing line of old oak trees that stood some 80-feet tall ringed that forest, and on that particular day, there was something reflecting the sunlight above the tree line that caught my eye. I looked up to see (try to suspend your cynicism here) a motionless football-shaped silver object suspended about 100 feet above the oaks. Later, I would use high school geometry to triangulate its size at about 75 feet in diameter. So clear was it that day that I could make out distinctive construction features on the surface. Since the thing wasn't moving, I raced inside to get our Polaroid, which, regrettably, was out of film. When I returned to the yard the UFO was still there, so I jumped the chain-link fence and roused my neighbor, Miss Marion, and pointed to the woods.

"Is that what I think it is?" I asked.

"Oh, my God!" my fifty-ish homemaker neighbor replied.

Beyond that, we just stood there looking up in stunned silence until about a minute later, when the craft decided it was tired of Mr. Lancelotta's oak trees and shot off, disappearing in an eyeblink. Of course, an experience like that is a life-changer. For years thereafter, I obsessively scoured UFO photos in the tabloids, looking for the version we observed. Finally, in 1975, when the Air Force released its Project Blue Book Files[‡‡‡], I saw one of its photos reproduced in the National Enquirer scandal sheet, and it was virtually identical to the one we saw that summer afternoon. Although the photo (at left) was widely concluded to be a fake, it nonetheless was a fake that coincidentally looked just like the real UFO that hovered over. Lancelotta's trees. Adding to the coincidence was the date of the photograph: June 16, 1963, the same summer I had my experience. From that point on, in fact for years after our family relocated, Miss Marion and I, looking for verification

[‡‡‡] Project Blue Book was the Air Force UFO investigation that lasted from 1952-1970.

of our sanity, asked each other countless times, "Did we really see that thing?" It seemed we had. §§§

The Norwood Heights Yankees stayed champions both years that I was eligible to play, and in my second year I was voted team captain. Usually after a game, Mark and I worked on our music, all of this without parental input, since my father, again with the only car, was drowning his sorrows in work, and my homebody mother was becoming borderline agoraphobic, only going out for Sunday dinners and on our July trips to Atlantic City. (My parents never attended my games or musical performances). I never even saw Mark's parents. We were learning to create our own world, independent of our elders. And our world was pretty inexpensive. I have no memory of constantly craving special clothes or other material goods — I had a working guitar, the newest Trio record, a baseball glove, the Pratt Library, and Ted's. What else was there to want? My entire joyful world cost less than a one-month cell phone bill for today's youth. However, I soon did find one more possession to add to the list: a tennis racket.

Tennis came to me as a high school freshman in 1963. One of the great things my parents did for me was to send me to a superlative all-boys Catholic high school, Irvington's Mt. St. Joseph's "College." (In those days, for reasons unknown to me, many Catholic High Schools referred to themselves as colleges). Although my parents struggled mightily to afford just the basics, they found a way to pay $250 tuition not only for me, but also for my two younger brothers (today it's $11,000) for this high academic institution overseen by the stricter-than-strict Xaverian Brothers. They found the tuition money by painstakingly tube-rolling the bags of quarters that my father brought home from the bar every night – for years. My mom remembers dad in the kitchen cutting out cardboard inner soles to stuff into his perforated shoes, instead of buying new ones, so that he could save for my schooling. It would have been so much easier to send us to the free public school a block from our home, but they just deemed it unacceptable. If my father said it once, he said it a hundred times that he wanted us to have a better education than he. I was sure that would be the case, if only because I didn't have his right hook.

The Xaverian order was founded in the Netherlands in 1837, with its chief calling being the teaching of immigrants in the US and Native Americans. The US headquarters was in Baltimore, and the

---

§§§ The photo was snapped by Apolinar "Paul" Villa, Jr. on June 16, 1963, in Peralta, NM.

center of activity was "St. Joe," founded in 1876. The grueling academic standards (not to mention requisite short haircut, sport coat and tie) were loathed at the time, but within just a few years, I was more than appreciative of what those imposing clerics had accomplished and instilled in me. The knowledge I acquired also would make it a lot easier to hook classes later in college.

I was soon to learn that going to any school crammed with only pubescent boys required that the students develop creative ways to burn off all the energy and hormones coursing through their bodies. Thus, pranks ran out of control, despite the severe consequences, and occurred on an almost daily basis. Without girls there to impress or distract us, the creativity normally focused on mating rituals was channeled to making each other laugh.

On the very first day, I was introduced to one of my favorite gut-busters. One of my classmates, who will remain anonymous (Bobby Matikiewicz), had painstakingly studied our school year calendar in "The Mount Book," and subtracted every weekend and holiday to determine precisely how many days were to be actually spent at school until the following summer's last day. Then, he snuck into first period class before the teacher and wrote on the chalkboard in gigantic font:

282

The next day the board read:

281

And so on, every day — for the next four years! Eventually the teacher would enter the room, and without even looking at the board, just order, "Erase it!" Every student knew who the culprit was (Bobby Matikiewicz), but we never ratted on him.

Our class "Homeroom 111," actually became infamous for having behavior problems — mostly in good-natured quests to have a giggle — and we took a strange pride in being known throughout the school for our absurdist bent. Many times the principal would announce over the PA: "At 1 p.m. we will be having an assembly music concert, so please make your way there now — class one-eleven, don't bother coming."

One-eleven had an amazing collection of genuine characters: I recall Justin, who used to fight for the seat farthest from the teacher, so that he could snooze. The poor boy needed his rest so much that he usually brought a small pillow with him on which to rest his weary head. Then there was Ravella, who abused our elderly English instructor horribly. Our home English assignment consisted of writing a book report every week. For at least two years, Ravella alternated just two books every other week (*The Jim Thorpe Story* and *Ben-Hur*), never getting caught. He also became famous for razor-cutting the entire contents of a book into small bits, shoving them into his pockets so he could fish for answers during a test. I actually devoured the reading list; St. Joe was where I discovered the world through the eyes of Mark Twain, James A. Michener, Herman Hesse, Harper Lee, Norman Mailer, and William Faulkner.

For about two years, our French class toiled under a new standardized testing method, with our exams administered in the new audio lab, via multiple-choice oral exams fed into our headsets. At some point we learned that another Catholic high, Cardinal Gibbons (renamed from Babe Ruth's St. Mary's alma mater), used the same test tapes, but for some reason, scheduled their tests a week before St. Joe's. In no time at all we dispatched an emissary and obtained the list of correct answers shortly before our test day. The list would read: "1 - C, 2 - A, 3 - B, etc." Just before a French exam, we'd all meet in the boys' room and post a lookout, while our emissary read out the answers. We took better notes in that lavatory than we ever did in the actual class (since, of course, we took none in the class).

From there, it was just a matter of getting a few answers intentionally wrong, since 30 guys all achieving a score of 100% might make the school wise (ya' think?). This chicanery was employed on countless tests, until, unbeknownst to us, the school learned of the gambit. Without warning, on the next test our French teacher announced that the tape player was malfunctioning, thus he would have to read the test aloud. What he didn't tell us was that he was reading the questions in reverse order. Of course, we never knew it because we never listened to him, having filled in all forty or so answers before he had arrived at the third question. Our scores on that test ranged from about 4% to 11%, about the same odds of a monkey accidentally getting a couple answers correct. Suffice it to say, that marked the end of our new standardized tests.

Our poor Theology teacher, a young Xaverian novitiate, was so taken aback by our Marx Brothers-type lunacies that he quit the brotherhood soon after our graduation; I am certain Class 111 played a major role in his decision.

The student body at St. Joe was an interesting mix of middle, and lower middle class kids from every segment of the city. Just as in other high schools, there was a powerful drive to be accepted, and even hip. However, the strict dress code, as spelled out in "The Mount Book," made that quest exceedingly difficult:

> *There is no regulation uniform at the Mount. However, there are certain rules which must be observed in regard to dress. All students must wear suit coats, with lapels and of a conservative color, shirts with collars designed for wearing a tie. A necktie is to be worn. Students are to wear suit coats and ties at all times during the school day. Exceptions are made to the above rule on suit coats for those students who have earned a varsity letter or an "M" letter for scholastic achievement and have attached the letter to an official school sweater. The trousers must be of the sport or suits type but need not match the coat. Peg or "drape" pants are not permitted. Dungarees are not permitted. The shoes may be brown, black, white or any combination of these colors. Loud or exceptional suedes are not permitted. Boots and other noisy and distracting forms of footwear are not allowed. The so-called "desert boots" will not be tolerated. "Drape" and other unusual types of haircuts are not allowed at the Mount. Bleaches, dyes, and the like are not permitted. Mustaches are not permitted.*

Finding some form of individual identity within these strictures was a daunting challenge that we rose to on a daily basis. Essentially, we had two clear style routes to acceptance: "Joe College" and "Deaner." The Joe College crowd, about 80% of the students, slavishly dressed in herringbone tweed jackets, button-down shirts, Bostonian wingtip shoes, and paisley ties, as they advertised their goal of getting into an Ivy League college. The Deaners, on the other hand, modeled their look on the "Drape" styles worn on the local Buddy Deane dance show: skinny ties, skinny pants, sharkskin jackets (as opposed to tweed), and pointy boots. Obviously, the Deaners pushed the "Mount Book" envelope, and were regularly sent home to change clothes.

As for me, I fell in with a group (less than 5% of the school) that relished our own style creations, sort of like jazz musicians. My band of a half-dozen pals was borderline existentialist, vowing that the more something was "in," the more we reviled it. Whereas our classmates went to inter-school dances, wanted to be jocks, and listened to the Top Forty, we favored jam sessions, Marx Brothers movies, Roger Corman, Ed Wood, and basement listening parties that featured Captain Beefheart, Frank Zappa, Wild Man Fisher — virtually anything that cracked us up.

Deaner classmate Dave Jarboe was a talented musician, who in his sophomore year was given a chance to play bass in a hot local band, The Marquis. The band's lead guitarist, John, who attended Loyola "College" on the other side of town, was a brother of our classmate, Jerry Hall. Jerry was a curious brainiac, who was often seen in the company of the clerics, usually at an assembly or at lunch, and we were all curious about it since it went way beyond the accepted norms of "brown-nosing." Years later I learned that Jerry, in fact, was hearing "the calling," and eventually became a Jesuit priest. His brother John, whom I met many times at various musical functions, went on to found the band Orleans, for whom he wrote classic pop songs such as *Still the One*, *Dance With Me*, *Power*, and my favorite, *Tongue Tied*. Unbeknownst to me at the time, John's musical travels and mine would take us on a strangely parallel journey in the 1970s.

Getting back to Jarboe, the only way Dave could join the Marquis was if he owned professional equipment, which he didn't. So Dave came up with a plan: one-by-one he approached fellow students with a chance to "buy stock" in his career by contributing one dollar to his Fender bass fund. Somehow, in exchange for a piece of paper noting the "stock" purchase, Jarboe accumulated enough money to buy that bass. Although we never saw any cash dividends from our investment, we got to hear lots of terrific music — Dave was a talented player and deserved the break.

My anarchist high school pals (Rick standing, Mike with useless guitar, and Doug thinking of ending it all.)

In addition to studies and good-natured mischief, another St. Joe requirement was extracurricular activity. Since I was a big fan of the

Baltimore Colts and Johnny Unitas, I tried out for the freshman football team. The only real football experience I had was the neighborhood "mud bowl," a pick-up game that was organized the day after we'd had a monsoon-like rainstorm — maybe three a year. Within thirty seconds of a mud bowl kickoff, every player would have crud wedged into places he didn't even know existed. We looked like a black-faced minstrel show with a football instead of a banjo; the scene was so chaotic that we had couldn't identify our own teammates, with pass interceptions being thrown more than forward completions, the result of throws to the wrong man. I looked so forward to a rainstorm, since playing the mud bowl made us laugh until our sides hurt.

But the mud bowl did nothing to prepare me for real football at St. Joe. I had never felt so much physical pain as in those tryouts, and I still haven't. To make matters worse, every day, bloody and bruised, we'd jog by the tennis team in their spotless whites, who appeared much more civilized than the muscle mutts who were squashing my face into gridiron for two hours at a time. I didn't even wait for the first cut to be made, I just stopped showing up.

Now, with no after school sports activity, I began watching the tennis team play matches. At that time, tennis was a throwaway sport; nobody seemed to care about it, and nobody was interested in funding it. The tennis coach worked like mad to keep them in shape, but the four dirt courts were just barely playable. You read it right — dirt. On a hot day, when the wind blew, it was like playing in a dust bowl, which actually made for a distinct home-court advantage.

Nonetheless, I was quickly drawn in to what I would later conclude is the greatest of all sports. When played properly, tennis is the most balanced sport imaginable, embodying grace, skill, power, fitness, sportsmanship, intelligence, and strategy. It is the only sport where a player calls his opponent's shots, teaching young people about the honor system every time a point is played. Tennis allows for no coaching, time outs, or substitutions, making it the purest sport in terms of judging the athlete's innate ability to find a way to win. As exercise, singles tennis can't be beat. It is the equivalent of a two-hour boxing match without the bruises and corner men — jabbing, probing, feigning, pacing, and creating misleading patterns of shot making before finally going for the kill. The bottom line was that the game had class, just the kind of sport the Trio might play when not cranking hits out of the Capitol Tower! Oh, and did I mention that Angie Dickenson played tennis?

It happened that my madman algebra teacher, Brother Carey, was also the tennis coach. Carey, rumored to have been a Golden Gloves boxing champion, brandished his Popeye-sized forearms the first day of class, threatening to use them on any "wise acre" student.

Brother Carey, C.F.X., sketching plans for electronics class

A wiry, five-foot, ten-inch dynamo, Brother Carey was a brilliant mathematician, tough teacher, and an eminently fair man, but he did use those forearms occasionally in those days of sanctioned corporal punishment.**** I asked him about the team, and he suggested I try out in the spring, since it was too late for the fall team. Although I had no experience, he was encouraging, and suggested I start reading *Man With a Racket*, about Pancho Gonzalez, and watching Rod Laver if I ever had the chance. He also suggested finding a copy of tennis icon Bill Tilden's *Match Play and the Spin of the Ball*. "Then find a good wall to hit against, like Pancho did," Carey said. "And start getting your arm in shape," he added, as he once again rolled up his sleeve to give me an example.

Back to the Pratt...

At this time our family lived in a new row house community, built on a slope just a quarter mile from the county line. At the top of the hill sat a new Baltimore City school, Rock Glen Junior High, a thug-riddled institution that I had nothing to do with until I set my sights on tennis. Once I absorbed Brother Carey's prescribed books and obtained a cheap wooden racket, I needed to find a wall. I had read that Gonzalez spent untold hours, as a similarly poor tennis aspirant in Los Angeles, banging balls against a wall from close range. He wrote that there existed many useful variations of wall drills for those who couldn't

---

**** It seemed that once a week, a classmate was beaten, slapped, or pushed against a wall by a teacher. One day, an apostle of Christ loaded up his fist and sent a roundhouse towards a seated classmate who had talked back. The 14-year-old ducked, as the holy man's fist came crashing into the wooden desktop, breaking it into pieces. When a kid was particularly mischievous, a Brother would take him into the cloakroom located in the back of the class, where he could pound away without witnesses, while the class heard the kid howling. Students often emerged with red faces and bloody noses. Minor infractions landed one in 'jug," or two hours after school with a couple of dozen others. Jug, which I only recently learned was an acronym for "Judgement Under God," usually consisted of manual labor around the grounds, or writing thousand word essays on impossible subjects, such as "The Thoughts of a Fly as it Crawls along a Screen," or "The Love Life of an Eraser." And you couldn't leave until you had filled ten loose-leaf pages. Additionally, the writing quality had to be approved, lest the prefect admonished, "Sloppy — do it again."

afford an instructor, and I knew from having scaled the eight-foot chain link fence that encircled the Rock Glen property that the massive brick building's parking lot butted up against a thirty-foot high wall that was practically windowless —*practically* being the operative word here.

My daily after-school rituals now included negotiating said fence after tossing my racket and ball can over, then spending about an hour waging war with that wall. Since it was a tennis maxim to hit to your opponent's typically weaker backhand, I concluded in a flash of insight that if my backhand was stronger, my opponents would be playing right into my strength. Thus I would hit five or more backhands for every forehand. To this day it is my most potent weapon. I also remember endlessly trying out the spins that Tilden wrote about, until one spin shot got so out of control that I smashed the nearest window, which caused me to race off and lay low for a few weeks before going at it again.

The fall of 1963 seemed carefree, and especially joyful for the Russo clan: my second brother was born that September (my other came into the world four years after I), and, surprisingly, the hysteria that accompanied the previous year's nuclear showdown in the Caribbean with the USSR had faded in memory (mine at least). Meanwhile, my obsession with books continued unabated, and was now joined by a growing interest in comedy (especially the Marx Brothers and Steve Allen), and tales of adventure (notably television shows such as Michener's Polynesian-themed *Adventures in Paradise*, and *Route 66*.) But we were all about to be jolted out of our illusory reveries in a way no one anticipated.

Chapter Three

The End of the Innocence

I WAS IN a corridor of St. Joe's new Ryken Hall on my way to eighth period biology class with one of the school's few lay teachers, Mr. Hall, when I caught this buzz among other scampering students. At first it was unclear what was going on, until finally I heard from a breathless upperclassman that had learned some details, if mangled, from a transistor radio.
"Kennedy's been shot by some Russian guy!"*

My first thought was: another prank (Bobby Matikiewicz). But my second thought was: "Now the nukes are really going to fly." When we took our seats in class, the word had not yet reached our teacher, who began his usual sleep-inducing lecture on protozoan culture. However, he was soon interrupted by the crackling of the little speaker over his head, a sign that we were soon to be addressed by our principal, Brother Bartel, a rarity outside of ninth period homeroom. Although ecstatic about the interruption, quickly we began to wonder: Could this Kennedy rumor actually be true? His exact words are lost to memory, but in the most somber voice I had ever heard emanate from that tiny speaker, Bartel announced that President Kennedy had been seriously wounded, and that all class work was suspended. We were instructed to go to our homerooms where our teacher would lead us in group prayer.

We walked in dead silence back to our homerooms; it was the only time those halls were silent in my four years at St. Joe. It felt more like a morgue than a high school. Shortly into our recitation of The Lord's Prayer we were again interrupted by that goddamned speaker. We knew this had to be bad news. With his voice choking, Brother Bartel now directed us to pray for the soul of President John F. Kennedy, the man I met at Westview Shopping Center three years

---

* Bizarre coincidence: On April 19, 1994 I was back at St. Joe, giving a presentation to the alumni association about my recent two-year stint as an investigative reporter for PBS's *Frontline* series, where I helped produce a three-hour special on the life of Lee Harvey Oswald. After the speech, I was chatting with fellow alumni out on the pathway near Ryken Hall when someone interrupted and told us the news of Jackie's Kennedy's death from cancer that night. Thus, I was within thirty feet of the spot where I heard of her husband's death thirty-one years earlier.

prior, and who had been pronounced dead at age 46 in Dallas. The date was November 22, 1963.

How to describe the effect of the murder of the first Catholic President on a classroom of Catholic boys who practically worshipped him? There sat about thirty of us, at the supposed zenith of our testosterone reserves, sobbing like six-year-old girls. I looked up from my own pit to see if our star jock, Dave, had succumbed to emotion. Surely that muscle mutt wouldn't be crying? But he was perhaps the worst of all, practically inconsolable. It is a certainty that this scene was mirrored in all the other four-dozen St. Joe homerooms, not to mention much of the free world, so widely was Kennedy revered.

Artists everywhere vented their feelings of loss the best way they knew how, and my California musical heroes wasted no time. Hours after the assassination, in San Francisco, the Kingston Trio's John Stewart, who had spent time with Kennedy in the White House, penned the haunting "Song For a Friend" and, with only Dean Reilly's upright bass accompaniment, and recorded it three days later, on the day of Kennedy's funeral. With a breaking voice, Stewart memorialized a haunting lyric that remains the best expression of how it felt to live through November 22, 1963:

Song for a Friend

When you sit and wonder why things have gone so wrong
And you wish someone would tell us where our friend has gone.

Look then in the hills when there's courage in the wind
And in the face of freedom and those who look to him.
And search within the heart of every young man with a song
Then I think we'll know where our friend has gone.

Summer takes the winter as the good years take the pain.
There'll be laughter in the land again but hearts won't be the same.

And I know I'll remember when a chill wind takes the sky
And speak of the years he gave us hope for they will never die.
And as we gaze at brave young men when yesterdays grow long,
Then I think we'll know where our friend has gone.

When you sit and wonder why things have gone so wrong.
It's then that we'll remember where our friend has gone.

(©John Stewart, November 22, 1963)

The brief song, played *lamentoso* on a Martin guitar de-tuned to the key of G-flat, was the emotional highlight of the Trio's masterpiece album, *Time to Think*, a decidedly pensive, un-Trio-like effort that also featured gems such as "The Patriot Game," "Hobo's Lullaby," and "If You Don't Look Around." It was released just a month after Kennedy's death, which only amplified its poignancy. Likewise, John Stewart's friend and co-writer of several Trio songs, John Phillips, wrote a melancholy song in the days after the assassination entitled "Monday, Monday."[†] At the time, Phillips headed the folk group The Journeyman, whose Ohio gig was cancelled the night of the killing. Although not directly inspired by Kennedy's death, Phillips later told me that he wrote it as a snapshot of the general malaise that had set in not only in the country but also in his personal life.

Two days after the Trio's album was released, Capitol Records' other chief moneymaking machine, the Beach Boys, recorded their expression of grief, also written the night of the tragedy. The band had tried in vain to cancel a November 22nd performance in Yuba City, California. There, after a moment of silence for Kennedy, the group played to a screaming, record-setting number of fans. Back at the El Dorado Hotel at 2 a.m. that night, still wired from the recent roller coaster of emotions, Brian Wilson wrote the stunning, plaintive melody for "The Warmth of the Sun." When his lead singer and lyricist Mike Love overheard the work-in-progress, he said, "That's one of the most spiritual songs I've ever heard." He then proceeded to write an accompanying metaphoric lyric. "It was a spiritual night," Love would later say. "We got going and a mood took over us. I can't explain it…We wrote that song about losing someone close. We wrote that song until three in the morning, crashed, and went to sleep." On New Year's Day 1964, they committed it to tape.

For the next few days, although the tears subsided, the national sadness lingered on. Throughout the weekend, my family walked around the house like zombies, unable to do anything but dwell on the tragedy (a clear affront to my new baby brother), and stare at first televised national wake on the old black and white until we were bleary-eyed. It was the first time that America was literally glued to the television for days on end, as technically ill-equipped news reporters created the "breaking news" genre on the fly. Predictably, the early

---

[†] Stewart would later be pivotal in helping Phillips' next group, The Mamas and the Papas, land a record deal. Coincidentally, Phillips would become a friend of mine in the 1980s, where we had great times playing music together in upstate New York, and Stewart and his wife, Buffy, would also become friends in the nineties.

reports were riddled with errors, some of which led to the birth of modern American conspiracy paranoia. We quickly learned that my classmate got it wrong about the "Russian" assassin; he was an American who had only lived in Russia. This somewhat eased my fears of nuclear annihilation, but did nothing to lift the gloom.

After two days of watching the suspect being hauled between interrogation rooms of the Dallas City jail, various scenes back at the White House, and the new president trying to calm things down, our family finally left the house for a one-hour interregnum: we went to Sunday morning mass. My only memory of that convocation was that it was all about the tragedy two days previous. Within seconds of returning to our home, the TV was back on, after being allowed only an hour or so to cool down. Still reeling from the effects of what felt like the first death in my "family," I was now hit, almost before the set warmed up, with the emotional coup de grace. As the alleged assassin was being transferred still again, something went horribly wrong, and seemingly in slow motion. Before my very eyes, the killer was himself killed with one shot from a bystander in the jail's basement. To this day, despite the ubiquitous presence of camcorders, the murder of Lee Harvey Oswald by Jack Ruby remains the only execution broadcast live on national television. We had now progressed from the tragic to the surreal — and I didn't even know that word yet.

The melancholia dragged on for weeks, right into 1964, but in February we would get the word from midtown Manhattan that it was OK to have fun again. Since it was Ed Sullivan who shaken us out of our musical coma in 1956, it was only fitting that he lead the nation out of its prolonged period of mourning over JFK. Three weeks before the Dallas tragedy, Ed Sullivan's return flight had been delayed at London Airport because of the chaos surrounding the arrival back in the UK of that country's latest pop band heroes. A week later, a now curious Sullivan signed the diminutive quartet for three performances at $3,300 each. He had no idea what a deal he was getting. From the time Sullivan accidentally encountered the group on the London tarmac until their February 1964 first appearance on his show, the working class Liverpool musicians went on a concert tear throughout Scandinavia, England, and France, propelling their mere popularity into fame.

Word traveled quickly across "the pond," where by January 13, 1964, their first single, "I Want to Hold Your Hand," was selling 10,000 copies an hour, topping one million copies sold since its release on December 26. On February 9, 1964, two days after their touchdown at the fittingly renamed John F. Kennedy Airport in New York, The Beatles debuted on the Sullivan stage as the proud holders of the number one song in the country.

For myself and my small circle of musician friends, the Beatles had all the earmarks of a flash in the pan; although they had some good original material, their first albums were filled out with recycled American pop by Little Eva, the Marvelettes, Chuck Berry, The Isely Brothers, Carl Perkins, Little Richard, and so on. The original music was fun, but I heard nothing initially that made me the least bit curious. The harmonies were basic, mostly lifted from Motown and Everly Brothers styles, and their lead guitarist was good, but no Duane Eddy or Ventures.

When later that year the "mop tops" played in Baltimore's Civic Center, just ten minutes from my house, I couldn't have been less interested. With all the 13-year-old girls gushing over "the cute one" and "the quiet one" and clamoring for tickets, it seemed a virtual certainty that musical depth was not part of the Beatles' equation. As a young musician becoming more interested in vocal arrangements and songwriting, I was aghast that anyone could see songs like "Twist and Shout," "Love Me Do," and "Chains" as being in the same universe as the Beach Boys' "Warmth of the Sun," "Girls on the Beach," "A Young Man is Gone," and "Keep an Eye on Summer." But this was just the start of my contrarianism: in future years I would be the guy who preferred McGovern to Nixon, Beta to VHS, dbx to Dolby, Fender to Gibson, and Mac to PC.

The Beatles' ascension in February was also a matter of great timing, given that the country was looking for an excuse to snap out of its assassination melancholia. But it was terrible timing for Brian Wilson and Co., whose own response to the overlong wake came a month after the Liverpudlians' breakout TV appearance. Although the Beach Boys rushed their fifth album to the stores, containing pop diamonds including "Fun, Fun, Fun" and "Don't Worry, Baby," *Shut Down, Vol. 2* was only able to peak at number 13.[‡] The Beatles had already, to use a 21st century cliché, "sucked all the air out of the room." And although they had stolen the Beach Boys' (and everyone else's) airwave thunder, the Beatles' triumph on Sullivan would mark the beginning of the greatest, and most enriching, rivalry in pop music history.

That spring I tried out for, and made, the JV tennis team. The varsity team would prove far tougher to crack, since its starters were

---

[‡] The Kingston Trio's masterwork, *Time to Think*, peaked at number 7, then quickly disappeared after the Beatles' arrival.

country club-trained kids with refined games I couldn't quite catch up to. As the great Rod Laver used to say, even with serious effort it takes a minimum of five years to become a tennis player; my own game wouldn't ripen until I was in college, where I played on the varsity team for four years. Nonetheless, I would play one semester of varsity tennis at St. Joe before my graduation.

At this time I was making small change playing folk music with Mark, and was beginning to wonder how I would afford a quality guitar and *any* car in the next couple years. Thus, thanks to a recommendation from a neighbor whose window I must have broken, I took a brief summer job in a sweatshop that had a government contract to make valves for gas masks. It was such an awful experience that I vowed never again to earn money by doing something that I didn't love, or at least wasn't part of a great adventure. So far, I've been true to that vow, so the tribulation paid off in the long run.

Although the gas mask job paid well, we worked in the un-air conditioned basement of a converted Baltimore City row house. Baltimore in the summer resembles a blast furnace, albeit with twice the humidity, and we toiled over a bench with nothing but a rotating fan to keep us from passing out. (A popular Baltimore bumper sticker read: "I know Hell is hot, but what about the humidity?") The other ten employees I shared the basement with were inner city blacks with whom I got along well. One day I noticed a couple of them singing along with the radio, and sounding pretty good. I had the idea to get them gathered around the large, multi-speed fan during our lunch break and sing into it á cappella to achieve varying degrees of vibrato. Over the next few weeks, I would teach them harmony parts, and as we improved we all looked forward to singing into that fan. It made the drudgery almost bearable. And you haven't lived until you've sung "Surfer Girl" with a group of people who have zero interest in "riding the surf together" and who possess a completely different definition for the word "woodie."

My guitar playing was now entering a new phase. Having grown disenchanted with my old-school teachers, who showed no interest in the new music that was exploding onto the pop scene, I quit taking lessons after two years at the Maryland Studio of Music. I had concluded that I had learned the rudiments of reading and ear training, and thus had the tools to learn the modern styles on my own. My arrogance was almost immediately jolted by the 1964 release of a hypnotic LP entitled *Getz/Gilberto*, the monumental pairing of 37-

year-old American jazz tenor saxophonist Stan Getz and 33-year-old Brazilian guitarist/vocalist/composer, João Gilberto.

The young guitarist, discovered by Getz on a recent trip to Brazil, had, with the help of genius pal, done nothing short of creating a new musical genre, using his own newly invented guitar technique and the songs of 37-year-old Brazilian composer, Antonio Carlos "Tom" Jobim. The essentials were that Gilberto and Jobim blended traditional samba rhythms with completely non-traditional jazz chords, and Jobim's stunning melodies, which he crafted meticulously. Additionally, they eschewed the standard Brazilian percussion instruments in favor of a percussive guitar plucking style that became known as *violão gago*, or "stammering guitar." Getz's beautiful sax lines, for me at least, were just the icing on the cake.

The Great João Gilberto

What was so mind-blowing to me about Gilberto's playing was his chord work, often featuring just three notes so well chosen that they quietly launched the melody into the stratosphere — but not just any notes. Gilberto plucked substitute notes that were only implied by the composed chord, tricking the listener's ear, through a process termed "psycho acoustics," to hear notes that weren't even being played. The resultant effect, which took a formerly poverty-stricken Gilberto years to develop, was more effective than all the "power chords" played through 300-watt amplifiers.[§] (Other greats who "got it" were Count Basie, Django Reinhardt, Freddie Green, and the Four Freshman.) It was my first exposure to the musical concept that "less is more," and started a lifelong musical exploration of how the brain processes the strange vibrations we call music.

Of course, I knew none of this when I first heard Gilberto's wife, Astrud, a housewife thinking she was just cutting a dummy vocal track, singing Jobim's "Girl From Ipanema" on the album. All I knew was, no matter how many times I lifted and replaced the needle on those poor record grooves, I had absolutely no idea what chords Gilberto was playing, even though I had no difficulty with rock or pop songs. I purchased the sheet music for "Ipanema", only to find that the

---

[§] During one eight-month stretch, João practically locked himself in the humid, tiled bathroom of his sister's apartment, where he re-voiced his guitar chords countless times before he was satisfied.

published chords sounded nothing like those played by Gilberto. Eventually, I saw him play the song on television, and I was transfixed, trying not to blink, lest I miss something. However, I recognized not one of Gilberto's chord grips — it was a major ego buster. Worse still, in the days before any sort of video recordings, I had to get it in one viewing, and I failed completely. For a time I felt like throwing my guitar out the window. I didn't, but I stopped playing for weeks, until I slowly began getting the courage to tear into that record, and one-by-one, I started to pull some notes out.

Of course, I was fortunate — kids of my generation, unburdened by a nonstop onslaught of digital distractions, had the ability to sit still for hours, focused on concepts like nuance and quality, and actually get good at something, or even get lost in books. If it happened once it happened a hundred times that my parents were having some friends over and I stayed in my room practicing, unable to be coaxed downstairs lest I'd lose my place on the section of vinyl grooves I was deciphering. Some of these guests later told me that they thought I was shy. Of course, they hadn't seen me in action sneaking into the Edgewood Theater. It was a hobby that, unbeknownst to my parents' guests, had recently shifted into second gear.

My musical passions now included trying to meet whatever successful musicians I could in order to try to get an insight into how they did it. To this end I began perfecting techniques for not only getting into shows for free, but also scamming my way backstage. At the time there was much written about famous "gatecrashers," and I gleaned what I could, combined with my original schemes, in furtherance of my goal to get closer to the action. My Saturday matinee successes in illegal entry at the Edgewood movie theater gave me all the confidence I needed. Over the next two decades, crashing became a hobby of sorts, and I prided myself on having a 95% success rate. I started at the Marine Ballroom on Atlantic City's Steel Pier.

My first successful crash occurred at a 1965 show starring Gary Lewis and the Playboys, then riding high with the Al Kooper song, "This Diamond Ring." Gary

John West and his Cordovox gizmo (2nd from right)

happened to be the son of superstar comic Jerry Lewis. I was particularly interested in an instrumental sound they obtained which sounded like nothing I had heard before; I was determined to ask them how they did it. Like any good gatecrasher, I arrived early in order to "case the joint." I entered service doors that were clearly off-limits and were also clearly unguarded. Inside one storage area I encountered another door that opened onto a narrow, rickety wooden walkway on the outside perimeter of the pier, thirty feet above the churning Atlantic Ocean. About 100 feet along this walkway, towards the end of the pier, there appeared a deck with picnic tables butted up against a railing over the ocean. Sitting at those tables were Jerry Lewis's son and his Playboys! It had to be the coolest backstage area in the world.

I carefully made my way to the "back deck" where I was warmly greeted by the band, whom I suppose got a kick out of this 15-year-old interloper. I told them I was a guitarist, and that I thought "This Diamond Ring" was amazing. One player, John West, explained where they got their secret sound; it was from his newly invented Cordovox, an Italian "electronic accordion" that predated polyphonic synthesizers by at least ten years, but created similar tones.

They let me watch the show from the wings, where I was mesmerized by that Cordovox (and stunned by Gary's pitch-challenged voice), and when they came offstage, Gary, who was somehow named by *Cash Box* magazine as 1965's Male Vocalist of the Year, [**] asked me if I knew where he and his California buddies could surf the next morning. I told him I had been coming here since I was born, and knew just the place, about three piers down. They thanked me and went their way, and I was due back at the Shoreham Hotel. The next day, the word on the boardwalk was that Gary Lewis and the Playboys were busted by the beach patrol for surfing at a "No Surf" beach. Sorry, guys.[††]

That summer was also the first time that I saw the Beach Boys in concert. It happened that my mother's brother, Phil Cascio, invited us to spend a couple of days with his family in Long Branch, New Jersey. Uncle Phil worked for American Totalisator Company, which calculated and displayed the betting at racetracks, and during the summers he was stationed at Monmouth Park Racetrack, near Long Branch. We had visited Uncle Phil at Long Branch before, and I was always amazed that

---

[**] A quick listen to Gary's recordings provides evidence of a "guide vocal" provided by great LA session singer Ron Hicklin, whose group sang on TV themes from Batman, to That Girl, Laverne and Shirley, and Happy Days. Hicklin's ubiquitous group also ghosted vocals for The Monkees, The Brady Kids, the Partridge Family, and Paul Revere and the Raiders, to name just a few. Too bad Ron didn't tour with Gary Lewis.

[††] Others that I met backstage at the pier included The New Christy Minstrels and The Association.

the beach culture there was so different from Atlantic City. Here there were genuine beach babes my own age, bottle-blond guys who fantacized about "Surf City," surf shops where the Beach Boys' 45's were on permanent rotation, and a strange, but sweet smelling smoke I had never experienced at those AC Turkish Taffee shops. The locals somehow even managed to surf those gnarly East Coast waves. At last, East Coasters who knew what "woodies" were.

On our 1965 trip I learned at a surf shop that The Beach Boys were playing at the Asbury Park Convention Hall, about eight miles south on Ocean Avenue. I persuaded one of my cousins to go with me to the show and I immediately hopped a transit bus to go purchase tickets in Asbury Park. My rising passions for music and adventure were driving my super-timid homemaker mother crazy with worry.

"You were out of control," mom told me recently. "We got into town, and five minutes later you were gone! Fifteen-years-old! We had to go out looking for you."

Although we went to the show, I was dismayed to see that the Beach Boy I really wanted to meet, Brian Wilson, was nowhere to be seen on the stage. Unbeknownst to me, he had suffered a nervous breakdown seven months

Glen Campbell (left) with the Beach Boys

earlier and no longer toured with the band. Standing in his place, playing bass, was LA session guitarist Glen Campbell. The show was a typical sixties screamfest, but fun nonetheless. And although I missed the main man, his absence was put to great use, as he was in an LA recording studio creating sonic miracles that would soon surface on Beach Boys' records. After the show, I continued honing my gatecrashing skills, making my way to the private parking garage in time to meet Carl Wilson, Dennis Wilson, and Glen Campbell as they approached their limousines.

Perhaps the result of my humiliating reckoning (thanks to João Gilberto) that I was a mediocre guitarist, I briefly flirted with the idea of pursuing something other than music as a profession. At the time, the only other career that seemed as captivating was the one that promised close associations with the likes of "Tatiana Romanova," "Honey Rider," "Domino Derval," and, last but not least, "Pussy Galore." Maybe I could be Agent 008? "Russo, Gus Russo." Thus, in late 1964, fifteen-year-old Gus Russo offered his services to the Central Intelligence Agency by

> CENTRAL INTELLIGENCE AGENCY
> WASHINGTON, D. C. 20505
>
> 4 January 1965
>
> Mr. Gus Russo
> 213 Boswell Road
> Baltimore, Maryland 21229
>
> Dear Mr. Russo:
>
> We have received your recent request and are enclosing a brochure which concerns employment opportunities within this Agency.
>
> Thank you very much for your interest.
>
> Sincerely,
>
> E. D. Echols
> Director of Personnel
>
> Enclosure

scribbling a letter asking what he had to do to become a spy. I still have the response letter and brochure they sent back two weeks later, which suggested I study science or linguistics in college. What the —? I didn't want to be "Q" or "Miss Moneypenny." I wanted to be Bond — you know, the guy who snorkels in the Bahamas, drives a Bentley, and plays no-limits *Chemin de Fer* in Monte Carlo. No wonder the Brits had a better intelligence service — they had their priorities right. And given my awful grades in Mr. Hall's biology class, and my complete dependence on my friends at Cardinal Gibbons for the answers to French tests, I concluded that the CIA and "Agent 008" were not a good fit. Not long after my earth-shaking decision that would surely result in **S.P.E.C.T.R.E.**'s conquest of the planet, NBC Television, as if to rub salt in my wound, ran the series "I Spy," in which "Kelly Robinson" was a touring tennis pro by day and a spy by night. Another teasing lie — I knew because I had that namby-pamby brochure and it said nothing about tennis-playing spies!

By 1966, disabused of the romantic notions of making gas mask valves in a Baltimore sweat shop or offering my covert gatecrashing skills to the CIA as a summer intern, I returned to the Pratt in search of ways to earn money playing music as a sixteen-year-old. A kindly librarian who knew me from my constant music searches directed me to a guidebook on summer jobs in resort areas. "They often hire young musicians as staff, you know, like waiters," she explained, "then they entertain the guests at night." I must have written letters to dozens of resorts that advertised for just such musicians. Most of these were in New England or the Poconos. Of those that sent back brochures and job applications, I most wanted to be hired by The Pococabana in Minisink Hills, Pennsylvania.

The Pococabana's Technicolor brochure advertised a beautiful pool (with Bond-like babes perched nearby), tennis courts, rock and roll, hootenannies, and Broadway show productions with an actual Broadway director who summered there (no need to wait for Guffman).In those days, the Pocono hotels usually had a slogan, and the Pococabana's was "Just for the Fun of It!" I couldn't have agreed more. It even had its own cartoon mascot, "L'il Poco," a foreshadowing of a yet-to-form band that would have a huge influence on my music in the coming years. The resort's name, a play on New York's swinging Copacabana Club, sounded like a place that 007 or the Rat Pack might frequent – a virtual light year from gas masks in a 120-degree Baltimore row house!

The ads even showed a kid who looked like me playing a guitar that looked like mine to an enthralled gaggle of well-dressed guests by the fireplace — a good omen if ever there was one. Like the CIA brochure, I still have that booklet from the Pococabana (OK, I am the original pack rat).

Before I could complete the job application, I had to first obtain a Pennsylvania youth work permit, which I did, returning it with a downright wonderful facsimile of my father's signature. When the permit arrived, I sent off the application, attaching a photo of my CYO talent show trophy ("one of many," I lied), and shortly thereafter I was ecstatic to learn that the resort in fact hired me as an "entertainer/ kitchen apprentice." I couldn't have cared less about the kitchen work, since I envisioned just the pool, the tennis courts, the music, and the babes, and I was confident they would kick me out of the kitchen once they realized not only my great skills as a guitarist, but also that I had a rare allergy to domestic work. Sadly, I still suffer from it.

That poser has my job!

Of course, I still had to break the news to the parents, who in the stern Italian way my father had mastered, let me know in one terse sentence that my dreams were to be dashed: "Not a chance — end of discussion," my father pronounced. I knew better than to ask a second time, since that sort of disrespect was usually met with another short sentence that I must have heard a thousand times: "Because I'm your father and I said so." To pursue it beyond that was to invite something painful to happen — to me. I was certain that my father was just doing my mother's bidding, since her kids were, and remain, her whole life. To be fleeing the nest at sixteen was probably about twenty years ahead of her schedule, but with Mark Twain, James Michener, Siddhartha, and all my musical heroes whispering in my ear, I had to up the ante: I decided to spend an entire night out on my own to let them know how serious I was; the point being that unless they relented, I would just run away. Of course I wouldn't have followed through, but it was a bluff I thought might work. And it did.

Where to stay that night? I remembered a place near the Pratt, adjacent to the only lit tennis courts around. Since I had been trespassing on their courts for months working on my game at night, I might as well use the facility next door. Thus, after a night spent on a couch at the University of Maryland's student union, where I blended in with napping college students, I returned unwashed to my first class at St. Joe the next morning (I might run away from home, but I *really* feared the wrath of those Xaverians!). There I was immediately escorted to the principal's office to await my parents, who had called the school. The rest is a bit of a blur, but the bottom line was that I would be allowed to work at the Pococabana that summer. It was the official beginning of the rest of my life.

The end of the 1965 school year saw me packing my bags (especially my tennis racket and guitar) for the Poconos, only a four-hour bus ride from Baltimore, yet a place I had never even seen in person. I stared at that brochure the whole way there, daydreaming about the world outside Irvington.

My first glimpse of the hotel was heartening — it actually looked like the brochure, albeit with slightly less saturated colors. The owners seemed nice, the dorm was reasonable, the tennis courts and pool in great shape, and the girls were cute — of course my taste in girls was likely pretty forgiving since I spent most of the year in St. Joe's all male zoo. Then I was introduced to the dungeon I was supposed to call my workplace for the next three months: the tucked away steamy corner of a smelly, hot kitchen run by a madman Slavic chef known to throw butcher knives from one side of the kitchen to the other in fits of rage. Oh, and he was always enraged. My nook (or was it a cranny?) was where a non-stop stream of dirty pots, pans, plates and glassware from over a hundred diners were stacked for me and one other "pearl diver," as we were called, to race through almost nonstop. What happened to "Just for the fun of it"?

The job was such a drudgery that I tried to lift my spirits by pretending that dishwashing was an elite position, attempting to trick my brain by referring to my new career as a "Culinary Utensil Hygienist." Soon I was creating vaunted job titles for the rest of the staff: chambermaids became "Habitation Control Engineers," and groundskeepers were christened "Topographical Systems Analysts." Part of my motive was that I reckoned that when I returned to school in the fall, it would be more impressive to say I spent my summer as a Culinary Utensil Hygienist than as a lowly dishwashing pearl diver.

Although I did get to play guitar by that fireside, my hands were such a mass of cuts from broken glass that I had to invent my own minimalist chord grips, although not as brilliant as João Gilberto's. After a couple of weeks spent with "L'il Poco," I had had enough. Having learned of a waiter job available at the Pocono's grandest four-star resort, I packed up my stuff and hitched over to the gorgeous Shawnee Inn, situated not far away on the banks of the Delaware Water Gap.

The main building was breathtaking, boasting a huge concrete and white plaster façade that overlooked the Delaware River. Opened in 1911, the Inn was known as a golfer's paradise, with a championship course built on an island and designed by the legendary A.W. Tillinghast. This "Gem of the East" hosted the first PGA National Championship in 1938, and featured members such as Jackie Gleason and Art Carney, Ed Sullivan, President Eisenhower, and George Gobel. It was at Shawnee that Arnold Palmer met his wife. At the time I arrived, the Inn was owned by the famous choral conductor and recording artist Fred Waring.

Unlike the Pococabana, the kitchen at the Inn was pristine and the waiters and waitresses in their starched white uniforms were treated with great respect. I felt at home immediately. And if I hadn't been sold on the place already, I was a couple days later when I was alerted by a fellow worker to go to the rec room. There stood "The Great One"

himself, Jackie Gleason, putting on a pool exhibition, this just a few years after Gleason had starred in the terrific film, *The Hustler*. I watched as he ran three racks, but apparently I had missed the first half-dozen!

Everything was going swimmingly in the Poconos, but apparently not in Baltimore, where my mother had put out an all-points bulletin for her MIA 16-year-old son, who somehow had disappeared from the Pococabana, where she had called to check on him. That's right — yours truly had forgotten to alert his parents to his change of locale. At some point I called home to let the folks know I had seen Gleason, but before I could say "Hi," my mother broke into hysterics. That's strange, I thought. Then — oops! My oversight hit me. Then my father got on the phone, and it wasn't pretty. The bottom line was that a bus ticket would be waiting for me tomorrow at the Stroudsburg, PA Trailways depot, and if I weren't on that bus, there would be hell to pay. For some reason, my Huckleberry Finn bravado had now deserted me. Actually, I knew the reason: my father was no stranger to corporal punishment and downright fits of rage. To me, the first-born of his kids, he could be terrifying. He mellowed exponentially with my two younger brothers, but I had to run the gauntlet. I later learned that oldest son Brian Wilson had a similar experience.

Although I returned from the resort world, I had seen the light, and would soon return with a vengeance. The rest of that summer was spent jamming with musician friends from St. Joe, trying to find an electric version of my folk success. My folk partner Mark had no interest in "going electric," but I wanted to move on, in the absurd hope that I could create an East Coast version of the Beach Boys. My maternal grandmother Rose (not to be confused with my paternal grandmother Rosina) was the first to really get my passion for music and stunned me that summer with by far the priciest gift I had ever received: she took me to the Mecca for local musicians, Chuck Levin's Music Store in Wheaton, Maryland, and told me to pick out a guitar and amp.

I almost hyperventilated as I hypnotically marched to the Fender display case, where, unable to speak, I pointed to a Fender Jaguar (just like the Beach Boys' Carl Wilson's guitar, only in sea foam green). I then turned and pointed to a Fender Deluxe Reverb amp. My grandmother then went off with the salesman to negotiate, while I waited to wake up from this dream. If it was a dream, I have yet to awake, because Rose had somehow stashed away some money and purchased that rig for what was, for us, a king's ransom. It was somewhere in the vicinity of $400 ($1600 today), but I was never told the exact amount.

Although this new equipment allowed me to audition for local bands, I, being a typical (or so I am told) take-charge Virgo, had my own ideas for starting a band. My first attempt was a short-lived five-piece combo we called The Eastwinds, my East Coast attempt at a surf band. What I didn't grasp was that beach music was completely undanceable, especially when compared to the tracks coming out of Stax, James Brown's Smash Records, and Motown — so it was very hard to get gigs at those teen centers and CYOs. Eventually I would compromise, just to get jobs, but my aversion to playing "dance music" would plague me throughout my career. Bands like mine almost had to get recording contracts to stay afloat, thus I began trying my hand at writing songs. And pop songwriting was entering a new phase of sophistication.

For Baltimoreans not obsessed with pop music, 1966 was the year of the Baltimore Orioles baseball team. Me being a member of the Orioles Junior Advocates, I too was caught up in the frenzy of our first championship contender since the team's founding in 1954. Having spent many a Saturday afternoon in Memorial Stadium's bleachers, I vowed I was going to be there as well, when the team played its first ever World Series home games. Security in those days was virtually non-existent, and having already honed my gatecrashing skills on the Steel Pier, I had no doubt that I, and some of my fellow advocates, would find a way in. In the weeks leading up to the Series, we were able to determine that the fence behind the right field bullpen was completely unguarded. On their first home game, after the Os won the first two in LA, a couple of us jumped the fence and raced for the bleachers, where the usher recognized us from the dozens of games we had attended. He told us to just find a place to squeeze in and he would look the other way.

We thus witnessed the madness as the Orioles won the next two games for a four-game sweep of the heavily favored LA Dodgers, who boasted pitching icons Sandy Koufax and Don Drysdale. Although the Dodgers pitched brilliantly, the Os pitched even better in two tense 1-0 games. The last game was decided by a solo blast off the bat of Frank Robinson. Having blown my shot at the UFO, this time I made certain I was ready by purchasing a cheapo Polaroid "Swinger" camera that took horrible black & whites, including one of Frank rounding the bases. (See www.gusrusso.com)

Chapter Four

"Something's Happenin' Here"

WE NOW ENTER the era in which culture and politics seemed to coalesce, reach critical mass, and implode. The assaults on the collective psyche were occurring so fast that the period quickly became a blur for those who lived through it. As my old friend Papa John Phillips used to say, "If you remember the sixties, you weren't there." Well, friends, this is the period he was referring to.

By 1966, I had finally hooked up with a good working band, consisting of myself on lead guitar and three upperclassmen on bass, rhythm guitar, and drums. The band had three decent singers and an amazing drummer who spent most of his time playing along with Gene Krupa on his gorgeous pearl Slingerland kit. Don, our bassist, came up with our name when his teacher at St. Joe chastised his class for not paying attention: "What is this, a drawing room society?" Thus we became The Drawing Room Society, a name that fit in perfectly with the British invasion, which supplied most of our repertoire.

In those days, most teen bands were compromised, since they always included at least one mediocre player who was only allowed in because he could afford a PA system. Our band wanted no such weakness, so we had to improvise on the PA business. Luckily, Rick, our other guitarist was an electronics wiz, so we all pitched in for a Heathkit build-it-yourself amplifier, which he assembled, saving us hundreds. Next we needed speakers. One of our bandmates, who will go unnamed, had a summer job on a construction site where they were building the new city of Columbia, between Baltimore and DC. Apparently, the job site had an outdoor speaker system mounted on poles. They were loud, and obviously indestructible. Thus, at one rehearsal, I remember frantically the band painting two mysterious "horn speakers" green over their original gray.

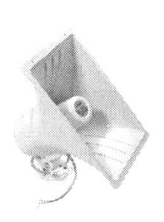

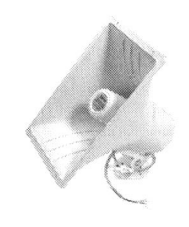

I asked no questions.

Although those speakers were workhorses, they had less dynamic range than the system used by Tokyo Rose in WW2. And that amplifier broke down all the time, causing Rick to race mid-song from the stage, while we jammed, and ingenuously patched that thing together with whatever bailing wire was handy. We'd be up there taking solos and laughing our butts off while Rick struggled to crank that thing up before the dancers passed out. Although we could have stopped the song, Rick wouldn't hear of it, seeing it as a personal challenge to fix that thing in under five minutes so we could end the song properly.

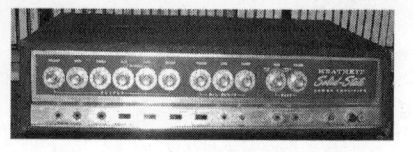

The "DRS" specialized in Brit-rock with good harmony vocals, covering many songs by the Beatles, the Hollies, Spencer Davis, the Bee Gees, and the Zombies — but mostly Beatles. It was amazing to be in a "Beatle band" while the real thing was still cranking out hits. In those days, singles were usually released on Fridays, and we'd schedule a rehearsal right after school that day in order to learn a new release so we could play it that night at a teen center.

The PA thieves rehearsing

There was a certain swagger in being the first band to play a new release, especially by the Beatles. This became very challenging when the new release was "Strawberry Fields," and we had to buy it, learn it (on a turntable), and adapt it in one afternoon. I'll never forget the night we played "Penny Lane" to the members of the St. Williams' CYO on the day it was released. The kids were stunned, and we had to reprise it a couple more times that night. A particularly proud moment came when we won a huge "battle of the bands" against six other groups. Although we had no keyboard, we took a big gamble and closed our set with the Doors' "Light My Fire," on which I had worked for days trying to cop Ray Manzarek's iconic baroque organ riff on my guitar. That vinyl had practically melted by the time I was done with it, but we won that contest going away, and it led to many more jobs.

On a macro level, as John Phillips alluded to, it was an incredible time to be growing up. From London, to Washington, to LA, to San Francisco, socio-politics and pop culture were in overdrive. The fuel was an explosive mixture of the civil rights movement, disgust with the war in Vietnam, Boomers entering both their college years and their draft age, pot smuggled back from 'Nam, LSD smuggled out of research labs, the sexual revolution, the first generation of teens with disposable income, a best-selling book that said the Kennedy assassination involved a government cover-up, and the decisions of Brian Wilson and the Beatles to "turn on." Those of us in mid-high school were on the periphery of it all, but it was seeping into us by osmosis nonetheless. The atmosphere was charged and inescapable.

After his late 1964 nervous breakdown, studio-bound Brian Wilson began smoking pot to help him relax, but the drug had an unforeseen positive effect on his artistic growth. In March 1965, his band released *The Beach Boys Today!*, an album of such musical nuance and beauty, especially the side two "ballad side," that it had the unwanted effect of driving a wedge between the band and the average teen musicians who couldn't begin to play these 150-second masterpieces. Twenty-three-year-old Wilson, the first rocker allowed to produce his own music, was now employing uncommon (for rock) instrumentation, impossible (but elegant) chord progressions, and the most complex (but listenable) pop vocal arrangements on earth, essentially asking: "What if the Four Freshmen turned on with George Gershwin?" The combination virtually guaranteed these songs would not be played at teen center and CYO dances. It also guaranteed that my vinyl copies would disintegrate in record time, as I tried to plumb the depths of this remarkable new sound.

Elsewhere in Los Angeles, a vortex of rock synergy was developing on the Sunset Strip. The Whisky A Go-Go had opened there in 1964, followed by the Action, the Galaxy, the Sea Witch, Ciro's, Pandora's Box, and The Trip, all great concert clubs within walking distance of each other. A few blocks off the Strip was the Troubadour, another key musical melting pot. When Ciro's house band, The Byrds, hit with a remake of Dylan's "Mr. Tambourine Man," the scene really caught fire. Musicians now gravitated en masse to "The Strip" from all points to play showcases or just to meet other players in order to form new combinations. This primordial soup of pop fostered or gave birth to an incredible amount of hit-makers: the Mamas and the Papas, The Association, The Eagles, The Turtles, the Seeds, Love, the Lovin' Spoonful, the Buffalo Springfield, the Standells, the Strawberry Alarm Clock, Moby Grape, Iron Butterfly, the Mothers of Invention, and the Doors. The city's summer 1966 closing of Pandora's Box on Sunset and Crescent Heights instigated a riot on the Sunset Strip in which 300 protesters were arrested. The event inspired guitarist Stephen Stills, then smarting from his failed audition for The Monkees, to write one of the first great rock anthems, "For What it's Worth."

Brian Wilson's Liverpool rivals, also starting to enjoy the wacky weed, replied to the *Today!* release with an album that made converts of many US musicians (including this one) that had been on the fence. *Rubber Soul*, released nine months after *The Beach Boys Today!*, was the first Beatle album not saturated with teen love songs. Not only were the lyrics now considering more complex human interactions such as jealousy, sexism, loneliness, and even prostitution, instrumentally the band began experimenting with sounds unattainable with their Rickenbacker, Gretsch, and Hofner guitars. "The boys," under the guiding hand of classical producer George Martin, were now immersed in tape speed experiments, synthetic sound processing, sitars, faux harpsichords, "fuzz bass," and string quartets. As icing on the cake, their songwriting skills were growing exponentially. There were no "fillers" here, as there were on all previous pop albums ("A whole album with all good stuff," Brian Wilson humbly called it, as if there was much filler on his *Today!* album). Although they were not in Wilson's league from a harmonic standpoint, the Beatles' increasingly nuanced melodies and superior metaphoric lyrics (an admitted Wilson weakness) more than kept them in the game. But *Rubber Soul*, with its wall-to-wall great songs, pushed Wilson, working in isolation just blocks geographically but a light year musically from the scene on The Strip, to create what many critics have named the greatest pop album of all time. That was exactly what Brian had told his wife he would do.

My relationship with *Pet Sounds* began the day it hit the stores, Monday, May 16, 1966. I was such a fan that I had marked my calendar weeks earlier noting the date of the release; the *Today* album had been so stunning that I couldn't wait for new Wilson material, even if it were only half as good. Although I had my driver's license, I did not yet own a car, and on that particular day I convinced my mother that the closest Montgomery Ward department store was due for a family visit after my father came home from work. On arrival I bounded up to the fourth floor record department, only to find no new Beach Boys album. I worried that it had already sold out. But the salesman said he had not sold one all day, and happily agreed to see if it were in the back, as yet unboxed. Within minutes he returned with a Capitol Records box and a Sunny's Surplus box-cutter.

Out came the most bizarre looking "rock" record I had yet seen: On the front, the five Beach Boys were pictured feeding animals at a petting zoo — not a surfboard or a car in sight. On the reverse, the band was seen in full Kabuki Theater Samurai wardrobe. And the title, *Pet Sounds*, was no less arcane. I plunked down a hard-earned $3.99 and we headed home, a tad concerned that Brian had gone too far this time.

Within a minute of arriving home, the needle hit the grooves, and I was simultaneously mesmerized and confounded. The music was as new to me as João Gilberto's chords had been two years earlier — only this music held dozens of layers of such heavenly complexity. There was no use picking up my guitar to try and play along. Even had I been able to decipher Wilson's musical code, this was a symphony with no place for a Fender Jaguar. As a listener, you were transported in the first seconds by some sort of arpeggiated string instrument (actually a custom-made 12-string "mandolin guitar" in the hands of jazz great Barney Kessel), recorded with the most sumptuous echo chamber you had ever heard.* This four-bar intro to "Wouldn't it Be Nice" was in the key of A, yet the verse opens in F, while the bridge is in D. And the rhythm is not kept by predictable rock guitars and drums, but by two accordions, doing a painful non-stop "triple bellows shake," and tympani. And this was one of the most accessible songs on the album!!! Twenty-three-year-old Wilson somehow made these bizarre leaps of tonality and logic sound completely natural, so much so that when released as a single, its infectious genius was irrepressible. No other rock

---

* It is rarely noted, but Brian treated the echo chamber like another instrument, and his painstaking settings played a major role in the sound of the Beach Boys.

single had ever been so odd, yet it hit the pop charts with a bang, residing there for three months, reaching Number Two in the UK.

From the first song's fade-out, the sonic palette grew even more stunning, more beautiful, and more creative. It seemed like the work of genius. Here were gorgeous songs being interpreted by tack pianos, harpsichords, bicycle horns, Theremins, kettle drums, buzzing Hammond organs, dog whistles, bass harmonica and banjo duets, French horns, violas, upright basses, accordions, vibraphones, ukuleles, empty plastic water bottles, and slide trombones — all building to what remains the strangest rock coda ever: the sound of Brian's two dogs barking as a train roars by (???) With Gershwin's *Rhapsody in Blue* as his guidepost, Wilson made it all work. The Beatles may have had their sitar, but Brian had everything else. With no George Martin coaching him, Wilson had now raised the musical ante into the stratosphere.

Beneath this succulent sheen were more traditional pianos, strings, horns and guitars, handled by LA's "Wrecking Crew" session wizards, but they were placed far back in the mix. What most impresses me now, having since spent thousands of hours in recording studios, is how Brian managed to keep this musical menagerie from sounding cluttered or forced. The album breathes effortlessly, never jarring, and without a hint of ego (the lyrics accentuated that point). This was not some rich kid showing off how many instruments he could afford to hire; everything, including that lush echo chamber, was chosen to service the emotional core of the song at hand. And those emotions, fed by nervous breakdowns, not narcissism, were breathtaking.

Brian was just hearing brilliant new instrumental and harmonic concoctions that even the most jaded session players promised him wouldn't work – that is until they heard the playback. An oft-repeated account tells how a sixty-something session violinist from the LA Symphony quietly advised a twenty-something Wilson that the notes on his chart clashed so badly with another instrument that it would never blend. A smiling Wilson told him to wait until he recorded another sound he was hearing in his head and all would be just fine. When that actually occurred, the violinist knew he was in the presence of someone special and never raised an objection again. "How he heard all those combinations in his head was beyond me," the yeoman string player later gushed.

There was obviously way too much going on here to take in on the first listen, thus I replayed that album repeatedly until I passed out in the wee hours of the morning. Within two days I had played it so much that the already-scratchy grooves were practically screaming to me to give them a break. Although I kept my original copy, I replaced over a dozen worn out copies until the CD *finally* came out in 1990. Although I now own thousands of great recordings, *Pet Sounds* is far and away my favorite; nothing else even comes close. I persuaded my band to work up a reasonable facsimile of "Wouldn't it Be Nice" and "Sloop John B," but for the most part, local musicians ignored it, favoring hipper, rougher-edged fare. Although I felt, once again, like an outsider, I would eventually learn that I was far from alone in my astonishment at what Wilson had delivered to the world.

The accolades were at their most intense in the UK, where Rolling Stones manager Andrew Loog Oldham and Paul McCartney had heard an early acetate of the record, brought over by LA record producer Lou Adler. Oldham said, "That first listen changed our lives." When the album was soon released, Oldham took the unprecedented step of taking out a full-page ad in *Melody Maker*, wherein he named *Pet Sounds* "The greatest album ever made." Who drummer Keith Moon thought the album was going to change the world, and set about corralling the rest of his band, the Brit press, and Lennon & McCartney at the Waldorf, where they listened to the album twice. John and Paul quickly walked over to the piano and tried to figure out some of the intricate chords, and on leaving the hotel room, the two Beatles exclaimed, "We'll tell everybody!"

In the ensuing years, McCartney has been consistently effusive in his praise, saying, "It was *Pet Sounds* that blew me out of the water. I love the album so much. I've just bought my kids each a copy of it for their education in life ... I figure no one is educated musically 'til they've heard that album ... I've often played *Pet Sounds* and cried. I played it to John [Lennon] so much that it would be difficult for him to escape the influence ... it was the record of the time.... sends shivers up my spine." He even called the album's standout ballad, "God Only Knows," "the greatest song ever written."

Other artists echoed McCartney. Eric Clapton: "I consider *Pet Sounds* to be one of the greatest pop LPs to ever be released. It encompasses everything that's ever knocked me out and rolled it all into one." Elton John: "For me to say that I was enthralled would be an understatement. I had never heard such magical sounds, so amazingly recorded. It undoubtedly changed the way that I, and countless others, approached recording. It is a timeless and amazing recording of incredible genius and beauty." Beatles producer George Martin: "Without *Pet Sounds, Sgt. Pepper* wouldn't have happened... *Pepper* was an attempt to equal *Pet Sounds*." Bob Dylan said of Brian Wilson's talents, "That ear — I mean, Jesus, he's got to will that to the Smithsonian."

The press, often belatedly, shared the opinions of the music makers:

• *In 1995, nearly thirty years after its release, a panel of top musicians, songwriters and producers assembled by MOJO magazine voted it "The Greatest Album Ever Made."*

• *It was number one in New Musical Express's list "The 100 Best Albums".*

• *Critics of the German magazine Spex voted it the best album of the 20th Century;*

• *In 2001 VH1 placed it at #3.*

• *The London Times magazine ranked it greatest album of all time.*

• *Rolling Stone placed it at #2 on its list of the 500 greatest albums of all time behind only Sgt. Pepper's Lonely Hearts Club Band by The Beatles.*

• *In 2004, it was one of 50 recordings chosen by the to be added to the National Recording Registry.*

• *According to Acclaimedmusic.net, Pet Sounds is the most acclaimed pop album of all time by music journalists.*

• *In 2006, the album was chosen by TIME as one of the 100 best albums of all time, ranking number two on their list.*

These Johnny-come-lately accolades were often decades too late. Capitol Records hated the album with its "undanceable" music, and refused to promote it. And although a couple single releases did well, the LP was the first Beach Boys release in years to not go Gold. The effect on Brian was said to be devastating, further accelerating his descent into full-blown depression.

As much as I loved what Brian had done, I was likewise simultaneously taking a huge ego hit: this guy was only seven years older than I! And there was just no way I could get from here to there by the time I was twenty-three. It was the "Gilberto Effect" all over again: I did not exist in the same musical universe as artists such as Wilson, so what was the point? Brian and I were in separate funks, on opposite coasts, over the same recording — but for very different reasons. My dismay, however, was soon overtaken by the fact that our band was having a rip-roaring great time, while putting smiles on a lot of faces. Even some of our parents began to loosen up: it just might be possible to make a career of this rock thing after all. I might not be Brian Wilson, but the scene was just too electrifying to quit because of one amazing record.

Pet Sounds propelled my interest in songwriting and producing, and thus I soon owned a cheap reel-to-reel deck that I picked up in a pawn shop on Baltimore's infamous "Block," and began making what, in retrospect, were horrible demos; my early songs were nothing more than cut-and-paste jobs, borrowing riffs from my favorite songs while hoping no one would notice — pretty much the way most writers start out. When I felt I had five or six commercial songs, I made my first ever 4-hour trek, via Trailways bus, to Manhattan — in those days a round-trip ticket from Baltimore to New York cost around $20.

Like all new arrivals in the Big Apple, I was overwhelmed by the bustle, from the swarms of racing commuters at the gates to the cavernous Port Authority above, which in those days had as unofficial greeters massive herds of prostitutes, pimps, and drug dealers. There were even more of them out on the street — the terminal is located on Eighth Avenue and 42nd Street, which was the national epicenter of flesh and drug peddling. It was a bitter cold February day when, tapes in arm, I ran the gonorrhea gauntlet of 42nd St. for the first time and turned north on Broadway to my goal, The Brill Building.

Located at 1619 Broadway, the Brill since the 1930s was the legendary, one-stop location for meeting publishers and record execs, cutting demos, and meeting radio promoters. Many hundreds of Top Forty classics were sold and produced within that structure. Eyeing the frontage of the eleven-story building for the first time, I felt like Dorothy seeing the Emerald City: a marble and polished bronze Art Deco entranceway, with an actual Wizard overlooking, signified that just beyond those doors dreams were made.

It turned out that the façade was just that— a façade. The inside of the building looked like any Baltimore low-rent office building: drab and completely utilitarian. The interior was a warren of small offices behind black wooden doors, on which were painted names of publishing firms I had never heard of. It was eerily quiet on most of the floors, and completely unlike what I had expected. So where were Carole King and Burt Bacharach? After reading the directory, I made some inquiries and quickly learned that the Brill building actually represented the old school

"Tin Pan Alley" types, living off royalties from Broadway Shows, Sinatra songs, the Big Band era, and other songs found in my parents' and grandparents' record collection. The real action, it turned out, was across the street and up two blocks, at 1650, the "Not Brill Building."

Inside 1650, the atmosphere was electric, with young musician wannabes clogging the halls with their acoustic guitars or tapes in hand, while waiting for someone to allow them inside a tight cubicle for an audition. Meeting all these young talents and soaking up the scene was a reward in itself, and knowing there were others like me showed me that I wasn't alone as a "Dreamer on the Rise," as John Stewart would call us. Back in Catonsville, I was an oddball, but here I felt legitimized, and I just knew that some of these scruffs would be rock stars, perhaps even me.[†]

Here the directory was more than familiar, the offices were a fountainhead of music royalty, names like Aldon Music, which alone employed dozens of music giants — names like Burt Bacharach and Hal David, Tommy Boyce and Bobby Hart, Neil Diamond, Gerry Goffin and Carole King, Ellie Greenwich and Jeff Barry, Jerry Leiber and Mike Stoller, Barry Mann and Cynthia Weil. All told, over a hundred producers who could change your life in an instant were in this very building. These were all names I knew and that I would kill to work with or sell a song to. I wound my way up the stairs, past open doors where someone was pounding out a new song on an old upright (was that Carole or Burt, I wondered?), and started knocking on doors like all the other kids in the hallway. Unlike today, appointments weren't needed, but timing was. Often a gruff cigar smoking publisher would dismiss you with, "Sorry, kid, too busy today. Come back tomorrow, or next week, or never. I don't care." But occasionally, someone would allow you in and sit you down with a curt, "Watcha' got, kid?" This would lead to your tape being cued up and played for perhaps twenty seconds, then "Sorry, kid. Come back when you got something else. Next."

I remember desperately trying to get into see one particular producer and was turned away so fast that I must have looked stunned when I headed for the stairs. I heard a voice down the hall call to me.

"What's the problem, pal?" the dark haired Latino asked.

"I just spent all day on a stinking bus from Baltimore, and this guy wouldn't even let me in the door," I replied.

[†] To get a sense of it, see the 1996 movie *Grace of My Heart*.

"Got it. OK, go back in there and say you cleared it with 'Hatchet Face.' You'll get in. Good luck." And with that he was off. I went back in and dropped the name.

"You know Tony Orlando?" the producer asked. "He knows what he's doing, so you must have something. OK, come on in." At the time, Orlando was a demo singer in the building and would achieve huge success in a few short years, but his friend wasn't buying that day.

Surprisingly, the rejections didn't depress me, especially since everybody else in the elevator had gotten rejected too. I was just glad to be that close to the *possibility*. Excitement was in the air, as they say, and I vowed to return to Baltimore, write better songs, and keep coming back to 1650. Over the next three or four years, I'd make the trip once or twice a year. I came very close with Bee Gees producer Robert Stigwood, who had just opened a New York office. I even entered my band's tapes in a Warner Brothers talent search, and they brought us to their New York studios to record top quality demos. At the time, the Warners stable included Peter, Paul, and Mary, the Association, Joni Mitchell, James Taylor, the Bee Gees, and Van Dyke Parks, among countless others. I remember double parking our junkers on Madison Avenue while we off-loaded our gear for our day of sessions in the iconic studios. Alan, the engineer for our sessions jangled my nerves with remarks like: "That's the same outlet that Jimi Hendrix and Neil Young used," or "Here, this is the stool that Dylan sat on when he recorded his audition tapes here," or "Here, try this mic — Barry Gibbs loves it." We didn't get the deal, but we had a blast, and the recordings sounded amazing.

In June 1967, the Beatles responded to Brian Wilson with *Sgt. Pepper's Lonely Hearts Club Band*, a stunning achievement that pushed the envelope of acid-inspired musicality. Like a modern day James Cameron, the band threw every technological trick available at the project, all kept within the bounds of accessibility by the adult supervision of producer George Martin.

On the heels of *Pepper*, the Monterey Pop Festival, held June 16-18, 1967, kicked off the "Summer of Love," which was based in the center of "Flower Power," San Francisco. The festival, produced by Papa John Phillips and his producer Lou Adler, launched the careers of many who played there, making some of them into stars virtually overnight. Acts such as The Who and Jimi Hendrix, which had each already been sensations in the UK and Europe, now exploded onto the American scene. Others who rose to popularity following their appearances at Monterey included Janis Joplin, Laura Nyro, Canned

Heat, Otis Redding, Steve Miller, Buffalo Springfield, and Indian sitar maestro Ravi Shankar.

In the fall of 1967, I got a taste of the Summer of Love in Baltimore, as a concert came to town with a playbill that, although at the time was unremarkable, in retrospect was one-in-a-million. On November 26, I went with some friends to see the Beach Boys at the Baltimore Civic Center. Due to the failure of *Pet Sounds*, the arena was only half full, so after the lights went down, we were able to sneak up to one of the front rows.

The first act was Sam the Sham and the Pharoahs ("Wooly Bully"), followed by the Soul Survivors ("Time Won't Let Me"). Then things got real interesting with a new group called The Strawberry Alarm Clock ("Incense and Peppermints"), who blew our minds. We retrieved our minds just in time to have them totally obliterated by the next act, which featured three guys in suits and ties, one Flower Child, and one guitarist so enveloped in hair and buckskin fringe that he was hardly visible. Then with crystal clear harmonies and three lead guitars, they treated us to one amazing song after another. "What was that??" we asked each other, shell-shocked. "That" was the Buffalo Springfield, featuring a bunch of youngsters named Richie Furay, Stephen Stills, Neil Young, Jim Messina, and Dewey Martin. As much as I dug the Beach Boys, it was pretty obvious they had a tough act to follow, especially with Brian not there. But they did a bang-up job, and half way through their set invited the Springfield to jam with them. Pretty amazing night for just $3.50 a ticket.

Back at band rehearsals, our drummer Mike and I persuaded Don and Rick that "Country-Rock" was the new big thing. We went on a tear, learning numerous undanceable songs by the Springfield, a decision that cost us yet more teen center gigs. Years later, I got a laugh from Springfield founder Richie Furay when I told him of the only Springfield clone band in Baltimore. "I hope you lasted longer than we did," he said. We didn't. Both bands had a lifespan of about three years, the Drawing Room Society breaking up when we went off to different colleges.

Of course, all this teen music mania did not go unnoticed on Madison Avenue, where agencies and their banker clients made the calculated decision to lionize all things "young," at the cost of all things wise and experienced. It may be the first time in history that being inexperienced was touted as being superior (read: profitable) to the opposite. In the wake of this decision, many true talents were pushed aside. Tony Bennett and Count Basie were playing to 1,500 people, while the Strawberry Alarm Clock filled 15,000 seat arenas. Believe it or not, Grammy awards were once given to geniuses like Henry Mancini, Ella Fitzgerald, Cole Porter, Duke Ellington, Aaron Copeland, etc. But this standard would soon be eroded as an homage to "youth."

The invention of 300-watt amplifiers allowed less talented young rockers to create the illusion of musicality by just turning up the volume. It was faux gravitas, courtesy of Marconi, Edison and Tesla (but mostly Tesla). Things have now digressed to the point where, four decades after "the youth revolution," the Grammy statuettes for pop are bestowed upon recipients who can't write or read music, play an instrument, or sing without computer assistance. Many current Grammy winners don't even attempt to sing, instead merely screaming incessantly about their manhood into a digital recorder. Those who do compete as songwriters, with no knowledge of the real masters of the art, are worse than mediocre. Cole Porter sharing the same artistic award with a Ms. Swift or Spears or Mr. Diddy borders on the insane.

But that's another book...

As you might have heard, political upheaval in the sixties matched the musical maelstrom beat for beat. We high schoolers saw ourselves as waiting in the wings, ready to take our part when we became collegians. The atmosphere was set by a small group of brave souls who refused to settle for second-class citizenship any longer. One by one, the great grandchildren of slaves, supported by white "Summer Freedom" volunteers, decided they would sit in any bus seat they wanted, dine in any restaurant, and play for any sports team. So, with water cannons in their faces, attack dogs at their flesh, lynch mobs and gun-toting racists making a forceful (if unintentional) case against inbreeding, the "colored people" made a stand. Why that individual and collective courage came to the fore then and not earlier is a mystery to me, but it was four hundred years overdue. The Civil Rights Movement, led by such as Rosa Parks and Rev. Martin Luther King, Jr., supported by most of the youth movement, and attended by countless casualties, signaled the birth pains of new America. Many would argue that the country is still in labor four decades later.

Gasoline was thrown on this societal fire in 1966 with the publication of *Rush to Judgment* by attorney Mark Lane. "Lane," whom I have on good authority was born Marcus Levin, presented the book as a legal brief on behalf of the innocence of his deceased "client," Kennedy assassin Lee Harvey Oswald. To those of us as yet unschooled in the ways of wily defense machinations that are capable of nit-picking any murder case to death, Lane *seemed* to make a good case that the government covered up the truth of the crime, and was likely even a participant in it. But Lane was merely using a deft legal scalpel to surgically take his "evidence" out of all context, which of course was his right as defense counsel. To place it in modern perspective, it was as if Oswald had hired Johnnie Cochran and Alan Dershowitz to vindicate him. With chapter after chapter of "Mark Fuhrmans," Lane's bestseller ignited a generational accusation against the US government, and later the CIA specifically, for its culpability in the most heinous crime imaginable.‡ Not long after, rogue New Orleans District Attorney Jim Garrison also twisted the evidence to link Kennedy's killer to the CIA.§ Now, the bureaucrats who denied equal rights to blacks were also the killers of their own president. And we were soon to learn what horrors they were inflicting on people of a different color 8,000 miles away.

At this time, the military draft was no longer something off in the distance to be ignored, or dealt with by unlucky teenage guys (mostly blacks) without college deferments. Over 400,000 US military were now completely bogged down in a guerilla-style civil war that had nothing to do with the US, with casualties mounting, and no end in sight. With rumors running wild that college deferments might be suspended, many young men saw the protest movement as a matter of life and death. Anti-war protests were gaining steam around the world

America's horrific misadventure in Vietnam, foisted almost exclusively on the backs of the young poor, placed even more attention on the youth culture. With the spotlight on them, they took advantage of the opportunity by escalating the anti-war rallies that had begun in 1963. In October 1967, with almost half-a-million troops in Vietnam, 50,000 protestors marched on the Pentagon, a charged event chronicled by Norman Mailer in his Pulitzer Prize winning book, *The Armies of the Night*.

A seminal moment for me came on March 2, 1968, when Senator Robert F. Kennedy delivered his keynote speech on Vietnam from the Senate floor. Kennedy actually did the politically unthinkable and admitted that, as an aide to his late brother, he was wrong about Vietnam. "If fault is to be found or responsibility assessed," Kennedy said, "there is enough to go around for all — including myself." Incredibly, it would take another twenty-seven years, and 2.5 million bodies, for even one

---

‡ Not coincidentally, some of Lane's mentors (perhaps unknown to Lane himself) were connected to the KGB, and were just doing their job in tearing down the CIA.
§ Like Mark Lane, Garrison was also duped by the same KGB operation that aimed at planting evidence against the CIA. Garrison was further deluded by his own madness.

more senior official from the era to make a similar admission regarding that war[**]

Two weeks later, RFK announced his candidacy for the presidency. Kennedy's admission struck me as so brave, even braver than the great Sen. Gene McCarthy, who had been running the gauntlet as the first anti-war candidate, that I became an envelope-licking, door-knocking volunteer as soon as his Baltimore office was set up.

Kennedy's stance reminded me of a similar act of courage a year earlier, when heavyweight champion Muhammad Ali, at the height of his prowess, abdicated his boxing throne, and refused induction when he was drafted. He explained to the press, as only he could: "We [Muslims] don't take part in Christian wars," adding, "The Viet Cong never called me nigger." For almost four years Ali could not fight, as he appealed his case right up to the Supreme Court, where he won with a unanimous ruling. Beach Boy Carl Wilson had to similarly suspend his career, missing a European concert tour while he successfully fought the draft board for his conscientious objector status. Another 100,000 were now living in Canada to escape the war.

At the time of RFK's decision to run, I was a first year student at what was then a commuter college, the one-year-old University of Maryland Baltimore County (UMBC). To say that UMBC was my first choice of schools would be misleading, for — to paraphrase legendary NFL coach Vince Lombardi — it was the *only* choice. The way many of us saw it, getting into college for that coveted draft deferment was a matter of life and death. I had too many dreams to play out, and I was not about to come home from Southeast Asia in a pine box at age eighteen. Interestingly, without the draft, I might have been happy to skip college and move to California, where I could mix it up with my musical heroes, but it just wasn't an option, and UMBC was the least expensive decent school I could find.

It really hit me in the spring of my senior year at St. Joe: I had three months to come up with $2,000 ($13,000 in 2011 dollars) in tuition fees — or die in Vietnam. My grades at St. Joe were only fair, but good enough to qualify me for a number of schools, had my bank

---

[**] In his 1995 book, *In Retrospect*, former Secretary of Defense Robert McNamara wrote, "We of the Kennedy and Johnson administrations who participated in the decisions on Vietnam acted according to what we thought were the principles and traditions of this nation. We made our decisions in light of those values. Yet we were wrong, terribly wrong." Almost a decade later, in the documentary film *The Fog of War*, McNamara stated what had been obvious to so many of the protestors young enough to be his grandchildren: "We do not have the God-given right to shape every nation in our image or as we choose." Duh.

account held enough of a balance, or for that matter, had it come into existence yet. My father had already informed me that the only way I was going to college was if I paid for it; he believed he had fulfilled his financial requirement by paying for St. Joe, and my inability to obtain a college scholarship was my failing. In addition, he was a WW2 vet, and he saw nothing wrong with military service, or the war in Vietnam, for that matter. The arguments I had with him and my uncles, also veterans, over that damn war only increased the emotional gulf between us, and often left my mother in tears. We were not alone: countless other families were torn apart by the "generation gap" that Vietnam had exacerbated -- just one more tragic legacy of that war. In one ear we heard our musical avatars singing about love, and in the other Uncle Sam was ordering us to burn villages with the inhabitants still inside and to murder 14-year-old North Vietnamese regulars.

SIGNAL THE LEITMOTIF MUSIC: "Back to the Pratt."

In the library's reference section, I frantically poured over the books on scholarships, loans and grants, and when I hit upon "Maryland Legislative Scholarships," I was intrigued. I don't know if it is still in force, but in those days, a member of the Maryland legislature could, by the mere stroke of a pen, grant a scholarship to a worthy candidate in his or her district. My mind was racing on the bus ride home: who was our district legislator? Then it hit me: He was none other than the father of Brian McGuirk, the star pitcher on our championship Yankees little league team. Even better, Senator Harry J. "Soft Shoes" McGuirk, was a known a Democratic Party "boss," whose deal-making legerdemain in the State Senate earned him the moniker "The Fixer." Harry had been a sponsor of our team, and I had actually been to his house, about a mile from ours, for team meetings six years earlier.

Almost immediately I walked over to the sprawling McGuirk rancher and re-introduced myself to The Fixer.

"Mr. McGuirk, I need a favor," I explained at the front door. He ushered me back to his home office, the first I had seen, and I explained that I had just graduated from St. Joe, and was interested in a $2,000 Legislative scholarship so that my first year at UMBC would be covered.

"St. Joe is a great school," he said. "How were your grades?"

"Pretty good, and UMBC has already accepted me."

With that, McGuirk scribbled some words on a piece of paper, I suppose a note to himself, and said, "Done!" The Fixer was a man of few words — and obviously quick action. (Perhaps not coincidentally, four decades later I would write a book about a similarly terse man with the same "Fixer" nickname, Sidney Korshak.)

As I took my leave, I remember Senator McGuirk saying something to the effect of:

"Great job at first base, Gus." I think I may have helped his son win some games and it stuck in his mind. Walking home, I couldn't get over the fact that it took me just five minutes to earn what would have taken my father a year. Once again, the idea that anything is possible was reinforced. My first year was in the bag, giving me plenty of time to come up with a scheme for my sophomore year. Two weeks later, I received my tuition bill from UMBC. At the bottom it read: "BALANCE DUE: $0." For me it meant that I was not going to lose my precious guitar-playing hands to a "Bouncing Betty" land mine in the Asian jungle. Thanks, Harry. I was the first in my family to graduate high school, now I'd be the first to graduate college. I was beginning to feel like Huckleberry Finn, desperate to rise above my station while simultaneously living a grand adventure.

UMBC had quickly established itself as the intellectual younger brother of the University of Maryland's hard-partying College Park main campus. Although its academic standards were very high, its architectural standards couldn't have been worse. In 1968, the campus consisted of a half-dozen unremarkable, rectangular red brick buildings, situated between rivers of mud due to the ongoing construction — I have yet to see a more unattractive campus. My high school, set on a beautiful sprawling green campus, seemed like Club Med by comparison. It would take decades for the UMBC campus to be completed. And even still…

Chapter Five

The Real World

I WAS DISMAYED to learn that there was no music major program at UMBC, and that even if I transferred to the College Park main campus, there was a strict classical music requirement in their program; however even if I played classical guitar it wouldn't have mattered since at that time guitar was not an instrument accepted by the school as "classical." In my freshman year I gravitated towards Poli-Sci, which was where I eventually received my degree, with a minor in music. I also played on the varsity tennis team for all four years.

My first, short-lived, college band was called Siddhartha, named after my favorite Hermann Hesse character; I also figured that the Hesse-rock connection had been successfully broached by the band Steppenwolf, and wondered why more bands didn't raid his titles for names. At the time, UMBC had a thriving student union scene that hosted good concerts on a regular basis. Not only did Siddhartha play there, but so also did a brilliant young guitarist from suburban Maryland who, in addition to his guitar wizardry and great songwriting skills, was a competitive gymnast who loved to explode off of mini-trampolines and do flips in the middle of his solos. Decades later, Nils Lofgren would have to have both hips replaced as a result. [*]

I remember playing a gig at a hip DC club called The Emergency. Sometime later, I ran into Nils, who told me that he played there just a few days after us, and who walked in but Stephen Stills and Neil Young, two of my heroes from the Buffalo Springfield. To make matters worse, Young was blown away by Nils (who was fronting his three-piece band, Grin) and brought him to California to play on his next album. Nils said that Neil felt that Nils's great guitar skills so overshadowed Neil's rudimentary style on the first song recorded that he "strongly suggested" that the young hotshot play piano instead on the next cut. Nils's work can be heard on the seminal Young album, *After the Goldrush* (1970). From there, Nils' career exploded, working with a *Who's Who* of rock royalty during the seventies before landing with Bruce Springsteen's E Street Band. But as he told the *Baltimore*

---

[*] Many Nils "flips" cane be seen on Youtube, e.g. here:
http://www.youtube.com/watch?v=5mcnQQuxDv8

Sun in 2009, "We [Grin] cut our teeth in Baltimore and at UMBC. A lot of great memories of Baltimore." The point of this digression is to call attention to the concept of serendipity-meeting-talent; I have often wondered how my life might have been different had Young and Stills walked into the Emergency a few days earlier when Siddhartha was on stage — especially since we played some Springfield songs. Oh, well, Nils deserved it. He is a huge talent, and in another universe, Springsteen could easily be playing in *Nils's* band.

Nils and me in 2010

When Siddhartha wasn't gigging, which is to say most of the time, I moonlighted in a quartet that played to older crowds — weddings and such. Because I was underage, I became a serial lawbreaker with this act, often playing in country-western bars around the Glen Burnie area. I had previously played some country clubs with the Drawing Room Society, when we were all underage high schoolers. It was in one of these dives that I saw my first stage that was protected from the bottle-throwing drunks by floor-to-ceiling chicken wire (yep, that scene in *The Blues Brothers* was real, kids.) From behind that wire, I saw some gargantuan bar fights; I recall one in which some drunk thought his girl was dancing too close to another guy. The drunk pounced on the poor soul, then dragged him out to the parking lot — followed by the entire audience! We played the next couple of songs to a completely empty bar, craning our necks to watch the fisticuffs through the large window. I also played a dozen or so dates on Baltimore's notorious "Block," made up of a couple large burlesque houses and dozens of dank strip clubs. Playing those skin joints provided quite an education for this 18-year-old.

At UMBC, I experienced a different kind of serendipity than Nils had at the Emergency. For years, I had been basically teaching myself how to play tennis, but when I landed on UMBC's team, I had the good fortune of having a dedicated coach, who was also a ranked player and a devoted tennis teacher.

On a daily basis, Doug Moore, formerly ranked number one in Maryland singles, refined my game, correcting strokes that fell short of the textbook style. Thanks to Doug, who passed away suddenly during my fourth year on the team, I had almost four years of priceless coaching from a master. Like Ted Martini, I owe much to Doug Moore.

The tennis scene in 1967-68 would be virtually unrecognizable to today's players — of any sport. Thanks to international tennis rules put in place at the time to maintain the game's "purity," players were forced to remain amateurs if they wanted to play in any of the "Major" events (the Wimbledon, French, Australian, and US Championships). The open secret, of course, was that many of the top "amateurs" found ways to get subsidized under the table. With most tennis stars craving those major trophies, only a handful of players chose to go pro, if only out of need to support their families. Small pro tours, bankrolled by wealthy businessmen, barnstormed the globe while lobbying to bring the archaic rules into the modern world. It was these exhibitions, needing to find ways to play in enclosed facilities that fostered the development of the first synthetic playing surfaces (such as AstroTurf) that are taken for granted today.

(l. to r.): B. Gassaway, J. Frost, S. Sullivan, S. Eisenberg, G. Lintzeris, S. Grossman, D. Moran, S. Lazinsky, C. Nelson, R. Wobbeking, L. Jordan, G. Russo, Doug Moore (coach).

In the spring of 1968, Coach Moore arranged for one of those tours, owned by tennis loving Texas oilman Lamar Hunt, to come to UMBC to practice with the team. Hunt's tour, which was named "The Handsome Eight," consisted of some of the greatest players on earth, and I got to hit with all of them.

Among the standouts were Tony Roche (who won many majors as an amateur, and went on to coach the great Roger Federer), Cliff Drysdale, and John Newcombe.[†] Being on the receiving end of one of Tony Roche's famous crushing volleys taught me a great life lesson: there is no better way to gauge your true talent than to jump into the shark tank with the best. I learned more about where my game really stood in a couple hours with the Handsome Eight than I would have in thousands of hours of college or rec field matches. Since that experience, I have always tried to work and play with the best, not only to keep my abilities in perspective, but also to pick their brains. Life is too short to live in a fantasy world.

Just weeks after the Eight hit with us at UMBC, the International Lawn Tennis Association opened up the major events to professionals, and almost overnight all the good players turned pro. That fall marked the first US "Open" tournament. But the sad fact remains that gut-wielding greats such as Rod Laver, my tennis hero, had been prevented for years from winning more majors; Laver won eleven of the coveted titles, but was not allowed to compete for six years after he turned pro in 1962. The men's record at this writing is sixteen, held by Coach Roach's charge, Roger Federer. But had not his best years (ages 24-30) been taken away, Laver likely could have garnered two-dozen or more major trophies. As it is, he is still the only man to win the calendar Grand Slam (all four majors in the same year), and he did it twice!

Looking back, it is now clear that for many of us, the winter and spring of 1968 represented the last vestige of a more innocent time. Although the Kennedy assassination and the war in Vietnam had taken a toll on the "Happy Days" illusion, it still seemed possible to carve out a sunny, unfettered parcel of the American Dream, free from the concerns of most of the real world. Life could still be unrealistically uncomplicated. Our suburban world was still insulated from the army draft and was almost crime free; it was still the era of unlocked cars and homes, the time before the National Rifle Association began peddling guns to anyone who could pull a trigger. Most urban turf disputes still were resolved by fistfights, and had little impact on the outside world.

It seemed everyone over sixteen hitchhiked, and I don't mean just to an Orioles game, but cross-country. It was not even uncommon

---

[†] The balance of the Eight was Nicki Pilic, Butch Buchholz, Dennis Ralston, Pierre Barthes, and Roger Taylor.

to see a pretty Hippie girl hitching solo — many adventures to be had there. Not a weekend went by that highway overpasses weren't lined with teens "riding their thumbs" and bearing hand-printed signs reading "NYC" or "LA" or "Chicago." The placards often bore embellishments such as peace signs or flowers. I was a frequent participant in these road adventures, quickly realizing that by specifying an exact destination, hitchhikers were giving drivers and excuse to pass them by. A sign reading "Miami" could meet with a driver's response ala: "Sorry, I'm only going as far as Ft. Lauderdale." Thus my signs read: "North," "South," "East," or "West." It was hard, I assumed, not to be going to one of those destinations.

For my mates and me, our world consisted of music, tennis, adventurous summers, and, of course, girls. I finally owned my first car, a beat up old Chevy that broke down every couple of weeks (requiring still more hitchhiking), so I felt completely liberated. I had the added distraction of spending two or three nights a week in the downtown Baltimore offices of RFK's presidential campaign, licking envelopes, and working the phones. Although Maryland didn't have a primary that year, we still hoped to get a head start on the general election and sent volunteers to help out the East Coast states that did hold primaries, such as New Jersey and Pennsylvania. The volunteers were excited when word arrived that the Kennedys would be hosting a cookout for the campaign workers at their Hickory Hill, Virginia, spread right after the June California primary, which was a must-win in his bid for the nomination. For me it also meant a chance to play tennis on Hickory Hill's storied clay court, perhaps with Bobby himself.

I had my own agenda mapped out for the summer of 1968: for some time I had been orchestrating my return to the Poconos. I had persuaded one of my neighborhood buddies, Chris, who was still a senior at St. Joe, to join in the adventure. After consulting the same employment guidebooks I had used two years earlier, we were both hired as groundskeepers and musicians by a small resort, and we looked forward to making the drive north in Chris's white Corvair convertible immediately after the Hickory Hill bash. The funny thing was that Chris had absolutely no musical skills, and was hoping to finesse the situation by lip-synching or blending in with an unplugged "air guitar," hoping that the owners would never notice.

With no warning, this bucolic fantasy world was smashed hard against the wall of reality, thanks to a series of events that commenced in April 1968. At the time, Coach Moore, always looking for new ways to inspire and instruct his charges, had arranged for our college team to play a scrimmage match against a tennis club that played on the city's only red clay courts, located in the only oasis of an urban ghetto that had developed many years after the park had been created. The Clifton Park Tennis Club was the last holdout in a rapidly deteriorating black neighborhood, but we were enthused, since most of us had never before even seen the dreaded red clay, the source of so much misery at the French Championships. Although we knew that clay was ungodly slow and very receptive to spin, our team felt very confident, given that the Clifton Park Tennis Club players ranged in age from fifty to eighty years of age. It would turn out that the lesson Coach Moore had planned for that day was "humility." There would be many other unscheduled lessons learned that day.

Our match was set for Sunday, April 7, 1968. Almost 800 miles to our south, a lifelong petty crook had something else scheduled for April 4, a ghastly undertaking that would see the Clifton Park neighborhood, and thousands of others, become engulfed in flames.

I don't recall exactly where I was when I heard the news, but I remember being riveted to the television on the night of April 4, watching the coverage of Rev. Dr. Martin Luther King's assassination in Memphis. Dr. King had arrived in the city six days earlier to lend support to striking sanitation workers. I had followed King's work from a distance over the years, fully aware of his civil rights marches in DC, and his early opposition to the Vietnam War. Now, pundits worried, his death might incite an American race war; for the last couple years, small scale riots had broken out in black ghettos, usually to be stamped out by King and his message of non-violence. Now, with arguably their only role model gone and seemingly proven wrong about pacifism, African-Americans felt sucker-punched and soul-shattered. They took to the streets in an orgy of existential anarchy, determined to take what they now knew they would never be allowed to own.

As soon as Bobby Kennedy was informed of the murder, he gave a brilliant speech, often called one of the greatest in US history, in Indianapolis, attempting to forestall the predicted riots. Bobby's speech worked in Indianapolis, but nowhere else. Nonetheless, his stunning exhortation is worth recalling:

> Ladies and Gentlemen — I'm only going to talk to you just for a minute or so this evening. Because...I have some very sad news for all of you, and I think sad news for all of our fellow citizens, and people who love peace all over the world, and that is that Martin Luther King was shot and was killed tonight in Memphis, Tennessee.

Martin Luther King dedicated his life to love and to justice between fellow human beings. He died in the cause of that effort. In this difficult day, in this difficult time for the United States, it's perhaps well to ask what kind of a nation we are and what direction we want to move in.

For those of you who are black — considering the evidence evidently is that there were white people who were responsible — you can be filled with bitterness, and with hatred, and a desire for revenge.

We can move in that direction as a country, in greater polarization — black people amongst blacks, and white amongst whites, filled with hatred toward one another. Or we can make an effort, as Martin Luther King did, to understand and to comprehend, and replace that violence, that stain of bloodshed that has spread across our land, with an effort to understand, compassion and love.

For those of you who are black and are tempted to be filled with hatred and mistrust of the injustice of such an act, against all white people, I would only say that I can also feel in my own heart the same kind of feeling. I had a member of my family killed, but he was killed by a white man.

But we have to make an effort in the United States, we have to make an effort to understand, to get beyond these rather difficult times.

My favorite poet was Aeschylus. He once wrote: "Even in our sleep, pain which cannot forget falls drop by drop upon the heart, until, in our own despair, against our will, comes wisdom through the awful grace of God."

What we need in the United States is not division; what we need in the United States is not hatred; what we need in the United States is not violence and lawlessness, but is love and wisdom, and compassion toward one another, and a feeling of justice toward those who still suffer within our country, whether they be white or whether they be black.

> So I ask you tonight to return home, to say a prayer for the family of Martin Luther King, yeah that's true, but more importantly to say a prayer for our own country, which all of us love — a prayer for understanding and that compassion of which I spoke. We can do well in this country. We will have difficult times. We've had difficult times in the past. And we will have difficult times in the future. It is not the end of violence; it is not the end of lawlessness; and it's not the end of disorder.
>
> But the vast majority of white people and the vast majority of black people in this country want to live together, want to improve the quality of our life, and want justice for all human beings that abide in our land.
>
> Let us dedicate ourselves to what the Greeks wrote so many years ago: to tame the savageness of man and make gentle the life of this world.
>
> Let us dedicate ourselves to that, and say a prayer for our country and for our people. Thank you very much.

Within hours of King's murder, for which no one had been arrested, the first of 125 cities began to blow up. Baltimore City, just two miles east of where I lived, was one of them. As over two thousand local police watched impotently, tens of thousands of angry blacks looted, then firebombed, thousands of downtown businesses. We stayed glued to the television, as the Governor requested and immediately received, thanks to President Johnson's intervention, over two thousand US Army and National Guard reinforcements. It would be just the first wave. The police call-up put a powerful exclamation point on the changes Baltimore was undergoing: the last time police were brought in to break up a huge city crowd was in May 1960, when 2,000 kids had assembled in the 1800 block of Rosedale Avenue, not to loot, but to organize the largest line dance to the song "The Madison," popularized on the local Buddy Deane Show. It was a different world, to be sure.

The day after the assassination, a man who couldn't be more different from Kennedy, succeeded in preventing the riots from spilling over into the Kennedy bastion of Boston. Motherless, fatherless, and raised in a brothel, soul icon and convicted ex-felon James Brown was due to perform a concert on Thursday, April 5, in Boston, the very city where Dr. King received his PhD. and met his future wife Coretta Scott. By Thursday, the nearby black enclave of Roxbury had already succumbed to the rioting, and the city's leadership was desperate to save the city center. Unbeknownst to Brown, Boston Mayor Kevin White had instructed the local PBS station WGBH (which hastily advertised the show as "The Jimmy Brown Concert") to broadcast the concert live, hoping to keep the black population off the streets. Of course this move prompted thousands of Brown's fans to have their tickets refunded so they could watch the show at home, safely, for free. Brown, the farthest thing from a pacifist (and so he had told Dr. King), was infuriated when he heard how the Mayor was taking money out of his pocket. The singer threatened to walk, but after a tense negotiation, Brown agreed to go on with the show in exchange for $60,000. [‡]

Brown started the show by asking the viewers to be calm and to not destroy their community.

"We're Black," the Godfather of Soul said. "Don't make us all look bad. You're not being fair to yourselves, to me, or your race." Brown then informed his fans that Black Power didn't mean violent power.

I'm still a soul brother," he said, "and you people have made it possible for me to be a first-class man in all respects. I used to shine shoes in front of a radio station. Now I own radio stations. You know what that is? That's Black Power."

The one-night buffer did the trick; the Roxbury riots ended, never spreading to downtown Boston. After the show, Brown traveled to Washington, D.C. the next night, and gave a televised speech that ended riots there. He did the same at his next gig in Rochester, NY.

Unfortunately, most of the country, which included Baltimore, wasn't so lucky. Every day, the torchings and lootings spread despite the early influx of 2,000 federal troops into Charm City. Thus, by the weekend, "Task Force Baltimore" peaked at 11,570 troops.

[‡] In his autobiography, Brown wrote that he only balked at the concert because he was signed to previous television contract that prohibited another performance. He never mentioned the $60,000.

Scenes from the Baltimore riots

At some point in all this madness, I remembered that we had a tennis match set for ghetto-surrounded Clifton Park on Sunday, the 7th. Of course it must be cancelled, right? Wrong. I called Coach Moore, who informed me that the match was still on; many of our scheduled opponents were World War Two vets who couldn't be frightened into missing a tennis meet by mere looting. Additionally, Clifton Park was the safest place in Baltimore, since the Army had set up its base camp there. After we hung up the phone, it struck me that I had to somehow *get* to Clifton Park in one piece — *that* was the challenge! The only route to Clifton Park was along impoverished, incinerated, and smoldering North Avenue.

On Sunday morning, with the riots in full swing, I donned my tennis whites, threw my rackets into the backseat of my 1962 Chevy Impala and headed into center city. I hardly drew a breath as I slowly drove around burnt-out cars, assorted detritus, and angry Blacks cursing me as I prayed nonstop that my balding tires would stay inflated, my carburetor would not get one of its frequent vapor locks, and the "E" on my gas tank wasn't accurate. Then I realized that if I did get stranded, my tennis whites virtually branded me as the enemy. I would be as good as dead.

I didn't take this picture of the North Avenue riots, but I could have. This is exactly what I drove through on the way to Clifton Park.

Amazingly, I made it to the match alive, only to be thoroughly eviscerated by those cagey older vets who worked the red clay like masters. With stop-dead drop shots, perfect lobs, side-spinning chips, and cuts that often bounced backwards, our whole team was slaughtered by guys who were old enough to be our fathers, or in a few cases our grandfathers. The next impression was the stark contrast of looking up to your service toss against the backdrop of smoke from the burning city. As if the scene weren't surreal enough, we were playing in the midst of thousands of pup tents, tanks, jeeps, and military on break. Our team's destruction therefore also made for entertainment for the armed troops who watched us from the surrounding slopes. It seems we were the laughing stock for all. Of course, our team later told everyone who would listen that we lost only because we were somehow preoccupied with one thought: we still had to dodge the mobs and burning buildings to get home in one piece after the match. I still think it was a reasonable excuse.

Coach Moore had not only taught us humility, but also the value of playing a thoughtful game as opposed to the brute force that comes naturally with youth. Of course, I learned other lessons, such as: keep gas in your tank and tread on your tires!

It took weeks for Baltimore, and the nation, to lower the pressure caused by King's death.[§] Just as the city began to return to normal, my sleepy little neighborhood, Catonsville, became national news, when Father Daniel Berrigan, his brother Philip and seven others visited my draft board, located about a mile from both my home and UMBC. There they made a non-violent gesture, perhaps in honor of King, aimed at bringing attention to the war in Vietnam. Seven months earlier, the Berrigans had raided the downtown draft board and poured chicken blood, purchased from a local market, on draft records.

[§] The Baltimore riots ended as quickly as they had begun when Baltimore's civic leaders begrudgingly appealed to the city's heroin kingpin, Melvin Williams, for help. According to those who were there, Williams went into the heart of the ghetto, where he was worshipped, and said one word: "Enough." And it stopped almost immediately.

Now out on bail, the "Catonsville Nine," as they became known, grabbed hundreds of records (not mine, regrettably), took them out to the parking lot and burned them with homemade Napalm. Afterwards they released a statement: "We confront the Roman Catholic Church, other Christian bodies, and the synagogues of America with their silence and cowardice in the face of our country's crimes. We are convinced that the religious bureaucracy in this country is racist, is an accomplice in this war, and is hostile to the poor."

It seemed as though the world had descended, almost overnight, from a relatively peaceful place, albeit with the occasional tragedy, into the opposite: a dark abyss, albeit with an occasional uplifting respite. As depressing as the spring of 1968 seemed to this point, it was about to get even worse.

On Tuesday, June 4, when not daydreaming about returning to the Poconos, I spent much of the evening in the UMBC library, cramming for the next day's final exam in psychology. RFK was ahead in that day's crucial California Democratic primary, but there was nothing the Baltimore volunteers could do to help. Sometime after midnight I was back in my room with the radio on, listening to Bobby's victory speech in Los Angeles. Minutes later I crashed, and probably dreamt of Kennedy's presidency and an end to the war. The next thing I knew my radio alarm was going off — time to go to that dreaded exam. But before I could even shake off the cobwebs, I heard the first words from the radio: "Senator Kennedy should be coming out of surgery any minute." What the ??? What does he mean, "surgery"?

My first reaction was to hope and pray that I was either still asleep, dreaming, or I was only half-awake and misunderstood the reporter. What word sounds like "surgery"? Perjury? No, that made no sense. As I crawled out of bed the reporter clarified the situation by repeating that awful sixties mantra: "He had been shot in the head." Just like JFK, just like MLK, just like that Vietcong prisoner whose street execution was filmed for the world to see. I was not allowed to dwell on my sorrow, since I had to get off to that psychology final. I took that exam in a trance, with tears in my eyes, completely focused on what might be happening in Bobby's Los Angeles recovery room. How I passed that test I'll never know.

Racing home from UMBC, I soon heard the news that the worst was confirmed: like his beloved brother, Robert Francis Kennedy was dead at the hand of a lone assassin. Although far from a perfect analogy, I finally got some sense of what Blacks felt weeks ago when King was killed. Bobby was the only politician I trusted, and with him gone, I felt, albeit temporarily, like tearing down the system too. America seemed beyond redemption, so what was the point of obeying its laws? Of course, my peers and I ultimately retreated from the brink of anarchy, probably because our convictions were muted by our relatively cushy lifestyles, and decent futures were at least possible for us if we could avoid the draft. I've come to learn that this is why America has been immune to revolution, or even a long-overdue rewrite of the Constitution: it is materialism — not religion — that is the opiate of the American masses. By keeping a bare majority of the populace satiated with goods, the informed, righteously infuriated minority can never gain a foothold.

I don't consider myself an overly greedy or materialistic person, and certainly in the sixties all I needed was a good guitar and a good tennis racket to be perfectly content. But I knew that someday I'd want that James Bond lifestyle and I couldn't have it in a war torn country. Others such as the Weather Underground believed differently, acted on that belief, and were predictably squashed. Although the timing seemed right to go for the Big Lebowski, most of us decided to keep trying to change the system, not tear it down. History may prove that to be a monumental error. We'll see — and soon I think.

In any event, my politicization and activism became elevated after Bobby's death. I persuaded my friend Chris that we had to do something before heading off for the summer. We decided on making a stink about gun control. My first constitutional law courses had convinced me that Founding Fathers put the word "militia" in the second amendment for a reason. If the militia had nothing to do with gun ownership rights, then why were they mentioned at all? These men weren't prone to needless florid language. But if it were meaningless, then why choose the word "militia" over any other meaningless word, say, "sailor" or "blacksmith" or "apple pie"? It was about time We the People put the National Rifle Association (NRA) in its place, i.e. out of the business of promoting the trafficking in arms. We crafted a simple petition asking for stricter gun laws, mandatory registration, the end of mail order sales, and the abolishment of "Saturday Night Special" handguns. We had to be among the first take on the NRA.

THE REAL WORLD   85

At first we went door-to-door, but then the thought emerged that we needed to confront high-profile people, as well as venues that would get more attention than suburban neighborhoods. Thus we made a beeline for Memorial Stadium, where we bought tickets to a soccer game and trundled about the upper decks soliciting signers for over an hour before we were tossed out. From there we staked out the Mayor's office, and the local television and radio stations. We wanted well-known people to be put on the spot on the issue. Surprisingly, the iconic Baltimore City Comptroller Hyman Pressman and Colt's manager Harry Hulmes signed for us. We also had a couple of members of the Orioles sign on. Soon we began to attract media attention and were interviewed for the *Baltimore News-American*, and later for one of the local news shows, a great moment of pride for our families.

> **Have 500 Signatures**
> # Baltimore Boys Push Gun Control Petition
>
> *June '68*
>
> Two Baltimore teenagers have entered the controversy over the right to keep and bear arms. Their weapon is another right the right to petition.
>
> Chris Scherf and Gus Russo have to totaled more than 500 signatures including those of City Comptroller Hyman Pressman and Baltimore Colts manager Harry Hulmes— in their fight to restrict the sale of firearms.
>
> The college boys, who had hoped to campaign for slain presidential candidate Robert F. Kennedy, said they were upset that they "never got a chance to."
>
> Concerned that a U.S. Senator a civil rights leader or a Baltimore bus driver could be shot with an easily obtained weapon Chris and Gus began their petition drive last Wednesday. It will end next week at Senator Joseph Tydings (D.-Md.) office.
>
> THE PETITION calls for "registration of all firearms and their owners, and prohibition of the mail-order sale of guns. It also supports a ban on gun sales to persons with criminal records or histories of mental illness."
>
> Chris and Gus, who wear khaki pants and striped short-sleeve shirts, plan to spend the weekend at area shopping centers. Last Wednesday they hiked through Memorial Stadium getting signatures from soccer fans. Thursday and Friday they visited City Hall, radio and television stations and Charles Center.
>
> Chris, 17, who will enter the University of Maryland this fall, recalled that at Charles Center "We couldn't get people to stop and listen."
>
> Gus, who is 18 added, "They'd look at us and say, 'I've already paid,' or . . . 'I don't want my name on any list.'"
>
> THE PAIR had better luck at E. J. Korvettes' Rt. 40 store, where over 200 shoppers took time to read and sign the petition.
>
> "People are either emphatically for it or violently against it," Gus remarked. "Some people think it (the petition) is a Communist plot. Others expect another World War."
>
> Chris interjected, "Some help a pistol is gonna be in World War III."
>
> A teenage boy who said he possessed both a criminal record and a gun, willingly signed the restrictive petition. "He said he'd start carrying a knife," Chris jested.
>
> Gus, a liberal arts major at the University of Maryland, Catonsville campus, reasoned, "You have to register a car. But you still have the right to own one."
>
> The petitioners also observed that in Europe, where their are tight gun controls there are few gun murders.

Eventually we delivered about 2,000 signatures to Maryland Senator Joe Tydings in Washington. Of course, my political activism once again went nowhere; the NRA's deep pockets bought (and still buys) too many votes. The fact was that progressives were, and remain, a small minority in the US. Thus we couldn't end the war, elect Bobby, or defeat the NRA, but there was some solace in knowing we tried. I would continue to support the anti-gun movement for the rest of my life. Someday, if we're lucky, the NRA will lose its grip on official Washington.

Chapter Six

Henryville

SOON AFTER THE SEMESTER wrapped, Chris and I set out on our summer adventure. By this time I had junked my old Chevy, so we loaded up the front trunk of Chris's white, rear-engine, air-cooled Corvair convertible and headed up I-83N to the Poconos.

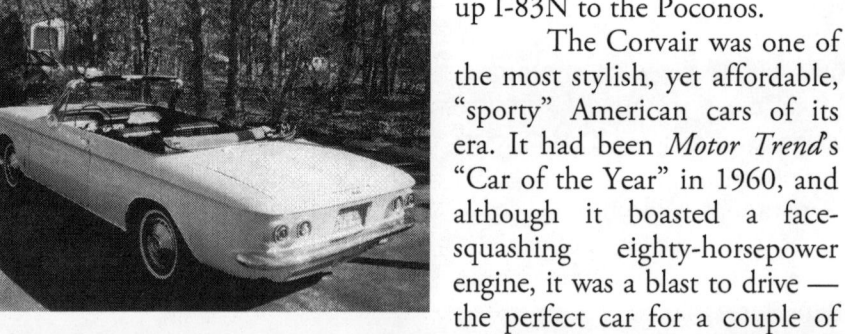

The Corvair was one of the most stylish, yet affordable, "sporty" American cars of its era. It had been *Motor Trend*'s "Car of the Year" in 1960, and although it boasted a face-squashing eighty-horsepower engine, it was a blast to drive — the perfect car for a couple of teens on a summer vacation trek. In a few years, design flaws that encouraged oversteering and rollovers saw the end of Corvair's production run. By midsummer, Chris and I would discover a less dangerous, but nonetheless infuriating design flaw.

Hitting the highway outside of Baltimore, we started calling each other "Tod" and "Buzz," the monikers of the two lead characters from the iconic TV series *Route 66*, an hour-long drama with a bizarre premise: two young guys with no discernable background just driving across the country in a gorgeous Corvette in search of adventure. The show had nothing to do with the actual route, since their adventures took them across the country, and even into Canada – places where Rt. 66 never touched. But who cared? It was a popular series that only added to my wanderlust, and even though we had the poor man's sports car, we had the right attitude.

Pulling up to our new place of work on Rt. 191, Henryville House, we first encountered a beautiful main lodge built in the 1800s as a fly-fishing retreat for nearby Paradise Creek. Thanks to that creek, Henryville Lodge, as it was then called, became so popular over the decades that four US presidents (Calvin Coolidge, Benjamin Harrison, Grover Cleveland and Theodore Roosevelt) stayed there. Henryville's entertainers from the glory days included Annie Oakley, Buffalo Bill

Cody, John L. Sullivan, and Judge Roy Bean's fantasy girl, Lily Langtree. Nestled on a ridge overlooking the main building was a long row of perhaps twenty single-story motel type rooms. All told, the lodge could accommodate about 200 guests. Behind the main lodge there was a pool, recreation Quonset Hut, and miniature golf course, all adding up to a slogan that radically set it apart from the Pococabana's "Just for the Fun of it." Henryville, on the other hand, boldly carved out its own Pennsylvania turf with the unique catch phrase, "Fun on Parade." (In fact, it turned out that most of the Pocono resorts included the word "Fun" in their slogans.)

Chris and I pulled up to the front entrance in our cool ride like happy-go-lucky "Tod" and "Buzz," and bounded up the stairs and into the office where we met "Ziggy" Ziegler, the mid-thirty-ish manager of the hotel owned by his dad, Alvin Ziegler. To our dismay, Ziggy was curt, and all business. He immediately pointed out the cork bulletin board in his office where our maintenance chores would be posted every morning. Chris and I looked at each other. Maintenance? We were here to cut the lawn. The only thing I knew how to maintain were my guitar strings, and Chris, who hoped to become a sports journalist, knew even less. Ziggy clarified for us:

"Oh, yeah, you must have misunderstood the ad. You guys will do everything that needs to be done. You know, roof repairs, plumbing, painting, electrical shortages — just the standard stuff. You didn't think you were going to just cut the lawn once a week then lounge by the pool the rest of the time?"

Oh, no way, not for the grand $75 per week we'd get *before taxes*. Ziggy, obviously noticing that we were in the early stages of shock, reminded us that our meals and lodging were free, so we should be excited. Not only that, the staff was free to use all the facilities on their off hours and were encouraged to mingle with the guests. I guess the blood had sufficiently returned to our faces, so Ziggy decided we were stable enough for the big shock.

"OK, then, I'll show you to your rooms," he said. I caught glimpse of his wife's eyebrows being raised while she quickly turned away to avoid our gaze, as Ziggy led us around to the back of the main building and pointed up a small hill to what looked like a large storage shed suitable for storing things you didn't value — a ramshackle, almost-windowless firetrap that a serious sneeze could blow over. The first floor consisted of a garage that stored lawn mowers, and large gas and propane storage tanks. The second story looked like an oversize doghouse.

"Is our dorm behind that shed?" Chris asked.

"That *is* your dorm," answered a peeved Ziggy. "They call it Bedlam."

We would soon learn that the reference to the infamous British home for the insane would actually be fitting. Whatever blood had returned to our faces was now completely MIA. Now numb, we walked up a dozen unsupported, rickety stairs onto a porch constructed with rotted boards that felt as though you'd fall through if you weighed over 150 lbs. Luckily, Chris and I were both skinny.* Looking through Bedlam's front door was not unlike looking into a dimly lit, rat-infested haunted house from a William Castle movie or a poem by Edgar Allen Poe. Inside was a "hallway" with "walls" constructed of a beaverboard type material, known commercially as homasote,

Jamming on Bedlam's porch

and usually reserved for sticking thumbtacks into. This same material was used to partition about ten tiny two-cot rooms (or cells?) where the inhabitants (inmates?) resided. Most rooms had no doors. The beaverboard walls were so thin that they were full of holes made by crazed staffers punching fists through them (the inmate who resided on the other side of the wall next to my cot used to get a kick out of ramming knives through the wall, luckily

---

* Come to think of it, everybody was skinny in those days, and not the "stare in the mirror, gym-induced six-pack" kind of skinny. We just didn't overeat, and we were in a state of constant, calorie-burning, motion. I'm glad I grew up in the last generation that was not sentenced to stare at video display terminals of some sort for eight hours a day.

missing me by inches. I think he missed because he could see me through the wall when a light was shined on it.) Thus, the entire interior of Bedlam looked like stale Swiss cheese — and smelled worse.

We had last choice of rooms, second on the left. I couldn't initially understand why our room was still available, but I soon realized that the spot where I rested my head was two feet above the gasoline storage tank on the bottom floor. Well, I rationalized, at least if the tank exploded, I wouldn't have to dodge blades emerging from the wall any longer. The kid across the hall from Chris and me, Pesky, tried his hand at interior decorating to make his room livable. He did so by stealing cans of paint from the storage room below, after which he went to town, manically flinging the paint against the wall to achieve a sort-of Jackson Pollack-meets-Ken Kesey effect. Of course, there was no label on the rusted cans, so it was only later that we learned that Pesky had accidentally painted his room with Rustoleum primer, which stunk and stayed tacky for the rest of the summer. The resourceful Pesky, however, made the best of a bad situation and bragged about how before going to bed he could take off his clothes and fling them against the wall where they would stick until the next morning — a great feature for drunks. We would often look into his room and marvel at how much weight Rustoleum could hold. We ran tests by throwing tennis balls and other objects into Pesky's room to see if they would stick. We felt like POWs trying to stay sane. The sticky fun came to an end when someone affixed a poor squirrel to the wall.

Chez Pesky

Above the main floor was an attic, which we never even peeked into, that was reported to house bats the size of ultralight planes, while the basement was home to rats that looked like they could commandeer Chris's Corvair for a night on the town — if there was a town. We surmised that the humans on the central main floor were the buffers that were there to prevent warfare between the two rodent species. Sort of a Pocono DMZ.

My half of our room   Me trying out my new door

Down the hall was nestled a cozy, unlit, un-tiled shower and a toilet with no seat. Ziggy often joked that if we were good, he'd get us a seat. We weren't, and he didn't. But all of the above paled in comparison to our worst fear: we soon learned that Bedlam had caught fire both previous summers, both times in the middle of the night. The firefighters raced to extinguish them before the gas storage tanks exploded, and their investigation determined, on at least one occasion, that one near conflagration was caused by copper pennies placed in Bedlam's circuit box in order to save money on those pricey .75 cent fuses. It occurred to me that the only way this building passed any housing code was if the inspector was Ziggy's relative. I never resolved that mystery.

I remember meeting one staffer who had worked there in previous years telling us about the "Henryville Ghosts." All told, nine spirits (a child, three men and five women) roamed the halls of the main lodge. Many had died, not surprisingly, in fires, but one female ghost, a maid who committed suicide by hanging in Bedlam's garage basement was allegedly fond of waking the male staff by screaming in the middle of the night. Great. Not exactly our fantasy of girls screaming in the night for an entirely different reason.

Come to think of it — where were the girls, we asked? Another staffer pointed to the main lodge, where the female staff lived in relative palatial splendor on the top floor. Chris and I made a beeline to meet the girls, whose collective attractiveness convinced us to stay on. The girls' rooms were clean, well lit, with no bats, rats, exploding fuel tanks, or ghosts. Thus the obvious goal was to connect up with a girl as soon as possible to avoid spending much time in Bedlam — not that a teenaged boy needed any more incentive to get some female action.

Susie, a cute office secretary showed us around the girls' abode, sarcastically complaining that her pink wallpaper was peeling— hell, the boys barely had walls!

As I tried unsuccessfully to fall asleep that first night, I actually began to pine for those good old days making gas mask valves in a Baltimore sweat shop. Sometime in those first few days I carved a sarcastic "Fun on Parade" into Bedlam's hallway entrance.

After that first sleep-free night of listening for bats, rats, ghosts, and fires, we made our way bleary-eyed across the dirt path to the staff dining room for breakfast around eight a.m. Our co-workers all seemed nice enough, but once again I heard whispers that the cook was a certified lunatic. It was a pattern I would see again and again in the eastern resort areas: it appeared that mental illness was a prerequisite for becoming a resort hotel chef. After breakfast Chris and I made our way to our corkboard-posted assignments in the front office. The first note read: "Gus and Chris, repair the ice machine in the kitchen." Chris and I both stifled laughter; this was like asking Truman Capote to rebuild your Chevy V8. On the way down the guest hallway, Chris, ever the comedian, grabbed a Gideon's Bible from an empty room — he planned to pray over the ice machine while I kicked it.

With our un-callused hands, it must have been obvious to all that we were, in the words of comedian Chris Elliott, "fancy lads," not maintenance men. The only calluses I owned were from playing guitar and tennis. Thus a crowd of doubting staffers encircled us as we approached the gigantic commercial icemaker. I opened the lid and reached in to a pool of warm water where there should be ice.

"It definitely has a problem," I diagnosed, to the laughter of all around. Chris cracked open Gideon, and, finding nothing appropriate for electrical miracles, read something — I believe — from Revelations. With that I started kicking the infernal machine. Nothing.

"I think you should check out the internal recindicator," Chris suggested (for the rest of the summer, he would distinguish himself with his ability to invent authentic-sounding mechanical lingo.)

"Of course, the recindicator," I agreed. I noticed that we now had the waitresses in stitches. Not bad.

I climbed into the waist-high ice retrieval door as Chris held my feet. I reached back as somebody handed me a flashlight. What happened next went a long way to convincing Ziggy to keep us employed, although Ziggy (and everyone else), busy in the front office, never learned the secret. With my butt hanging out from the icemaker, I noticed a reset switch in the back of the machine's interior. The switch said, no lie, "On/Off." It was set in the off position. I yelled back for Chris to read something from the New Testament, and I made some repair-like noises, before resetting the switch. Miraculously, the machine came to life. Chris pulled me out, to the sound of the applauding waitresses, who were also somewhat in a state of shock — as was Chris.

"Praise be to God," Chris and I said in unison, as we made the sign of the cross.

Now a startled Chris looked at that Bible, likely contemplating a move to Lourdes. I pulled him aside and confessed about the power switch. It would be our secret, but we would bring Gideon to all our repair jobs the rest of the summer, hoping that he would lead us to more on-off switches. Our toolbox consisted, literally, of a hammer and a Bible, as we became comic relief for both staff and guests. My worship of the Marx Brothers was finally coming in handy.

That evening we found out that we were on call, and were directed to an elderly guest's room in the main lodge. "She needs her heater fixed," Ziggy informed us. Early summer evenings actually got quite chilly in the Poconos, and the rooms were furnished with pre-Civil War forced-air steam heaters, which of course, Chris and I knew zero about. Since I had "repaired" the icemaker, it was now Chris's turn to perform a miracle. He grabbed a hammer; I grabbed Gideon. Before we knocked on the door, I broke open the Good Book and read another completely inappropriate entry. When the woman came to the door, I asked her to wait out in the hallway while Chris went in, telling her it might be dangerous. In truth, I didn't want her to see Chris scratching his head and whacking her heater with a hammer. From the hallway we could hear my partner banging away. Once again, to our surprise, another miracle occurred; it seemed that the heater had some sort of vapor lock from not having been used since last summer, and all it needed was Chris's nuanced touch. He emerged from the room and explained to the thankful woman.

"It was just the rotating flamistan," Chris assured her. "Sometimes they get stuck between the paddock and the furlong. It happens all the time." Chris was a racing fan and occasionally tossed in bits of track lingo.† The woman insisted on tipping us, and as we made our getaway, she gushed, "I certainly can sleep safe at night knowing you guys are around."

With that, Chris and I raced for the exit, so as to not burst out laughing in front of the poor, misguided woman.

We gave the entire motel section a show after our corkboard boss told us to "remove the hornet's nest from the door above motel room # 42." Now, Chris was allergic to bee stings and I was allergic to pain in general, so this really required some thought. We decided to revive a pickup truck that sat in the garage under Bedlam for the task. This jalopy was at least twenty years old and didn't have enough horsepower to qualify it as a prop in *The Grapes of Wrath*.

In any event, after much planning, Chris and I decided to do a drive-by assault on the nest, which was situated on one of the in-line motel units on the top of the hill. First we hammered some poles together, creating a 15-ft. attack jousting rod. On the end we fashioned some oil-soaked cloth, effectively turning it into a gargantuan torch. We both wrapped cloth bandanas around our foreheads, long enough to blow in the breeze like Harpo in the chariot race climax of *Horsefeathers*. We slowly drove by the motel unit to see what we were up against. The nest was a whopper, forcing us back to the garage to extend our weapon even further. We didn't want to get near that thing.

As a crowd began to gather, I read something from Gideon about plagues of insects, we then lit the torch, and with Gladiator Chris hanging from the right side running board, I drove the truck past the motel room while Chris extended our ridiculous weapon toward the hive. By the time the bees came out, we were a hundred yards down the parking lot. The crowd cheered. Somebody gave us Caesar's "thumbs down" signal and we drove by a few more times until that nest was engulfed in flame. That's when we realized we were about to burn down the entire motel unit.

"Holy shit!" Chris screamed as he ran from the truck to retrieve a hose. As he bravely fought the blaze and I torched the bees, I now saw that the guests were rolling in laughter. It must have seemed to them like a live Three Stooges stage show, with Gus, Chris, and Gideon subbing for Larry, Moe, and Curly. Thus, for our next hive removals, I came up with something less destructive: Easy Off Oven Cleaner. I just sprayed the bees, and they instantly fell to the ground, their wings disintegrated. (Tip: make sure you're upwind when you try this.)

---

† Chris would go on to become President of the American Thoroughbred Association.

After our hornet roasting success, we repaired back to Bedlam where we busied ourselves trying to build a door to our "room." The result was far from a perfect fit, but the gaps seemed small enough to keep Rodan and his bat buddies from flying in. The next morning, our to-do list began with "Repair and paint the entrance to motel room #42." That became the leitmotif of our summer job – repairing what we had destroyed the day before. Pure job perpetuation. A good example of this was the day our work list said, "Mow the front lawn." Finally! We were beginning to wonder when we would be asked to do something we actually knew how to do. So confident were we about this assignment that Gideon was allowed to even take a day off. Big mistake.

We had a blast learning how to work our first riding mowers, racing around the giant trees on the front lawn of the lodge. After an hour or so, we looked over our work and congratulated ourselves on a job well done. The next morning our work list included replacing the lightbulbs in the trees in front of the lodge, which we did repeatedly, to no effect. Strange. All the bulbs had somehow gone bad at the same time. Then one of us noticed an exposed length of electrical cable near the base of one of the trees — you know, the cable we must have ridden over yesterday when we were racing our riding mowers. Oh, well, one more thing added to our list.

Perhaps the best example of our self-perpetuating chores came on the day we were told we would spend the next week painting the exterior trim on the dining room's window frames. Of course, these were no ordinary windows, but something more like an elaborate

French window design, and there were dozens of them.

Out came the paint, brushes, and ladders, as we spent a hot summer week scraping and painting those windows. At $75 a week for our salaries, I can only imagine how much Ziggy thought he was going to save. The day after we finished the job came the note to scrape all the splattered paint off the windows. That took two or three more days, followed by a note telling us to remove and replace all the windows we cracked during the scraping.

Our summer of '68 was fleshed out with the standard teen romances that came and went, "riding our thumbs" around the Poconos on our days off, and playing in the hotel's sing-along style hootenannies. At least three nights a week, a dance band entertained the guests, usually Polkas or square dancing, and the staff was encouraged get the old-timers out of their seats. The star performer was a bizarre song and dance man known as "Smilin' Sam the Rubber Legs Man." Much like scenes in the movie *Dirty Dancing*, we had to dance with the guests until they were tired, then we danced with each other.

As the summer wore on, Chris began having mechanical problems with the Corvair — specifically, it burned and leaked oil at a pace only matched two decades later by the *Exxon Valdez*. By the end of the summer, we'd typically pull into a gas station and tell the attendant, "Please fill up the oil and check the gas." They thought we were joking, but we were dead serious. When Chris's birthday came to pass, all the hotel staff bought him cans of oil. We even found five-gallon cans for the occasion. I think it lasted two weeks.

All in all it was a great summer; too bad it ended strangely. On a personal level, the strangeness began with spending my late summer birthday recovering from a visit to a Stroudsburg hospital emergency room, the result of my otherwise entertaining lack of mechanical skills. It all started when a guest reported foul smelling liquid bubbling up from the putting surface of the miniature golf course. As it was Chris's great fortune to have the day off, I arrived on the scene alone with the hammer and Bible, both of which proved surprisingly useless in dealing with the situation at hand. What I confronted was the most foul-smelling eruption imaginable, and a source of confusion for this suburban youth. In situations where we were stymied, we'd typically bring out Ziggy, who was actually quite the handyman.

"Oh, no, not again," he said upon arriving at the putt-putt site. "This happened about ten years ago, and it's no fun at all. We'll have to rent a snake." No less confused, I asked him what was going on, and why on earth we'd need a reptile.

"The septic lines are clogged," Ziggy answered. The "snake" was a coiled plumber's snake that would have to be inserted at numerous points along the underground pipeline, whereupon it would be electrically rotated to free the clogs.

With that pronouncement I was about to experience the most disgusting week of my life – to this very day. While Ziggy procured the needed "snake," I went back to Bedlam to change into my most disposable clothes (not an easy choice, actually). There I found my roommate sleeping in. On occasion, if the job was too big, we'd have to forfeit our day off, and when Chris heard what was up he bolted out the door. "I want full credit for getting up and out of there in less than 30 seconds," Chris recently recalled, "when you came into the room swearing — the only time I heard you do so — about the sewer line being broken." Chris jumped into the Corvair while still getting dressed, and raced to Stroudsburg, far out of Ziggy's reach. "I think I set a record for sitting at a Woolworth's fountain counter for eight hours, reading and consuming ice cream sodas. Somehow, Ziggy suspected my absence wasn't a coincidence."

However, Chris was only able to avoid the first day of what was to take us a tortuous week toiling in human waste. During that time, Chris and I walked the entire grounds searching, and sniffing, for the gory geysers. Once one was located, we dug a ditch three feet deep through the sewage muck, and with human waste all over us, we carefully unpacked the tensely coiled metallic snake and inserted it into the broken pipe; we had been warned to be careful, as the snake was prone to whip free if not coiled or uncoiled properly. We then jumped out of the hole and turned on the roto-rooter and unclogged the workings. At the end of the workday, we felt like we needed to walk through a car wash repeatedly to remove the stench. Even after a thorough scrubbing, we didn't feel fit for human contact. This was our life, eight hours a day, for at least five days. I found it impossible to believe that some people actually do this for a living.

As though to put an exclamation point on the week from hell, on the last hour of the last day, bone tired, I lost concentration for a second and paid the price. While Chris was filling in a ditch, I set about to coil up the thirty-foot long snake for the last time. Just as I wrapped the final section, the feces-covered device whipped open and uncoiled with frightening force, catching my lower lip on the way. Had it caught my eye, my orbit would have ended up in orbit, so I suppose I'm lucky. As it was, my lip was cut deep enough to require a couple stitches, but the gash was now filled with guess what. And the rest of my face was covered with "guess what" as well. As I was being scrubbed down, sutured, and shot up in the emergency room, I was frustrated by the thought that this couldn't have happened five days earlier, sparing me a few days of work.

The national scene unfolding on television was almost as revolting as the week we spent in those "Fun on Parade" ditches. We arrived back at Henryville from the hospital just in time to gather around the television in the front office and witness the uncoiled rage of the Chicago Police Department. On August 28, 1968, a group of 10,000 anti-war protestors, with legal permits obtained by activist Abbie Hoffman, stood in Grant Park, just off Michigan Avenue, demanding that the Democratic National Convention adopt a plank for ending the war. Since Hoffman's "Yippies," the SDS, and the National Mobilization Committee to End the War in Vietnam, had announced their plans a year earlier, the Chicago PD had plenty of time to prepare, but it seemed that all they did during those months was practice splitting open coconuts, because that was how they dealt with the skulls of the unarmed protestors.

Gathered around the hotel's only public television, we learned that early in the afternoon police beat a young boy for lowering Grant Park's American flag without permission. In response to the police brutality, the protestors pelted the police with food, rocks, bags of urine, and chunks of concrete. The police then answered with Billy Clubs followed by so much tear gas that it burned the eyes of Vice President Hubert Humphrey who was showering in the Hilton. Much of the carnage was captured live on national television. When Chicago's "Gestapo tactics" were decried from the convention stage by Connecticut Senator Abraham Ribicoff, Chicago Mayor Richard Daley could be seen on the convention floor cursing back at him, "Fuck you, you Jew son of a bitch! You lousy motherfucker! Go home!"

The final toll came to 101 protestors treated for undisclosed injuries in area hospitals, and the resultant federal investigation concluded that the melee resulted from a "police riot." The consensus back in the Henryville lobby, and in many corners of America, was that none of this would have happened if the Democratic Party had favored the brilliant anti-war candidate, Senator George McGovern, over Johnson's pro-war standard-bearer, Vice President Humphrey. I began reading up on McGovern and was so impressed that I vowed to work for him in some capacity in the future.

Soon the Henryville staff was saying their goodbyes, most of us deciding that we wouldn't tempt fate by spending another summer in the firetrap known as Bedlam. On the other hand, Chris and I loved the summer resort lifestyle and decided to find another, slightly less flammable, locale for our summer of 1969. After packing the Corvair to the brim and filling up on 10W 30, we headed back to Baltimore in early September. Predictably, all along the way we passed scores of other sign-bearing teens hitching homeward — we barely had room for our legs, so we had to pass them by.

Some of the Henryville girls

Unbeknownst to me, my favorite band, the Beach Boys, was similarly encountering kids hitching rides in far away Los Angeles. The band's drummer (and anointed sex symbol), Dennis Wilson, regrettably, had enough room in his Rolls Royce that summer when he stopped to pick up two comely hippie girls named Yellerstone and Marnie, both of whom would share his Beverly Hills bed later that day, setting off a chain of events that would rock the country.[‡] The girls turned out to be friends with a guy, named "Pigpen" for his abhorrence for soap, who was surrounded by over a dozen more drug-addled, but beautiful, young girls with names like "Sadie Glutz" and "Squeaky." The insatiable Dennis invited the entourage to live in his rented mansion in exchange for sex on demand with the girls. Over time, Pigpen, the girls' Svengali, revealed himself to be a somewhat gifted musician, who hoped to sell his songs. Soon Dennis was bringing the aspirant, whom Dennis called "The Wizard," to the Beach Boys' studio to cut demos, two of which ("Be With Me" and "Never Learn Not to Love") were in fact recorded by the Beach Boys under Dennis's name. He next took the aspiring star to Byrds' producer Terry Melcher's rented house at 10050 Cielo Drive in Beverly Hills. Although Melcher, the son of actress Doris Day, promised to help the swarthy, unwashed, songwriter, he never followed through. Dennis also introduced Pigpen to Melcher's landlord, show

---

[‡] Dennis would later write a song about his habit of picking up female hitchhikers, the unreleased "I'm Going Your Way."

biz manager Rudi Altobelli, who wasn't so polite, sending the disheveled singer packing.

    Melcher and Altobelli were just two of the people Wilson set up with Pigpen. On another occasion, when Wilson was hitchhiking home, he was picked up by psychotic drug dealer from Dallas nicknamed "Tex." Wilson brought Tex into his mansion madhouse, introduced him to Pigpen, and Tex accepted an invitation to make the classy commune his new home. In the coming months, Wilson's squatters cleaned him out of almost $200,000 in cash and expenses (which included totaling Wilson's brand new, uninsured, Ferrari, valued at $21,000.) And Pigpen became increasingly violent, even putting a knife to Dennis's throat, as it became apparent that Melcher and Wilson were not going to make him a star. Wilson became so terrified that he abandoned his own home to them. There they remained throughout the fall of 1968 until they were evicted for non-payment of the rent. It only further infuriated the quickly deteriorating Pigpen, who next summer would order his acolytes to deliver a grisly message of revenge back at the Melcher-Altobelli property. That's when the rest of the world would learn the true names of Dennis Wilson's hitch-hiking house guests: "Marnie" was Patricia Krenwinkle; "Yellerstone" was Ella Jo Bailey; "Sadie Glutz" was Susan Atkins; "Squeaky" was Lynette Fromme; and "Tex" was Charles Watson. And they would do anything for "Pigpen," whose real name was Charlie Manson.

Chapter Seven

Blue Water, Pt. 1

SO IT WAS BACK to school, the tennis team, and playing music. Not long after the fall semester began, the Catonsville Nine were convicted of the destruction of US property and sentenced, collectively, to eighteen years in prison. At the time of his sentencing, Fr. Daniel Berrigan wrote, "Our apologies, good friends, for the fracture of good order, the burning of paper instead of children." His sentiment rang true with me and my fellow classmates at UMBC, a campus that was quickly becoming Baltimore's ground zero for collegiate protests.

Given the spring 1968 assassinations, the King riots in Baltimore, the civil rights and war protests in the nearby nation's capital, and the Catonsville Nine travesty in our back yard, it was small wonder that the UMBC campus became quickly radicalized, hosting its own chapters of the SDS, Black Panthers, and countless other leftist interest groups. To put an exclamation point on things, we elected a radical, pro-student power, pro-civil rights, and anti-war student government at UMBC. In the September 30, 1968 edition of the campus daily, *The Retriever*, SGA president elect Daryl Hagy spoke to the students of UMBC urging activism: "The problems which are now frustrating the United States are not separated from this university by ivy-covered walls," Hagy intoned. "They are just down the street. We have demonstrated against them. We have marched. We have protested--but what have we offered as solutions to them and how deep is our commitment to work towards their solutions? This is the new beginning students must now make, and that I believe it is the destiny of students this year."

UMBC students of 1968 staged rallies and made bus trips to DC's Independence Mall rallies at the drop of a hat, and there were frequent takeovers of campus buildings to call attention to issues that ranged from the war to women's rights to black power – you name it. The school's administration had now made it clear that the young campus favored research professors (so-called "grant machines") over teaching professors, and the classic "publish or perish" debate saw many of our best teachers fired, which lead to "sleep-ins" and takeovers of UMBC's Hillcrest administration building. The black student union, demanding more black professors at the institution, organized one takeover of the besieged administration building. The worst repercussions of the radicalism were the firing of several sympathetic faculty members who took part in the protests. Today, the university's 12-1 p.m. "free hour" is a direct result of this past, created when we student protestors convinced administrators to give them a period during the school day to organize.

One of my professors at the time, Fred Pincus, assistant professor of Sociology, is still teaching there at this writing. He recently bemoaned how the UMBC climate has changed over the years. "There is much less student activity today," Pincus said. "The Internet has changed things and now there is a question of what is more effective, protests or the Internet...Personally, I think 100,000 people in the street is more effective than 100,000 people in a Facebook group." More disturbingly, students today are much more concerned about finding jobs than past students have been, Pincus added. As a result, fewer students take the time to be activists and more are focused academics and jobs.

Thanks to a wishy-washy Democratic nominee (Vice-President Hubert Humphrey) and a secret deal in which the South Vietnamese delegation agreed to stall going to the October Paris Peace Talks, the reviled Richard Nixon became President in November. Compared to the horrors of the previous spring, 1969 began as a relative walk in the park. Although there were over 500,000 troops in Vietnam, most of the protests— and there were many— ended with minimal bloodshed. In addition to protests at various University of Maryland campuses, UMass, Berkeley, Howard University, Penn State, and the University of Wisconsin made newsworthy shows of anti-war solidarity.

Meanwhile in New Orleans, a stark-raving mad DA named Jim Garrison finally saw his protracted two-and-a-half year witch hunt against a local community leader fall apart in shambles. On May 1, 1969, it only took forty-five minutes for a Big Easy jury to exonerate businessman Clay Shaw for the preposterous, completely unsupported charge that he organized the assassination of President Kennedy for the CIA (the foreman said it might have taken half that time except that a number of jurors took a restroom break.) Like Mark Lane before him, the paranoid, self-serving Garrison had been unknowingly duped by the Soviet KGB into helping drive another wedge between the CIA and the American public. In that regard, both Garrison and the KGB were successful. Shaw was not so fortunate: despite his courtroom victory the liberal, civic minded Shaw was financially destroyed by a heartless public servant, and he died not long after his acquittal, but not before a civil court excoriated the out-of-control DA.

Aside from politics, music and other art forms were still a powerful force in our lives, and our campus was a primordial soup for countless student musicians, poets, dancers, painters, and bands.

On any given warm day, musicians stirred that soup in the common area outside the cafeteria. A major part of UMBC's dynamic music scene while I was there was the concerts that the school hosted, among them: Bossa Nova great Charlie Byrd, 12-string folk icon Tim Buckley, the vastly underrated singer-songwriter Biff Rose, Nils Lofgren's trio Grin, and Chicago Transit Authority (later shortened to Chicago.) Of course, I often volunteered for the entertainment committee as a way to have a say in upcoming shows and to go to the concerts for free. A half mile away, the local community college also had a robust concert schedule that featured acts such as the Eagles and Poco.

When Poco arrived in 1970, I made certain I was in the center of the action, obtaining backstage passes from a friend. Before the show, the band was in the gym locker room, sitting on Anvil flight cases while warming up vocally. I remember joining in the action when they did "Kind Woman," which my current group also covered. After the show I drove Richie and Tim Schmit back to their hotels before we all went out for food and drink. After Richie stored his guitar in his room, he turned on the TV before we headed out. I asked him about the TV and he informed me that, having spent years in hotel rooms, he had learned that keeping the TV on was a great form of security. I have done the same ever since.

That's the night I heard the true story of "For What It's Worth," the Buffalo Springfield's first hit single. I can't be certain, but I'm fairly sure that it was ex-Springfield member Richie who told me the tale of how the single found its way onto the coveted rotation of KHJ radio station in Los Angeles — it became the launch point for the record's success. At the time of the song's recording, the Springfield's best friends, some say mentors, were the Byrds, whose guitarist, David Crosby,

Richie and me in 2009

happened also to be great friends with the Beatles — as well as their pot connection when they visited LA. In early 1967, Crosby returned from London armed with an acetate of the as yet unreleased Beatles opus, "A Day in the Life," which had been personally given to him by the mop tops. Fully aware of Crosby's hedonistic excesses, and as yet unable to get their own song played on the radio, the Buffalo Springfield conceived a brilliant piece of "honey-trap" spycraft; they engaged the services of a young woman of easy virtue, armed her with the best drugs they could collect, and sent her David's way with one mission: Get that acetate!

In short order, the Hippie Mata Hari seduced Crosby, had him play her the recording, and after he passed out, brought the disk back to the waiting Buffalo Springfield. The band then trucked over to KHJ and made them an offer they couldn't refuse: in exchange for an exclusive airing of the centerpiece from a future album by biggest band in history, the station would agree to place "For What It's Worth" in heavy rotation for the next few weeks. For the station it was a no-brainer, and "For What It's Worth" went on to have a three-month ride on the charts, peaking at Number 7 nationally, in part because the public mistakenly believed the protest lyric was a reference to the anti-war rallies. The Beatles' "A Day in the Life," was released five months after FWIW, as the climactic song on the LP, *Sgt. Pepper's Lonely Heart's Club Band*.

Back in 1968-69, the airwaves hosted an explosion of musical creativity, with every conceivable genre, from soul to folk to standards to psychedelic to jazz to movie themes, represented in the Top Forty list. Between 1967 and 1969, the Beach Boys recorded four terrific LPs (Smiley Smile, Friends, Wild Honey, and 20/20), and the Beatles delivered *Sergeant Pepper's Lonely Hearts Club Band* and the double disk "white album," which drove Dennis Wilson's already crazy house squatter "Pigpen" Manson to violent insanity.

By the spring of 1969, Richie Furay's new band Poco had released their first album, *Pickin' Up the Pieces*. It was another brilliant Furay concept, fusing rock and country genres with three killer tenor vocalists and the insane pedal steel guitar virtuosity of Colorado's Rusty Young. I was so stunned by this new "Country Rock" sound that I began the search for kindred spirits with whom I might form a similar new group. My seeming foolhardy search for a pedal steel guitarist in Catonsville further isolated me from the club-gigging mainstream bands, but I couldn't have cared less. I have always followed my musical muse without the slightest consideration of the marketplace.

Amazingly, I found what was probably Baltimore's only young steel player, and together with three others formed a new group, Destry, that covered songs by Poco, Springfield, New Riders of the Purple Sage, and Gram Parsons. We actually sounded pretty good, although we were undanceable and thus completely out of place in Baltimore, and therefore almost impossible to book. However, the skills I learned in Destry would serve me well as I moved on after college.

One day that winter, I headed back to "my" library to begin the search for the next resort that would be the lucky recipient of my vast musical and handyman skills. Being financially strapped as always, summer in Europe was out of the question due to the cost of airplane tickets. (Unlike today, flying was still a bit of a luxury in 1969 and my feet had yet to even leave the ground.) Thus I focused on the best locales within driving distance. Thumbing through the 1969 resort guidebooks, I stumbled upon photos of a stunning lake resort that was nestled between two mountain ranges, appearing in photos as a mini version of that favorite Bond getaway, Lake Geneva. The 32-mile long, 200-ft. deep lake, formed by bedrock glacier melt, is situated 200 miles north of New York City on the Vermont border, and is actually the largest spring-fed lake in the US, giving it crystal clear waters on which rest some 300 small islands.

Virtually unknown to Baltimoreans, Lake George was a major summer vacation draw for New Yorkers, Canadians, and various New Englanders, but like "our" Atlantic City, it featured low-priced carney distractions in the south-end "Village," and more upscale refinements as one headed to the sparsely populated north. That's where the lakeside "Millionaire's Row" mansions (with private clay tennis courts, I might add) were inhabited by the spawn of 19th century American titans with names like Rockefeller, Whitney, Trask, Peabody, and Carnegie. Additionally, a number of celebrities owned lakeside getaway retreats. But the real draw was, and is, that gorgeous lake. All told, there was clearly infinitely more potential for adventure here than in Henryville, and the lodging *had* to be better than Bedlam. My pal Chris agreed, and so we sent away for job applications.

We were hired by the most promising resort in all the brochures, Blue Water Manor, which specialized in musically talented staff who entertained the guests seven nights a week. Every night had a different theme: Staff talent show, Broadway Musical, hootenanny, jazz, dance band, game night, and special solo concerts. All the staff (waiters, chambermaids, lifeguards, etc.) was expected to perform at least three nights per week, making for a robust learning experience for us musicians. I would later find out that the Manor was deluged with a thousand applications per year, many from up and coming Broadway understudies, for the sixty open positions. I was lucky to be hired, and how Chris finessed the application I'll never know. My day job was described as "cabin boy," in actuality a male chambermaid (since the grounds were so severely sloped, boys were hired to push the heavy towel, sheet, and soap carts around the resort to service the rooms.)

In mid-June, Chris and I hopped into his newest jalopy (the Corvair died immediately after the Poconos) and made the eight-hour trek northward, once again to a place neither of us had ever been. Making our way past the summer hitchhikers up the Rt. 87 "Northway," Chris and I saw no hint of a lake as we approached Exit 22, supposedly just a quarter mile from the water.

Peabody "cottage"

Only a few hundred yards off the highway, we *would* have had a glimpse of the water, except that the horizon was obscured by the "summer cottage" of George Foster Peabody, the iconic financier and philanthropist. That's right, the 19th century barons who summered here referred to their lakeside manses as "cottages" in a weak attempt at humility. Gazing at the Tudor-style edifice, one of us remarked, "We're not in Henryville anymore!"

Making our way up the western shore past the Peabody Estate, we finally saw it — the bluest, most gorgeous body of water we had ever laid eyes on. Driving up the Lakeshore Drive switchback, I was astonished that the beauty of the lake actually exceeded the photos. No Technicolor Pocono-style retouching needed. I immediately understood why Thomas Jefferson called it "...the most beautiful water I ever saw." Poor Chris almost drove off the two-lane road as he tried to take in the seascape. On this

Basin Bay

western shore were situated all the resort hotels and restaurants, while the eastern side was reserved for a very few private lakeside estates purchased before the entire area was subsumed into the *six-million-acre* Adirondack Park, the largest state-owned park in the US. About seven miles north of the southern tip's Lake George Village was Blue Water Manor, located on Basin Bay, one of the most serene, protected locales on the lake.

Since most of BWM's two-dozen outlying buildings were nestled among seventy-foot high trees, all we saw from the road was the hotel's welcome sign, almost driving by it. Turning onto the driveway, the first thing we spotted was a lone tennis court (Yes!), followed by an indoor pool building that was connected to the main office. Behind the pool building was the co-ed dorm (Again, Yes!). Trees and cottages obscured any view of the lake, a couple hundred yards down the sloping property. We walked into the office and introduced ourselves to the co-owner of the resort, sixty-ish Ellen Shukis, like Ziggy, another stern, all-business taskmaster. The entire lodge, including the magnificent Stone Manor House, had been built decades earlier by her parents, Lithuanian immigrants Dominic and Appolonia Slivynas. Dominic himself built the cabins and laid the Manor House stones.

Ellen informed us that the resort would open to guests in about two weeks, thus allowing us time to rehearse our various musical combos. Additionally, we were expected to try out for the season's once-a-week musical, *West Side Story,* directed by a genuine Broadway hoofer. However, Ellen said that when we were not rehearsing or working, we were permitted to use all the resort's amenities, including the tennis court, boats, water skis, lakeside sauna, indoor pool — whatever. Once the guests arrived, we had to naturally differ to then. After depositing our gear in our dorm room (which barely contained one bunk-bed, but was an infinite improvement over Bedlam), we set out to survey our newest domain, proceeding down the cabin-lined tarmac walkway to the Manor House on the edge of the lake.

Inside the stunning castle-like stone and timber fortress was a large meeting room that featured a grand piano and what we were told was the largest stone hearth in America. Atop the massive edifice was the mounted head of some poor moose, which would become the object of a drunken, and dangerous, late-night decoration ritual that was known as "shooting the moose." It would be against the hearth backdrop that our nightly entertainment would be staged.

Exiting the back door of the Manor, we found ourselves on a fifty-foot high cliffside deck with the most beautiful view I had ever seen. Looking over Basin Bay and out across the lake proper, we were almost speechless at the beauty of the Vermont mountain range — dominated by the stately Black Mountain and Buck Mountain — that ringed the lake on the eastern shore. On one magical starlit night that summer I would be on that deck observing the purple curtained beauty of the Northern Lights as they swayed high above the lake near Black Mountain. I have yet to see this breathtaking celestial light show again.

Looking over at the eastern shoreline and simultaneously below to the unused canoes, Chris and I decided it was time for our first adventure. After all, we had been here over an hour and had yet to have our first catastrophe. Thus we made our way down the most rickety wooden stairs imaginable, affixed to the cliff wall many decades previous, past what would be Chris's lakeside snack bar, to the four resort docks, where we commandeered two six-foot long canoes from the boathouse.

Of most importance here is that neither Chris nor I had ever been in a canoe before. But how hard could it be? Row once to the left, once to the right, and repeat. If Huck Finn could do it, so could we. Equally important

Scaling Buck, with Basin Bay in the background.

is the fact that, although the clear mountain air made the opposite shore appear to be a half-mile away, it was actually *six times that far*, through North Sea-style whitecaps that only became apparent after exiting the misleading serenity of Basin Bay. Once in the lake proper, the water below sank to a depth of 200 feet, or about 198 feet more than it would take to drown both of us non-swimmers. Oops. Oh, and one other thing: we launched our mini canoes at 4 p.m., thinking we'd be back in an hour, with daylight to spare. Double oops.

One hour later we found ourselves in the middle of a turbulent lake that had suddenly grown exponentially in width. But we were undaunted, as determined to touch the opposite shore as the Apollo 11 astronauts were to touch the lunar surface later that summer. By the time we arrived at our goal, it was almost dark, and our hands were blistered and swollen. As we came about, our hearts stopped upon the realization that we had to make our way across this huge lake in the dark, towards a destination we had never seen at night, and for only a minute by day. We could be out there rowing in circles until the sun came up, an aquatic version of *Exodus*. Overhead was the most star-filled sky we had ever seen; too bad neither of us happened to have a sextant in our jean pockets.

Making our way back was terrifying: the rough water was freezing, and large Donzi speedboats and Chris Craft yachts — piloted, we later learned, by rich, drunk kids — raced past us creating wakes that almost sank our canoes. Somehow we made it back to the dorm alive and collapsed.

The following morning provided a welcome wakeup call. As I made my way down the dorm hallway and into the gym-style group shower room, I was jolted from my morning brain-fog by the sight of a comely lass showering just a few feet away. "Hi, I'm Beth," she offered as she held out her hand. The sight of me standing there in shock prompted her to ask: "Need some shampoo?"[*] Oh, this was going to be a fun summer!

At eight, the teenaged workforce assembled in the staff mess hall for breakfast, whereupon Ellen set out the itinerary and introduced us to our various supervisors, adding that tryouts for the various shows would commence later that morning. For the next couple hours, "General Annie" gave the cabin staff a militaristic seminar on how to properly clean a room and make up a bed — both firsts for me. Sadly for us cabin boys, Annie's idea of a clean room put the operating suite at the Mayo Clinic to shame. Every inch of the room had to be virtually sterilized, and Annie would, unannounced, spot-check every

---

[*] The dorms weren't *intended* to be coed, as the boys and girls sections were separated by a section of drywall. However, on the day the first boy arrived, the first order of business was to "tear down that wall," creating our own underground railroad of hormones. During the off-season, that wall would be re-installed, only to have it demolished on the first day of the next season.

nook and cranny of a room with perverse glee just to make sure. Any sign of dust, dirt, or hair would require a start-to-finish do-over.

Later, we all assembled in the Manor House to meet Bobbie, a woman with much experience producing shows in New York City. Having no interest in acting or dancing, I took the option of performing in four other nights of entertainment, so I was out of there until the musicians met up that evening. Poor Chris, with no musical ability whatsoever, was nonetheless forced to sign up for the summer's weekly production of *West Side Story*, the tender tale of two warring "Loisaida" street gangs who surprisingly sing and dance while they blow each others' brains out. Chris hoped to hide in the back of the stone hearth for the duration of the production, at the farthest recesses of the singing, dancing, and "rumbling" chorus. He almost succeeded, landing the role of "Chino," who had only one line, no vocal solos, and just one key skill to master: pulling the trigger of a pistol once, accented by a well-timed drum rimshot, killing the hero, "Tony," in the climax. What could go wrong? Plenty, it turned out.

The first two weeks at the resort, before the late June opening, were a blur of musical rehearsals, guest room cleaning, swimming, boating, tennis, and partying. On off-hours, the dorm became our Sunset Strip, with non-stop jamming and partnership-forming. For the remainder of that summer, virtually every stroll down the hall of the un-chaperoned dorm was accompanied by sweet aromas of pot and incense, mixed with the sounds of music and mating. "Safe sex" was virtually unheard of in the Sixties, as all girls seemed to receive their first birth control pill packets as a twofer with their driver's license on their sixteenth birthday. And sexually transmitted diseases weren't even a consideration; Boomers reached sexual maturity in a unique time — the only thirty-year span in human history, 1950-1980, when unprotected sex could be engaged with no repercussions, i.e. after "the pill" (which prevented pregnancy) and penicillin (which cured any pesky infection), but before AIDS, which has yet to find its own "magic bullet."

Drugs were everywhere, predominantly pot that the staff purchased from the neighboring trust fund kids, who seemed to import it by the boatload. LSD was around as well, but was seen as more of an occasional luxury. As far as drugs were concerned, I was a bit of a teetotaler; I never enjoyed the "pot high," and only did it a few times. I did acid once, and had such a remarkable eye opening experience that I felt I never needed to do it again. It was as though I was given such a permanently-imprinted new perspective on life and the universe that I had no need to revisit it: I got it. Furthermore, the acid we had available to us at that time was pure — and safe — pharmaceutical grade from Sandoz in Switzerland. In short time, as acid sadly became more "recreational," kids began using tainted homemade versions that you couldn't pay me to dabble with. The truth was I was a bit of a health nut, very serious about my tennis game, and I had no desire to clog my lungs with pot smoke, or play a match in a state of bliss. But that was my trip. My trio mates loved to indulge, so much so that I used to introduce our hard-partying lead singer to the audience as "Ol' Red Eyes."

After a night of jamming in the dorm, we'd often repair naked to the dockside sauna bath, followed by a heart-stopping skinny dip in the cold waters of Lake George. The complete late night ritual became known as "The Seven S's": "Shit, shower, shave, smoke, swim, sauna, and sex."

"It's lovely to live on a raft. We had the sky up there, all speckled with stars, and we used to lay on our backs and look up at them, and discuss about whether they was made or only just happened." — Mark Twain, *The Adventures of Huckleberry Finn*

We took long boat rides in one of the resort's three Boston Whalers, exploring the many scenic islands of The Narrows, the Calf's Pen diving cliffs, and countless hidden alcoves, such as the sublime Paradise Bay, located in the island strewn Narrows. In Paradise Bay we'd float on inner tubes, while sipping Margaritas that were refilled by our on-board mates. Occasionally, we'd even be allowed to take out the beautiful all-wood longboat, *The Daina*, named after Ellen's 20-year-old Bohemian "wild child" daughter, who drifted in and out of the resort all summer with her boyfriend, renowned jazz flautist Jeremy Steig.

Whenever they popped in, Jeremy would play free-form jazz while Daina performed an exotic-erotic bellydance, much to the shock of the elderly guests and to the wild applause of their pubescent grandsons.

Stopping at various docks along the lake, we began making friends with the local trust fund kids, many of whom were living along Millionaire's Row. Soon, our floating party would spread the length and width of the lake. It was as though 1967's Summer of Love had been reprised in upstate New York two years later.

It was the first time I experienced "tubing" and sailing on those little two-man "sunfish" sailboats. Occasionally, we'd be sailing in the middle of this huge lake when the wind disappeared. With no way to get back in time for the evening gig, we often had to put our thumbs out and hitch to a powerboat. This became especially harrowing because when the wind died suddenly, it was usually due to an approaching storm. Watching the lightning approach our unmoving metal-masted boat was heart-stopping.

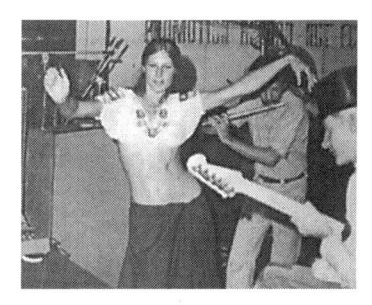

Daina and Jeremy doing their thing in the Manor House.

With the exception of Chris, the staff possessed amazing musical talent, and many went on to have big careers in music.[†] I began rehearsing an acoustic harmony act with Will Beemer and Dave "Ak" Atkinson. It was a well-balanced combo: Will, a bit of a Lochinvar, was a great frontman, guitarist and baritone; "Ak" was not only a gifted tenor

---

[†] One notable was Bostonian, Bill Goebel (later changed to "Gable.") An accomplished, singer, guitarist, cellist, pianist, and composer, Bill enthralled the guests during his weekly "solo night" performances of original material. Bill, a frequent tennis partner of mine, later moved to LA, where he wrote for Chicago, the Yellowjackets, and DeBarge, before releasing his own recordings. He built a terrific home studio that hosted the likes of Brian and Carl Wilson, Jackson Browne, America, and countless others.

with a soulful voice, but also one of the greatest blues harmonica players I have ever heard. I filled out the middle, singing second tenor, playing lead guitar, and arranging the vocal harmonies.

Our trio had the vocal blend I had always been searching for, the one that can't be forced, but only happens when the right set of vocal chords are matched up — pure serendipity. I remember when we first crammed into Will's room to try and harmonize. Seconds into our first song we all smiled and looked at each other as if to say, "Oh, this is special!" Our acoustic trio blew audiences away with our spot-on deliveries of songs like CSN's "Suite: Judy Blue Eyes" and the Hollies' "Bus Stop." I also played in the staff rock band, which did great covers of songs by Hendrix, Zeppelin, and the Allman Brothers, in addition to playing in what we called "the straight band," which played oldies for the adults.

Four-part harmonies inside the hearth

The Lake George vacation season is remarkably short, in large part because the icy waters only become warm enough for swimming after mid-summer; thus the guests started arriving at Blue Water Manor just before the Fourth of July. Much more so than at Henryville, the scene at our Lake George resort encouraged the forming of relationships with the guests (and their daughters), most of whom stayed for a week or two. If a guy couldn't score after taking a girl for an inebriated float in Paradise Bay, or a moonlight sauna, he was hopeless. At the end of their stay, the guests would leave a tip envelope in their emptied rooms.

The staff was so talented that the guests often gravitated to us as though we were rock stars, and it made sense for us to perform at our peak, since the more the guests were impressed, the bigger the tips at the time of their departure. Although our wage was about $65 a week, we could earn five times that much if we performed both our day *and* night jobs well. Although the staff genuinely liked many of the guests, there was no escaping the fact that the more we bonded with our audience, the bigger the payday. Many of us visited the guests (and their daughters) in the off-season, and remained friends with them for many years.

A typical day at Blue Water Manor went like this: a quick "co-ed" shower, breakfast at eight a.m., servicing the first of your dozen-or-so cabins until lunch, then finishing up by two o'clock. If your rooms weren't full, or if you worked fast, you could be completely finished by lunchtime. However, sometimes General Annie would spot-check your work and order you back to do it all over again. From there it was down to the beach, where we'd hang with the vacationers, who often took us out in their private boats, which they had towed from the city. Given the calm waters of Basin Bay, the resort was a Mecca for water skiers, and Ellen served them well with an anchored ski raft and free ski tows all day by a staffer — usually my bandmate Will Beemer — that manned one of the whalers. Often our ski boats had to dodge the Donzi speedboats of the neighboring rich kids who raced them recklessly around the bay while high on ganja. One close call involved a reckless trust kid who, high as a kite, accidentally raced between our towboat and the skier being towed, cutting the tips of her skis. Amazingly, this activity even took place at night, with only the moon

BWM staff photo (guys with their roach —holding hands raised are saying "I'm stoned")

to light the proceedings. Although there were some gruesome injuries, it's amazing no one was killed.

A weekly highlight for the water ski crowd was the hotel's water spectacular put on by the local hot-doggers and a couple of our most athletic staff. The star of the ski show was Donald "Bobby" Borth, who had skated in the famous Wisconsin Dells extravaganza. The zero-body-fat Bobby was an astounding athlete, not only on the wake jumping slalom ski and the jump ramp, but also in his bare feet. Unlike most bare-footers, who stood up in a slalom ski that they later dropped, Bobby could actually "get up" without a ski. He not only skied forward, but backwards, on his ski-less arches — and he could do it seemingly forever. Another crowd-pleaser was Bobby's black Lab, who skied with him on a custom-made board. The show closer was the six-person, flag-waving, pyramid, which often featured the owner's striking, belly-dancing daughter, Daina, in the pinnacle position. I was there the day that Daina hoisted herself to the top, only to have her bikini bottom became ensnarled on one of her second-tier lifters. But free spirit Daina was insouciant, as she stood aloft, smiling and waving to the horrified families (including hers) who rushed to cover their children's eyes. The incident became known as the "other" moon over Basin Bay.

Bobby Borth wins another skiing trophy

Of course, many of my afternoons were spent on the tennis court, or the beachside courts in the closest town, Bolton Landing, about a mile further north on Lakeshore Drive. I fell in love with Bolton, which had its own unique charm, featuring a packed calendar of free, and often quirky, public events.

On the Fourth of July, Bolton hosted the annual Great Bolton Bed Race, in which business owners sponsored staff double beds on wheels being raced for a block down the main drag in pairs of two or three. Although they are more common now, in 1969, there was only one other bed race, in Honolulu, so the event was a major tourist draw. Huge crowds, plied with cocktails from the outdoor cafés, lined the street as each local establishment enlisted its four burliest males to push its cutest female staffer, who sat atop the bed, down the long block to the finish line. I remember that years later, a local nurse I was dating told me how one reveler leaned in too closely to the view the race, whereupon she was hit by a bed, breaking her leg. My nurse friend told me how bizarre it was at the Glens Falls Hospital, when the emergency room orderly filled out the Blue Cross form, which asked for the cause of the injury: "Hit by a speeding bed."

The town seemed to host special activities almost daily in the lakeside Rogers Memorial Park: arts & crafts festivals, free movies in park, the annual talent show, the "Bolton Open" tennis tournament, and, last but not least, the absurd "Miss Bolton Beauty Contest."

Blue Water Manor's winners in the 1969 Bolton Talent Show

At five o'clock, the whole BWM staff reassembled for dinner (if we hadn't eaten elsewhere), then the kitchen staff went back to work, while the rest of us got ready to put on the evening's entertainment. After the Manor House staff shows, the musicians would usually hit the adjoining bar, where we'd party for an hour or so with the guests, then it was often down to the lake again (via that rickety cliffside stairway) for a midnight sauna and skinny dip. Countless teenage girl guests found themselves down at the hotel's tiny sand beach, under a moonlit sky, where they were willingly seduced by the boys who entertained them just an hour earlier. This led to a common ailment known as "sand burn." The day after, it was easy to tell which sexual position had been favored the previous night just by the position of the bright red patches of skin. I can tell you from experience that one night of passion in the sand was usually enough to learn one's lesson, and future trysts were taken elsewhere. In that regard, we cabin boys had an advantage, knowing which rooms were vacant — and possessing keys to all of them — we often snuck our girls back to an unused guest room, careful to return the room to its pristine condition early the next morning. It was a special treat when a "Triple A" room was available.

Unlike the cabin staff, which could anonymously work off their wounds and hangovers the next morning in empty rooms to be serviced, the wait staff often had to greet their breakfast clients looking like hell. By the end of the summer, we were all bone tired from the non-stop hedonism of it all. We couldn't wait to get back to class where we could get some much-needed sleep.

Without question, Blue Water Manor's weekly entertainment highlight was the Saturday night Broadway musical presentation. As mentioned, in 1969, the show, with a six-piece band, a cast of two-dozen, and many costume changes, was the Leonard Bernstein-Stephen Sondheim masterpiece, *West Side Story*. Although the lead performers were wonderfully talented, the staging for such a serious undertaking, in front of a stone hearth and underneath a comically decorated moose head, made the whole thing a bit surreal. With no curtain, each scene would be accompanied by a total blackout, as the cast scurried off in the dark to a side closet to change costumes and get back into place before "lights up."

The show was so fraught with potential danger or embarrassment that those of us who weren't in it made certain we were in the audience in case hilarity or chaos ensued. What danger? Consider that this particular show featured a number of gang rumbles between "the Sharks" and "the Jets," which our intrepid staff had to act out on a stone floor, against a stone hearth that barely had room enough to stage a flea circus. Bloody noses and black eyes were common, as some actors forgot to pull their punches; this often led to retribution in the following performance. My pal Chris, 140-lbs. soaking wet, used to literally ride out the rumble scenes safely by jumping onto the back of a 200-lb. "Shark" nicknamed "Bear." One night Chris failed to find Bear and paid the price. It was an unfortunate coincidence that his bloody nose came just before a scene blackout that preceded his big scene in which he shot "Tony" in the climax. Ever the trouper, "Chino" Chris dashed out, gun drawn with one hand, handkerchief to his nose with other, and head tilted back, shot the young lover as the audience howled. Chris had tried to yell his line, "Take that, Tony!", but it was muffled by the handkerchief and clotted nose. After that show, Chris's character was reduced to a non-speaking role. On some occasions, the ultimate moment was ruined by a distracted drummer who delivered his rimshot either a second late or a second early. Once, "Chino" pulled his trigger to the sound of silence, then he comically pointed the barrel to his face as if to see what was wrong, as the sound of drummer Dale's rimshot finally rang out. The audience roared again, while director Bobbie cringed in the back row, wishing Chino would shoot her.

On another occasion, a post-rumble blackout cut to tender scene in which "Tony" romances "Maria" on her "balcony," which was actually a rickety, one-foot high tree stump. Pretending Maria was twenty feet above him, Tony started to sing the gorgeous ballad "Maria," but froze in place when — lights now up — he saw the unconscious body of a "Jet" at his feet in the middle of the hearth. It seemed that the unfortunate thespian had banged his head against the hearth wall in the all-too-real gangbang, and had knocked himself out. When the blackout came, everyone had dashed off but him.

What embarrassment? How about the time that "Maria" sang the stunning "There's a Place For Us" while a giant bat flapped its way into the Manor House. With children crying, all eyes, including Maria's, were riveted to the roofbeams as she warbled on, terrified. Owner Ellen ordered her to keep singing while she swatted at the thing with a broom.

By August, an interesting dynamic had developed: the staff shows became so key to the resort's success that the owner had to think twice before firing anyone for poor job performance or hedonistic excess in the dorm. The irreplaceable leads in the musical were virtually untouchable and could get away with murder, as the increasingly ad-libbed show deteriorated late in the summer. Much as George S. Kaufman decried what the Marx Brothers had done to his screenplays, there is little doubt that Bernstein/Sondheim would not have recognized their masterpiece at the end of the summer of 1969.

Almost every afternoon found me working out with another staffer on the resort's lone tarmac tennis court. In 1969, tennis was still below the radar as far as the masses were concerned, thus the court was hardly used by guests. This was before the tennis explosion of the Seventies, when the glitterati and media glommed onto the likes of Connors, McEnroe, Borg and Evert. (Truth be told, I'm certain that one reason that I made my high school team was the mere fact that hardly anyone tried out for it.) And with Blue Water Manor's great water-skiing venue, that's where most guests and staff headed immediately after lunch. Consequently, I had actually begun to think of the court as my private piece of the resort.

Thus, I was a bit taken aback one July day when a family of four commandeered *my* court for hours, and hitting pretty crisply I might add. They were quite a sight, a striking family of four, all with great shocks of blond hair — father, mother, teenaged son and daughter. The father was at the net, drilling his kids, while mom sat courtside reading a book. After waiting in vain for them to finish, I walked over to the office to inquire about this bizarre family: who were they, and hadn't anyone told them about this neat lake just down the trail? The office manager Kathy pulled their card for me and showed me their names, which frankly looked liked gobbledygook.

"They're Lithuanian friends of Ellen's from the city," Kathy explained. "The father is a travel agent and sends a lot of Lithuanian immigrants here on vacation packages."

We had grown accustomed to seeing a fair number of people of Ellen Shukis's heritage here over the weeks. I would later learn that this husband and wife had arrived in the US during the great Lithuanian immigration wave after World War II, when the Soviets occupied the country. Some 780,000 Lithuanians had died during the war, and another 30,000 died trying to take back their country from the Soviets after occupation. Even more disappeared in the Siberian Gulag. Like all these new *Dipukai* immigrants, New York City's Lithuanian population was fairly clannish, and Blue Water Manor was a favored retreat for them.

Kathy added that the family would be here for two weeks, and that they were *really* into tennis. This was a disaster; I could only play in the afternoon because I had to play music in the evenings, and time was a-wastin'. I decided to do what tennis players all over the world do: I would ask them if they needed a fourth for doubles; although I preferred singles, it would be better than nothing. I looked back at the reservation card: the father's first name was "Vytautas," and I gave up entirely on the surname, which began with a "G." As I walked over to the court, the skinny son, about 15-years-old, began to look familiar. Then I remembered that he had been at our rock band performance in the Manor House the night before, eyes riveted to us guitar players. He seemed to be the leader of a pack of Lithuanian boys who were also there with their parents.

As I approached courtside, the smiling matriarch put aside her book and we introduced ourselves, with her apologizing about the pronunciation of her last name. "Everybody just calls me 'Mrs. G'," she said. Mrs. G mentioned that her son, who loved playing guitar, had raved about our band last night. I asked if "Mr. G" might be interested in a fourth for doubles, and she called out to him in Lithuanian. Mr. G happily waved me on to the court and introduced me to his son and his younger daughter. I noticed that his longhaired blond son and I both used the same model racket (and the same one used by Laver), the beautiful Dunlop Maxply Fort. Although Mr. G and I won a spirited doubles set against the brother and sister, I was well aware that the kids' strokes were far superior to mine, and once their bodies grew into their game, I'd be lucky if I ever won a point from them again. I was correct; when young Vytautas "Vitas" Kevin Gerulaitis became a pro in a few short years, his game went into the stratosphere. He would also become the Number 3 – ranked player in the world. But when I managed to scratch out a solitary singles victory over Vitas in that summer of 1969, I knew it was only because I towered over him in both height and weight. Or maybe it was just because he was anxious to hit the water skis (he was a gifted skier as well.)

But the key thing for me was that, in the years after Vitas became a star, I was honestly able to brag that I had what amateur tennis players used to call "indirect wins" over everybody that Vitas beat. It went like this: Vitas went on to beat McEnroe, Connors, Gonzales, etc., and *I had beaten Vitas*, which gave me "indirect wins" over the same players. Pretty cool, huh? Self-delusion is a wonderful thing, which reminds me of an expression we used to have back then: "I might live in a fool's paradise, but it's a paradise, nonetheless."

Over the course of the next two weeks, I felt as though I had been adopted into the Gerulaitis family: we played matches every day, followed by boat rides, and many guitar lessons given to young Vitas, who could only be described as a force of nature. This was my first experience meeting someone who had "that something special."

Vitas, appropriately named after a Medieval Lithuanian king, already exuded charisma, and his young Lithuanian posse followed him around like he was Peter Pan. His smile and outgoing spirit were already electrifying, but it was nonetheless bizarre to see his pals treat him like a rock star at age fifteen. What would become the legendary Vitas Gerulaitis party train was already in full locomotion long before he achieved fame. The staff began to treat Vitas as one of our own, bringing him and his boys along on a couple of late night boat rides down to Huddle Beach or Blue Lagoon for skinny dips with the girls. His father was amused when he saw his son's legs scratched from the bushes at Blue Lagoon, and he worried that it would be a dead giveaway to his mother. "At least, stay out of the bushes, Vitas!" he admonished. It became a running joke.

I learned that Mr. G was a former Lithuanian Davis Cup player, and its national champion for four years running, until World War Two intervened. Teamed with his young bride, Aldona, Vitas, Sr. had won a mixed doubles table tennis championship in Germany, and he strongly believed that Junior's tennis would allow him to travel the world for free, as it did him.

Seeing the world was a key reason that he owned Litus Travel Insurance Agency in Queens. It was never about making money. Hell, there was no money in tennis at the time. It was all about having a happy-go-lucky life, while making friends on the four corners of the globe. Junior was obviously a willing recipient of Senior's *joie de vivre*. In time, he would take it to a new level.

Gerulaitis family in the late fifties

It was a sad day when the Gerulaitises packed up for their return to Queens. Out of left field, they invited me to come visit them in the city before I returned to school. They made the offer irresistible when they added that Junior was a ball boy for the US Open, which at that time was played on the luxurious grass of the West Side Tennis Club in nearby Forest Hills. Mr. G was also on the club's Field Operations Committee, with junior helping the grounds crew, and had easy access to tickets for the entire two-week tournament. I could stay with them as long as I liked and go to the matches with them every day. It was the definition of a no-brainer. The fact that I was due back at school in early September hardly mattered, as I began to count the days until late August, when the tournament began.

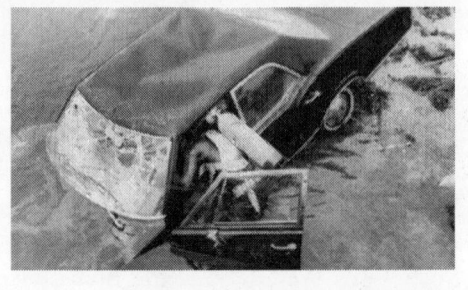

By mid-July an easy, dream-state sort-of rhythm had set in, only to be jarred by a four-week series of events that make the period the leading candidate for the most incredible month of headlines I have yet lived through. The chaotic cascade began on July 18, when Bobby Kennedy's younger brother Teddy, Senator from Massachusetts, dashed any chances for another Kennedy presidency. Partying with Bobby's former campaign workers ("The Boiler Room Girls") on Chappaquiddick Island, off the coast of Martha's Vineyard, the married Kennedy left the reunion at 11:15 pm with one of the girls for what seems to have been a typical assignation for one of the conspicuously carnal Kennedy clan. Although Teddy later claimed he was merely offering twenty-eight-year-old Mary Jo Kopechne a ride to the ferry (five minutes away), the fact was that she never said goodbye to her friends, and left her purse and keys behind, as though she meant to return. An hour-and-a-half later, a local sheriff saw Kennedy's car parked on Cemetery Road, but his approach to the vehicle spooked Kennedy, who started the car and drove off. A few minutes later, just before 1 a.m., Kennedy drove his car off a small bridge into two feet of water, on the opposite end of the island from the ferry dock. The car rolled over, and started taking on water. Short version: Kennedy saved himself, but left a healthy Mary Jo to die slowly without even reporting the accident.

When the car was discovered eight hours later, Mary Jo was indeed dead. At the inquest held the following January, John Farrar, the diver who extricated her body stated, "It looked as if she were holding herself up to get a last breath of air. It was a consciously assumed position. — She didn't drown. She died of suffocation in her own air void. It took her at least three or four hours to die. I could have had her out of that car twenty-five minutes after I got the call. But he [Ted Kennedy] didn't call."

There was no autopsy, and Teddy got off with a six-month driving suspension — case closed — and an end to any dreams of living in the White House.

The tragic news of Mary Jo's death by negligence first broke on July 19, just as much of the world was holding its collective breath in anticipation of man's first setting foot on another celestial body. Almost impossibly, just eight years after President Kennedy set the goal for Americans to walk on the moon, astronauts Neil Armstrong and Buzz Aldrin were within a day of doing just that.[‡] There wasn't much that could divert the Blue Water Manor staff from its hedonistic idyll to something as boring as sitting still in front of a television, but Armstrong's first step on the lunar surface did just that. When word got out that one of the staff had hooked up a 15-inch black & white in his dorm room to watch the event on the night of July 20, over a dozen of

---

[‡] Although Kennedy publicly rationalized the venture because it seemed the best way "to organize and measure the best of our energies and skills," the truth was that it was all done to try to demoralize his Cold War adversary, the USSR.

us crammed into the tiny hovel and stared at the poor quality image from the moon, as a high quality joint was passed around.

The combination of an inferior transmission from the lunar lander, the cheapo TV we were staring at, and the smoke-filled room made for a picture that was so indistinct that, for all we knew, we could have been viewing an underexposed film of two hippos mating. But then we heard Armstrong's first words as he stepped onto the Sea of Tranquility's West Crater: "That's one small step for man, one giant leap for mankind."[§] Since the phrase made no sense, I found it quite telling that in one instant, Homo sapiens had simultaneously displayed both their technological prowess and their intrusive flaws. A few moments later, Buzz Aldrin followed Armstrong down the ladder, but, as we found out later, before he could say anything at all, he pee'd his spacepants. But the moment was still so profound that our Blue Water staff cheered loudly. I am certain that it was the only time I watched television that summer.

Just over two weeks later, I picked up the morning paper and read the gory climax of Dennis Wilson's un-kept promise of stardom to Charlie "Pigpen" Manson.[**] Although we wouldn't know for five long months that Wilson's hangers-on were responsible for the Cielo Drive murders of actress Sharon Tate and four other prominent Beverly Hills friends, the gruesome slaughter in fairy tale land was unprecedented. Years later, Papa John Phillips, who at the time lived not far from Tate and her husband Roman Polanski, told me how, overnight, Beverly Hills changed from blissfully insouciant to flat-out terrorized.[††] Fearing they were next, most celebrities stopped celebrating, and stayed locked-down in their compounds. Phillips was even accused by Polanski, who was overseas during the carnage, of being the perpetrator. Polanski believed Phillips committed the murders in an act of revenge for Polanski having slept with Phillips' "adventurous" wife, Mama Michelle Phillips.

[§] Of course, Armstrong meant to say, "That's one small step for *a* man, one giant leap for mankind."

[**] The motives for the Tate killings can never be known for certain, but having read most of the accounts, I conclude that when a Manson follower named Bobby Beausoleil had earlier been imprisoned for a gruesome murder, Manson decided to make him appear innocent by committing a similar crime while Beausoleil was in stir. He chose the Melcher/Tate house because Watson had already been there, and Manson was still fuming at Melcher for not getting him a record deal.

[††] Manson's "Family" murdered at least three others that summer.

That summer's final earth-shaker took place in our New York state backyard, just a three-hour drive south of Basin Bay. For over a month we had been hearing about a massive outdoor music and arts festival set for August 15 — just a week after the Tate killings — on a 600-acre farm near the sleepy hamlet of White Lake, in the town of Bethel. Tickets were going for $8 per day, and the advance word was that it would be an East Coast version of 1967's Monterey Pop Festival, which drew about 60,000 people a day for three days. I had planned on going to the fest with other BWM staff, but as the big day drew near, I decided to take a pass for a number of reasons: first, on the day before the festival kickoff, New York State was hit with a front of rainstorms that made me wonder whether it was worth getting drenched for three days to hear acts like Arlo Guthrie, Sweetwater, Mountain, Ten Years After, and The Grease Band. Although there were some acts I was interested in seeing (Crosby, Stills & Nash, Sly & the Family Stone, and Creedence Clearwater Revival), I was more drawn to the bands that had performed at Monterey, like the Buffalo Springfield, Otis Redding, The Byrds, The Association, The Mamas & Papas, etc. In fact, the Doors declined an invitation to Bethel for much the same reason. According to Doors' guitarist Robby Krieger, his band passed because they believed it would be "a second class repeat of the Monterey Pop Festival."

300,000 at Folk-Rock Fair Camp Out in a Sea of Mud

By BARNARD L. COLLIER
Special to The New York Times

But perhaps my chief reason for staying behind was the fact that for every staffer that defied Ellen's order not to go, someone else had to pick up their workload — and their tips! I was going to need the extra money to buy souvenirs at the US Open a couple weeks later. When Friday the 15th rolled around, I was certain I had made the correct choice; the sky was overcast, and radio reports said that the Northway was becoming a parking lot and was going to be closed. I walked back to the parking lot after breakfast to see off over a dozen tie-dyed staff in two VW microbuses.

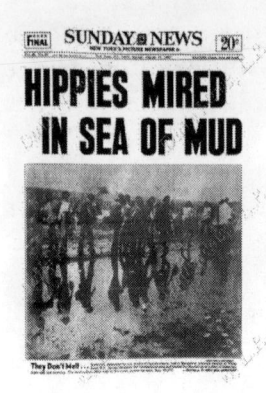

"See you in a couple hours," I quipped, figuring they'd turn back once they hit the clogged highway. I didn't see them until four days later. It turned out that the road was mostly gridlocked in the northerly direction, up from New York City; those heading down from upstate fared much better. As you can imagine, the next day I awoke to the newspaper headlines screaming about the piece of history I had missed. Although the stories emphasized the horrid conditions, it was still clear that I missed a big one – over 400,000 weren't so foolish.

When our encrusted colleagues returned, they looked like they had been through a war: dirty, hungry, and bone tired, but, unlike battle-fatigued soldiers, smiling from ear to ear! I don't remember much of their recap except that the word "Awesome" was heard a lot as they trudged off to the showers. I do remember hearing that one of our pals had a "bad trip" on the free acid that was being passed around. The event is remembered as "Woodstock," although it took place in White Lake, some sixty miles from the town of Woodstock.‡‡ Over the next ten years, the aura created by the festival drew many musicians to upstate New York permanently. And although I missed the big show, I would be one of those making the pilgrimage.

That summer saw me in the best shape of my life, thanks to the non-stop swimming, sailing, tennis, girl chasing, and performing. The learning and growth curves were mind-boggling. Too soon, it came to an end. By the end of August, the staff shows went into disarray, as kids started returning to college ahead of the Labor Day finale. Ellen begged us to stay on, but many were ready to return to some semblance of normalcy, or maybe just sleep. My pal Chris chose to stay on to help close up the resort, as I made my way by bus down to Queens, the Gerulaitises, and the US Open.

---

‡‡ Coincidentally, one of those in Beverly Hills lockdown after the Tate-LaBianca killings was ten-year-old James Schamus. Confined to watching television all day long, he became absorbed with the Woodstock coverage. Forty years later, he wrote and produced what is to my mind the best theatrical recreation of that Upstate New York summer, *Taking Woodstock*.

Keep in mind that most Baltimoreans were jacked up over the upcoming 1969 World Series between the powerhouse Baltimore Orioles and the upstart New York Mets, but all I could think about was watching Rod Laver attempt to complete the first-ever professional tennis Grand Slam. As someone who had only been in the borough of Manhattan, I was also excited to visit Queens, where Vitas lived. I was given the address of 159-23 99th Street in Howard Beach. Fantastic, they even lived on a beach! Meanwhile, back in Catonsville, my mother was frantic about me getting home in time for the start of school. Although I promised her that I would be there in time, I knew I wouldn't. The second week of the Open coincided with my first week of classes, which I had signed up for by mail. Oh, well. I'd just have to play catch up.

I arrived in Queens a couple of days before the Wednesday, August 27th opening day of the tourney and checked in with Mr. G at his travel office, a small storefront quaking under the elevated trains on Jamaica Avenue. This being my first experience with the "El," I wondered how people didn't go crazy from the noise.

When Mr. G later drove me to his home, I quickly realized that Howard Beach was no sandy resort town, but was instead a working class neighborhood much like my own in Catonsville. In fact, in all the years I would visit Howard Beach, I never saw a beach. We arrived just in time to see Vitas leaving to catch the Long Island Railroad on his regular trek to tennis lessons. In addition to taking lessons from his dad, Vitas was enrolled in the three-year old Port Washington Tennis Academy, located twenty miles away. The school was run by none other than Rod Laver's former Aussie coach, Harry Hopman, formerly the captain of 22 Australian Davis Cup teams between 1939 and 1967, winning a still-unmatched 16 times. Other players then under Hopman's wing were greats such as Tony Roche, John Newcombe, Fred Stolle, Ken Rosewall, Lew Hoad, and Neale Fraser. Vitas was in good hands, indeed, and I envied him. An all-around athlete, Vitas was an A student at Archbishop Molloy High School in Queens, a sports powerhouse. Vitas told me that he was not initially excited about tennis, still considered a sissy sport in the sixties; all of his pals played for Molloy's baseball, football, and basketball teams. Always the outgoing center of the party, Vitas envied the team-sport camaraderie. "Do you know how many people played tennis in Queens?" Vitas once asked. "Me and my dad."

Over the many days I would be a guest in his home over the years, I was witness to Vitas's hyper-kinetic schedule: he'd arrive home from school around 3:30, then quickly off to the train stop, sandwich bag and rackets in tow, for the ride out to Port Washington near the north shore of Long Island, then back in the late evening to hang with his posse for a bit before hitting the books until the wee hours. Next day, same thing. On the weekends we'd all hit with Mr. G on nearby public courts.

The private school and the private tennis lessons did not come cheap, and the Gerulaitis family was not rich. Far from it — Mr. G worked long hours in the travel office so that he could provide for his wife Aldona, Vitas and Ruta. And the kids understood it. — As Vitas began making friends in Port Washington — like John McEnroe and Mary Carillo from Douglaston — he began to really enjoy the game. That's when he began to take off.

My first night in the Gerulaitis house was a doozy. The Gs had set up a cot for me in their basement, where I was up against Vitas's wall of amplifiers and guitars, while across from me was a table supporting the highest stack of neatly washed and folded tennis whites I have ever seen. Whenever Vitas had a few minutes, we jammed, but he always regretted that his busy schedule left little time for his beloved instruments. He really wanted to be a rocker. After we all said goodnight, it wasn't long before I was jolted out of bed by what I though was an earthquake, followed by another one a few minutes later. This went on all night! The next morning, shaken, I stumbled upstairs, where Mrs. G offered me breakfast.

"So, how did you sleep?" she asked.

"Are you kidding? Didn't you hear what was happening?" I shot back.

"What do you mean?"

"Are you kidding? Every fifteen minutes there was this gigantic roar. Don't tell me I was dreaming."

At this point, the whole family cracked up.

"Oh, that's just the jets," Vitas said. "You get used to it in a few days." Soon it made sense why this immigrant family settled in Howard Beach. Far from the "beach" idyll that I had imagined, Howard Beach bordered the westernmost runways from JFK Airport, and the Gs were two short blocks from the runway where the largest jets took off and landed. In exchange for that deafening nuisance, houses were available for a fraction of what they would cost just a mile away. I tried to imagine how Mr. G dealt with those planes roaring above his head by night, and the elevated subway thundering above his travel office by day. Surprisingly, both his hearing and his nervous system seemed just fine.

The other curiosity of the home was the water. That first morning I filled a glass from the tap, only to have Mrs. G grab it from me just as I raised it to my lips. She then grabbed a lemon slice, which was at the ready in a bowl on the kitchen counter, and squeezed it into the glass. It was my first experience with "hard water." I have come to learn that I was fortunate that Baltimore has near the best municipal tap water in the country.

On the appointed starting day of the second US Open ever, I went with the two Vitases to the scenic Queens enclave of Forest Hills Village, home to the West Side Tennis Club. Founded in 1892 on the West Side of Manhattan, the club was forced to move to Queens in 1914, due to the need for more room to accommodate its growing membership. Two years later, the committee built a stunning Tudor-style clubhouse for $25,000.

I followed Mr. G as we walked through the Village, stopping at a grocery store two blocks from the club. There we bought sandwiches and soda, which we bagged to take onto the grounds of the Open. Both the vendor and the clubhouse food were too expensive, I was informed, so this was how the regulars did it. That grocery store visit would become a ritual over my next nine years going to the Open at West Side. (In 1978, the tournament moved out to Flushing Meadows, where everything changed, including the camaraderie and the food rules; now it's taboo to bring food or beverage into the Open, so a hungry fan is forced to pay $12 for a burger and fountain soda, and $8.50 for a slice of pizza — and that's just the vendor food. The ground's restaurant prices are astronomical.)

We turned a corner and there it was, Mecca for the tennis world, the clubhouse entrance to the 14-acre, fenced-in, West Side Tennis Club. The inside of the clubhouse was like nothing I had ever seen before: sumptuous wood-paneled dining rooms on the first floor, which opened onto large awning-covered terraces and patios, where the rich and famous sipped and supped. Up an exterior stairway were the second floor players' lounges and lockers.

After introducing me to some members, Mr. G. found some day passes for us, giving me full access to almost any available seat in the famous horseshoe stadium and full clubhouse privileges, not to mention the side court action. In a daze, I ambled onto the terrace and observed a view that actually rivaled the one from Basin Bay: dozens of beautifully manicured grass courts, where players were hitting in a

silent ballet that can only be experienced on courts that make no sound when one runs, drops his racket, or bounces a ball. For someone who learned to play on the wall of Rock Glen Junior High and the dirt courts of Mt. St. Joe, it was positively dreamlike.

Vitas walked over to chat with former Davis Cupper Gene Scott, whom I later found out was a sort-of mentor to both Vitas and even younger John McEnroe. Scott was toting a bizarre new stainless steel

Wilson T-2000 racquet, recently invented by René "the Croc" Lacoste, who forty years earlier had invented the collared cotton shirt, now a ubiquitous design used by tennis players, golfers, and the non-sporting public. Although Lacoste's "Polo" shirt was a winner, this new racquet, and all the synthetics that would follow, heralded mostly negative changes to the core game of tennis (more on that later.) For now, thank God, most players still used wood-laminated "bats."

It seemed everywhere I turned there was another superstar, just casually hanging out: Arthur Ashe, Stan Smith, Pancho Gonzales…the women were also represented over on the other side of the terrace, where the likes of Billie Jean King, Margaret Court, and Virginia Wade chatted up club members. As I turned to the terrace bar on my left, I began to feel faint, as fully half the Australian team was standing at the bar, putting down massive amounts of Foster's Lager. "Newk" Newcombe, "Tony the Tiger" Roche, and "Muscles" Rosewall all came and went. Then I saw *him*, a diminutive redhead (5'9", 155 lbs.), with a distinctive left forearm that was twice the size of his right appendage. It was the Rocket himself — thirty-one-year-old Rodney George Laver, the greatest player to ever wield a racket.

I quickly determined that I might as well pretend that I belonged there, just like everyone else, so I walked over to Roche, who had hit with me at UMBC six months previous, and re-introduced myself. After some chitchat, I let on that I wanted to meet the Rocket.

"Hey, Red," he called out to Laver, "you've got an actual fan over here." Laver walked over and, down-to-earth as could be, shook my hand and spoke with me for a few minutes. I remember asking a silly question about what grip he used on the toughest shot in the game, the high backhand volley. He just laughed and said, "Oh, whatever comes to mind at the time. There's a lot of grips that work." What I took away from it was that too much emphasis is put on grips. What matters is hustle and hand-eye coordination. When we spoke of the tournament at hand, he said he was anxious because his pregnant wife was back home in California, and was due during the second week of the Open.

From there, I was off onto the main grounds, gliding between the grass courts, stopping whenever I saw a match I wanted to watch. Later that day, I sat with Mr. G as we ate our bag lunches in the

14,000-seat stadium. I swear that every usher knew Vitas, and they treated us like VIPs. The atmosphere in those days, before the boom, was much less frantic, and everyone seemed to know each other. On a couple days I got to hit with Vitas on the grass, which was as alien to me as the lunar surface was to Armstrong. The balls bounced only as high as your ankles, unless they hit a chalk line or a divot, which caused them to jump into your face. Although it was fun to be able to dive for shots, I couldn't believe that three of the four Slams were played on this stuff.

On the pathways as in the clubhouse, players mingled effortlessly with the fans and club members, stopping to talk whenever approached. Back then the only other "feature court" was the grandstand, which was nothing more than a bleacher section. That was my favorite venue, since you could sit close to some of the best matches. There was one additional perk: Vitas told me to wait until the bleacher was filled, because the grounds crew, which he volunteered for, allowed the overflow to actually sit on the grass, just feet behind the court. Consequently, I sat courtside behind matches featuring Newcombe, Ashe, Laver, Gonzales, and others, often catching errant serves.

Observing the greatest players on earth at such proximity was like being in a classroom with Socrates. Perhaps the key insight I took away was that the game is overwhelmingly in the legs — something not many teaching pros will tell you, with their mind-numbing focus on grips and stroke perfection. Unless you see these talents at close range, you can't understand how their hustle and preparation are the single biggest differences between them and the rest of us hackers. Vitas later told me that, in all the years he studied under Laver's coach, Harry Hopman never said a word about his strokes. "He just ran me to death," Vitas said. "He used to say that anybody can learn to hit standing still, but few can do it while on the run." This concept drastically improved my game, and made me a better tennis teacher in years to come.

Between matches, it was back to the clubhouse to hang with the players. Life was good, indeed.

I went to the first week of the Open, then, not wanting to overstay my welcome in the Gerulaitises' basement, I set off for a few days to visit other New Yorker friends I had made that summer, before returning for the semis and finals.

I toured all around Long Island, then had a couple of nights in Manhattan, celebrating my 20th birthday at the beautiful Park Avenue apartment of one of BWM's upscale guests. The owners were away, and their gorgeous Swedish nanny let me and a couple other staff crash there. While slumming in this million-dollar pad, I caught my first musical, the off-Broadway production of *Jacques Brel is Alive and Well and Living in Paris*. I was very excited to see this 24-song review, since Brel's great songs had been recorded by the Kingston Trio and many other folkies I admired.

Brel's compositions were painstakingly translated from the French by Brill Building icon Mort Shuman ("Save the Last Dance for Me"). The show was a mind-blowing four-part harmony performance, full of Brel's trademark wit and pathos, not to mention his virulent anti-war stance. I was hooked. Those of us who liked it loved it, and became like acolytes. New York Brel-ophiles went to the show almost weekly. Over the next few years I must have gone a dozen times. We also became evangelists for this chanson genius, who refused to come to the US because of the Vietnam War. If he had done the US media tour, I have no doubt that Brel would have become a household name, so great was his talent. After that first show, I took a bag of "Go to Brel" buttons in order spread the faith when I returned to university. §§ Speaking of which, somewhere off in a distant land, UMBC was starting the fall semester and my mother was becoming hysterical. Why couldn't she understand?

On the weekend it was back to West Side and the Gerulaitis clan. We saw Laver defeat defending champion Arthur Ashe in the semis, which stretched out over two days due to rain. Unlike Wimbledon, West Side had no tarps or tents to shield the lawns from the weather, thus the postponed championship, between Laver and my UMBC "Handsome Eight" hitting partner, the much more muscular Tony

---

§§ The revue played nearly 2,000 performances, becoming one of the longest-running off-Broadway shows in history.

Roche, finally took place on Tuesday, with only 3,700 fans there to witness it. The club hired a helicopter to hover over center court to dry out the grass before we were allowed in, but the surface was still in terrible shape.

Laver, wearing spikes, defeated his teammate Roche 7-9, 6-1, 6-2, 6-2, while his wife was overdue three thousand miles away. After taking a set to get used to the footing and the bad bounces, Laver obliterated Roche, and in doing so, won the first, *and only*, professional calendar grand slam. (He had already won it as an amateur in 1962, and Don Budge did likewise in 1938.) For this historic feat, he took home a staggering $16,000. (The female Open victor, Margaret Court, pocketed $6,000.) Today's men's and women's purses are $1.6 million each, a 100-fold increase. After the match, Laver shed a few tears as USLTA President Alistair Martin presented him the champion's trophy and check for $16,000, saying, "You're the greatest in the world ... perhaps the greatest we've ever seen." As soon as he could hand off the trophy, Laver borrowed a dime from writer Bud Collins in order to place a collect call to Mary. She gave birth to their son ten days later.

"The Rocket" hoists his 1969 US Open trophy

As for me, it was back to Baltimore, Poli-Sci courses, traipsing through the UMBC mud...blah, blah, blah. After the summer I just had, there was no way I could ever settle for the mundane again, and from now on, every day spent in class would feel like Purgatory, as I awaited my "Get Out of Jail" card called a diploma. Three months on Basin Bay was that magical. OK, so I missed Bethel (Woodstock), but thanks to the extra money I earned at Blue Water during the festival, I witnessed something that was, for me, just as historic: tennis's first professional Grand Slam. I also met many of the pros with whom I would stay friends for two decades, and solidified my relationship with the Gerulaitises.

* * *

As I recount these memories of the summer of '69 here in the winter of 2011, I feel compelled to inform the reader of a truism that is stuck in my brain, unable to be dislodged. One of the harshest results of aging is the way that time perception becomes drastically altered. In

1969, every day seemed to last a week, and held a dozen adventures; each week felt like a month, and so on. An eternity existed between June and September, and I was thus a much different person when I returned to school than I was when I left it just ninety days earlier. By contrast, this past summer of 2010 has gone by in the wink of an eye, and with exponentially fewer adventures. The point: don't waste your "long summers" doing nothing, because they won't stay "long" forever. As Maxwell Anderson famously wrote, "It's a long, long while from May to December, but the days grow short when you reach September."

Chapter Eight

333

I RETURNED FROM the lush, manicured greens of the West Side Tennis Club to the sloppy mud paths of still-under-construction UMBC just in time to catch Yippie Abbie Hoffman's road show — talk about going from the sublime to the ridiculous. The school's Cultural Committee, every bit as radical as its Student Government Association, brought Yippie leaders Hoffman, set to stand trial in five days for last summer's riot in Chicago, and Paul Krassner, who also founded the left-wing satire journal, *The Realist*, to the campus on September 19, 1969. To UMBC they brought their brand of righteous demagoguery, while I brought my bag of "Go to Brel" buttons, hoping to start my own kind of movement.

At 9 p.m., a wild-eyed Hoffman performed to a crowd of about 2,000 outside of the Academic Building. Dropping F-bombs in almost every one of his anti-establishment sentences,* Hoffman also instructed us on how to make Molotov Cocktails, which he wanted us to bring to Chicago next week and throw at "the fuckin' pigs" and the "fuckin'" federal courthouse building. Accentuating his remarks with the occasional cartwheel, he came across like a manic standup comic. His schtick may have seemed funny at the time, but since, as we later found out, the FBI had infiltrated the gathering, Hoffman's Molotov bit was reported to the prosecutors, who then entered it into evidence when the "Chicago Eight" trial opened five days later. UMBC had arrived! After his rant, I gave Hoffman a Brel button, which he thought was absurdly hilarious. He pinned it on his vest, and promised to wear it at the trial, if only to get under the judge's skin.

The subsequent trial was nothing if not a continuation of the three-ring circus, with Hoffman staying in the same gear as he had been at UMBC. Although I didn't make the trip to Chicago — I was still decompressing from my non-stop summer — apparently many did, as the National Guard was called in for crowd control outside the courthouse. Almost immediately after the proceedings commenced, Black Panther Bobby Seale laid into Judge Julius Hoffman (no relation

---

* The local TV reporters who had come to cover the event were incensed because their profanity-laced footage, including their interviews with Hoffman, was unusable.

to Abbie), calling him a "fascist dog," a "pig," and a "racist," just for starters. The judge famously ordered Seale bound and gagged, eventually severing him from the trial altogether (turning the defendants into the "Chicago Seven.)

That left defendants such as Abbie Hoffman and Jerry Rubin to continually mock the court: one day they dressed in judicial robes, and, after removing them on the orders of the judge, they revealed Chicago Police uniforms underneath; on another occasion Hoffman yelled at the judge, "You are a *shande fur de Goyim* [a disgrace in front of the gentiles]. You would have served Hitler better." After being cited for profanity, Hoffman replied, "Your idea of justice is the only obscenity in the room." Another defendant curtly summarized: "This court is bullshit." The trial extended for months, with many celebrated figures from the American left counterculture called to testify (including folk singers Phil Ochs, Judy Collins and Arlo Guthrie, writer Norman Mailer, LSD advocate Timothy Leary, and Reverend Jesse Jackson).

Five months later, five of the defendants were convicted of crossing state lines with the intent to incite a riot, and sentenced to five years in prison. At sentencing, Abbie Hoffman recommended that the judge try LSD, offering to set him up with a dealer he knew in Florida.

The convictions were eventually reversed, and although the defendants were convicted of contempt of court (duh) in the retrial, the new judge did not order jail time. Two sad endnotes: of the eight police officers indicted in the matter, seven were acquitted, and charges against the eighth were dismissed. And I never found out if Abbie wore the Brel button.

On the local scene, Baltimore had little interest Hoffman's high life — the city was more interested in a sports high: its Baltimore Bullets basketball team hosted the NBA All-Star Game, and reached the league playoffs, just weeks after the vaunted Baltimore Colts football team, led by icon Johnny Unitas, played in the third Super Bowl. And now the Baltimore Orioles baseball club had made it to the World Series. The two previous championships had frustrated the local fans, with the Bullets losing to the New York Knicks, after the Colts (favored by 18 points) lost to the New York Jets by a score of 16-7, in Super Bowl III, in one of the greatest sports upsets ever. So far this year in sports, New York had Baltimore's number. Now, incredibly, Baltimore was given a third post-season chance against a New York team in one year, as the heavily favored Orioles were matched against the lowly New York Mets. A Mets pitcher summed up the odds by saying, "If the Mets can win the World Series, the United States can get out of Vietnam." He was tragically proved wrong.

Thus the local fans sank into a deeper funk when the Mets beat the Os, four games to one. Years later I found out that my early musical inspiration, the Kingston Trio, played an indirect role in Baltimore's misery. Over a decade earlier, Trio member Dave Guard had dated a California girl named Katie whose parents once played a song for him that they had learned on their Arizona honeymoon in 1932. With Katie and her nine-year-old brother, Tommy, listening, the parents sang the jazzy ballad, for which they never learned the composer's name. The trio was enthralled by this great saloon song, which they recorded in 1958. "Scotch and Soda" went on to become the trio's most requested song, and Dave Guard sent the royalties back to Katie and Tommy's parents, who used the money to put their kids through school. And little Tommy Seaver did so well at Fresno City College and USC, that he went on to get signed to the pros, where, among other things, he beat the Orioles in game four of that 1969 World Series — after making that metaphor about Vietnam and the Mets.

That fall, while our radicalized campus tried to make the loudest noise possible, universities on the other side of the continent were very quietly putting the finishing touches on their own revolution, one that arguably had a more lasting impact than all the college protests combined. At 10:30 p.m. on October 29, 1969, the first two "connection nodes" of something called the ARPANET were activated between two engineering schools in California. Under contract to the Defense Department's Advanced Research Projects Agency (ARPA), a communications link was created between UCLA and Stanford University, in part to allow ARPA-sponsored scientists to exchange research findings rapidly. Nineteen years later, this powerful research tool would be unleashed on the public, who quickly turned "the internet" from a research portal into a pornography cesspool. Not long after the ARPANET "breakthrough," the first mobile "radio" phone call was made from a researcher at his "cell" at Motorola to a rival at Bell Labs. Bell raised the de-evolution ante by then creating the fundamental science behind low fidelity MPEG recordings, trumping the work of the Japanese firm Denon, which first digitized music. The convenience revolution was now poised to overtake the quality renaissance of the first part of the century, and the first generation of electronically addicted "digital natives" soon came into being.

Oddly, one of the first things I think about when bemoaning the smothering digital chatter mediocrity that now envelops us, is my summers on Lake George. Recalling those sublime late-night lakeside get-togethers and the solitude — even with a dozen people there — of Paradise Bay floating tubes, crystallizes for me just what we have lost. Sadly — no, *tragically* — I cannot imagine such gatherings being able to occur today. For it is now virtually impossible to have such a shared group experience without the interruption of one or more Blackberry devices or cell phones. Equally absurd, modern digital natives will connect to their MPEGs via "iPod ear buds" when in the presence of nature's monumental serenity, listening to horribly compressed recordings instead of the soothing breaking waves, or just the sound of the breeze. Digital natives are now so hooked on nonstop electronic connections and Facebook's faux "friends," so out of touch with the natural world, that their truncated attention spans render them unable to read books, master a musical instrument, or even see and feel the beauty right in front of them. The very thought of trying to enjoy the tranquility of Basin Bay while someone on a nearby Adirondack chair barks into his "yell" phone is beyond depressing.†

But I digress.

About two weeks into classes, I was already bored to tears. Thus when a call came from one of my BWM colleagues living in Boston, I was packing my bags that same night. Tim K. had uttered the two

---

† A 2010 study by the Kaiser Family Foundation concluded that today's youth, ages 8-18, spend an astounding 8 hours per day on digital media. Incredibly, this study did not take into account "texting" and "tweeting" time (an additional hour-and-a-half daily). In South Korea, internet addiction is so pervasive that interventionist "boot camps" are springing up. The subject of Digital Natives is now being studied in an interdisciplinary collaboration of the Berkman Center for Internet & Society at Harvard University and the Research Center for Information Law at the University of St. Gallen. It aims to understand and support young people as they grow up in a digital age. http://www.digitalnative.org/#about. For more on all of this, everyone should read *The Dumbest Generation*, by Mark Bauerlein, *The Cult of the Amateur*, by Andrew Keen, or anything by Cliff Stoll.

words that my generation had no comeback for: "Road trip!" Back then, when gas was .35 cents a gallon and all cars were V-8s, we took great joy in the open road. In college, we frequently entered weekend "road rallies," in which dozens of car-packed teens, armed with sets of themed clues, made their way around the Maryland countryside, hitting various checkpoints along the way during the daylong contest. The rallies were safe because the winner was determined not by speed, but by the mileage registered on the odometer. The car with the fewest wrong turns thus won a cash prize. Each car's crew consisted of a driver, a navigator, and two experts armed with encyclopedias, sundry almanacs, and reference books in the back seat. My gang, well prepared by the many sneak-ins at the Edgewood Theater, did pretty well on the "Movie Monster Rally." But the actual result was inconsequential; the event was a daylong laugh riot.

Somehow Tim had acquired a used, but gorgeous, British car made by Hillman. Anxious to road test it, he suggested that we do a "Southern swing," motoring south from Maryland, all the way to the Florida Keys, then back up through Alabama, Mississippi, Louisiana, etc. We hoped to transect about a dozen states, most of which I had never seen, in two or three weeks. I was especially excited about seeing Cape Kennedy.

Need I tell you what my poor mother thought of this idea? With me having already missed the first week of school thanks to Gerulaitis, Laver, and Brel? Well, the way I looked at it, since I was taking care of my own tuition, they had no money in the game, and thus, no room to complain.

I informed my instructors that I would be away for a while, but back in time for midterms. I took my course syllabi and textbooks, and would try to read when Tim was driving. I promised the profs Florida oranges (which I delivered on.) A few days later, after borrowing someone's sleeping bag, I piled into Tim's car and we were off. The trip was wonderful, and if my memory were better, I could fill a book with the details. The Southland is beautiful that time of year, and we squeezed as much of it in as humanly possible in that brief time: Skyline Drive, the Smokey Mountains, Civil War battlefields, Savannah, James Brown's hometown, the Suwanee River, Cape Kennedy, South Beach, New Orleans, Nashville. All along the way we piled on the pounds thanks to the nonstop barrage of Southern deep-fried diner foods.

Mixed in with the predictable tourist memories of Florida beaches are a few not-so-typical incidents. Tim and I had decided to memorialize our road trip by collecting (read: *stealing*) local signage. I started by taking the metal, three-ft. long "Suwanee River" sign from above a small bridge over that river. Soon, we had over a dozen signs stashed in the rear seat foot-wells. We were so excited to hit Ft. Lauderdale at three in the morning that we decided to make off with the massive wooden "Welcome to Ft. Lauderdale" sign, which was bolted to two poles in the highway median. That task was a complex operation, given that the sign was fixed by dozens of bolts and cars were driving by at about one a minute. About a hundred yards in either direction were red lights that we could use to our stealthy advantage.

We parked the Hillman on the other side of the highway and lifted the hood, as though we had broken down. One of us — the lookout — pretended to work on the car, and when the red lights cooperated, the other would race back and work on a bolt. When the lights changed, we'd both be back under the hood of the car. This went on for over an hour, and when we finally unhinged that beast, we realized that we had neglected to plan where we were going to stash it in our small vehicle. So for the next hour, with the sign lying under the car, we unbolted the back seat from the flooring so that we could hide the sign under the seats. Off we went.

I remember driving after midnight, west from Miami through the Everglades to Ft. Myers via the just-opened, laser-straight, "Alligator Alley." Entering The Alley, you are met with giant warning signs, advising that you had better check your tires and gas tank, as there are no stations along the then-two-lane, unlit, 84-mile long, *alligator-infested* road.

I was initially fine with the whole alligator thing, but Tim must have had a phobia because he wouldn't shut up about the gigantic bloodthirsty monsters that were lurking just inches from our well-worn British tires. He claimed that he had heard tales of stranded motorists who had been dragged off to the netherworld, never to be seen again. Within fifteen minutes he had me likewise spooked, as I kept my eyes glued to the roadside, which quickly tapered off, shoulder-less, into the glades. The road, littered with rusted-out vehicles and the occasional Indian camper, was so straight and flat as to become quickly hypnotic; we could see car headlights coming at us from many miles away.

We had just begun to settle in when we hit a snag – minor anywhere else but in this realm that would have frightened Danté: bugs. Bugs the size of parakeets blasting our windshield. The British wipers, apparently not designed to clear away anything over a metric gram in weight, were no match for the creature splatter that was now obscuring our vision, and might cause us to veer off the embankment, into the everglades and...

    into...

        the...

            mouths...

                of...

Faced with this potential catastrophe, we knew that someone had to get out of the car, take his chances with the reptilian monsters, and clear the windshield — about every 15 minutes! That first negotiation was a doozy, and from then on we alternated. After the bug assault subsided, Tim, hypnotized by the road, needed me to spell him behind the wheel. Of course, neither one of us wanted to leave the safety of our vehicle, having just seen an abandoned car in the swamp just a few minutes before, its owner likely eaten alive. But with Tim unable to maintain a straight line, we had to do something. The simple answer was to crawl over the shifter, and each other, to the opposite seat, which we did. Try to picture two guys over six feet tall, making their way between bucket seats in this tiny British motorcar. We laughed our butts off at the absurdity of the scene, which we nonetheless repeated three or four times.

We arrived in Ft. Meyers under cover of darkness, and after locating a suitable grassy park, pulled out our sleeping bags to get some much-needed shuteye. Since we didn't want to be seen from the road, we deployed our bags behind a large dirt mound and crashed. The next thing we knew, we were jolted awake by metallic flashes and shrieking sounds directly over our heads. I started to stand up and almost had my head taken off. It seemed that our camping spot was on the down slope of a dirt ramp that was very popular with a local gang of 12-year-old dirt bikers. Had the first wave of jumpers missed their mark, Tim and I would have been seriously crunched in our sleep. Thank God these kids knew what they were doing. I don't know who was more startled by the simultaneous discovery — the kids or us, but soon we were all laughing hysterically.

After breakfast, we began slowly winding through central Florida, while eight hundred miles to the north, my fellow UMBC classmates, whom I barely knew, were dozing off in "Con Law" class. And my mother — you know the rest.

While driving north through central Florida towards Tallahassee and the Florida State University dorm of a couple of hot sisters we knew from the lake, we noticed that all of the small towns had town name signs of a uniform design. It gave us the twisted idea of exchanging them in order to confuse tourists. We spent the better part of a night removing town signs and replacing them with one from miles away. I have often wondered how many future Sunshine State visitors scratched their heads in bafflement, as their driving map indicated they were entering Ocala, but the sign read "Brooksville."

On the near-tropical FSU campus, I was struck by the dissimilarities to my still-under-construction UMBC alma mater. Whereas UMBC students were trudging through the mud between classes, and taking over buildings in protest *after* classes, the FSU "eds and coeds" existed in a sunny parallel universe that recalled *Gidget* and the fifties: on the campus quad, with nary an "End the War" button in sight, groups of tanned blonde coeds played Frisbee while their shirtless "BMOC" boyfriends played touch football. On one campus expanse I was stunned to see teams of students practicing on trapezes. It turned out that these were members of FSU's "Flying High Circus" trapeze team, founded in 1947 as an activity for male and female students to participate in jointly. The only requirement to be a member of the FSU Circus is that one must be a degree-seeking student registered at the university.

Rivaling a professional circus, the FSU Circus is primarily an aerial and stage presentation with student performers rigging all of their own equipment. A *credited* "Introduction to Circus" course is offered to students and includes the basics of juggling, walking the high wire, aerial ballet, and rigging. I learned that students who did well often moved down to Venice, Florida after graduation to do post-grad work at Ringling Brothers' "Clown College." This was at the same time that UMBC students were being taught how to build Molotov Cocktails by Abbie Hoffman. I just love contrast.

Wending our way through Georgia provided still more memories. The Hillman decided to give out on a Sunday night in a remote rural area in the middle of a driving rainstorm. Tim and I put out our thumbs, just as we would in Yankee-land, but here in the Deep South, our longhair non-patriotic Hippie style didn't exactly endear us to passing motorists. One pickup-driving red neck slowed, and rolled down his passenger window just long enough to utter, "Now, don't y'all worry. It's a dry rain," laughing as he sped away.

The incident reminded me of another story of a disabled vehicle in the South, one experienced a couple of years earlier by my cousin Phil as he and a friend were, coincidentally, also driving north from Florida to Baltimore. As Phil and friend traversed North Carolina late at night, they saw a broken down car on the road. Stopping to investigate, they saw a frightened, middle-aged black woman behind the wheel. She obviously thought the two white kids were going to harass her — or worse. Once they assured her they were friendly, they offered to help the woman, named Maria, with her flat tire. She explained that she didn't have a spare.

"No problem," Phil said. "We'll just drive you to the next town and find one."

With this, a stunned Maria watched as Phil removed the wheel from her car, threw it in his trunk, and drove them all in search of an all-night service station. Eventually they found one, had the tire repaired, and returned to Maria's vehicle just as dawn was breaking. It was not long before they had remounted the tire. At this point, Maria reached into her purse, offering to pay the boys for their time, but they adamantly refused.

"Please," she begged. "Let me give you something?" Again they refused. They only relented when Maria asked for Phil's address, so that she might send a card of thanks. A couple days after arriving back in Baltimore, Phil received that card — and it was attached to something. He was called to the front window as a large delivery truck pulled up, and two men delivered a heavy box to Phil's front porch. Phil's mother signed for it. Inside was the largest color television set made in the mid-sixties, a time when hardly anyone we knew owned one (only 3% of US households had one in 1964.) Attached to the set was the following note:

> "Dear Phil,
>
> I can't thank you enough for helping out a stranger in need. Colored people down here aren't used to that yet, I guess.
>
> With all good wishes,
>
> Maria (Mrs. Nat King) Cole"

Maria Cole

Years later I learned that the virtuoso's second wife, Maria Hawkins Cole, had grown up in Sedalia, NC, raised by her aunt, Dr. Charlotte Hawkins, and that she often returned to visit relatives.

I was hoping that Phil's karma might transfer to us, but no such luck. Regrettably, we longhairs had to wait even longer than Mrs. Cole for assistance, but eventually we were picked up and taken to a service station, whose owner lived above the shop. When we told him we needed an alternator belt for a 1965 Hillman, he laughed harder than that damned "dry rain" pickup driver. The good ol' boy then explained that he didn't get many requests for parts for a foreign [read: communist] car. This was Detroit-made pickup country, after all.

"And if I can find it, it's gonna' cost ya," he warned. He made a few calls, during which he continued giggling. Two hours later the rubber belt was delivered, price tag $100, the equivalent of $500 today — for a belt! We were now running on monetary fumes, but the final insult was just half a day away.

More than ready to return home, we raced along rural roads that rarely posted speed limits. In fact, often all we saw were *minimum* speeds posted. The day after buying our $100 rubber belt, we were rounding a soft curve at well over 60 mph, when out of nowhere a 25 MPH speed limit sign appeared, behind which sat a motorcycle cop who must have pulled over tourists like us as fast as he could get back behind that sign. It was a classic hidden speed trap. As we began to pull over, it hit us: the stolen signs! At least a dozen were on the rear floorboard, and the humongous Ft. Lauderdale greeting was pushing up our back seats at a noticeable angle.

Tim thought fast and got out of the car before the cop had alighted his bike and could tell him not to. We couldn't let him see the interior. Tim looked at the rear of the Hillman as the cop approached.

"Officer, I promise to get that brake light fixed just as soon as I get to Massachusetts," Tim lied. The cop explained that he was pulled over for speeding and that the brake light was fine. I waited in the car, certain that the cop would eventually search the vehicle. But we finally got a stroke of luck — the cop wrote a ticket and took off without ever searching the car. We made it to Baltimore where Tim had some gas money wired to him so he could make it back to Boston. We divided up the stolen signs; Tim took the large Lauderdale sign since neither of us wanted to empty the car and remove the seats to get to it. Years later, Tim told me that he added legs to that sign and turned it into a kitchen table. However, when he moved, he tied the sign to the top of his car, and as he was driving cliffside on a New Hampshire "notch," a gust of wind tore it loose and sent it careening into the valley below and smashed into a hundred pieces.

Not long after returning (and delivering Florida oranges to my teachers), I went to movie night at UMBC to catch Paul Newman in "Cool Hand Luke." The blood rushed from my face as I watched the Florida chain gang fate of Luke, who had defaced municipal parking meters. Now Tim and I had just defaced over a dozen Florida municipal signs — in fact we had stolen them! Had that Georgia cop searched our car, I could have ended up just as dead as Luke! I vowed never again to steal anything. As Luke said in the movie, "Sometimes nothing can be a real cool hand."

Finally back in Baltimore, this twenty-year-old, now with a bit of perspective, began to appreciate the wonderful quirkiness of this blue-collar town. And it was an especially unique era for the city. At the time, I was dating a gorgeous 18-year-old, half-Italian, Blue Water Manor guest who lived in northern New Jersey. Kim and I saw each other about two weekends a month; I would drive my old Chevy up the Jersey Turnpike (Exit 10), while both families held their breaths each time, worried that the wheels might fall off at 70 mph. We'd stay in each other's families' guest rooms — but just until we were certain everyone was asleep, of course. For me, it was a perfect relationship that allowed me (and my girlfriend) significant free space to deal with school and our muses, of which there were no shortage in the blocks that surrounded the central Pratt Library.

Within walking distance of the library there were, in addition to Ted's Music, countless counterculture venues that were always bursting with activity, including the many clubs along the "Charles Street Corridor," the party scene on Bolton Hill, and the "head shops" of Read Street (Baltimore's own "Haight-Ashbury".) About a mile north along the corridor was folk impresario George Stevens' Blue Dog Cellar, which featured folkies such as Josh White, Arlo Guthrie, and Tom Paxton. The "Dog" was where George Carlin famously played to a completely empty room in 1965.

My favorite Blue Dog performer was the indescribably bizarre, yet completely genius, Paul "Biff" Rose, who usually accompanied his *avant garde* folk creations on a banjo, but who turned out to be a stunning throwback-style stride, yet melodic, pianist when I first heard him banging away at one of his infamous parties on John Street in Bolton Hill. Biff, it seemed to me, had achieved the impossible: a blending of musical brilliance with Marx Brothers lunacy. And I loved every note and lyric of it. A former New Orleanean who only lived in Baltimore briefly, Biff hit it big when Tiny Tim covered his song "Fill Your Heart," which he co-wrote with future Grammy winner, Paul Williams.

Biff's potent combination of anarchist humor, outgoing personality, and brilliant musicianship would soon make him a regular on *The Tonight Show* and the *Smothers Brothers Comedy Hour*. He became a joke writer for fellow Blue Dogger, George Carlin, and his first album, *The Thorn in Mrs. Rose's Side*, was a huge influence on the emerging David Bowie. Years later, when I came to spend much time in Biff's Big Easy, I completely understood how such a mentality was nourished. There are many "Biffs" prowling the French Quarter.

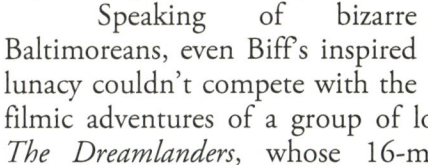

Speaking of bizarre Baltimoreans, even Biff's inspired lunacy couldn't compete with the filmic adventures of a group of locals known as *The Dreamlanders*, whose 16-mm. excursions usually premiered in the basement of Mount Vernon's historic Emmanuel Episcopal Church, built in 1854, in, just a couple of blocks from Ted's and the Pratt. One of the Dreamlanders' crew, a twenty-something Catonsville neighbor of mine named Pat Moran (whose family had gotten me that awful gas mask job), had gone on and on about her crazy friends, and let me know when they were having screenings. In an early offering, Pat played "Dorothy" in a send-up of "The Wizard of Oz," called "Dorothy and the Kansas City Pothead." In this telling, the winged monkeys were winged junkies and the Wicked Witch of the West was a wicked narcotics agent.

Led by twenty-something "auteur" John Waters, who had recently been expelled from NYU for smoking pot in his dorm, the twisted "acting" troupe boasted members such as Glenn "Divine" Milstead, Mary Vivian Pierce, Mink Stole, and Edith "The Egg Lady" Massey. Waters had graduated from Calvert Hall "College" (high school), the East Side's version of St. Joe, three years ahead of me. Not unlike my

The Dreamlanders

attraction to the Fender guitar given me by Grandmother Rose, John fell in love with an 8-mm. film camera given him by his grandmother, Stella. His experiments with that camera led to the short films that three dozen of us squeezed into the church basement to screen with John and the Dreamlanders: *Hag in a Black Leather Jacket* (filmed on his parents' Lutherville roof), *Eat Your Makeup* (in which Glenn played Jackie Kennedy), *Mondo Trasho* (during the filming of which the entire cast was arrested for indecent exposure near Johns Hopkins University), *The Diane Linkletter Story*, and *Multiple Maniacs* (in which the 250-lb Glenn, in full drag as "Divine," gets raped by a giant lobster). It brought smiles to all of us that these vulgar, envelope-pushing flickers were ironically unspooling in the basement of a church.

The fact that the movies were downright awful in no way mitigated the fun we had watching them with this group of harmless lunatics, who usually sat in the first row of folding chairs, decked out in full hashish-inspired regalia (John, often dressed as a cowboy). If someone would have told me that Waters would go on to make millions in Hollywood and on Broadway, with Pat Moran by his side as casting director, I would have laughed even louder than I did at these early efforts. It still amazes me, and I think it does the self-deprecating John as well, whom I still occasionally run into at screenings at the Charles Theater, just blocks from the still-functioning Emmanuel Church. After John, I think the Church no longer screens movies without seeing them first.

But without doubt, my favorite hangout was the musty, quirky, "only in Baltimore," Peabody Book Shop & Beer Stube, located on Charles Street, just four blocks north of the Emmanuel Church and two blocks from the famed Peabody Conservatory of Music and Ted's Music, in the shadow of Baltimore's *original* Washington Monument.

Founded in 1927 by an Austrian immigrant, the three-story townhouse, laid out to replicate a Viennese *bierstube*, must have functioned for my generation, and previous ones, in much the same way that Mona Best's Liverpool house/club Casbah did for the pre-Beatles Beatles: three floors of rooms in a former family home, crammed with books, young musicians, magicians, and sing-along piano players, all topped by a dimly-lit atmospheric barroom, where local intelligentsia batted around the great issues of the day. One local writer described the décor thusly: "a cluttered caricature of its humble origins with ballet slippers hanging from the wrought-iron chandelier, and a stag's head above the brick fireplace competing for attention with mounted animal horns, ceramic busts, figurines and framed pictures of waterfowl."

Among its early patrons were Veronica Lake, Dorothy Parker, Rudy Vallee, and F. Scott Fitzgerald. But its most regular habitué in the early years was none other than the "Sage of Baltimore," the brilliant beer-loving essayist for the *Baltimore Sun*, H. L. Mencken.[‡]

It was said that Mencken, an amateur pianist, sometimes used the venue for his weekly musical "Algonquin Round Table"-style jams known as the "Saturday Night Club."[§] Many members of the club, which existed for over forty years, were instructors at the nearby Peabody Conservatory, or members of the Baltimore Symphony. The Club would typically play for a couple hours and then break off into discussion groups.

By the 1960's, the Peabody had become a magnet for Hopkins medical students, Peabody Conservatory music students, and visiting celebrities (Dustin Hoffman was a regular) who wanted some privacy. Although each room was stuffed with sundry bric-a-brac, they differed in theme: one room was a beer hall replica, with fireplace blazing as "El Duko" sat at an ancient, wonderfully un-tuned upright piano and played old songs for sing-alongs; another room was more sedate and perfect for conversation; still another, overlooking Charles Street from the third floor, featured young acoustic musicians and poets. All the entertainers played for tips.

[‡] For those unfamiliar with the works of the great Mencken, the title of the book you are reading is an homage to him: among some of his published titles were *Happy Days, Newspaper Days,* and *Heathen Days.*

[§] Four club members, Gustav Strube, Theodor Hemberger, Emma Hemberger, and Adolph Torovsky, composed over 650 songs.

Gliding between all the rooms were new owner Rose Pettus, who acted as a hostess/ringmaster, and the white-bearded "Great Dantini,"** who performed classic magic tricks, such as "the mystery of the Chinese rings," during the musicians' breaks.

One of the regular guitarists who came by to play was a humorous student/teacher at Peabody with whom we spent countless nights at the stube, jamming on the Beatles, CSNY, and Dylan. Years after we all left Baltimore, Michael Hedges went on to become one of the world's greatest acoustic guitar stylists, employing unique tunings and finger-tapping techniques. But when I played with him, it was straight-ahead folk-rock. In fact, when I heard his breakthrough CD, *Aerial Boundaries*, years later, I thought it was a different guy with the same name. Then I saw the cover and immediately knew that my old mate had indeed transformed his playing in the intervening years, utilizing not only new techniques, but inspiration from the classical composers he studied at Peabody. I recently went through an old address book and found Michael's homemade business card:

Michael Hedges

Tragically, Michael died in late 1997 at the age of 43, when his car skidded off a California highway. The next year he was awarded a posthumous Grammy Award for *Best New Age Album*.

The Peabody Book Shop became my home away from home, and I spent at least a couple of nights a week jamming there with new friends, finishing the night bar-side, and arguing politics. Without knowing it, we young Peabody players of the late Sixties repeated that same paradigm established by the great Mencken and his Saturday Night Club. In hindsight, it was a privilege indeed to sit at the same old wooden tables as the great Mencken, similarly discussing the great

---

** True name Vincent Cierkes, he arrived at his stage name by combining **Dante** and **Houdini**.

issues of the day after indulging in the most powerful force in the universe, music.

Tragically, the great stube was shuttered in 1986 after Rose passed away. It's doubly sad because there is nothing remotely close to it in Baltimore today. I was no longer in town when the doors were locked for the last time, but I read where, in the waning days, regular patrons often gathered around the old upright and sang along as El Duko played Mary Hopkins' hit, "Those Were the Days." It was an apt choice. "Once upon a time there was a tavern…"

Meanwhile, as time went on my long-distance relationship with Kim required more and more ingenuity. Between liaisons, we kept in touch by phone, which in 1969 was not an easy thing to do. As hard as it is to conceive now, long distance phone calls were once a great, and expensive, luxury. With "Ma Bell" operating as a telephone line monopoly, a fifteen-minute call from Baltimore to Exit 10, New Jersey could cost twenty dollars or more. And I have yet to meet the teenaged girl in love who can talk for just fifteen minutes to her boyfriend, whom she only sees twice a month. I had to scramble for a solution, and I found many in the "phone phreaking" hippie underground and the writings of none other than Abbie Hoffman.

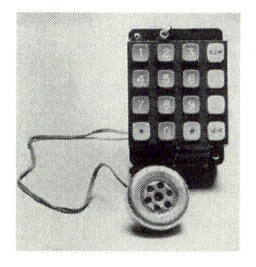

In lefty journals like *Ramparts*, Hoffman and others dispensed numerous tips, from the elegantly simple to the arcane, on how to rip off Ma Bell. Over the course of my two-and-a-half years courting Miss New Jersey, I went through any number of methods to make free long distance calls, usually (and ironically) from "pay" phone booths: using slugs (#14 brass washers, as I recall) in the coin slots; jamming precisely-measured cardboard slivers down the quarter slot repeatedly to add on credit: spitting on a penny and spinning it counter-clockwise as you drop it into the nickel slot; jamming one end of a bobby pin into the mouthpiece and the other to a "ground" on the door frame to get a dial tone. Sometimes you could just get an operator to give you credit by claiming the machine swallowed your money. One of my favorite Hoffman inventions was useful on the older style pay phones with a rubber cord between the mouthpiece and the box: jam a thumbtack into the cord, then touch the flat end to the metal frame, and voila, instant dial tone. Worked like a charm — for a while. Once Ma Bell caught on, she started covering the rubber cords with tack-proof metallic wrap. The more sophisticated methods included the use of tone generators that mimicked the exact ringtone frequency made as a quarter hit the mechanism and the use of the mythic "Blue Box," which operated on a similar principal. Some of the more infamous high-tech pranksters were Apple Computer founders Steve Wozniak and Steve Jobs.

On one occasion Wozniak used his Blue Box to dial up the Vatican, then, identifying himself as Nixon advisor Henry Kissinger (while imitating Kissinger's exaggerated German accent), asked to speak to the Pope, who was sadly sleeping at the time.

Phone Phreakers Jobs and Wozniak at work

However, it was all a cat-and-mouse game with the phone company, and although they created defenses for every scheme we used, it seemed the phreakers were always a step ahead. I think the challenge of playing this early electronic game was infinitely more fun than the calls themselves (sorry, Miss New Jersey). Many thousands of us across the country became players in the phone phreaking wars, and we rationalized it with the knowledge that AT & T's "Bell Telephone Company" was, after all, an illegal monopoly (which the feds would finally break up in 1982).

Hoffman soon elaborated on the idea of free phone calls when he published a 1971 *Ramparts* article on how to get free *everything*, entitled "America on $0 a Day," which was then expanded into the literary classic, *Steal This Book*. This counterculture guidebook, the pranksters' subversive prequel to the works of Matthew Lesko, had the most outlandish table of contents, which noted chapters such as: Free Food, Free Clothing, Free Transportation, Free Land, Free Housing, Free Education, Free Medical Care, Free Money, and even Free Dope. I still have my well-worn, underlined copy, which was like a Bible to me when I went on the road as a traveling musician after college.

My telephone gambits reached a zenith (or nadir?) when, during one of my many trips to catch a concert at our main campus in College Park, I was informed of something called the Wide Area Telephone Service, or WATS, a Bell service that allowed large institutions to make unlimited long distance calls to certain states for a flat fee. I was told that the University's main campus had many department phones hooked up to WATS lines. After a period of recon, I found such a phone in the basement of the psychology department, which stayed open into the night, but was usually unoccupied after 6 p.m. For the next few months, whenever I was in College Park, I'd call Kim and we'd chat for hours.

The party only ended when some sharp-eyed university accountant spotted all the calls on an invoice, and then called Kim's home to see what business they had with the school. Oops. I had no idea the calls were logged. After some tense negotiating, the school agreed to a small repayment (a fraction of the many hundreds of dollars it would have cost with traditional calls), some of which was paid by Kim's disgruntled father.

Looming over all the fun and games of late 1969 was the specter of Vietnam. With more and more of us Boomers set to graduate from college (losing our II-S deferment status), and with fighting levels at their peak — over half a million in Vietnam — we male students were about to learn exactly who would be drafted the day after graduation. Until this point, men were conscripted daily in an order based on a wide variety of characteristics (age, skills, marital status, etc.) Now, the Selective Service decided to turn the system into a simple one-time lottery, the first in twenty-nine years, so that every non-deferred man born between 1944 and 1950 and whose birthday was among the first 195 birthdates drawn would be immediately inducted, thereby eliminating seven years of uncertainty.[††] Our day of destiny, the draft lottery, was set to be televised nationally on the upcoming December 1st, just a month away.

Since I had never won a drawing before, I assumed the worst and began to panic. To think that in just a few weeks I had gone from sipping Margaritas in Paradise Bay, and hanging out with Rod Laver at the plush West Side Tennis Club, to the dark, but realistic, prospect of dying in a rice paddy in Southeast Asia was almost incomprehensible. Even for someone who relishes contrast, this was too much. But the bottom line was that there was just no way was I going to kill other young people 8,000 miles away who were so obviously no threat to me, in a war that was immoral at its core. Thus I contacted a very anti-war left-wing young couple that I had befriended when they were guests at Blue Water Manor, and who regularly smoked grass with the staff. Gilles and Danielle, from Rimouski, Quebec, graciously offered to put me up in their small home until I got settled in Canada, should it come down to going into exile.

Simultaneously, I began researching various ways to fail the induction testing process (I quickly concluded that there was no way I would qualify for the coveted, but rarely awarded, Conscientious

---

[††] The number 195 was based on algorithmic projections that concluded that enough men would be available in the first 195 birthdates to meet foreseeable military needs. The number was to change slightly every year, depending on the conditions in Vietnam.

Objector, or 1-A-O, status that cost Carl Wilson and Muhammad Ali a fortune in legal fees to defend.)

Most ploys involved scamming the physical test by pretending you couldn't hear, or could barely see. Others feigned weakness: a fellow UMBC student confidently advised: "When the guy in front of you has his blood drawn, start holding your breath. You'll pass out as soon as they jab you with the needle." Another popular approach was to just act insane (a tactic employed successfully by fellow 1949-er, Bruce Springsteen): we all knew of guys who barked like a dog, or defecated in their pants, while others checked off the box on the psychological form that said "I am a homosexual." Not surprisingly, the Army had devised brilliant counter-strategies for most of these gambits, and only the best of the best fooled them. I had to assume that I wouldn't be one of them, so I informed my parents that if I received a low lottery number that I was off to Quebec the next day.

None of this went over well with my Battle of the Bulge-veteran father or my patriotic WWII veteran uncles. Our family dinners, like millions across the country, suddenly became tense affairs that now substituted heated arguments about politics, patriotism, and morals for idle chatter about Orioles statistics. Many of these episodes brought my apolitical mother to tears. Eventually, it became easier to just find an excuse to miss family dinner altogether. Thus, for our family and many others, Vietnam cemented the end of the "Ozzie and Harriet" illusion of the all-American family. Although the father-son rift subsided somewhat over the ensuing decades, the relationship sadly never returned to what it once was, which, due to my father's work/escape modus, wasn't much to start with. I was now spending even more time on the tennis courts and at the Peabody.

On November 15, 1969, I boarded a charter bus at UMBC and trekked down to DC, where I joined over 250,000 in the largest anti-war rally in U.S. history. The fast-approaching draft lottery had obviously brought the issue to the boiling point. (I have often wished that the draft were in effect during our current adventures in Iraq and Afghanistan; it might be the only way to engage today's digital natives in something other than Facebook and iPhones.) On the stage performing that day were prominent, and impassioned, artists such as Arlo Guthrie, Pete Seeger, Peter, Paul & Mary, John Denver, Mitch Miller, and touring cast of *Hair*. The mood in the crowd was electric, and I came home more resolute than ever to move to Canada if necessary. If memory served, there were a lot of good musicians hailing from the Great White North,‡‡ so I was certain I would find my niche.

On the dreaded evening of Monday, December 1, 1969, I threw a small suitcase on my bed and began throwing in the essentials. In a cardboard box I placed more material that I would send for from Canada.

At 8 p.m., much as society was about to put a figurative fork in the happy days of the fifties, CBS fittingly cancelled the televised version of the illusion, *Mayberry, RFD,* in order to broadcast the historic drawing. With me and my entire family riveted to the small black & white in silence, Rep. Alexander Pirnie (R., NY), the senior Republican on the House Armed Service Committee's special subcommittee on the draft, with little fanfare, reached into a clear glass bowl and withdrew the first of 366 small plastic cylinders. As he handed the tube over to a representative of the Selective Service, I was certain that the rolled-up paper inside contained the date August 30, my birth date. But it didn't.

"September 14. Zero, zero one," came the revelation, denoting that the poor souls born between 1944 and 1950 on September 14th would be the first to go. The remaining tubes were pulled by young men and women representing the Selective Service's youth advisory committees in various states. For over an hour we watched, almost without breathing, and still no pronouncement of August 30. As the organizers approached the all-important 195th draw — the last of the inductees — I worried that my date would be attached to that pull, the most painful one of all, just one pull from freedom.

The drama was excruciating as the young man reached in for the 195th extraction. Time seemed to slow down as he handed the all-important vessel over to the adults to be read aloud.

"September 24. One-ninety-five."

I stood up and yelled. With my stern father sitting there I stifled

---

‡‡ Among those who came to mind were: Burton Cummings, Neil Young, Gil Evans, Joni Mitchell, Ian & Sylvia, Gino Vanelli, Randy Bachman, the Wainwright Family, Lenny Breau, Leonard Cohen, Rick Danko, Hank Snow, John Kay, Richard Manuel, Denny Doherty, Galt Macdermot, and the McGarrigle sisters.

the desire to scream out, "Fuck you, Nixon!" My mother, predictably, had tears in her eyes. The feeling of relief was overwhelming: I would not be among the next 850,000 sent off to the killing fields. We kept watching, curious to see when my date would be drawn. As the night was drawing to a close with no announcement of August 30, I began to worry that we had all missed something; was my number already drawn? Keep in mind that there was no DVR rewinding in 1969. And then we heard it.

"August 30. Three hundred, thirty-three." Very heavy number, I thought. I wondered if it was as mysterious as 666, but all I knew was that it saved my Italian-American skin. In the end, nearly 3.5 million men, drafted from a pool of approximately 27 million, would serve in Vietnam, and I would not be one of them.

I jumped into my car and drove over to one of my classmate's homes, where I was happy to learn that most of my pals had likewise escaped the reaper. And Paul, the only one with a low number, had a sympathetic doctor who guaranteed he would get him excused because of a bad back. It was a great night. The next day back at school was a different matter altogether. I remember walking into my first class that morning, where, initially, guys were high-five-ing each other and yelling out their high numbers. Then we noticed the others — sitting at their desks, head-in-hand, almost on the verge of tears. They were the lottery's losers. The celebration stopped on a dime, as we knew we were rubbing salt in the wounds of the not so fortunate.

UMBC's collective experience with the draft lottery was not without great poetic justice, to wit, the talk of the campus quickly became the dual facts that the president of the school's small "Young Republican" faction was born on September 14 (drawn first), whilst the SDS chapter leader just happened to arrive on June 8th (the last drawn.)

I soon made my way to the school library where I perused some books on numerology, curious about the strange, cultish, lottery number assigned to me, 333. Interpretations were numerous, but the ones that stood out referred to the number as the "Magical Sign of the Triple Threes," — I couldn't argue that 333 was magical for me — which meant that the Archangels are with you and that you are on the path to enlightenment (again, Siddhartha?) Another reference noted that, in one of her messages given to Don Stefano Gobbi of the Marian Movement of Priests, the Virgin Mary wrote: "333 expresses the mystery of the unity of God." There was, in fact, so much historical interest in my number of liberation that I began to wonder if there might be something to it. Regardless of its rumored powers, 333 gave me the sweetest Christmas ever.

Chapter Nine

Hot Shots and Sweet Spots

THE SPRING OF 1970 brought big musical news. In early April, Paul McCartney announced to the press that he was leaving the Beatles. Although a shocker at the time, it was later learned that the band's dissolution was long in coming. In fact, John, George, and Ringo had actually all quit the previous year, and ironically it was Paul who convinced them to not go public. Thus, Paul's stealing of the climactic headlines eroded whatever was left of their friendships, at least in the short term. But at least the band went out in style; the final studio album, *Abbey Road*, was their most stunning. And what other band, after recording over 300 mostly love songs, saved their best, and most appropriate amorous line for the very last: "And in the end, the love you take is equal to the love you make"?

That amiable philosophy fell on deaf ears in the ranks of the Ohio National Guard. One month later, after President Nixon – the man who had secretly scuttled the Paris Peace talks in order to defeat Humphreys in the 1968 election – announced a US military "incursion" (read: invasion) into Cambodia, American campuses, including UMBC, erupted in protests led by students and academics labeled "bums" by Nixon. By calling the blatantly illegal action an "incursion," Nixon tried to make it sound like a holiday, an *excursion*. His administration's use of euphemism typically took the linguistic device to absurd heights (or depths.) In Nixonland, lies became "inoperative statements." The bastardization of the English language for the purpose of acceptance of otherwise objectionable activities would only accelerate in the coming years.[*]

On May 4, after four days of protests at the northeastern Ohio campus of Kent State University, the Ohio National Guard snapped: twenty-nine guardsmen fired 67 rounds over a period of 13 seconds

---

[*] By the 1990's, bad and vulgar poets would be called "musicians," and win Grammys; teen heiresses who made bedroom sex tapes became "reality stars;" bettors no longer traveled to Las Vegas for the gambling, but for the "gaming." After gaming, a sucker no longer went to a strip club, but to a "gentlemen's club." While at the club, our gamer saw no cocaine-addled prostitutes, just "escorts." Prostitutes — I'm sorry, escorts — who agreed to be filmed were labeled "adult film stars," or "porn stars," and would be revered on *Oprah* and *Entertainment Tonight*; These "stars" didn't work for mob-connected pornographers, but for "adult industry executives." Cute teenaged boys with no musical ability whatsoever, could have their voices "Auto-tuned" in order to form vacuous "boy bands." I could continue ad nauseam. Nixon would be proud.

into a crowd of 2,000 protesting, but unarmed, students, killing four of them. The dead had been shot in the neck, face, and chest, while nine others were wounded, including one who suffered permanent paralysis. The impressions of one eyewitness spoke for many of us. Kent student Jerry Casale was friends with two of the victims, and witnessed one of them lying bloody in the aftermath.

"I saw Allison [Krause] lying there after she was shot," said Casale. "I saw tons of blood on this bright sunny day, and sat on the grass because I thought I was gonna pass out." The trauma of the event was so deep, Casale said, that it completely altered his worldview.

"That changed me from being this kind of laissez-faire hippie into 'No more Mr. Nice Guy,'" he said. "It changed my view of how things work, because what I saw was that truth doesn't matter, money and power and politics create and sustain reality, and that history is a bunch of lies retold over and over by the people that have the power."

After graduation, Casale formed a successful band with fellow student Mark Mothersbaugh, and their lyrical expression of mankind's increasing inhumanity made his group, Devo, a favorite of mine and many of my friends.

"We wanted to take the horror and trauma, and address the flaws of the human condition in a humorous way," Casale remembered. "If I couldn't have brought humor into it, I would have turned into an assassin. I wouldn't have started Devo unless [Kent State] happened."

In the immediate wake of Kent, four million students went on strike across the country. UMBC was among 450 other schools that closed down for a couple of days. For me, it was back down the Baltimore-Washington Parkway to D.C. on May 9, 1970, just five days after the shootings, where I joined over 130,000 people, mostly students, demonstrating against the Cambodian *excursion* and the Ohio National Guard. It was an incredible gathering, considering that it came together almost overnight — and we did it without the internet!

Surprisingly, we were allowed to stage the protest on the Ellipse, just south of the White House. The organizers seized on this proximity to aim some of the PA speakers at Nixon's fortress, which was dubbed "The Outhouse." Thus he couldn't avoid hearing the chants of "Fuck Nixon," as he pretended to watch a college football game on television. His bemused bravado was a feint: the 82nd Airborne was stationed in the basement of the Executive Office building to protect him from the "bums," while busses formed a barricade between the Ellipse and the White House, and thousands of soldiers, National

Guard, and DC police encircled the entire site. Although the scent of pot was everywhere, the cops seemed to give it a pass.

It was an unusually warm day for early May, the temperature flirting with 90°, as we listened to speakers such as Coretta King, and the Chicago Seven's David Dellinger and the ubiquitous Abbie Hoffman who lead chants of "Power to the People!"

We embraced Nixon's disparaging description of us with signs reading "Bums Against the War." Actress Jane Fonda made her way up to the podium where she saluted the crowd, saying, "Greetings fellow bums!"

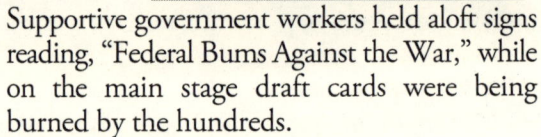

Supportive government workers held aloft signs reading, "Federal Bums Against the War," while on the main stage draft cards were being burned by the hundreds.

As the afternoon progressed and the temperature soared, many of us made our way over to the Reflecting Pool to cool off, then we just rolled up our pants and waded up to our knees or sat on the rim, dangling our legs in the water. A couple dozen or so, still riding a Woodstock high, jumped in "starkers" until the cops showed up to arrest them for public nudity. In those days, hardly anyone – myself included — carried a camera, but I wish I had brought my Polaroid Swinger for what happened next. As I sat on the ledge with a couple of UMBC pals, one of the skinny dippers, a stunning pixie-ish babe, emerged from the pool just a couple feet away. But this was no truant Columbia University dance major. It was "Barbarella" herself. That's right, thirty-two-year-old Jane Fonda, who had just starred in the cult classic, was standing just six feet away in the altogether. She smiled at us, and one of my friends offered her a hand getting out (I was, sadly, transfixed to the point of paralysis). Jane was able to put on her clothes before the cops caught her. And off she went. God, I miss the old days.

By mid-afternoon, the crowd began to disperse, as some of the more radical headed toward the Justice Department complex. After someone yelled, "To the White House!" I found myself following a group of thousands walking behind marchers carrying black-draped coffins up

15th St, trying to find a gap in the barricade. I know that at least one coffin, marked "America," was thrown over the busses onto the White House lawn. Some of the group, harassed by police, then began carrying the caskets towards Arlington National Cemetery.

Late in the afternoon, things began to turn ugly after some protestors started smashing windows on H Street. Apparently, things were even more violent on the George Washington University campus. The military responded with tear gas and 300 arrests. When the first gas canister was tossed at our location, my friends and I high-tailed it back to Baltimore, while the Prez, obviously worried he might get hit by a rock thrown a quarter mile, made tracks for Camp David.

That spring, as I prepared for final exams and my return to Lake George, there was one more memorable event. On May 30, I attended a concert by Crosby, Stills, Nash, & Young at Baltimore's Civic Center. The place was jammed, as CSNY was at their peak after Woodstock and the recent release of their stunning first album as a quartet, *Déjà Vu*. The reason this show stands out among the blur of great concerts we all attended was the encore, featuring a new song that represented the most timely, emotional, even cathartic, performance I have ever seen.

"I just wrote this a couple days ago," Neil Young announced. "We haven't recorded it yet. It's called 'Ohio'"

With that, Young and his bandmates launched into a fever dream in D minor about the murders of students just like us at Kent State only four weeks ago. The audience was in tears and holding aloft thousands of lighters and lit matches, as though they were candles for the dead. By the tag line, we were all singing — make that screaming — the phrase: "FOUR DEAD IN OHIO, FOUR DEAD IN OHIO..." over and over for many minutes, until both the band and the audience were completely drained, vocal cords shredded.

With the UMBC tennis season — I mean semester — over, I was on my way back to Blue Water Manor, where this season's musical to be butchered was the Damon Runyon-inspired *Guys and Dolls*. The story, which took place during Prohibition in Chicago, featured bootlegged "hootch" in almost every scene. Although the cast was supposed to be drinking iced tea, they smuggled the real thing — including a beer keg behind the prop bar — onto the stage every night, becoming completely sloshed by the third act. That summer was a carbon copy of the previous year's hedonism-by-the-lake. The big difference was that the musical's director, Bobbie D., decided that she needed a larger performance space than the Manor House hearth, where so many staff had been banged up recreating the *West Side Story* rumbles. However the new site only added to the theater of the absurd that the staff so relished. One of BWM's draws was that it included one of the only indoor pool facilities on the lake, thus guaranteeing that a long-planned vacation would not be completely rained out. It was decided that the weekly musical would be staged in the pool building, with the performance on one side of the long pool and the audience across the water sitting on bleachers.

The combined effect of the indoor humidity (which kept the piano permanently out of tune), the choking smell of chlorine, and the performers who slipped, jumped, or were pushed into the pool made the production rival the Marx Brothers' destruction of Verdi's *Il Trovatore* in *A Night at the Opera*. Bobbie, a trained Broadway hoofer who took her work seriously, was often moved to tears – not by a great performance, but by seeing her life's work being turned into a joke by a bunch of pot-smoking hippies. It reminded me of one of my childhood heroes, movie director Ed Wood, who passionately, but completely unsuccessfully, tried to make good art out of schlock.

I stayed in regular contact with Vitas, now 16-years-old, throughout the year, but he was fast becoming a junior champion and couldn't make it to the lake that summer. His game was distinguished by its textbook form, punishing volleys, and perhaps the quickest feet in the history of the game – inherited from his dad, who, in his youth, was nicknamed "The Rabbit." In July, Vitas was honored to be chosen to play an exhibition doubles match at Madison Square Garden with another junior, Steve Geller, and icons Pancho Gonzalez and Pancho Segura (Vitas and Gonzalez won).

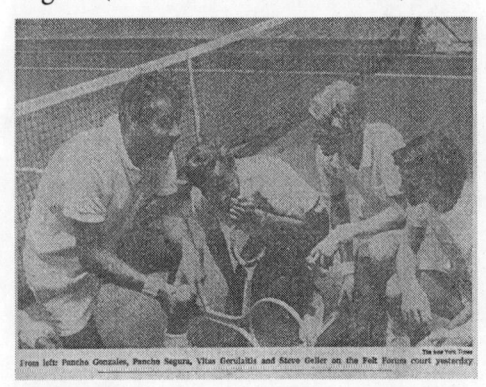

The match was a prelude to a championship between Laver and Rosewall, which Laver took in three straight sets. Vitas was so proud that he sent me a clipping of his photo in the *New York Times*. At summer's end, I once again stayed with the Gerulaitises for the US Open fortnight in which

Rosewall beat Roche for the men's championship. By this time, young Vitas, who had shot up in height, was devoting so much time to his game that his guitars and amps were gathering dust in the basement.

Another vivid memory had to do with tennis's original "bad boy." At most championships, when the pros aren't actually playing, they schmooze in the clubhouse (usually playing backgammon at the Open) or back at their hotels, leaving their coaches to scout the competition's matches. By my second trip to the Open I began to notice that there were two exceptions to this rule, one obvious, and the other perhaps a surprise. I remember numerous times in the old players' lounge when the announcement came that one of these two players was due out for their match, and quickly a dozen or so other pros would rush to the stadium to get a good seat. The players were Rod Laver and Ilie "Nasty" Năstase, at the time ranked number six in the world.

The Romanian Nasty, also referred to by the press as the "Bucharest Buffoon," was perhaps the most gifted man to ever wield a racket, possessed of grace, elegance, speed, power, spin, touch – you name it. He seemed to glide over the court as though gravity didn't exist. The pros never called him Nasty or Buffoon, they instead used reverential names like "The Magician," or "The Wizard," or "The Sorcerer." Many were the times that I sat with Vitas and his pro friends such as little Johnny McEnroe in the stands marveling at Năstase's genius. When he played doubles, it was as though the other three players didn't exist — we were just riveted to Nasty, waiting for him to do something amazing. But we also watched him for the hysterics, because the Romanian was also quite mad.

Egged on by his Fu-Manchu mustachioed mentor/coach from Transylvania, the hulking, non-smiling, Ion "Count Dracula" Tiriac, Năstase was compelled to entertain the crowd (and himself), or to mimic other players or the referees that he regularly warred with. In his zeal to entertain by mixing in unorthodox and unpredictable but dazzling shots (like today's Fabrice "the Magician" Santoro), the original tennis Magician often lost focus on actually winning matches. He thus short-circuited his own legacy, which likely would have dwarfed even Laver's. That's how brilliant was his gift.

I witnessed some great Năstase antics personally. I often attended post match press conferences (and usually asked questions), and at one such gaggle, Năstase excoriated the attendees to their faces for their "unfair" treatment of him. He labeled them "lazy bums," "scum," and muttered assorted expletives while storming out. We stayed in our seats awaiting his opponent's entrance when half a dozen waiters arrived, trays aloft and loaded with dozens of martinis, courtesy of The Magician. During one hellishly hot day in late August, players for the first time began changing shirts courtside, prompting Nasty to change his *shorts* in the center of the court, to the howls of the crowd. When the umpire scolded him, Ilie adopted his "foreign man" ploy, looking confused and pretending he didn't understand what he had done wrong. When an umpire scolded him for giving the finger to a linesman, Năstase again feigned innocence, saying, "What? This? [giving the finger to the ump] This is Romanian peace sign. I just show love." The crowd was in hysterics again. The fake insouciance was used when Wimbledon decreed that all doubles teams dress exactly alike, a ruling that chafed Nasty (like all the others.) Thus, when he paired with Arthur Ashe, he pretended that he believed the rule had to be taken literally, thus he walked onto the hallowed court looking exactly like Arthur — right down to his black-face makeup.

If Năstase saw that an opponent was going to smash a ball to make it bounce into the stands, the wild man made a beeline for the bleachers well before the ball was struck, and waited for it in the fifth row, to his opponent's shock, and occasionally returned it. This even brought one of his opponents to his knees with laughter. He went into the stands often, as in the time he was irked that an umpire refused to call a rain suspension. Ilie adapted to this inconvenience by jumping into the stands and absconding with a patron's umbrella. On the next point, he held the umbrella aloft in his left hand as he received serve with the racquet in his right.

Năstase showed his volatile temper when a bad baseline call sent him over the psychic edge that he virtually inhabited. On one such occasion I witnessed, the Open was being played on Har-Tru, a surface of finely ground basalt that had lines made of canvas tacked into the court with thousands of nails. After a particularly irksome call, Năstase proceeded to walk to the baseline, hack at the canvas tape until he freed it, then reached down and ripped the entire strip from the court before walking off to the laughter of the crowd and the screams of "Mr. Năstase!" from the umpire. He heard that scold so much in his career that he titled his autobiography *Mr. Năstase!*

There are hundreds of such Nasty anecdotes recounted by old-timers, but I'll just end with these two, told to me by Vitas. After a match between Vitas and Nasty in Salt Lake City, in a preplanned incident, the two walked up to the net to shake hands, then dropped their pants and mooned the thousands of Mormons in attendance. "You should have seen them," Vitas howled. "The parents tried to cover their kids' eyes. I thought they were going to have heart attacks." Vitas also liked to tell the story of when he and Ilie arrived late at an airport after another exhibition only to find their boarding gate had closed and their plane had begun to taxi. Undaunted, Năstase raced past ticket-taker and out onto the tarmac, where he began throwing his rackets, one by one, at the cockpit of the slow moving plane. It worked. The pilot stopped the plane and allowed the dynamic duo to board. Life was indeed different in the pre-Homeland Security world. Today that antic would land you in Gitmo.

In the context of hanging with Vitas and the top tennis pros, jamming with Michael Hedges, participating in real world political upheaval, and cavorting six feet from a naked Barbarella, my poli-sci classes at UMBC didn't stand a chance. What time I spent there was wasted staring out the window, imagining what I *could* be doing. It was about this time that I first learned the expression *Carpe Diem* – and all I could see were the diems that were not being carped. Thus my grades really began to suffer. And since my scholarship had expired, and I was now paying for my tuition via a $10,000 student loan, I decided to take a semester off to recharge whatever academic batteries were left. The fact that I dropped out just one semester from graduation struck some (read: my parents) as insanity. But I knew that I would fail my first courses ever that spring if my focus continued to unravel. Since my tennis coach had recently passed away, I also felt no strong pull to play team tennis.

Of course, I couldn't withdraw from school in the normal way. I had to put my own spin on the bureaucratic process. It occurred to me that if I formally withdrew, I would have to reapply for acceptance (far from a sure thing), and I would also forfeit my student loan. Thus when I received my course application for the spring semester, I had to think fast. I remembered what the Kennedy brothers had done during the 1962 Cuban Missile Crisis. At the height of the showdown, Soviet Premier Khrushchev sent a letter to the brothers stating that his country would remove its nukes if the US merely promised to not invade Cuba. But the next day a much more demanding letter arrived, also signed by Khrushchev, but really dictated by his hawkish puppet masters. The Kennedys decided to merely ignore the second letter, and agreed to the terms of the first. End of Cuban Missile Crisis. So I ignored the UMBC letter — I just went AWOL — and waited to see what would happen — which it turned out was nothing. End of UM Dismissal Crisis (sorry.)

In January 1971, South Dakota Senator George McGovern, the most statesmanlike and moral US politician I have ever seen, announced his candidacy for the Presidency. In the early sixties, George was practically a lone voice of opposition to America's military involvement in Southeast Asia, making him a bit of a folk hero to the rest of us who only caught up to him after LBJ's war escalation. In his January announcement, he decried "the loss of confidence in the truthfulness and common sense of our leaders," and the "dreadful mistake in trying to settle the affairs of the Vietnamese people with American troops and bombers." He not only promised, if elected, an immediate ending of the war, but also the waging of a humane war on "the plight of hunger, bad housing, and poor health services." And I vowed to be a part of his 1972 election push.

That spring, instead of hitting the books, I hit the road. I drove west with one of my Lake George co-workers this time, making it as far as Nebraska. The general theme was to drop in unannounced on people we knew around the country, many of them guests and staff from Blue Water. The looks of shock we got standing in a doorway in Wisconsin or Indiana were alone worth the gas money. One poor soul was standing over a stove cooking eggs as we appeared at the rear screen door. Turning towards us, he dropped a carton of milk into the hot pan, sending the flaming concoction in all directions.

I had decided to forego Lake Georgian hedonism for one year after learning of a summer tennis teaching program sponsored by Baltimore County. The Gold Cup was an innovative group instruction course that brought tennis out of the country clubs and into the lives of average kids. Five days a week, from 9 to 5, on the courts of over four dozen county high schools, Gold Cup instructors taught the game to thousands of new players every summer — for free! It was said to be the best public sports instruction program in the country, and competition was fierce to be one of the forty chosen instructors on the payroll of the county Department of Recreation and the US Tennis Association. The program was coordinated by the Baltimore Tennis Patrons, which at the time was mentoring youngsters like future champions Pam Shriver and Elise Burgin. In the seventies, world traveling tennis bums were popping up everywhere, and it seemed like a great career choice for someone not good enough to turn pro. Tennis by day, music by night. What's not to like? I was still determined to get the last laugh on the CIA, which had refused to hire me as the next "Kelly Robinson" (of *I Spy*).

Before going through a week of tryouts with about a hundred other wannabe tennis bums, I made a brief diversion back to my occasional hobby of gatecrashing. It so happened that on March 8, 1971, "the sweet science" was staging an international referendum on the Vietnam War. That is to say, Muhammad "The Greatest" Ali was going to challenge "Smokin'" Joe Frazier for his heavyweight championship belt. After two warm-up fights since his three-year forced exile, the twenty-nine year-old undefeated previous champ (31-0) was to get his title shot at twenty-seven-year-old Frazier in New York's Madison Square Garden, where $150 seats were being scalped for $1,000.

Other aspects of the event, referred to simply as "The Fight," were without parallel: each warrior would be paid a staggering $2.5 million; it was to be the first major closed circuit extravaganza, with viewing site franchises sold in 40 countries and 369 venues in the US. For the first time, there was no radio, not even radio updates — the first-ever global blackout of a sports event. Also, in an unprecedented move, the promoters tried to block overseas servicemen from watching or hearing the bout — a longstanding tradition. At the last minute, they reached a compromise wherein only troops stationed in Vietnam could listen to the event, and it was later said that the war was practically halted for two hours so the troops could listen.

Relentlessly hyped, the contest was billed as the "Fight of the Century," and in many ways it was. With the radio and television blackout, it was to be seen around the world only at the closed circuit venues for an average of $20 a ticket, a steep price ($100 today) for this anti-war/AWOL college student/musician/tennis bum. But, of course, I had no intention of missing the highly anticipated event, which was an instant sellout in predominantly black Baltimore city.

A little background here: Leading up to the fight, Ali, had denounced the Vietnam War and fought the Draft Board in court for three years, becoming a symbol of the anti-war movement. South Africa's Nelson Mandela spoke for many when he later declared, "Ali's refusal to go to Vietnam and the reasons he gave made him an international hero. The news could not be shut out, even by prison walls. He became a real legend to us in prison." Meanwhile, Frazier, a married, former dirt-poor slaughterhouse worker, became de facto mistakenly associated with the conservative, pro-war faction, having said that the only reason that he didn't go to Vietnam was that he was a father. Thus, the fight drew the attention of millions like me who previously had no interest in the bloody sport. It seemed like anyone who had a view on race, the war, and politics, was anticipating the cultural showdown.

But the Fight of the Century was also the con of the century, with millions of us hoodwinked by a master. Ali might have been a hero for his anti-war stance, but he was no domestic peacenik, willingly fanning racist flames leading up to the fight. Unprovoked, "minister" Ali repeatedly referred to Frazier as an "Uncle Tom," and nicknamed him "the Ugly Gorilla." (Ali had previously defamed Earnie Terrell with the "Uncle Tom" epithet and Sonny Liston with the "Ugly Gorilla" jibe.)

"I'm going to hit you on the head and straighten out your nose," spewed a rabid Ali. "Joe Frazier's so ugly his face should be donated to the Bureau of Wildlife." "You the white man's champ," Ali yelled at Frazier, who refused to call Ali by his adopted Muslim name. "I know what's going to happen the night before the fight," Ali told the *New York Post*. "That Joe Frazier, he's gonna' get telephone calls from folks in Georgia and Alabama and Mississippi saying, 'Joe Frazier, you be a white man tonight and stop that draft-dodging nigger.'"

All this, ironically, after Frazier had been in Ali's corner during Ali's painful, and costly, three-year battle with the federal courts. Incredibly, Frazier had not only supported Ali but he even lent him money. He even petitioned President Nixon to have Ali's right to box reinstated. But now, none of this seemed to matter to the former Cassius Clay. "I like to get under his skin." Ali told his trainer.

Although Ali's venom was labeled immoral and contemptible by insiders, few of us seemed to register what was going on, so much were we enthralled by Ali's skill, humor, charisma, and anti-war position. But Frazier knew better. His children felt the brunt of Ali's vitriol with attacks from their schoolmates, and Frazier received death threats, such as an anonymous note sent to him reading: "lose or else."

Pushed to the brink, Frazier eventually did his best to respond. "Clay is a phony," Frazier countered. "He never worked. He never had a job. He don't know nothing about life for most black people. He talks out both sides of his mouth. Doesn't act as he preaches. Lies to the public. Gets people riled up. Exploits race problems and real black pride. No real minister would act that way." † Frazier rightly pointed out the

---

† Far from being an exemplary Muslim minister, Ali fathered at least three children out of wedlock with his mistresses. His mentor and spiritual advisor, the "Honorable" Elijah Muhammad, had that beat: eight kids with six different teenaged girls. Muhammad's Nation of Islam (NOI) is controversial, to say the least. As for its effect on the world of boxing, Canadian champ George Chuvalo says NOI actually stared down the most powerful mob boss in American history, Tony Accardo of Chicago, forcing him to get his fighter Earnie Terrell to withdraw from a 1967 bout with Ali, who feared Terrell. According to author Mark Kram (*Ghosts of Manila*) Sonny Liston admitted taking a dive in his second title fight with Ali (1965) out of fear of NOI. After leaving his Kentucky home, Ali came up in the Mafia-controlled Philly fight scene, but the Mafia could never get its hooks into the young fighter, because, as one source told me, "Ange [Philly Mafia don Angelo Bruno] was afraid of the *schvartzers* [the Black Muslim NOI]." He was right to be afraid: throughout the period, the Philly branch of NOI ran "gangster mosques" for the violent, drug-trafficking Black Mafia.

hypocrisy of being labeled an "Uncle Tom" by a black man whose trainer was white. In his autobiography, Frazier called Ali's taunts a "cynical attempt by Clay to make me feel isolated from my own people. He thought that would weaken me when it came time to face him in that ring. Well, he was wrong. It didn't weaken me, it awakened me to what a cheap-shot son of a bitch he was."

Frazier's trainer later said that his man "wanted to actually kill Clay in the ring, he hated him so much." For Frazier, defeating Ali was thus about much more than retaining his championship; it was about restoring his honor.

Unbeknownst to many of us at the time, after Ali had come under the polarizing sway of the infamous Philadelphia chapter of the racial separatist Nation of Islam, he was turned into one of Sherwood Anderson's "grotesques,"‡ albeit still with a great smile and a legendary gift of gab. But the lighter-skinned contender was also an unmitigated bastard to the humble, blacker-than-black, Frazier.

So I was going to miss this? No way on earth. There were two possible venues in Baltimore: the 18,000-seat Civic Center, which sold out as soon as tickets went on sale; then it was announced that another site would be added, the old 7,000-seat Fifth Regiment Armory ten blocks north.

This staging, co-sponsored by CORE (The Congress of Racial Equality), also sold out. I chose the Armory to go see the fight, hoping that the CORE security volunteers would be more inexperienced than the Civic Center pros. I was right. A few days before the event, I went to a free boat show at the Armory in order to "case the joint." I quickly saw that the janitorial staff dressed in all-white slacks and shirts. That gave me a start; I owned both a white shirt — many, in fact, thanks to the St. Joe dress code — and a pair of white, "surfer" style jeans.

On the day of the big event, I decided to go very early in the afternoon, assuming the service doors would still be open to arriving staff. After putting on my costume, I retrieved my mother's best broom from the pantry. As I left the back yard, I passed my mother, who was sitting at the picnic table with some of her lady friends.

"Where are you going all dressed like the Good Humor [ice cream] man?" one of them asked.

"Oh, he thinks he's going to the fight tonight," quipped my mother. "He'll be back in an hour."

---

‡ In Anderson's groundbreaking 1919 novel, *Winesburg, Ohio*, he defines grotesques as people who have an obsession with some idea that blocks all other ideas or truths; once they believe in one truth, they can no longer see the other truths; they see all other truths as wrong.

I just smiled and said, "Wanna bet?" I showed her the broom.

"And you'd better have that with you when you get home!" mom ordered.

Leaving the broom in the car, I milled around at the Armory for a while, when I noticed that I was missing a critical piece of gear: the arriving janitorial staff were all wearing red armbands. I was able to determine that these were provided by CORE security. I therefore got back into my car and headed for a nearby Tommy Tucker's Department Store, where I purchased a similar swath of fabric in the "notions" department. Soon I was back inside the Armory with my shiny new armband and broom, looking busy sweeping (a skill I still retained from my Poconos experience) and setting up folding chairs. As fight time grew near I placed one chair about tenth row center and wedged my broom into it to signify that it was taken. I could have put it in Row One, but it seemed too close to the screen.

When the lights went down, off came the armband, and I plopped into my primo seat.

"Great seats, huh?" the well-dressed man next to me offered.

"Great," said I.

"We got these for a steal, seventy-five each. You?"

"Oh, uh, a hundred," I lied.

"Jerry Hoffberger," he introduced himself as we shook hands.

That would be *Jerry Hoffberger*, as in the owner of both Baltimore's iconic National Bohemian Beer ("Natty Boh") *and* the Baltimore Orioles. I recognized the name immediately. I told him how I had been a member of the Oriole Junior Advocates for years. And so it went for the rest of the evening, as "Jerry" bought hot dogs and sodas for all, including me, throughout the fight.

Meanwhile, at the live site in Manhattan, celebrities turned out *en masse*, from Miles Davis to Norman Mailer to Woody Allen to Frank "The Chairman of the Board" Sinatra, who, unable to land a ringside seat, stood *in front of* the ringsiders, taking photographs for *Life* magazine — he did it his way, I did it mine. Artist LeRoy Neiman painted Ali and Frazier as they fought, while a completely inexperienced Burt Lancaster, fresh from his starring role in the hit movie *Airport*, served as a color commentator for the millions worldwide. Funny, I thought, none of them wore a red armband.

Back at the Armory, at least, Ali's non-stop demagoguery had worked: 95% of the crowd, including myself and all of the blacks, seemed to be for Ali. When Frazier was lustily booed at the introductions, I actually began to feel sorry for the unpopular title-holder. As Michael Silver of ESPN described the scene years later: "While both fighters waited for the introductions Ali, gliding around the ring, twice brushed Frazier's shoulder as he moved past him. The crowd reacted with a roar. Frazier glared at Ali contemptuously. Then the house lights dimmed. The tension was almost unbearable. The fans were still on their feet when the bell rang. The fight was on!"

Ali possessed some notable physical advantages over Smokin' Joe: 8½-inches in reach, 4-inches in height (6'3" to 5'11"), and weighed 215 lbs. to Frazier's 205½. But Frazier was younger and much fitter; while Ali had been on the paid anti-war college lecture circuit for the past three years; Frazier lived in the gym, turning his body into a slab of unbreakable black granite. As though they weren't polarized enough outside the ring, the fighters were also complete opposites in boxing technique. Ali's speed, rare for a heavyweight, was mesmerizing, and his tactic had always been to dance in the ring to outmaneuver his dizzied opponents with moves such as the "Ali Shuffle." By contrast, in a style that predated Mike Tyson, there was no grace or nuance with the brute force reigning champion. With his head always down in a low protective crouch, Frazier was called "a pure puncher," relentlessly pressuring opponents with an endless series of ponderous, massive punches — and this pummeling machine never stopped unloading them until his opponent kissed the canvas.

It was obvious from the start of "The Fight" that Ali had lost some of his vaunted speed. Although he weathered the initial Frazier onslaught, by the end of the 11th Ali was clearly hurt, and Frazier sent him to his knees with a punch that would have knocked out another human. But Ali's pride forced him up and to his corner as the bell rang. As Silver noted, "Each man was fighting as if he had a point to prove. This was a genuine grudge match and it was being fought like one."

In the 15th, Frazier put an end to it, landing a monstrous left hook squarely on Ali's jaw, sending him hard to the canvas, flat on his back, legs in the air. Incredibly, Ali once again made it to his feet until final bell, but, to almost no one's surprise, he was pronounced the loser by unanimous decision — Ali's first professional defeat.

In the end, the fight lived up to the hype, and the after-action report was equally impressive: an estimated 300 million had viewed the brawl throughout the world (the largest broadcast in history); more people saw Frazier's hook landing than witnessed Apollo11's moon landing. The paid gate was reported to have grossed $20-million, by far the most in boxing history. Across the US, 90% of the 1.5 million available seats were sold. Thousands were turned away at Harlem's 369th Regiment Armory, where the 11,000 seats had sold out quickly. At the open-air Three Rivers Stadium in Pittsburgh, thousands watched the event outdoors, braving 17-degree temperatures. 20,000 attended the event live at the Garden, where one man died of a heart attack, while an additional 40,000 people milled about on the streets outside. There were riots at sites where the technology failed, such as the Chicago Coliseum.

My *après boxe* experience was a bit different. I was invited to drown my sorrows in some beers with my new friend Jerry and his pals at the new, alleged upscale strip club called *Club Les Gals*. Of course, I had been to "mammary Meccas" before; like most other teen males in Baltimore I had experienced a local rite of passage by going underage to skin joints on the infamous "Block" — I even had gigs in a couple of them. Now, having just turned twenty-one, and legal, they were already old-hat. But the chance to hang out with the Orioles' owner at a club that supposedly (unlike most of those on the Block) had beautiful dancers.

Jerry bought round after round – Natty Boh, of course – and our deep-pocketed group was like a magnet for the girls. As the booze loosened lips, I let on to Jerry how I had snuck into the 1966 World Series.

"You rascal," he laughed. "That was my first year with the team, and we were counting every penny." I bought the next round.

I made it home around three a.m., and the next day purchased a new broom for my mother.

The great success of the largest closed circuit television operation in history show altered the media landscape, and is credited with creating the market for closed circuit TV broadcasts of boxing matches, concerts, you name it. It was the precursor to today's cable pay-per-view. As Jack Gould then wrote in the *New York Times*: "The impact of the Joe Frazier-Muhammad Ali fight on the world of communications will extend far beyond tonight...Electronic life is going to change." He pointed out that previously free televised events were going to start to cost, leaving the poor out in the broadcast cold. He worried that the Fight of the Century would lead to a world where all televisions would be hard-wired with cables attaching them to "pay TV." He also wisely, and accurately, predicted that this future "cable television" would have to answer to no agency in its standards and practices.

Three months later, on June 27, 1971, by a vote of 8-0 (Justice Thurgood Marshall abstaining), the United States Supreme Court cleared Ali of the charge that he refused induction into the Armed Forces. The "Louisville Lip," aka "The Mouth From the South," aka "The Greatest," continued boxing for ten more years, with varying degrees of success. And the bad blood between him and Frazier persisted unrelenting for the next four decades, while a bitter Frazier bragged that he gave Ali his Parkinson's Disease (and he may have, with his countless thunderous blows to Ali's skull over three fights). Only in 2009 did Frazier make some statements that seemed to mark a softening of his understandable bitterness.§

With the specter of Vietnam removed from my future, I was given still another carefree summer. I was fortunate to have been granted one of the coveted tennis instructor jobs with Gold Cup, and my current band was playing pretty regularly. The timing couldn't have been better, as the Golden Era of tennis was on the cusp: Arthur Ashe, the great African-American player, was making history at the Grand Slams while fighting segregation worldwide and opening up the game to minorities; Jimmy Connors, Chris Evert, Bjorn Borg, and the elegant Aussie Evonne Goolagong were emerging, with Vitas not far behind; Hollywood celebrities were all over the sport.

---

§ See esp. the books *Ghosts Of Manila: The Fateful Blood Feud Between Muhammad Ali and Joe Frazier*, Mark Kram's *Ghosts of Manila*, and the documentaries, *Thrilla in Manila,* and the magnificent 2009 doc, *Facing Ali.*

I decided to celebrate by treating myself to my first hot car: a white 1965 Chevrolet Impala Super Sport convertible. It had a lot of mileage, and would need engine work within a year, but it was affordable — I think I paid about $600** for it — and it helped complete the illusion of a swinging, musician/tennis teacher. The red leather interior was killer, but that fancy new-fangled 8-track tape player was the icing on the cake.

In June, the newbie instructors were shuttled off to Essex Community College for a week of intensive training on how to teach group tennis, with emphasis on running tournaments and leading drills that would keep as many as twenty students going at a time. Each instructor was assigned a county high school. Rookies such as myself were given high schools in the poorer areas, while teachers with tenure held court at schools in the richer county districts, working with young players that had years of private lessons at the country clubs. By this time Kim and I had moved on; from my perspective, spending as much time as I did around single young girls, either in enticing tennis miniskirts, or dressed to the nines in nightclubs where we gigged, made monogamy an impossible challenge. And since I am a strong believer in fidelity, I had no choice but to break it off. This may have been when I began a lifelong investigation into the paradoxes inherent in modern human pair-bonding — I just find it impossible to ignore the paradoxes as though they didn't exist. But that's another book —

I had a fantastic time teaching tennis five days a week, and started to realize that I had a gift for communication with young people, and for teaching tennis specifically. Many of my students from this blue-collar area, who had never before touched a tennis racket, progressed amazingly over the course of just twelve weeks. A couple of them made it deep into the end-of-summer Gold Cup tournament, a first for this location.

** I recently saw that model on sale, restored, for $60,000.

For me, the key to being a good instructor was keeping the student relaxed enough to perform to his/her potential, and to observe carefully before correcting anything[††] — it's no coincidence that the best coaches just happen to have great eyes, and so do the best players. In conversations over the years with Vitas, his best pal, the Swede Bjorn Borg, Vitas's dad, and Bjorn's coach, the recently departed Lennart Bergelin, I learned that most journeymen coaches just talk too much, turning the student into a bundle of nerves. As Bjorn once told me, "If I was teaching, I'd just let them watch, very close up, for a while, then let them try it. My whole game is in my legs." I incorporated this by gathering students around me as close as possible while I hit ground strokes slowly against a wall. Then I told them to slowly start to move with me as I prepared, shuffled my feet, and hit the ball. Amazingly, the eyes and muscle memory of a relaxed student will be able to focus and subconsciously pick up the rhythm and start to mimic it. The body has its own innate intelligence and will usually figure out what to do. Then the teacher merely corrects whatever major flaws still exist in students with difficulty achieving a relaxed, focused state. And there was just one more secret. Recalling what Vitas had told me about Hopman's focus on fitness, I put the same question to Bergelin about Borg, and got the exact same answer. My job is to keep his legs in good

---

[††] One of the better methods for getting the athlete in such a relaxed state was developed by Timothy Gallwey in his seminal book, *The Inner Game of Tennis*. Gallwey later applied these principals to other sports, and went on to become the originator of the business coaching, life coaching and executive coaching disciplines.

shape," he added.‡‡ (He then recalled one specific fix: "I had him angle his left foot a little more towards the service line when serving. That was it. That's how I made my money," he laughed. Bergelin was, typically, modest: he took care of every aspect of Borg's hectic schedule, allowing the champion to focus solely on tennis.)   There must be something to this hustle thing: Borg became Number One in the world, and Vitas, briefly, Number Three. Thus, the major vocalizations I made that summer were just "Hustle!" and "Run!" Perhaps my most successful exhortation was actually the reverse of what most amateurs do: "Run hard, swing easy!" Uncomplicated. Try it. It works.

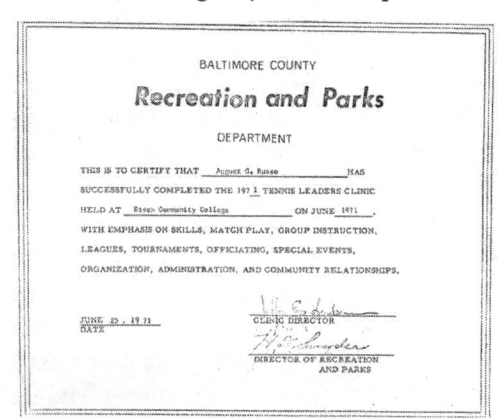

Another lasting memory from the tennis summer of 1971 was the day a strange looking man – older, slim, with a shaved head long before Vin Diesel made them hip — drove to my center and asked me if I would try out a new racquet he was developing. He had been driving to all the Gold Cup centers soliciting opinions. I said "Sure." He opened his trunk and brought out a couple of the strangest looking contraptions I had ever seen — flat black-painted aluminum tennis racquets, at 130 square inches exactly the twice the size of a normal one. He had fabricated the beast in the basement of his Roland Park home near Hopkins.

His name was almost as strange as his racquet, and had I paid any attention to the Blue Water Manor skiers, I would have been impressed: Howard Head. I later learned that the first person I had ever heard of with the name "Head," an engineer, had revolutionized skiing in the early fifties when he introduced first laminated, then aluminum skis to replace the cumbersome wooden variety. The patented design made him a multi-millionaire.

---

‡‡ After most matches and practice sessions, Borg received leg massages from Lennart that lasted between 60 and 90 minutes.

In the mid-sixties, after taking up tennis as a retiree, Head devised the first workable ball machine, "The Prince." However, his horrible game still failed to improve, so he assumed it must be the racquet's fault. The eccentric genius, unable to find his wood racquet's sweet spot, decided to make a bat with a larger sweet spot for gremlins who couldn't find that central four square inches that transmitted the most power with the least vibration and torque.

Howard Head

We rallied for about a half an hour with the cumbersome, far too light racquet with a humongous sweet spot (or "nodal point," as Head corrected) that sent many of my best strokes over the fence, and rendered net volleys downright impossible. I hated the behemoth, but was very polite and told the inventor (who still had a mediocre game) that I thought he should keep tinkering, maybe reducing the size and increasing the weight. Later that year, Head filed for a patent (U.S. Pat. No. 3,999,756) that eventually granted him ownership of all oversize racquets that might follow. And, boy, did they follow. His Prince Racquet was indeed reduced to 110 square inches (still too big for me), and made him millions, as he revolutionized another of his hobbies.[§§] Shows you what I know. But I am certain I was right in one respect: for me it was a failed revolution that ruined the pro game. More on that later.

As I hoped, in August my UMBC fall course guide arrived — with no mention of the fact that I failed to show for last spring's semester. I chose my final courses and would complete my Poli-Sci major (music minor) in December. At summer's end it was back to the US Open for the fortnight, a ritual that would continue unbroken for 16 years. On a couple of occasions, Vitas or his dad would tell me to bring my tennis gear to the club and we would rally on a side court for an hour or so. On one of these occasions years later, I was walking through the old West Side stadium with my rackets, wearing my warm up suit, when a young kid came running up to me, pen and paper outstretched, and asked me one of the most interesting questions I had ever heard: "Are you anybody?" I thought for a minute and responded, "I sure am," and signed his book "Jimmy Connors," who was then just a junior champion about to break out. I've often wondered if he still has

---

[§§] The last time I spoke with him in the late 1980's, Head was getting interested in scuba diving. I assume he invented some spectacularly aquatic.

"Jimmy's" autograph framed somewhere. I'm sure I stole the joke from Vitas, who signed Borg's name almost every day for kids who mistook him for his similarly longhaired blond buddy.

But my strongest memory of the 1971 US Open started out dreamlike before quickly turning nightmarish. One gorgeous afternoon on the veranda of the members' clubhouse, I couldn't help but notice a stunning brunette sitting alone at a table. Now there was nothing but beautiful women at the West Side clubhouse, but they were never alone. I made my way over and asked if I could join her. She smiled and said in an accent that seemed Eastern European, "Certainly. Be my guest." After a few minutes of strained chitchat (her English was very poor) in which she mentioned that she was in town to visit friends, I bought drinks — I likely had a Gibson, in hopes of reprising Cary Grant's conquest in *North By Northwest*, and my tablemate, Nikki, ordered something a tad more upscale. I was really on a roll. After a few more minutes a shadow wafted over our table from behind me, and I could swear the temperature dropped. I turned, and there they stood, glaring: Nasty Năstase and Count Dracula Tiriac. Năstase was only three years older than I, but he exuded the power of someone much older, worldly, and dark.

I frankly don't remember what, if anything, was said, but I was quickly on my feet and on the other side of the veranda. I looked back towards the table to see Nasty and Dracula, sitting with Nikki, and laughing. Another moment later a waiter handed me a cocktail, courtesy of the Romanians.

When Vitas appeared on the scene, I told him what happened, and he broke up. "That was Dominique," Vitas said. "Năstase's new girlfriend. You sure know how to pick 'em." He went on that Dominique was of royal lineage, maybe even a princess from some Eastern European principality.*** A couple of years later, Ilie and Dominique were married – the first of at least three marriages for the wild man, who would become the top ranked player in 1973, and inducted into the International Tennis Hall of Fame in 1991. In 1996, the devilishly handsome Năstase, who claims to have bedded thousands of women, ran for mayor of Bucharest, but was defeated. "Probably a very good thing for him <u>and</u> Bucharest," chuckled Tiriac, who himself went on to found a bank in Bucharest and become Romania's first billionaire. But

---

*** She was in fact Dominique Grazia of Belgium, whose maternal great-grandfather had built the Cairo metro and was made the first Baron Empain of Brussels. Her mother was Baronne Empain, half-sister of the current (1971) baron.

he was the first billionaire I ever met. I recall meeting only one other, Kirk Kerkorian, of Las Vegas fame.

After my no-ceremony December graduation I threw myself headlong into the nascent McGovern campaign, working locally out of the downtown Baltimore office. Interestingly, since the 1968 election debacle, McGovern had headed a group that would pave the way for changes facilitating his own bid: The Democratic Party's McGovern-Fraser Commission, trying to avoid a replay of the 1968 Chicago riots by voters who felt left out of the nominating process, advocated an expansion of the primaries and resulted in twenty-one such contests (including Maryland) in 1972, six more than before. Now, outsider candidates with wide public appeal, like McGovern, could appeal directly to the people for nomination with a grassroots campaign.[†††]

I had learned what I could about poli-sci in the classroom, but what I saw in real life turned out to be the true political education. This pre-internet, pre-computer, era was one of the last vestiges of decades of tried-and-true, old school politicking. In addition to the standard envelope stuffing, phone canvassing, and leafleting, we had to confront opposition tactics, which had reached an all-time criminal low in 1972. This was the year of the Watergate break-in by Nixon's "Plumber" henchmen. The Watergate Hotel complex housed our national party headquarters, and Nixon and his fellow crooks wanted to know what we knew about Nixon's numerous underhanded activities;[‡‡‡] Nixon's gophers had been conducting such break-ins almost since the day he was inaugurated in 1969. Although this latest Nixonian "incursion" at the Watergate garnered the headlines, those of us in the field for McGovern experienced countless other "dirty tricks" engineered by the same cabal. During the initial primaries, Nixon's gangsters targeted Democratic candidates like Ed Muskie and Hubert Humphreys, since they wanted to run against McGovern. After George's nomination, they focused all their criminality on our campaign. The shenanigans expressed themselves in a couple of typical forms: "McGovern rallies" would be arranged by the Plumbers, of course without our knowledge, only to have the candidate be a no-show; some

---

[†††] The "pure democracy" primaries are, of course, a double-edged sword, since an unsophisticated electorate is more easily hoodwinked by charisma than are hard-boiled, back room pols. Regrettably, the expanded primary system has given rise to "celebrity politicians" like Ronald Reagan, Sarah Palin, John McCain, John Edwards, and even, bless him, Barack Obama, to name just a few. Not what McGovern or the Founding Fathers had in mind.

[‡‡‡] Among Nixon's key fears were his history on the dole of billionaire Howard Hughes, for whom Nixon squashed anti-trust investigations, and Nixon's quasi treasonous 1968 deal with the South Vietnamese peace delegation to stall the peace talks in order to help him win the presidency.

of Nixon's tricksters imitated McGovern campaign chairman Gary Hart when placing harassing calls to newspaper editors or other influential targets; and flagrantly scurrilous anti-Nixon fliers were circulated on phony McGovern campaign letterhead.

In retrospect, it's fascinating how many of our unworthy opponents continued to poison the body politic decades later. Lucianne Cummings Goldberg, the New York literary agent who tipped the Republicans to President Clinton's intern paramour in 1997, was on the McGovern campaign plane in 1972 under the guise of a magazine writer, when in actuality she was being paid $1,000 a week to spy for Nixon's team. "They were looking for really dirty stuff," Goldberg later said. "Who was sleeping with who, what the Secret Service men were doing with the stewardesses, who was smoking pot on the plane — that sort of thing." §§§

White House documents released in 1996 disclosed that in 1972, then-thirty-four-year-old Nixon aide, and current cable television right-wing windbag, Pat Buchanan, "recommended staging counterfeit attacks by one Democrat on another, fouling up scheduled events, arranging demonstrations and spreading rumors to plague the rival party, all the while being careful not to run afoul of the Secret Service." Another memo quotes Buchanan as calling himself "a regular and enthusiastic member of the campaign 'Attack Group.'" Young Buchanan advised that his minions "should be able to help put demonstrations together, get leaflets out, start rumors, and generally foul up scheduled events — and add to the considerable confusion and chaos that will inevitably exist." He also suggested using IRS audits as a weapon against peace activists, left-leaning organizations, and other Nixon "enemies." As someone who was on the receiving end of this sort of neo-fascism, it is positively sickening to see him trotted out today as some sort of political wise man/analyst.

And there were others, such as twenty-two-year-old Texas "Young Republican" activist Karl Rove, who did all he could in that state to paint McGovern as a "left-wing peacenik," despite McGovern's World War II service piloting a B-24 bomber (in contrast, Nixon the alleged Quaker, saw no WWII combat and spent most of the war in Rhode Island, Iowa, and Philadelphia). Rove also worked as staff

---

§§§ Goldberg answered directly to legendary political trickster, Nixon advisor, and mob lawyer, Murray Chotiner. Chotiner, who was known in the Nixon camp by his code name "Mr. Chapman," had first helped Nixon smear congressional opponent Helen Gahagan Douglas in 1950. Chotiner, a close friend of the mob's *consiglieri* Sidney Korshak, arranged for Nixon presidential pardons for made Mafiosi. Goldberg and other campaign spies were referred to by the Nixonistas as "Chapman's Friends."

assistant to Texan George Bush Sr., then chairman of Republican National Committee (RNC), who was also busied helping his son, George, Jr., dodge the Vietnam draft. Rove's chief adversary in Texas was McGovern's Lone Star State campaign chairman, twenty-six-year-old Bill Clinton, from Arkansas. Two decades later, Rove would function as Bush's son's attack dog and continued Clinton canker sore.**** Most disturbingly, this far-right clique has succeeded in being perceived as "conservatives," which must cause actual conservatives such as Thomas Jefferson, John Adams, and even Bill Buckley to spin in their graves.

Despite what my textbooks illustrated, I was beginning to see how American politics played out in the real world. It was a discomfiting wake-up call that some might label merely "growing up." Regrettably, the system has continued to descend further into the partisan abyss in the decades that followed. True statesmen like George McGovern (or Republicans like Lowell Weicker and Charles Mathias, for that matter) don't stand a chance in what author Ronald Brownstein refers to as the era of "The Second Civil War."

We felt the repercussions from the pranks on a weekly basis, but somehow remained optimistic despite our uphill battle. My spirits were buoyed by one of my campaign responsibilities: I had volunteered to take some special chauffeur training so that I could drive various party dignitaries around when they came to town. Despite having participated in numerous war protests, I maintained a clean arrest record, and thus passed the Secret Service's background check. Although the Secret Service drove the candidate, I occasionally had the privilege of driving his wife Eleanor and the family of the VP candidate Sarge Shriver. On one mad dash down the Baltimore-Washington Parkway to the airport, with 16-year-old Maria Shriver and her younger brother Anthony in my back seat, I had to use my training when the lead car carrying McGovern came to a dead stop. The follow-up drivers had been instructed to veer left or right, depending on their position in the motorcade. I veered left into the median, as instructed, thus avoiding an 80-mph collision with the cars in front and behind. Not one car was scratched, and we made our way safely to the planes; I never learned what caused the stoppage.

**** Rove also introduced his "Dirty Tricks" mentor, Lee Atwater, to Bush Sr. Atwater later became a political attack dog for the Reagan-Bush team, and later still helping Bush Sr. become president, and himself RNC chairman.

On one trip to the airport, I managed to cajole a prickly Secret Service agent into snapping some photos of George and I on the tarmac. Looking at those photos now, it amazes me how true I remained to my musician/hippie ethos, even when driving in a presidential motorcade: there I was in my wild hair, John Lennon "granny" specs, patched jeans (the very ones on this book cover), flannel shirt, and clutching my faux cowboy hat! I defy anyone to find such a bizarre-looking driver in another presidential motorcade. But George was gracious as always.

Another highlight was escorting Eleanor to the blue-collar Bethlehem Steel plant in Sparrows Point. On the long drive past the slums of Baltimore to the hazy, thoroughly orange ash-tinted mini city, we had a wonderful conversation about the need to end poverty and hunger in America. For weeks thereafter, I stared at the passenger seat in my 1965 Chevy, amazed that a possible future First Lady had actually sat there. I was back at the post-Apocalyptic Beth Steel, alone, handing out "peacenik" McGovern fliers on May 15, when a particularly thick-necked steel worker started screaming "commie" epithets at me while some of his co-workers, luckily, restrained him. They told me I should leave before I got hurt. As I ran to my car, I asked a parking lot security guard what I had done.

"Didn't you hear?" he asked. "George Wallace has been shot in Laurel [MD]." The segregationist former Alabama Governor was apparently a favorite of the Beth Steel rank and file, who must have assumed that one of us "Jane Fonda Commies" had been behind it.[††††] The very next day, Wallace, shot five times and paralyzed from the chest down, won the Maryland Democratic primary going away, but the Maryland McGovern forces helped in other locales where we were successful, such as New Hampshire and Massachusetts.

Although we secured the nomination, held in Miami on July 13, we faced so many obstacles that winning the White House would

---

[††††] The shooter, 21-year-old Wisconsinite Arthur Bremer, didn't even have a political motive: he just wanted to be famous. He would serve thirty-five years in prison for the attack, and is last known to be living in Cumberland, Md.

have redefined the word "miracle." In addition to the Dirty Tricks crowd, we had strong opposition within the Democratic Party from the old backroom hacks who had been shunted aside by the new expanded primary system; some of these pols even deserted the party and worked for Nixon. Then there was the money: as Congressional investigators later learned, the Nixon forces were able to greatly outspend us thanks to hundreds of illegal corporate contributions that totaled in the tens of millions. And although Nixon won in a landslide, he would be forced to resign in disgrace (for covering up the dirty tricks) in a year-and-a-half. One week after Nixon's January 20, 1973 inauguration, both the South and North Vietnamese agreed to a cease-fire, and US ground troops were gone two months later. And two years after that, the country was finally unified, two decades after the French, then the US, created the false partition.

While Nixon spent much of the remainder of his life brooding in his San Clemente home, McGovern stayed in the Senate until 1980, later serving as U.S. ambassador to the United Nations Food and Agriculture Organization. In 2001, the World Food Program appointed him UN Global Ambassador on World Hunger. He is an honorary life member of the board of Friends of the World Food Program, and on August 9, 2000, President Bill Clinton presented him with the Presidential Medal of Freedom. And the key architects of the Vietnam War, such as Robert McNamara (see *In Retrospect*) and McGeorge Bundy (see *Lessons in Disaster*), eventually admitted that the war was a mistake from the get-go. The two million Vietnamese, the 58,000 US troops — they all died for no reason. We "Commie peaceniks" were right all along, but we take no joy in knowing that. We'd have much rather elected George and stopped the bloodshed.

Chapter Ten

A Banner Year

IT SEEMS THAT about every dozen years or so, I take a one-year sojourn from my frenetic lifestyle, recharge the batteries, and wait for a burst of inspiration that will fuel the next chapter. 1973 was that first such break. Although I continued playing in weekend bands, improving my songwriting skills, and giving private tennis lessons, I was still living in my parents' home and waiting for the next "Aha!" moment that would propel me into my first year-round apartment. In the meantime, I could think of no better place to gather my thoughts than Lake George, where Will, Ak and I reached a new level in our harmonic quest, and where the rest of the staff obliterated the Broadway show *Brigadoon*. Another blissful summer need not be recounted again, save for one incident that rose above the hedonistic rituals, which we staffers now had down to a science. This one didn't involve my original Lake George pal, Vitas, but another young thoroughbred that I happened to run into.

That summer I heard from my old Henryville partner in crime, Chris, who was now working as a sports stringer for the Associated Press out of New York. Indulging his love of the horse game, Chris managed to get assigned to work the summer meet at the stately, 110-year-old Saratoga Race Track in bucolic Saratoga Springs, a short drive south from the lake. The course was the home to four critical thoroughbred meets: the Travers, the Alabama, the Whitney, and the Woodward, and was the summer home for some of the wealthiest people in America. I had made the drive down occasionally to hang with Chris and his friend, the great race caller for the New York Racing Association, Marshall Cassidy.

One of the most prominent race callers in the country, Marshall's Wikipedia

Marshall Cassidy

entry notes: "He was best known for his accuracy, precise diction and upbeat delivery, especially early in his career when calling a close race as the horses ran down the stretch."

Marshall, who could have followed Sean Connery into the "Bond" role, allowed Chris and I to watch the races from his booth, or from above on the roof, away from the maddening crowds. I stood next to him in awe as he carried on conversations with Chris and me while simultaneously memorizing the dozen or so horses, colors, and jockeys for the next race. His memorization skills, which we tried in vain to match, were astounding. We also had the run of the paddocks and stables (this was before I learned of the cruelty involved in the race business.)

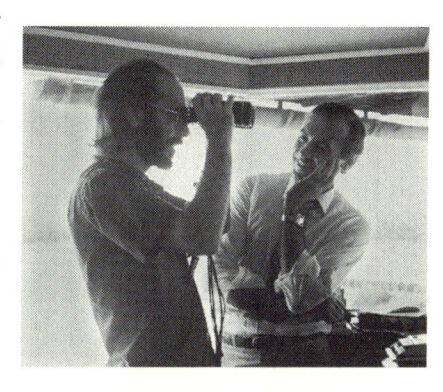

Showing Marshall how it's done. (My girlfriend Spike, who took the photo, instructed Marshall to "Look at Gus in awe.")

One day I asked a girlfriend at Blue Water Manor to attend the races with me. She got all dolled up in the high Saratoga style and we had a glorious day visiting Chris, Marshall, and the horsies in the stables. It was while walking through the betting lobby that I noticed a Black man looking frustrated as he struggled with the *Daily Racing Form* newspaper. I asked if I could help him read the microscopic newsprint, and he was most grateful for the assistance of younger eyes. He had been looking for a particular jockey that he liked, certain he was racing today, but forgot to bring his reading glasses. I found the jockey, and my new friend George was ecstatic and suggested I bet the farm on him — at the time, my farm consisted of about $20. We walked to the window together and betted on the jockey's horse. I bet my twenty and George put down about a hundred. We all walked out to the trackside viewing area, and screamed when the horse actually won. I cashed in for about $100 and George, obviously, five times that much.

For obvious reasons, we spent the next few races hanging with George and helping him with the *Form*. We all got on famously during a time (1973) and place (Saratoga) where you rarely saw Blacks and Whites socializing together. But I could care less about backward conventions, and we had a great day, celebrating our good fortune with a dinner together in the clubhouse, thanks to Marshall. Over food, George said he was semi-retired and just came up from Virginia to Saratoga to help a friend for a month or so. When the day ended and we were about to go, George wasn't ready for the night to end.

"I'd like to have you over my place for a drink," George offered. "My wife would love to meet you, and our place is right here in town."

I was all for it, but was surprised that my date felt likewise. We piled into my car and as our new friend George dictated directions I was becoming confused: we were heading directly into the heart of Saratoga's version of Millionaire's Row, where New York Blue Bloods (like Rockefeller, DuPont, Morgan, etc.) had their summer "cottages," mansions by anyone else's definition. And we were parking in front of one of the best. Except for athletes and musicians, I didn't think there were any Black millionaires in 1973, but I guessed I was wrong.

"Welcome to my home," George said. We were speechless.

We walked in the front door and were greeted by George's charming wife, who was oddly wearing an apron over what appeared to be a maid's uniform. As I looked around the living room, I saw some of the most beautiful horse oil paintings and bronze statues. Upon closer inspection, all of the artwork depicted just one equine, the one that had just won the Triple Crown, shattering speed records in the process: Secretariat. Now I was confused. George laughed and explained.

"We work for Mrs. Tweedy — I drive for her and my wife takes care of the house," George explained.

He elaborated that Virginian horse breeder Penny Chenery Tweedy and "Big Red" hadn't arrived for the season yet. After having a drink and getting a tour of Mrs. Tweedy's Secretariat collection, George invited us back when the boss was in town.

A couple of weeks later, I indeed spent the day with George, who took me to the big guy's stall, where I met the most beautiful horse I had ever seen — to this day I'm certain that anyone could pick him out in a herd of one hundred; his incredible physique, chestnut coat, white forehead "blaze," and three white "stockings" made the horse a superstar, even apart from his big racing heart.[*]

Later, George took me back to Penny's "cottage," for a cocktail reception, where I finally met the gracious lady as well as jockey Ron Turcotte. When things loosened up, I asked about the chances of

---

[*] In fact, Secretariat's 1989 autopsy would reveal his heart to weigh twenty-two pounds, nearly 3 times that of a normal thoroughbred, and the largest the autopsist had ever seen.

getting one of Big Red's lucky horseshoes the next time they were replaced. She laughed and said that, given that the shoes were only replaced every two months and the fact that many of her friends had the same idea, it might be a long time. Oh, well, it was worth a try.[†]

On August 4, 1973, Chris and I got a group together to sit on the roof and watch the big horse run in the Whitney Handicap. We held our breath as Secretariat was bumped against the rail and then lost by a length to Onion. Although Saratoga was known as "The Graveyard of Champions," it wasn't any curse that beat him: Penny later revealed that her beloved horse had been running a low grade fever on the day of the race, but she felt he could win regardless. I was so upset after the result that I tossed my betting ticket in the trash, but Chris wisely kept his as a memento.

Penny Tweedy and "Big Red"

Mercifully, Penny allowed the horse to retire early, at the end of that year — a very short career for a champion. I was honored to meet him.[‡]

Upon returning in one piece from the lake, I again spent two weeks in New York at the US Open with the Gerulaitises and some friends who had vacationed on the lake. By this time, Vitas had dropped out of Columbia University (where he had an academic scholarship) and turned pro; this would be his second year in the main draw at the Open. He was also becoming an astounding babe magnet, a trait that never left him.

Vitas's life was becoming so hectic that I was spending more time with his dad, "Mr. G," but over lunch at the clubhouse one day with junior, he mentioned that he had just signed up to play for a fledgling "Team Tennis" league that would draft the top pros to play

---

[†] Secretariat souvenirs were all the rage that summer, so much so that one groomer set up a bizarre tchotchke table near a fountain that dispensed famous Saratoga Springs mineral water, and placed atop it were dozens of brown paper bags, behind which a sign that explained "Secretariat Manure — $3 per bag."

[‡] At stud in Kentucky, Secretariat sired as many as 600 foals, including a number of major stakes winners, e.g. 1986 Horse of the Year, Lady's Secret, 1988 Preakness and Belmont Stakes winner, Risen Star, and the 1990 Melbourne Cup winner, Kingston Rule, who broke the course record in Australia's richest race. He also sired General Assembly, who won the 1979 Travers Stakes at Saratoga while setting a still-standing race record of 2:00 flat. His grandchildren: 2004 Kentucky Derby and Preakness winner Smarty Jones, Secretariat turned out to be a noted broodmare sire, being the broodmare sire of 1992 Horse of the Year and successful sire A.P. Indy. In 1989, at age 19, Big Red was euthanized after he acquired the painful, and usually incurable hoof infection, laminitis.

for sixteen franchised teams during the tennis tour winter off-season (he would eventually land with the Pittsburgh Triangles.) He added that that Jimmy Connors and Bjorn Borg were considering coming aboard. Billie Jean King[§], John Newcombe, and Rod Laver were among the league's other early signees.

My "Aha!" moment came when I returned to Baltimore and saw an article in the *Baltimore Sun* noting that one such World Team Tennis (WTT) team would be located in Baltimore, playing out of the Baltimore Civic Center.[**] Two prominent local lawyers had bought the franchise for $250,000 – big bucks in 1973.

That was it — I had to weasel my way into this operation.

I visited the lawyers/owners' downtown office — the team had no headquarters yet — and inquired about staff positions. The only thing that seemed to be remotely applicable was in Public Relations. A local TV personality had been hired to be the director of PR, but he was looking for an assistant director. The bad news was that the lawyers had been flooded with inquiries and applications. I filled out an application and left, wondering how I could separate myself from the pack. By now I had met more than my share of talented, soon-to-be-famous, people, and the thought occurred that perhaps a glowing letter of recommendation from one of them might do the trick. The trouble was that they weren't famous enough yet; Michael Hedges, Biff Rose, John Waters, even Vitas, would have little purchase with high-priced lawyers who needed someone with a special skill. I needed another "Soft Shoes" McGuirk. Then it occurred to me that there was one *extremely* famous person for whom I had busted my butt for free for a year in just such a PR capacity. Perhaps a recommendation from the recent Democratic Presidential nominee would grab their attention.

I cleaned up as best as possible and drove down the same B-W Parkway that was becoming my main thoroughfare. I have always felt fortunate to live in such proximity to the seat of government power, and I had taken full advantage of it over the years. In those days, as hard as it is to imagine now, it was relatively easy to meet with one's national representative. In the era that predated the infestation of thousands of professional lobbyists, the halls of the Senate office

---

[§] Elton John immediately began work on a theme song for Billie's team, the "Philadelphia Freedoms."

[**] The WTT would oversee a 44-contest season, with teams comprised of at least two men and two women. A match consisted of the first player or team to win five games, with a 9 point tiebreaker at 4-all, and no-ad scoring in: women's singles and doubles, men's singles and doubles, and mixed doubles.

buildings were relatively tranquil, save the "citizen lobbyists" there to promote a cause, such as ending the war, or having the documents on the Kennedy assassination released. Many were the time I had showed up unannounced to call on senior staff and occasional senators or congressmen to vent my own views.

I walked into the office of George McGovern, Democratic Senator from South Dakota, and told the secretary about my work on the campaign, and wondered if and when I might speak to the senator briefly. Luckily the Senate was in session, and I was told that when there was a break in the floor action — perhaps in a couple of hours — I could stop back and take my chances. She gave me a gallery pass and I proceeded to bide my time watching the tedious floor debate from above. When the break came, I raced back to George's office on the congressional subway and was waiting when he arrived. His secretary brought him over to me, and he immediately (or so he claimed) remembered me. I described my predicament, and he laughed and said something like: "If you think a recommendation from someone on the losing side of one of the biggest landslides in American history can be helpful, I think you're crazy — but I'm happy to do it."

We then walked back to George's inner office with his secretary. George said, "So, Gus, what should we say?" With that I dictated the most gushing letter imaginable, which George only slightly amended. After a hearty "Thanks!" I went with the secretary and waited as she typed it up.

I hand-delivered the McGovern endorsement to the lawyers' office and was hired on the spot (I assume they were Democrats). Soon, the new "Baltimore Banners" WTT franchise set up offices on the top floor of the Baltimore Civic Center. In our first staff meeting I suggested something I was passionate about: spreading the gospel of the greatest sport to the inner city youth. It was obvious that a sport as wonderful as tennis should not be the provenance of the country club set (as it now was), I told the owners, and the best shot the Banners had for success was to give it the same blue collar support as Baltimore's other pro sports teams. But that sort of fandom could only happen if the kids actually *played* the sport, and there were precious few tennis courts in the inner city. For a strapped city like Baltimore, it was a matter of economics: 78 precious feet of open city real estate could entertain ten or more basketball players or four tennis players.

Like Vitas, I was lucky to have found this game in a country caught up in team sports like baseball, football, and basketball. But at least those sports appealed to the melting pot. The paradox of so many formerly blue-collar tennis greats (Gonzales, King, Gerulaitis, Laver, Connors, Borg, etc.) entertaining only country clubbers at West Side reminded me just a bit of Ancient Rome — the stadium even resembled the Coliseum. I also saw the looks on the faces of the poor kids at my Gold Cup center who were stunned by the mental and physical challenges of this strange game. It was obvious to me that the sport could explode if some of the great inner city athletes took up tennis instead of a more traditional sport, and I dreamt of seeing the Civic Center overflowing with multi-cultural, multi-colored fans. It was agreed that I would spearhead an agenda that promoted the team, and the game, to the Mayor's office and the city's recreation and school boards.

Walter "Bud" Freeman, former Orioles promotion director, was brought in as Executive Director for the franchise, but I was most excited by the hiring of Aussie Davis Cup champ, 45- year-old Don Candy, who had played with Laver under the militaristic training of Vitas's coach, Harry Hopman. "The Candy Man" was a typical amber-drinking, storytelling, fun-loving Aussie, who had somehow ended up in the Baltimore suburb of Towson teaching at the Orchard Tennis Club. Often, before the workday began, Don would placate the owners and me with a round of doubles at Orchard. After these matches he would meet with a pair of 12-year-old wunderkinds, named Pammy and Elise for their intense "Hopman-style" workouts. Pammy, or "Curly Top," who stayed with Candy from age nine to twenty-four, was Pam Shriver, the fourth cousin of Maria, whom I had chauffeured during the McGovern campaign a year earlier. Her more diminutive pal was named Elise Burgin.

"Curly Top" Shriver

Interestingly, in junior competition two years later, Pammy was using one of Howard Head's jumbo basement creations that he had given to Candy. Two years after that (1978), the 16-year-old made it to the US Open final against Chris Evert, turning heads with her 6'2" height and her monstrous racquet. I hope Howard Head's bank was kind to her, because the success this unknown Baltimorean had on that day, with that frame, propelled the now green-painted monster into becoming one of the best-selling racquets ever. Both Elise and Pammy went on to have stellar pro careers, especially Pammy, who captured 21 singles and 112 doubles titles throughout her career, one of only five women to have won more than 100 career titles. With partner Martina Navratilova, she was part of one of the greatest women's doubles teams of all time.

The New Year 1974 started off with a bang. I had been toiling in the vineyards, giving clinics at schools with some of our players (Audrey Morse, Kristy Pigeon, Bob Carmichael, Betty Stove, etc.), when word reached that the Banners had signed our number one draft choice – and the number one player in the world — twenty-one-year-old pal of Vitas's, Jimmy Connors.

But behind the big announcement was a secret: the team was so anxious to make a deal that they allowed Connors to play whenever he felt like it, earning $3,000 a match ($14,000 today), win or lose. Of course, all Jimmy's expenses were paid, including an apartment, car, etc. I helped Jimmy move into his $300/month Towson apartment and drove him around the city once, but didn't really get to know him, as he was rarely in

speaking of sports—

It's the tennis racket!

The Baltimore Banners, a new World Team Tennis entry, held a tennis clinic at Harper's Choice Middle School last Thursday. Banner member Gus Russo (above), who handles public relations for the team, and tennis star Audrey Morse (below) were on hand to show Columbia youngsters the basics. The Banners meet Hawaii for their opening match of the season, May 6 at the Civic Center.

town. He skipped out on probably 60 or 70% of the matches — he was too busy training for the majors, courting Chris Evert, or had other sundry excuses. On two occasions I got the chance to trade ground strokes with Jimmy, once when he wanted to try out our synthetic court surface. Unlike today's loopy topspin game, Jimmy's strokes were like lasers, often with a bit of sidespin, taking them off the court. He was kind enough to hit down to my level, but it was clear to both of us that he could probably hit a winner at will.

One of the perks of my job was that, as a tenant of the Civic Center, I could come and go as I pleased, day or night, for concerts, concert rehearsals, sporting events, you name it. Between all the events I had crashed there previously and the shows I saw now for free as a tenant, I feel the need to say, "Thank you, Civic Center!" I made certain that the guards who worked the backstage door knew me and liked me, just in case my job ended prematurely — a good move, it would turn out.

A few days after the Connors signing I attended one of those many freebies, the January 28, 1974 Ali-Frazier rematch on closed circuit. This time I sat — with no broom — up in a restricted top level with the other Banner executive staff and watched the comparatively lackluster fight. Days before the bout, Ali had typically derided and goaded Frazier, calling him "ignorant," and this time it seemed to unravel the champ; Ali won in a decision. On another occasion, when the Harlem Globetrotters were in town, I planned a surprise for my 10-year-old brother Bob, who was turning into something of a wizard on his grade school basketball team, the Bulls. On a Saturday afternoon, I told him to dress in his sweat clothes and jump in the car, as he had so often before (Bob had been a regular guinea pig of mine as an eight-year-old, accompanying me to my Gold Cup center for tennis lessons. A natural athlete, he won his age group in my year-end tournament, despite never holding a racquet before.) I also picked up my little niece, Angela, then a tomboyish b-ball player herself.

As we walked into the Civic Center, empty save for a dozen or so black basketball players warming up, Bob went speechless when he recognized his Trotter idols, Fred "Curly" Neal, George "Meadowlark" Lemon, and Hubert "Geese" Ausbie. I walked Bob onto the court and Geese threw a ball at him and said, "Let's go one-on-one." Now Geese had no idea that this 3-ft.-nothing pipsqueak was a natural, and the star of his midget league. Bob took control of the ball, dribbled out just beyond the foul line, then turned, and threw up a one-hand jumper in Ausbie's face. The ball sailed over the six-footer, and swished.

"I quit, you're too good!" Geese said. Meadowlark and Curly posed for pictures with the kids, and then Curly taught Bob how to spin a ball on his finger and signed a wrist sweatband before we headed back home. Now the kicker is, Bob would wear that lucky sweatband to every Bulls game, even though his sweat caused Curly's autograph to run and fade into a blue blur. I remember when he'd proudly show off

Bob with Curly Neal

Angela and Bob meet Meadowlark

the memento to friends, who just had to take it on faith that the unintelligible inky stain was actually Curly's signature. But he still has the photo to prove it.

I wish all the Civic Center behind-the-scenes had been as much fun. To get to the Banner offices every morning, I entered the center on the ground floor backstage entrance, through the main arena hall over to the elevators, which I'd take to the top floor. Often I'd see a sound crew setting up for a concert, or the Zamboni machine getting the ice ready for a show or hockey

Bob practicing a trick Curly showed him

game — our tennis season had not yet begun. I'll never forget the day I came to work and got a whiff that almost knocked me out as soon as I entered the building: the circus was in town. What was far more sickening than the fecal stench of the livestock was the stench of their human trainers.

On that day my eyes were opened to the cruelty inflicted on the lower species by humans. I had always loved animals, but for some reason had never considered their plight. Watching the circus "trainers" as they put the horses through their paces running in the ring while whacking them in the shins with a two by four *on every rotation*, just to get them to fear their captors, made me ill. The elephants were put into submission by hitting them between the eyes with a brick. During my lunch break I visited the animals in their dirty stalls, and the forlorn look in their eyes tore my heart out. I have not been to a circus, zoo, national aquarium, or anywhere animals are caged, since that day. The experience led me to add these prisons to my protest list, and to become a donor to animal rights organizations. It also began a lifelong quest to determine if *Homo sapiens* are really all we're cracked up to be. The evidence, as I see it, isn't encouraging.

My favorite times working for the Banners were whenever the Pittsburgh Triangles, with Vitas, Ken Rosewall, and the beautiful 1971 Wimbledon champ Evonne Goolagong (yes, I had a major crush) came to town. After the matches, I took Vitas, Ken, Evonne, and our coach Don Candy out for some Foster's Lager at, where else, the Peabody Book Shop and Beer Stube. Watching the former Aussie Davis Cup teammates tie one on and swap tall tales was quite an eye-opener. Evonne, an Aussie with aboriginal roots, was no teetotaler either.

I thought it odd that Vitas usually had a Coke or 7-Up, but I was soon to find out that my friend was entering a dark time in his life regarding recreational drugs, especially cocaine; he didn't need the Foster's. By this time, Vitas had tuned into the all-time greatest partying bachelor, always surrounded by the most beautiful women at New York's Studio 54, where he was crowned "club pro." In Pittsburgh, he acquired the nickname "The Lithuanian Lion," for his manic partying as much as for his tennis. Vitas made the local news when he ordered the public-address announcer at the Pittsburgh Civic Arena to invite the crowd of nearly 11,000 to proceed from a match to his 20th birthday observance at a nearby hotel, where he had reserved the top floor. The result: heavy partying and at least one broken bathtub.

"Gus, you gotta' come visit me in Pittsburgh," Vitas implored. "There are more girls than I know what to do with. They wait for me in the lobby of my condo." For reasons I'll never know, I never made the trek to the Steel City — another adventure, like Woodstock (but perhaps more hedonistic), I didn't get around to, and I'll always regret it.

Vitas would go on to win, among others, the 1975 Wimbledon men's doubles crown (with Sandy Mayer) and the 1977 Australian Open men's singles title.

With the added income from endorsements, he bought a mansion in King's Point — a fitting roost for King Vitas — near the Long Island north shore, where he lived (when he was actually home) with his parents and sister.

His sister Ruta described the period to the press: "After Vitas won [his first ATP tournament] in Vienna in 1974, IMG [his management agency] told him to take the $150,000 and invest in a house. We moved from [blue collar] Howard Beach to [upscale] Kings Point. We were like the Beverly Hillbillies. We all moved into the house, including my grandparents, who lived above us in Howard Beach. The house had a tennis court and this little pool that was shaped like a tennis racquet. We were all part of the package. Where he went, we would go. Our lives changed very quickly." At the new home, Mrs. G treated Vitas's friends like family, and Borg like another son. As she had done for me, and all Vitas's pals in Howard Beach, she did Bjorn's laundry and gave him home cooked meals.

The Gerulaitises in the Seventies

Custom improvements to the new digs included an enlarged garage to house his collection of six luxury vehicles, including his iconic, mustard-yellow Rolls Royce Silver Wraith. But lest you get the wrong idea, one other thing must be said about Vitas: He was also the most generous person I have ever met. He was also quick to entertain and make everybody happy (his idol was Năstase). More about that later.

One day, out of left field, the Banners' owners invited the front office to an evening in New York City, all expenses paid. We would train up and attend a black-tie Broadway opening night and cast party. Unbeknownst to me, the attorney-owners were also minor investors in Broadway shows; two years earlier they had stakes in the mega-hit *Grease*, which must have made them a trainload of money. On March 6, 1974, they had a new show opening entitled *Over Here!*, starring the Andrews Sisters. I wanted to do this in style, so I shallowly decided to ask the most gorgeous girl I had yet seen in Baltimore to be my date. At the time, I was moonlighting some nights as a soundman for one of

Baltimore's top club bands, the Diablos; I was trying to learn more about audio and production, in expectation of producing my own music one day. At one of the best clubs we played, I had been flirting, somewhat fruitlessly, with Gail, a bartender who was a dead ringer for my all-time fav, Natalie Wood. For some strange reason, she didn't have a boyfriend — should have told me something — and for an even stranger reason, she said she'd love to go for the overnight.

On the train ride up, at least four guys made passes at Gail, even though she was obviously there with a date (me) — she was that ridiculously beautiful. One guy interrupted us in the dining car, and handed Gail his card, saying, "Excuse me, but if this guy (me) doesn't work out, would you please give me a call?" I had never seen anything like it. She was like a candle attracting moths. This craziness would not abate for the rest of the trip.

After checking into our Times Square hotel and changing into our formal duds — Gail was easily the most stunning girl that night — we strolled over to the Shubert Theater to catch the show. The "plot" — the two surviving sisters looking for a third voice — was just an excuse to play great Big Band music. After years of Blue Water Manor debacles, it was quite a revelation to see what Broadway shows were actually supposed to look like. Instead of a curtain call, the Andrews Sisters came out to the center of the proscenium and sang many of their hits. Great fun — except for the rented monkey suit that had me squirming in my seat by this time.

After the show we made our way across to Sardi's Restaurant for the party, where I wasn't high enough in the food chain to spend much time with the Andrews Sisters, so I settled for having cocktails with some of the bit players. John, the kid who played "Misfit," and sang the song "Dream Drummin," showed a lot of interest in — you guessed it — Gail. When he was chatting with her I spoke with a striking friend of his from the cast named Marilu. Both these hoofers had small roles in *Grease* two years before. The frivolity came to a screeching halt, when, in what must be roar-of-the-greasepaint tradition, everyone raced over to the small television set to watch Clive Barnes give his instant review on the local Ten o'Clock News. You could have heard a pin drop in Sardi's; in those days, the wrong word from the almighty Barnes could literally put a show out of business the next day. It was not a great review — somewhat mixed-to-good — but some of his accolades left the cast cheering. †† (In print the next day, Barnes wrote paradoxically, "As a musical it is preposterously bad, but also preposterously engaging.")

Within two years, "Misfit" John Travolta would see his career explode, with starring roles in *Welcome Back, Kotter* and *Carrie*, followed by *Grease* (the movie), *Saturday Night Fever*, and on ad infinitum (Yeah, but I went back to the hotel with Gail. So there!) And in 1978 his redheaded friend Marilu Henner would become a television staple in the hit series *Taxi*. Another *Over Here!* alum whose career soon took off was Treat Williams, who landed a lead role in *Hair* in 1979. The show also initiated my interest in Broadway shows (I was already into off-Broadway, courtesy of Brel), and a lifelong love of big band swing. When I returned home I thus began listening to a new guitar giant, Count Basie's legendary Freddie Green, the heartbeat of the band. I had to learn how to re-voice chords still one more time. I guess it never ends.

Marilu Henner and John Travolta

Back in the real world, the WTT was hemorrhaging money long before the first matches, and its failure to land a national TV contract made the situation all but impossible. There was also expensive litigation with the International Lawn Tennis Association, which was banning our players from competing in the French and Italian Opens. Jimmy was especially hard hit because that year he won Wimbledon, Australia, and the US Open, but was prevented from completing the Slam by the French ban. As the owners got frantic to sell season tickets, which were sagging terribly, all interest in urban youth tennis was dropped in favor of wine tastings at country clubs. Consequently, I lost all interest in WTT. The final straw for me came after our wonderful, and competent, office manager, Melanie, was fired, only to be replaced by a centerfold-style babe with a fraction of Mel's skill and personality.

On the early May opening night, Connors and the Banners beat the Hawaii Leis before a paltry announced Civic Center attendance of 2,722 — with nary an urban youth in the audience. The next match boasted an embarrassing 761 patrons in the cavernous arena. Similar totals were felt around the league. One wag wrote that,

---

†† *Over Here!* ran for about a year, and there has always been talk of a revival. In 2010, LA's Saban Theater announced the show would indeed get a new staging, with *Hannah Montana* star Cody Linley in one of the lead roles.

"There were more people on the team bench than in the stands." The situation was all the more remarkable because tennis was exploding everywhere but in the WTT. With staggering purses and attractive stars, the seventies were the golden age of tennis. After the September 20, 1973 (nationally televised) "Battle of the Sexes"[‡‡] between court hustler Bobby Riggs and Billie Jean King, racquet sales exploded, and every Hollywood celebrity had his personal court and tennis coach. But with the inner cities uninterested and horrible management,[§§] the WTT managed to snatch defeat from the jaws of victory.

The writing on the wall, I resigned early in the debut season, and Executive Director Bud Freeman left even before me. In the fall of 1974, after the Banners traded the big-ticket Connors to Pittsburgh, the Baltimore entry folded. Three years later, the Baltimore team owners were indicted on 27 counts of mail fraud involving false medical insurance claims; one was convicted and sentenced to five years in federal prison, while the other cooperated. Following the 1978 season, every WTT franchise but two folded, and the league ceased operations completely on March 8, 1979. Billie Jean King would get a new Team Tennis league going in 1981, but with tighter budgets and lesser-known players. It is still in existence, far below the sports radar. Despite our differences, two years after I resigned, owner Gerry Klauber was kind enough to write me a job recommendation.

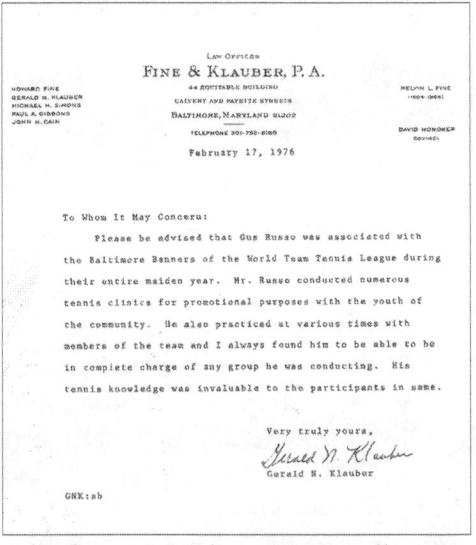

[‡‡] Twelve years later, at age 67, Riggs returned to the tennis spotlight when he partnered with my pal Vitas to launch another challenge to the opposite sex. His return to the public eye was short lived, however, when the men lost their doubles match against Martina Navratilova and Howard Head's muse Pammy Shriver.
[§§] The league was not particularly well run with four league presidents in four years and the joke in early 1976 was that the league would hire Sid Caesar so that they could claim they had had a Kaiser (Jordan), Fuhrer (Frank), King (Larry), and a Caesar as president.

My Team Tennis career kaput, I next considered investigative reporting as a backstop to my ongoing musical aspirations. It was a romantic notion during the era when the *Washington Post*'s Woodward & Bernstein were — it turned out mistakenly — lionized for their Watergate reportage. While at UMBC I had met the iconic syndicated columnist Jack Anderson, who had addressed my poli-sci class. Known to give many a youth their journalistic starts, Jack was very down-to-earth and approachable in the class, so now I decided to approach him in the real world. Jack sent back a personal response saying that he would keep me on file for future openings. (In fact, a decade later, Jack would be true to his word and give me my first work as a paid investigator.)

JACK ANDERSON
1612 K Street, N.W. Washington, D.C. 20006

May 20, 1974

Dear Mr. Russo:

Thank you for your recent letter and impressive resume. I don't have any vacancies on my staff at the present time. However, I've placed your application in the files and will be in touch with you should the situation change.

With best wishes,

Sincerely,

Jack Anderson

Mr. Gus Russo
213 Boswell Road
Baltimore, Maryland 21229

Chapter Eleven

A Magical Time in a Magical Place

"JUST THROW YOUR racquets and guitar in the car and get your ass *up* here!"

That was the command of one of my Lake George singing partners, Will Beemer. "Here" was Ithaca, a tiny 'burg in western New York State, about which I knew absolutely nothing other than it was a college town — exactly one thing more than I knew about Greece's Ithaca. Will had just relocated to Ithaca from the Arizona desert, where he was a construction foreman for environmental architecture visionary Paolo Soleri. Seventy miles north of Phoenix, Soleri and his band of volunteers were laboring to build Arcosanti, the world's first town (capable of housing 5,000) in total harmony with its environment. Now, Will had relocated to Ithaca's Cornell University to get his masters in the nascent field of "arcology," and Cornell had the best post-grad program in the field. But what Will hadn't anticipated was that in the 1970s Ithaca just happened to be the East Coast's version of San Francisco's Haight-Ashbury, albeit without the publicity and notoriety. Now his musical passions came to the fore.

Upstate New York, especially the zone about 100 miles northwest of Manhattan, had seen an influx of musicians, artists, and writers after the Woodstock festival. Among the new residents were Bob Dylan, The Band, Todd Rundgren, Thelonius Monk, David Bowie, Johnny Cash, Fagen and Becker (Steely Dan), Van Morrison, Pat Metheny, Bonnie Raitt, King Harvest, Orleans, and Carlos Santana. They were in addition to the countless less famous *artistes* who made the pilgrimage.

What wasn't as well known was that "the zone" reached its western boundary in Ithaca, 170 miles away, with a lot of concert clubs ("the circuit") in between. And because it was so confined (six square miles), Ithaca made for an even more exciting artistic and intellectual primordial soup than rural Woodstock. A scribe for the *Ithaca Journal* described it this way:

> "Ithaca's music scene rocked with such incredible intensity back in the 1970s that time seemed to swirl into one long sonic

joyride. An endless procession of major rock, soul, jazz, blues, reggae and folk performers passed through town in those days. Local bands used to pack clubs on a regular basis, and the pulsating environment produced groups who went on to garner national attention like Orleans, McKendree Spring, Elf, Country Cooking and the Rods. The counterculture was in full swing."

Of course, Orleans featured John Hall, a casual Baltimore acquaintance and the brother of my St. Joe classmate Jerry Hall. In Ithaca, John had formed his new band with former members of the super-talented Ithaca group Boffalongo, which wrote and recorded the first version of "Dancing in the Moonlight".* Former Ithacan talents included Harry Chapin, who wrote "College Town" about Ithaca, and Peter Yarrow, of Peter, Paul and Mary fame. Both Harry and Peter were Cornell undergrads who played at Johnny's Big Red Grill pizza house in C-Town. Ithacan guitarist Russ Barenberg joined with Peter Wernick, Tony Trischka, Kenny Kosek and John Miller to form the influential "new grass" group Country Cooking. In later years, Barenburg formed Fiddle Fever, whose recording of "Ashokan Farewell" was later used as the centerpiece for the soundtrack to Ken Burns' celebrated PBS documentary, The Civil War.

In Trumansburg, just to the north, inventor Robert Moog was beginning to market the Minimoog keyboard, a portable version of his Moog Synthesizer, first used on albums like *Switched-on Bach, Innervisions,* and *Abbey Road.* First-class musicians from around the world came to study at The School of Music at Ithaca College. Thanks to these international players, musical experimentation in Ithaca was rampant, leading to what became known as "The Ithaca Sound."†

Perhaps the earliest evidence of Ithaca's cultural impact was at the dawn of the 20th century, when the town was the center of the silent film industry, specializing in the use of its many gorges for "cliffhanger" serials. In those days, the town was nicknamed "Sodom," due to its reputation as a town of "notorious immorality," a place of horse racing, gambling, profanity, Sabbath breaking, and readily available liquor.

---

* Sherman Kelly, brother of Orleans drummer Wells Kelly, wrote the song in St. Croix while recovering from a near fatal mugging in 1969. Painfully laid up, Sherman was imagining "dancing in the moonlight."
† In recent years, notable foreign musicians who have relocated to Ithaca include Samite of Uganda, Mamadou Diabaté of Mali, and Malang Jobateh of Senegal.

In addition to musicians, artists, and filmmakers, Ithaca's intellectual heritage was fairly bursting at the seams with alumni such as Kurt Vonnegut[‡], Vladimir Nabokov, who based *Lolita* on schoolgirl conversations he overheard while riding Ithaca busses, and Alex Haley of *Roots* fame. The Nobel Prize winning head of the atomic bomb "Manhattan Project," Hans Bethe taught in Ithaca, as did his Nobel winning protégé, physicist Richard Feynman. Still there in the seventies were the *Twilight Zone*'s Rod Serling, who lived on Cayuga Lake and taught at Ithaca College, and astronomer Carl Sagan, teaching at Cornell. Predictably, with all its artists, intellectuals, and students (who, during the school year, swelled the population from 25, 000 to 50,000), Ithaca was and is perhaps the most liberal, and tolerant, city in the US. A popular local bumper sticker from the seventies read: "Ithaca: Six square miles surrounded by reality." In 1997, the perception of the city's uniqueness still held sway, when the *Utne Reader* named Ithaca "America's most enlightened town."

Of course Ithaca's main economic and cultural engines were the two hilltop schools separated by a couple of deep gorges: Cornell University, the engineering, hotel administration, and agricultural powerhouse, and Ithaca College, known for it's music and communication schools (the first female network news anchor Jessica Savitch was a famous alum.) Two decades earlier, my childhood hero, Gardner McKay ("Adam Troy" of the hit TV show *Adventures in Paradise*) had attended Cornell and earned a degree in art. Together, the non-sectarian "Godless university," Cornell, and the hard-partying coeds of IC contributed to the town's "City of Evil" nickname.

OK, so Will didn't tell me all this in his phone call (I'm sure the Pratt Library had something to do with it), but I could hear it in his voice: this place was special and I'd be crazy if I didn't hit the road. The icing on the cake was the fact that Will's new local friends, Bob Davis and Rich Krasnoff, were opening a premier concert venue, and with our third voice, Ak, making his way there from Montana, we were promised that we'd be the closest thing to the house band, opening for some of the most talented performers of the day.

Since my career as a team tennis exec had imploded in record time, and since Ithaca seemed like "the place to be," my first reaction was that I had no excuse for not migrating north and devoting myself to music full-time. No other excuse than "growing up," perhaps. I was

---

[‡] His books *Player Piano*, *Slaughterhouse-Five*, and *Cat's Cradle* all refer to Ithaca.

at that crossroads that all college grads experience, and although the majority of my classmates were well on their way to adulthood, getting a real job, getting married, etc., I and a few other Boomers still held onto a childlike curiosity — about everything — with little regard to the consequences, financial or otherwise. We were the first generation of young people to have the world practically handed to us. What to do with this amazing gift was the real question.

In addition to my fictional heroes, most of the real people I associated with or related to — Biff Rose, John Waters, Vitas Gerulaitis and the other pros, and countless great musicians — were all non-conformists, and seemed happier — and more alive — to me than my peers who were starting to move up the corporate ladder, taking out mortgages, and adding to the population explosion. The pressure on young men fresh out of college in the early seventies — I can't comment on today — was intense. The fork in the road was as clear as day, and the vast majority chose the conventional direction. To each their own; I make no judgments. We all struggle with the meaning of life, and honestly, none of us can claim to know the answer for certain. So, in the end we just follow our instincts and hope for the best. Some of us, for better or worse, also follow our bliss.

For me and my instinct, the choice was the definition of a no-brainer: I made a beeline for Western Auto and bought a road map that would lead me to Ithaca in the short term, but down the road less traveled in perpetuity. Will Beemer wasn't just inviting me to Ithaca, he was daring me to be bold — or crazy, I'm still not sure. So for all of you who wondered what it might have been like to live like a 20th century Siddhartha or Huckleberry Finn, hold on to your hats. The real adventure is just beginning.

Two tennis racquets, one guitar, and one suitcase later, I was off on the 300-mile drive through Pennsylvania coal country to Ithaca — once again moving to a place I had never seen. My mother remembers running down the street behind my car, imploring me to change my mind — in her insulated fantasy world, her children never left home. In contrast to Beemer, my mother had been encouraging me to become a sales manager at Rexall Drug Store two blocks from home (seriously). Her love was never taken for granted or unappreciated, but the sad reality was that if there were ever a poster child for the person who loves too hard, it would be my mom, whom I have never known to have any life outside her children. And I don't say that casually: no hobbies, no vocation, nothing. It wouldn't be a stretch to conclude that the subliminal fuel for my wanderlust came from my not wanting to end up like my father, bitter over the theft of a brilliant musical career, and my mother, practically housebound. That and the groupies.

On first sighting Ithaca, I was taken with its odd, yet natural beauty. The city was founded on "the flats," just south of the "finger lake" called Lake Cayuga, which drains to the north, and was itself formed behind the dam of a moraine that in turn forms dozens of glacial gorges, now loaded with world-renowned fossils. Some of the gorges still flow streams, usually with several waterfalls, such as Buttermilk Falls and Taughannock Falls. The city spread out to the adjacent hillsides (East Hill, West Hill, and South Hill), which, separated by the gorges, rise several hundred feet above the central flats, and on which sit the colleges.

I was quickly struck by the metaphor of the Ivy League students physically looking down on the salt-of-the-earth locals, with whom they rarely socialized. Ithaca's Blue Collar natives, not unlike Baltimorons, toiled in factories like the Ithaca Gun Company, the Morse Chain Company, and National Cash Register (NCR), while the students just studied and partied. Having attended a commuter school, I had never experienced the "collegetown" zeitgeist, but here it was, in all its philosophic and geographic depiction.

After settling into the guest room of Will's friends who taught at Cornell, I surveyed the town, and within days our trio was rehearsing in a beautiful restored barn at the back of the house. We worked hard on a 50-50 combination of original material and country rock covers. On hot days we'd repair to Potter's Falls, at the foot of Six Mile Gorge near the Ithaca Reservoir, where Hippie coeds sunbathed in the nude on giant boulders, taking the occasional illegal skinny dip. At the top of one gorge sat Eddy Street, in the heart of Collegetown, where Cornell students seemed to fall into two polar opposite categories: hard-partying frat boys and overly serious students who advertised themselves by the ever-present slide rules that didn't quite fit into their pockets. Many of the engineering students were Asians, under almost unconscionable pressure to get top grades, and almost on a monthly basis, one of these kids, distraught over a bad test score, would "gorge out" — jumping off one of the hundred foot cliffs to their deaths. These events were almost never reported in the news, but were the talk of Collegetown.§

---

§ After a period of decline in the Cornell suicide rate in the nineties, the numbers have sadly begun to spike in 2010.
See:http://www.theithacajournal.com/apps/pbcs.dll/article?AID=20103170399

Back in the barn, our only concern was the bane of every new band: coming up with a name. Since our sound was strongly influenced by bands like Poco, New Riders of the Purple Sage, the Flying Burrito Brothers, and other country-rockers, we began looking at maps of the western US for inspiration. Then it hit me that a great name would be the title of a song from John Stewart's most recent album release, an absolute masterpiece entitled *Cannons in the Rain*.** I had the vinyl on constant repeat playback, wearing out the grooves of the mesmerizing album. The track I had in mind recounted John's competition with Kris Kristofferson for a role in the Sam Peckinpah movie *Pat Garrett and Billie the Kid,* and John named the tune after the Colorado town where the film was shot. Thus we became "Durango." (Kristofferson became "The Kid.")

There were some setbacks in our master plan: the Unicorn Club was months behind on its opening, due to zoning issues over a noise variance. This circumstance saw us living very close to the bone — lots of peanut butter, tuna, and pasta — during those first months. After I moved into a commune on Buffalo Street in the flats, I was tipped by some locals that the local grocery giant, The Grand Union, placed unsold food out on the loading dock on certain nights for pickup the next morning by haulers. I remember my roomies and I setting our alarms to beat the truckers to the dock's huge boxes of non-perishables. For the better part of one year, we dined on ingenious variations of Velveeta Cheese, Doritos, and Ramen Noodles, all washed down by a glass of sugar water that went by the name of Wyler's Lemonade. We must have had a thousand free meals that year, but not one with any nutritional value.

** The album was produced by the great Nashville guitarist (and father of singer Deana Carter), Fred Carter, Jr. In addition to touring with Roy Orbison, Carter appeared on countless Simon & Garfunkle tracks, playing, among others, the iconic opening riff from "The Boxer."

Eventually my body demanded real food. Thus, for the first and only time in my life, I applied for unemployment insurance, based on my work for the Banners. (In line at the Ithaca unemployment office I met Marty Slutsky, the great guitarist from McKendree Spring.[††]) The compensation negotiations would be protracted, with me having to make a few trips to the Baltimore office over the next few months to get paperwork. Eventually Durango started gigging at places like the Stables Inn on Dryden Road and the legendary Rongovian Embassy in Trumansburg, and word got out that there was a new band in town, starting us on a great run. For bigger shows, we enlisted pedal steel virtuoso Jay Ganz and bassist Howie Kates.

The Rongo, by the way, had its own colorful history. Founded by Orleans manager Alex "Brooksie" Brooks in 1973, the Embassy featured a bartender named Ricky Jay, who had mastered the art of card throwing. From behind the bar he entertained by flinging playing cards fifty feet or more, hitting small targets, including spots on the map of "Rongovia," across the room. "During the daytime," Brooksie recently recalled, "Ricky taught the T-burg street urchins to hit the hubcaps of moving cars that passed through town on Rt. 96 with thrown standard playing cards. I remember one day arriving at the Rongo with the street littered with many decks of cards."[‡‡] Two doors down from the Rongo was Cosmos Vegetarian Restaurant, at a time when veggie restaurants were practically unheard of.

Word about Durango not only got out to the music lovers, but also to the musician's union (Local 132), which in those days seemed to have a vise grip on most of the good venues in New York state. We

---

[††] Slutsky went on to be the executive producer for the past two presidential debates as well as a technical manager for ABC, NBC, Discovery and FOX. He has won seven Emmy awards for technical excellence in the 1988 and 2002 Winter Olympic Games, 1989 New York Marathon, 1989 World Series and is still securing all technical aspects of countless television productions.

[‡‡] Ricky and Brooksie had previously been fellow Cornell students in the School of Hotel Administration. After graduation, Ricky worked in a rock club in St. Thomas that was opened by Brooksie, who adds, "While working the floor with slight of hand card tricks Ricky was attacked by a group of British Marines (who didn't like being so soundly tricked) and he decided to learn karate (back in Ithaca) for self defense. While doing that he opened the infamous "Deja Vue" nightclub on Seneca and Aurora."

were essentially forced to join, or there would be no work. And if we tried to work without a card—well, we'd just better not try it. Our friend from Blue Water Manor, the insanely talented Bill Gable, had told us about his frightening union experience in Niagara Falls. Traveling from Boston, where the union was not a force, for a four-night stand at the Holiday Inn, Bill was approached by a group of swarthy muscle men at the end of his first show. They asked to see his (non-existent) union card, and then told him that if he failed to join the Niagara Falls local immediately, he'd better not show up the next night.

Durango at the Rongo

Keep in mind, Bill rarely played in New York anyway, so the demand was just plain old extortion against a guy stuck 500 miles from home. To make matters worse, the exorbitant initiation fees and first-year dues would eat up 90% of his gig fee. Thus the conundrum: if he didn't play, he couldn't afford the gas home, and if he did play and pay the union "fees," he'd have only enough to get back to Boston, with no profit to show after four days work. Then the extortion turned into a threat: if Bill played again without joining up his hands would be broken so badly that he'd never play guitar again. The next day he joined. So did we.

Of course the union gave us absolutely no help when it came to booking jobs; it merely gave us the permission to *look* for work. (Gee, thanks.) While we waited for the Unicorn to open we continued to work the college scene — frat parties at Cornell, art openings at Ithaca College, and various bars in the flats. Other venues we covered were The Haunt and the North Forty. We played a Christmas Party for the local Hell's Angels chapter, who liked us so much that at 2 a.m. they ordered us to keep playing, regardless of the contract stipulation. At one gig, a diminutive man hauling a giant tuba made his way to the stage and asked if he could play some blues with us. And who were we to deny the great Rod Serling?

On Sunday afternoons I joined in great jam sessions at the Salty Dog, where John Hall and Orleans were regulars, as well as members of McKendree Spring, the Dean Brothers and the Zobo Funn Band. Speaking on behalf of his fellow Orleaneans, guitarist Larry Hoppen once said, "Ithaca is seminal to all of us." As far as I knew, John Hall and I were the only Baltimore musicians to migrate to Ithaca. There two years before me, John had already scored big when "Half Moon," a song he and his wife Johanna had written, was recorded by Janis Joplin on her *Pearl* album. They also had songs covered by Bonnie Raitt and Seals & Crofts. Throughout the seventies, his new band Orleans, based in Ithaca and Woodstock, cranked out some of the best rock songs in history. Among my favorites, many of which we saw them play in the Haunt and the Salty Dog, were "Dance With Me," "Let There Be Music," "Reach," "Power," "Love Takes Time," "Give One Heart," "Tongue Tied," and the song that made John wealthy in 1976, "Still the One."[§§]

Now here's the thing with me and John Hall: apparently we looked a lot alike at the time. We were both tall, lanky, with long faces and dark beards. We were mistaken for each other on the streets of Ithaca all the time. Whenever we'd bump into each other, John's first words were, "Are you John Hall?" To which I'd reply, "Yeah, are you Gus Russo?"

One of these guys is John Hall in the Seventies

Now I wouldn't bring this up except to say that there were some practical benefits to being mistaken for a local celebrity. My favorite perk was the girls who had a crush on the married John and were happy to settle for his look-alike. There was one special girl named Rocky… (Pardon me while I take a nostalgia break.)

OK — I'm back.

We became great friends with many of the local players, and I remember the listening parties thrown by the Brit-influenced Deans whenever Stevie Wonder released a new album. All the musicians would sit around the living room in stunned silence as we previewed albums such as *Innervisions* and *Fullfillingness First Finale*. Regardless of what genre we played, we all united behind a love of Stevie. He was also a great ego check for anyone who thought they were "all that." Another great party was held the night of August 8, 1974, when disgraced President Richard Nixon went on national television to announce his resignation. The booze and pot really flowed that celebratory evening.

[§§] According to Orleans guitarist Larry Hoppen, "Still The One" was inspired when someone that had been divorced, a friend of John and Johanna's, was over at their house and mentioned that everybody writes songs about breaking up, and it would be nice if somebody wrote something about staying together.

Will spent some of his afternoons exploiting the peculiar topography of the town — from 5,000 feet up! Due to its unique surface features, Ithaca is often covered in beautiful white cumulus clouds, magnets for hot air thermals, and therefore a Mecca for glider pilots. Will got his pilot's license and somehow persuaded me to be his first guinea pig — I mean passenger. That first ride was a mind-blower, since we caught so many thermal chimneys that we were up for hours, riding the columns up with the plane on its side, and my stomach in my mouth. Eventually I yelled "Enough!" and Will brought us down. But it was beautiful, up there silently with the birds and the clouds — BUT WITHOUT PARACHUTES. Landing was a bit of a heart-stopper, since a glider pilot has to perfectly judge his distance from the field and speed of descent, and since there is no power and no turning back; if you miscalculate, you hit a tree, or, more likely in Ithaca, a gorge cliff.

I spent much of my off time playing tennis, but when the brutal upstate winter arrived, I and my hitting partner Keith had to think of a way to keep working out. This was at the height of the 1970s "energy crisis," with gas lines, and conservation of lights and power. For years, thermostats were turned down across the country in efforts to forestall fuel shortages, and rooms were darkened the second they became unused.*** The sudden increase in energy costs mandated that indoor tennis courts had to raise their rates to a level we starving musicians could never afford. One winter day, while hitting against the wall inside Cornell's Barton Hall Field House, I noticed that, mixed in with the lines for basketball and volleyball on the rubberized floor, was the familiar outline of a tennis court. I was told that there was a net and posts, unused in years, in storage behind the bleachers. The question was: how could I, who didn't even attend the school, get to set that court up and use it — for free, no less?

Keith and I determined that there was no way we'd get in during the daytime, so we started coming by at night to case the joint. We learned that the last users of the building were the table tennis players, who broke their tables down after nine, then turned off the massive indoor lighting system. (I learned the hard way not to call them "ping-pong" players.) After they left, building security — basically one local guy named Ralph who sat just inside a rear doorway — protected the entire facility. We introduced ourselves and admitted straight up

---

*** In 1977, a bitter winter and a heating-oil shortage moved President Jimmy Carter to proclaim energy crises "the moral equivalent of war" and to create the cabinet-level Department of Energy.

that we were not Cornell students — we just wanted to play tennis at night. Alone all night, sitting by one lit lamp, reading the *Ithaca Journal* during the cold Ithaca night, Ralph was not a happy camper. He said he didn't even know about the tennis net.

So, after Ralph turned the lights back on, we dragged the netting out and set it up. By sheer coincidence, Ralph was curious about tennis, so we played a few points for him, and explained the rules. He really got into watching us blast shots that sounded like cannon fire in this immense empty room the size of Carlsbad Cavern. After a few minutes, we thought it best to not overstay this first visit. A couple of nights later we came back around ten with a bottle of Jack Daniels for our new friend. We were in. For the next couple of winters, for the price of a bottle of Jack once a week, Ralph let us play into the wee hours, burning all sorts of wattage and heating fuel — for just two people who weren't even students. I can't imagine how many thermal units it took to heat Barton Hall for two hours in the dead of winter. I remember Keith and I walking back through C-Town after working out, laughing about the "energy crisis." What energy crisis?

Occasionally I'd make my way over to Cornell or Ithaca College to audit courses being taught by astronomer Carl Sagan and tuba player/writer Rod Serling. Sagan had been director of Cornell's Laboratory for Planetary Studies there, and was the Associate Director of the Center for Radio Physics and Space Research.

In the mid-seventies his career was on fire: as a NASA advisor, Sagan assembled the first physical message that was sent into space: a gold-anodized plaque, attached to the space probe Pioneer 10, launched in 1972.[†††] Going against popular opinion, Sagan wisely challenged the decision to fund the dangerous, expensive, and minimally productive Space Shuttle program.

Rod, who grew up in nearby Binghamton, was already an icon. In addition to the groundbreaking *Twilight Zone* and *Night Gallery* TV series, he wrote award-winning screenplays such as *Requiem for a Heavyweight* and *Planet of the Apes*. After achieving success as a writer,

---

[†††] Pioneer 11, also carrying another copy of the plaque, was launched the following year. Sagan continued to refine his designs; the most elaborate message he helped to develop and assemble was the Voyager Golden Record that was sent out with the Voyager space probes in 1977.

he purchased a summer cottage near Ithaca. With his wife Carol, and their daughters Jodi and Nan, Rod lived in a lake house at the end of Kidders Beach Road in Interlaken on Cayuga Lake, 18 miles above Ithaca. Some of the most memorable Serling scripts in television history were crafted in Rod's Airstream trailer behind the Lake Cayuga house -- hence the name, Cayuga Productions.

I was especially drawn to Serling because of his strong anti-war position and his work for Gene McCarthy in the 1968 presidential campaign, a cause that led directly to the retirement of President Johnson. Before he moved to Interlaken, Serling lived in his conservative hometown of Binghamton, and recalled that, "For me to espouse this cause in Binghamton is a little bit like an Irish Republican Army officer being invited to a Black and Tan picnic." Serling didn't miss a beat when Johnson's successor, Richard Nixon, escalated Johnson's tragic error:

> *"The use of illegal wiretaps to spy on reporters and political opponents; the secret and illegal bombing of Cambodia; the authorization of 'plumbers' to burglarize and spy upon political opponents, the withholding of evidence in criminal cases, the defying of court orders, the obstruction of justice—this is the province of President Nixon and all the rest of that shabby crew who have written indelible chapters in the threadbare saga of the most corrupt, incompetent and downright immoral administration in the history of the American Republic."*

I had visions of getting to hang with Serling and company at his Cayuga Lake house one day, but it was not to be. Tragically, Serling, a heavy smoker who suffered from chronic heart disease, died on June 28, 1975 after emergency bypass surgery. He was only 50-years-old.

Rod's Lake Cayuga home

I also took in the occasional college concert, the most memorable being a particular Beach Boys show in Cornell's Barton Hall and Jackson Browne in Bailey Lecture Hall. I remember the Beach Boys show because of the poor opening act, a solitary piano player/vocalist who had to withstand the screams of 5,000 beach ball throwing, booing students who demanded to hear "Surfin USA." Whatever promoter double-billed a young Billy Joel with the SoCal juggernaut must have been high on bad pot.

When Browne walked onstage in the ornate, sold out lecture hall, he pulled one of the all time great diva moves: after putting his hand down on the nine foot Steinway grand piano, he stood up and declared it unplayable. The concert was brought to a halt as he walked off-stage. It was announced that there would be an intermission while the management tracked down a piano tuner. A half-hour later in walked a man with whom every band in Ithaca was familiar, an elderly German immigrant with a great ear — the best tuner in town. He slowly made his way to the instrument and proceeded to tune every string of that piano by ear, as the raucous audience howled for over an hour. Poor guy. He later told me that the piano was very playable, but he had to put on a show for the sulking prima donna backstage.

Another side interest managed to fill time while I awaited the Unicorn's opening. Along with many of my generation, I had been long interested in the mysteries surrounding the assassination of President Kennedy in 1963. It seemed that everyone I knew had devoured the conspiracy-tilted books and closely followed the 1969 trial of Clay Shaw in New Orleans. From the day it happened, national interest in the case ebbs and flows in a fairly regular cycle: about every five years or so, there is another flurry of attention on the tragedy due to some new revelation or investigation, and in 1975 there was a triple-whammy jolt to anyone interested in Kennedy's death.

First there were the findings of the Senate Intelligence Committee, chaired by Senator Frank Church (D-Idaho). In the committee's 14-volume report there were bombshells galore concerning the history of illegal activities of the CIA, usually at the direction of the White House. Among its key revelations were the extensive surveillance of American citizens, the assassination program within the CIA, and the shortcomings of the Warren Report, especially regarding the interest of Kennedy's assassin in Cuba and his possible contacts with Cuban agents in Mexico City seven weeks before Kennedy's murder. Church excoriated the CIA for not informing the Warren Commission of the possible foreign implications of the assassination, and then urged Congress to re-open the investigation, which it did three years later, under the banner of the House Select Committee on Assassinations (HSCA).

During the Church Committee's electrifying tenure, a handful of outspoken critics of the Warren Report were sent copies of a letter concerning his "position" from Lee Harvey Oswald to "Mr. Hunt," whom many took to be right-wing Texas oil magnate, acquaintance of Jack Ruby, and fierce Kennedy critic, H. L. Hunt.

The handwriting in the missive, supposedly written two weeks prior to the killing, had been verified as Oswald's by the top analysts in the US. (The fact that the KGB painstakingly forged the document over many months was not learned until two decades later. The Soviet spy agency had hoped that the public would assume that "Hunt" was CIA officer, Kennedy critic, and Watergate burglary mastermind, E. Howard Hunt. The idea was to turn the heat up on its archenemy, the CIA.)

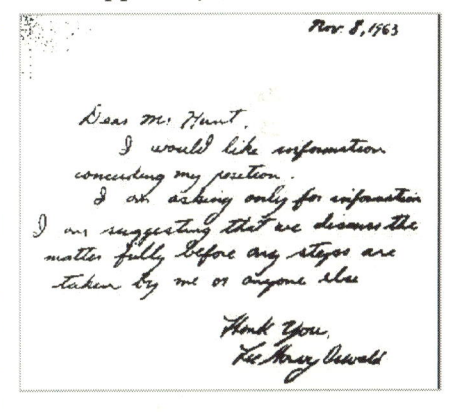

But without doubt, the most visceral assassination gut-punch came on the evening of March 6, 1975, when popular talk show host Geraldo Rivera unspooled on his syndicated program, *Good Night, America,* the long-concealed 18-second, 8-mm "home movie" made of Kennedy's death by Dallas dressmaker, Abraham Zapruder. Since the day of the killing, the government had refused to show its copy to the public, as did the private rights-holder, *LIFE* magazine. Until this night, all we had seen were still frames in the magazine, which obviously gave no sense of movement or direction. With rumors rampant that Kennedy had been shot from the "grassy knoll" located to his right front, critics had always assumed that the film would prove it.

It finally came about when Robert Groden, a high-school dropout and film lab trainee from New Jersey, let Rivera know that he, of all people, maintained a copy of the infamous "Z film," which he had stored in a bank vault for the last seven years. How Groden ended up with the film was a matter of being at the right place at the right time with the wrong ethics. In 1968, *Life* had hired a New Jersey film lab, Technical Animations, to make a 35-mm blow-up of the original 8mm Zapruder film. At the time, the lab's Vice President and General Manager, Moses Weitzman, a special effects film expert, employed 23-year-old Groden as a trainee and junior level staffer.

Weitzman made several copies, gave the best one to *Life*, and kept the rejects, one of which Groden surreptitiously copied and stored in a bank vault. Over the next seven years, using an optical printer, Groden made multiple copies, one of which he eventually showed on college campuses with comedian/activist Dick Gregory. Or as Weitzman later wrote in a letter to author David Lifton, "An employee of mine pirated a copy and made a career of it." (When that career started to fizzle, Groden, who had convinced the HSCA to use him as free consultant, similarly *acquired* Kennedy's autopsy photos and jump-started phase two of his ghoulish "career".‡‡‡)

When the studio lights dimmed and the silent film started, you could hear a pin drop, not only in the studio, but also in the Ithaca living room where I sat riveted with friends. As the dark blue Lincoln limo rounded the corner under Oswald's sixth floor perch, the sadness was overwhelming, not least of all because the First Couple never looked more attractive — JFK had just spent time in Florida and his

---

‡‡‡ Author Vince Bugliosi on Groden's acquisition skills: "In 2003, someone very high up in the HSCA hierarchy who wished to remain anonymous on this matter assured me he had 'firsthand knowledge'" of the fact that the FBI had investigated Groden and concluded Groden had stolen autopsy photos. "No federal theft prosecution could be commenced by the U.S. attorney's office against Groden because the photographs, as you know, were owned by the Kennedy family, not the government," he told me. 'However, the FBI took the matter to the Kennedy family contemplating they might want a state prosecution of Groden for theft where the Kennedy family would be the complaining witness. The family thought about it and decided against getting involved in a criminal case over the matter, and after consulting with their lawyers, also decided against bringing a civil action against Groden. But Groden had a close call.'"

tan looked perfect, while Jackie was resplendent in pink. Knowing what would happen in mere seconds — these beautiful people drenched in blood, skull and brain matter — gave us the urge to turn away. But we didn't. We had to see who killed our President.

When the horrific moment played out, the gasps in our living room were echoed by the audible gasps in the studio audience. Despite being a blurry fourth or fifth generation print, the film's colors were almost Technicolor-rich, a fact that made the fatal wound all that much more repulsive. Of course, what equally shocked us was the obvious backward head-thrust of the President, *toward* Oswald's perch. To the overwhelming majority of those who saw the film that night, it was clear that the American people had been the victims of a huge coverup, and JFK the victim of God-knows-who — but certainly not Oswald.

The experience only solidified what I had long believed, having read the works of Mark Lane and Edward Jay Epstein, who pointed out hundreds of seeming discrepancies in the case (it would turn out that only Epstein's work had any staying power.) But the film said in eighteen seconds what authors needed thousands of pages to drive home. Combined with the implications of the 1972 Watergate break-in, the Church Report, and the "Oswald letter," the "Z Film," which the government had in its possession since the night of the murder, was dispositive — or so we thought at the time.

I was now determined to learn everything I could about Kennedy's death, and, if possible, do something about it. At that time, there were three main sources of assassination-related information. In Canada, Dave Hawkins, who ran "The Collector's Archive," for which he placed small display ads in the back of *Rolling Stone* magazine, sold all manner of Kennedy ephemera, and was the first to sell bootleg "super-eight" copies of Groden's bootleg Z-Film — I purchased one immediately, even though I had no projector. I also obtained information from Carl Oglesby, the former President of the Students for a Democratic Society (SDS) who organized a Cambridge group called the Assassination Information Bureau, seeking "to politicize the question of John F. Kennedy's assassination." But most importantly, I began corresponding

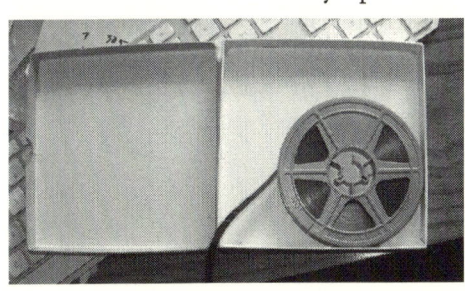

My bootlegged "Z-film"

with DC-based assassination researcher and Senate investigator, Bernard "Bud" Fensterwald. After defending State Department employees persecuted by Joe McCarthy in the fifties, Bud functioned as chief counsel for the Senate Judiciary Committee under Senator Edward V. Long of Missouri, and became close to Jackie Kennedy, and later, to New Orleans DA Jim Garrison. What most appealed to me about Bud was that he had no ideological predisposition regarding who might ultimately be behind the Dallas mystery. He was open to all possibilities, and sank much of his own money into following leads and encouraging young investigators (like yours truly) to follow their instincts. Thus, whenever I visited Baltimore, tried to spend a day at Bud's DC office, where he allowed me to rummage through his files and make copies to my heart's content.

Another mystery that enthralled me during the seventies was the world of a fascinating mob lawyer named Sidney Korshak. In 1976, the Pulitzer prize-winning *New York Times* journalist Seymour Hersh published a four-part exposé of Korshak, a Chicago-born lawyer who helped the mob infiltrate White Collar boardrooms. I was fascinated with this powerful millionaire, a man of few words who insisted on living in the shadows, yet was keen enough to make himself untouchable by law enforcement. It was clear that his command was so ephemeral and his associates so thoroughly muzzled that no book could be written on him. In the ensuing years, the nation's best investigators longed to write the book on Sidney, but were stifled at every turn. Little did I know it at the time, but I would eventually be the one crazy enough to take on "The Fixer's" story and write the book they said couldn't be written.

Eventually the Unicorn opened down in the flats, and our first gig there was as an opening act for an up-and-coming singer-songwriter from New Jersey who was out promoting her first album. Before the show, Phoebe Snow was a nervous wreck — so much so that her manager, Dino Airali, was worried that she wouldn't come out, especially after local favorite Durango had put in a killer opening set. But Phoebe did come out and her astounding voice blew the place away with songs like "Poetry Man" (which soon became the #1 Adult Contemporary single), "Shakey Ground," and "Harpo's Blues." We stayed in contact with Dino, who loved our music and said he'd help us get noticed in New York City.

We opened up for so many great acts, often for three-night

stands, that it begins to blur.§§§ A few, like the duo Aztec Two-Step, crashed at our house. I remember playing for a few days with James Taylor's brother, Livingston, who shared my love for Jobim. We spent time pre-shows in his dressing room jamming on Bossa Nova classics, with Liv on flute. One of the nights we opened for Liv, his brother James cancelled his show over at Ithaca College, so as not to hurt Liv's box office at the bottom of the gorge. Then there was the time that the Byrds borrowed my Fender Twin amp when theirs blew up on the first day of the gig; or the time George "Commander Cody" Frayne introduced himself by poking his head into our dressing room and uttering just one phrase: "Whatever you do, don't inhale the shit from Contac Cold capsules." (??) I remember when Tom Waits came in for a week of shows. I was so stunned that the second night I brought a pad and pencil, not to write down chords, but to remember his hysterical repartee, accented by rim-shots. I sat in the wings and wrote some down:

- "We been on the road so long, man, that when you get home everything in your refrigerator looks like a science project."

- "It's good to be busy, and we been busier than a pair of jumper cables at a Puerto Rican wedding, Jack. You know baby?"

- "This next song is unrehearsed, so it'll be rougher than a stucco bath tub."

- "I say, it's been cold on the road, colder than a Jewish American Princess on her wedding night, colder than a flat frog on a Philadelphia highway on the fourth of February. Cold, baby."

- "We just played in Philadelphia – you know 'the brother of lovely Sid.'"

    And, of course, the classic:

- "I'd rather have a free bottle in front of me than a pre-frontal lobotomy."

One afternoon I stopped by the club to check out the new PA system, and was recruited into helping haul furniture up to the main

---

§§§ Among the Unicorn stars, many of whom we opened for: Keith Jarrett, Roland Kirk, Billy Joel, Tom Waits, Martin Mull, Fleetwood Mac, Phoebe Snow, Don McLean, Commander Cody, Firefall, Michael Murphey, Livingston Taylor, The Byrds, Mary Travers, Chris Hillman Band, Roger McGuinn Band, Jackson Browne, David Bromberg, Aztec Two-Step, Little Feat, Gil Scott Heron, Orleans, Muddy Waters, Bill Gable, and Steve Goodman.

concert room, which was on the third floor of the building. What was so odd was that the furniture consisted of old plush easy chairs and sofas, unlike the room's décor. I found out that the act that night, guitarist-comedian Martin Mull, insisted on having the stage set up like his living room – he said he always sang better and felt more relaxed at home in his living room, so he just brought his living room on tour with him. (One of his early albums was entitled *Martin Mull and his Fabulous Furniture*.) He was actually quite a sophisticated guitarist. Patrons sitting in the front row that night noticed that when he played "bottle-neck" style, he substituted a dildo for a bottle. I was later told, but couldn't verify, that on that tour Martin stopped by the Rongo in Trumansburg, where he saw Ricky Jay, the guy behind the bar with his card-throwing act, and invited him to go on the road. Jay accepted, moved to Hollywood, and went on to have a big career as an actor and author.[****]

The predictable romances ensued between Unicorn waitresses and the musicians. Occasionally, even a patron participated in the goings-on. One such time was when my cousin Phil (from the Maria Cole incident) hitched up from Baltimore to watch Durango play the club. He was instantly drawn to waitress Debby, a dead-ringer for Joni Mitchell — in fact, "Joni" was my nickname for her. Phil must have had little going on in Baltimore because he just stayed in Ithaca flirting with Debby. On occasion Phil and I would hitch back to Baltimore together to visit family, get clean clothes, or, in my case, to deal with the unemployment compensation issue. Long story short — Phil and Debby dated, eventually moved to Baltimore, married, had a daughter, and stayed together for over thirty years.

[****] Ricky went on to star in a number of films by David Mamet, as well as writing books including *Cards as Weapons* and *Learned Pigs and Fireproof Women*. Mull recorded many comedy albums and appeared in countless movies and TV sitcoms, my favorites being *Mary Hartman* and *Fernwood 2-Nite*.

A MAGICAL TIME IN A MAGICAL PLACE   217

The only downer at the Unicorn was when a famous female singer (a tall blonde who used to be in a top folk trio with two guys) refused to let us get a sound check — she commandeered the stage all afternoon to make sure the lighting gels were perfect for her face. Then after the first night, she ordered the owner to fire us because we upstaged her (we got two encores before she came out and played a lame set.) Bob, the owner — God bless him — told her, "If they go, you go." Now we were really inspired, and she had to put up with us playing our hearts out for the rest of the week.

Durango was becoming the talk of the town, so much so that we garnered the front page of the *Ithaca Journal*'s entertainment magazine. I heard that the members of Orleans were none too happy about it since they had never gotten such a feature in the local paper.

Soon Doug McLean, the owner of the only professional recording studio in town, Sleepy Hollow Recording, noticed us. Sleepy Hollow was the recording home of Rod Serling, who created his narrations for the hit TV series, *The Undersea World of Jacques Cousteau* at the 16-track facility. Orleans and other locals had also cut tracks there. Doug's producing partner was Ray Repp, the top Christian songwriter credited with introducing folk music into Catholic masses. Doug and Ray believed our original songs were strong enough that, if we had professional recordings of them, could land us a major label deal. We signed a producing deal with McLean and Repp that gave us virtually unlimited studio time to record our best material.

During New England's winter ski season, Durango often hit the road, booking gigs in the scenic White Mountain notches of New Hampshire, and the Green Mountains of Vermont. In between "snow bunny" jobs, we hit Massachusetts music hotspots in "James Taylor country," like Pittsfield, Stockbridge, and Boston, then on to the seaport towns of Mystic, Newport, and Point Judith in Rhode Island,

and college towns like Burlington, Vermont. In James's Stockbridge hometown in the Berkshires, we played the legendary Music Inn.[††††]

What makes all this worth noting is that for many years musicians did not have to be famous to make a nice living on the various coffee house and concert circuits. There were literally hundreds of venues in the Northeast alone, apart from the dance clubs, that booked — and paid for — live music. In those spots songwriters and arrangers could hone their craft, invite record producers to hear them, and make their way up the showbiz ladder. Sadly, that world doesn't exist anymore. The few concert clubs that are left today can't support a fraction of the artists they did in the seventies. Consequently, few young people see a career in music as a viable career choice. And many of those kids have great talent that will never be allowed to flourish and bring out the great music that is in them.

In the spring we headed west, making it as far as Milwaukee, then down to Maryland where we worked with local favorites, Climbadonkey, whose members included Kyf Brewer and Glenn Workman. They would go on to form The Ravyns, which recorded "Raised on the Radio," used on the soundtrack of the 1982 hit movie *Fast Times at Ridgemont High*. Glen, who hasn't worn shoes in 35 years (including at a Kennedy Center gig), remains a good friend of mine.[‡‡‡‡]

Every band had war stories from the road — now *that* would be an interesting book — and ours were no more or less interesting than anyone else's, but I would be remiss if I didn't mention just a few. At the Maryland gig, the club owner said a friend had volunteered to put up the band in his large home. The friend turned out to be Baltimore Colts quarterback Bert Jones, heir apparent to Johnny Unitas, and that year's NFL Most Valuable Player. On the way to Milwaukee in our VV bus and VW Beetle caravan there was one moment of terror. Will and I were following the van in Will's Beetle, with all our guitars stacked on the back seat. On a long highway stretch in the middle of nowhere, the rear-mounted, air-cooled engine burst into flames. We jumped out

---

[††††] Among the many greats who played at Stockbridge's Music Inn: Louis Armstrong, Dizzy Gillespie, Duke Ellington and Count Basie. Pete Seeger, Woody Guthrie, Joan Baez and Odetta. Billie Holiday, Mahalia Jackson, Sarah Vaughan and Ethel Waters. The Rev. Gary Davis, John Lee Hooker, Sonny Terry and Brownie McGhee. The Modern Jazz Quartet, Coleman Hawkins, Miles Davis and Thelonious Monk. Herbie Hancock, Chick Corea, Weather Report and Dave Brubeck. Taj Mahal, Jimmy Cliff, Bob Marley and Muddy Waters. The Kinks, the Byrds, the Eagles, America, Bruce Springsteen, Lou Reed, Bonnie Raitt and Van Morrison.

[‡‡‡‡] See: http://freqsound.com/feet.html

fearing an explosion, when it hit us that everything we valued — our guitars – was in the backseat. Dare we risk our live for the guitars? In the millisecond we contemplated this, Will remembered that we had a thermos of iced tea behind the driver's seat. He raced to get it as I popped the rear hood. Will doused the engine with the tea and saved the day. We towed the car to a service station where the incinerated generator and melted rubber parts were replaced.

Before arriving at the venue, we stopped at an indoor mall to grab some supplies. Walking down the concourse, we heard the sound system playing a song that was one of our showstoppers, "Suite: Judy Blue Eyes." However, the version being played was not the original by CSNY, but our version from our demo tape. That was a bit of a rush. A mall cashier said the club had been playing it all week in advance of our gig. In Point Judith, Rhode Island we played in a huge two-story club right on the southern tip of the peninsula and a popular hangout for URI and Brown students. The place was so rowdy that the stage was enclosed in chicken wire, the first I had seen since the hillbilly bar gigs of my youth, and the owner had stacks of replacement windowpanes at the ready stored in the basement.

At the top of the Killington Peak in Vermont we played a ski resort that gave us pricey free ski privileges. However, I didn't want to hurt my knees, which I was trying to preserve for tennis. So I tucked my rackets under my arm and stuck out my thumb, and every day for two weeks I hitched to downtown Rutland to play indoors. It was quite a visual for the ski bums sitting in a long line of cars driving *up* the mountain, while as I stood on the other side of the road in two feet of snow with tennis rackets under my arm, going *down* the hill. Now that's commitment. When I heard what happened to our bassist, another skiing gremlin, I was glad I didn't cash in those lift tickets: on his first run, he couldn't stop and plowed into a huge rack of skis at the bottom, in full view of the lodge's restaurant patrons.

A highlight was when we played in Harvard Square at the legendary Passim Folk Club with our Blue Water Manor buddy, Bostonian Bill Gable. In the rear parking lot, as we loaded in, we watched a huge bus pull in near our van. We shared the lot that night with members of the *Rolling Thunder Revue*, which was playing a couple of doors down at the Harvard Square Theater. During breaks, we'd go back to the lot where Bob Dylan, Joan Baez, T-Bone Burnett, and Roger McGuinn (with whom we had played at the Unicorn) hung out before their show. The next day I made a beeline to Cambridge, where I met with Carl Oglesby and his associates at the Assassination

Information Bureau, who loaded me down with literature on the various political killings that had taken place in the US in recent years.

When the schools let out in June, the town emptied out, and Durango headed up to Lake George for the summers. Freed from the confines of Blue Water Manor, we now gigged up and down the lakefront. In the summers of 1975-6, we were the house band at Bolton Landing's Anchorage, a former Millionaires' Row lakefront mansion that had been converted into a bar/restaurant. The facility was adjacent to Rogers Memorial Park, with its beach and tennis court, and boasted its own beautiful three-acre lawn that ended at lakeside docks. We were given lodging on the mansion's second floor, so we could literally stumble down the stairs to our gig. We were such a big hit in Bolton that the crowds turned the place into a packed-to-the-rafters madhouse.

Three-hundred yards across Bolton Bay was the high-class Sagamore Resort where the vacationing Manhattan elite and many of the stars who gigged at the Saratoga Performing Arts Center outdoor "summer shed" stayed. We spent many an afternoon on the Sagamore's docks, sunning with those celebs, some of whom, like Billy Joel, were so taken with the lake's beauty that they purchased homes on the eastern shore. One summer, Billy bought a motorcycle from our bassist. Tennis great Ivan Lendl was said to have bought property after a stay at "The Sag."

One of our regular jobs was at a Village Club called Pour Richard's Pub, two blocks from the lakefront. We had a lot of regular fans there, but one group stood out. Most nights this group of a dozen or so commandeered three or four tables near the bandstand, and quickly got so raucously drunk that we worried things would get dangerous. They told us they were from the psychiatric unit of Glens Falls Hospital, and we naturally assumed that they were outpatients. It turned out that they were actually staff — psychiatrists, counselors, orderlies, and the like. They just really knew how to unwind.

Another bleary-eyed night at the Anchorage

The ringleader of this group was a wild-eyed young Latvian named Edgar (to this day the only "Edgar" I have ever met), and was a Director of Human Resources at the Glens Falls Hospital's Center for

Substance Abuse by day and a vodka-swilling amateur fiddle player by night. He often brought his fiddle and soloed with us on some Grateful Dead-type songs. Edgar says that when he jammed with us we became the only known "Holy Modal Rounders" tribute band (don't ask). I would become great pals with all the gang at these tables, but Edgar would soon turn up with a completely unpredicted musical offer — one that I couldn't refuse.

At summer's end, before heading down to the US Open, I received a great financial boost. For many months I had been traveling back to Baltimore to fight for my Banners unemployment insurance. When the state finally assented, they sent me all my back-checks at once. Thus I opened the envelope and out tumbled twenty-six checks for over $100 each (the equivalent of $10,000 today). I can't recall how all the money was spent, but some went to my student loan, some went to a new guitar, and a lot went to a two-week spending spree in New York while I attended that year's US Open. Most of that spending occurred either at the Westside Tennis Club or within a few blocks of Times Square: the seventies were the pinnacle of composer Stephen Sondheim's career, and I attended his musicals — *A Little Night Music, Sweeney Todd, Pacific Overtures*, and *Company* — repeatedly.

I managed to convince my brothers to come up for a day from Baltimore and meet me for a Saturday show on Broadway (likely *Sweeney Todd*). I told them to meet me at Rockefeller Center in the afternoon, where, unbeknownst to them, I had a plan to do a little gatecrashing. For the first two years of Durango, all we kept hearing about was this great new comedy-music show called *Saturday Night Live*. However, I never got to actually watch the show as we were booked most weekends, and this was before the age of VCRs. Now on break for the Open, I was determined to catch the show live. But this was at a time when it was the hottest ticket in New York. No problem — I merely relied on one of my most tried-and-true crashing tricks (alone worth the price of this book.)

Before the dress rehearsal, I merely walked to the security guard and told him my name was on the guest list, which of course it wasn't. He pulled the list out and while he scanned for "Russo," I searched for anybody's name with the number (3) next to it. After pretending to be shocked when my name was missing, I told the guard I'd make a call and see what the problem was. Instead, I walked back to my brothers and gave them the name "Fredericks," which had been listed as three guests of "Bill Murray." My brother went up, dropped the name and was promptly handed three passes. We then headed up the elevator to the eighth floor where a pre-show buffet was laid out for cast and guests. We mingled with the cast — I distinctly remember Lorne Michaels ladling some Swedish meatballs into my plate. I told Murray what I had done and he thought it was hysterical. He didn't particularly like the Fredericks anyway.

After we filled our bellies alongside Radner, Ackroyd, and the rest, we stayed for some of the rehearsal then had to bolt to our Broadway show.

Hanging at the Open with Mr. G, whose son Vitas was now a superstar pulled in a thousand directions at once, I noticed some changes. Up in the stands of the old horseshoe stadium, two rows stood out: there, standing out amongst the sea of white faces were about twenty black kids. When I mentioned it to Mr. G, he said they were "Vitas's kids." With no fanfare, Vitas had been inviting poor kids from Harlem to come to the Open — every day — at his expense. Vitas bought them all dinner and gave them racquets.

Soon he started dragging Bjorn and Johnny Mac into the Bronx and to the Central Park public courts, where they gave tennis lessons to the underprivileged. Eventually, all of Vitas's pro buddies pitched in: Connors, Billie Jean, Ilie, Arthur Ashe, and Vitas's sister Ruta among them. Vitas said his goal was to buy land, build courts for the kids, and help them get jobs. His work would evolve into the still-ongoing Vitas Gerulaitis Youth Foundation. A snapshot that typified Vitas was when he was finishing a lunch interview with a reporter, he beat three people to the bill, asking, "Who do you think you're with, Jimmy Connors?"

By this time, Vitas and Bjorn were best pals, a relationship that began after the two played a five-set semi-final thriller at Wimbledon in 1977 (Borg won), which many of us believe to be one of the greatest matches ever played. Sportswriter Mike Lupica described the after-match press conference with someone who should have been gutted by the loss: "Afterward, Gerulaitis was full of one-liners and sass, and filled that interview room with as much fun as it could ever know. Finally some old Brit in the back said, 'Vitas, you're pretty chipper for somebody who lost the match.' Gerulaitis, 23 that day and sure he would live forever, shrugged. 'This was my *winning* press conference,' he said. 'I hated to waste all this good material.'" Years later, Bjorn described to the press what happened the next day: "After I beat him in the Wimbledon semifinals, in 1977, he came to me right after the match and offered to be my practice partner to get [me] ready for the final," Borg said. "I mean, usually when a player loses, he leaves the next day. That's the kind of guy he is." Their friendship produced at least one downside: weeks later at the Open, Borg retired from a match against Dick Stockton with a shoulder injury. He explained that it was injured in practice, but in fact, it was hurt while he was water-skiing with his look-alike Lithuanian buddy off of Long Island Sound. The press never found out.

Although Vitas was his typical, eager-to please self, it was now well known that his happy-go-lucky personality knew no boundaries. His increasing drug use, accompanied by the usual entourage of sycophants, was now the talk of the clubhouse and the worry of his loving family, who was now living in his Long Island mansion. I made a conscious decision to not ask Vitas for passes, hoping to not appear like the vultures that hit him up constantly for favors, and I passed on the Studio 54 scene, least of all because I couldn't afford it and didn't want to leech off of Vitas. In later years, his family made it known to me that they, and Vitas, always appreciated that about me. Nonetheless, when I'd see Vitas on the grounds he refused to let me go without making me take stacks of front-row tickets that he kept at the ready in his gear bag. A typical conversation with Vitas went like this:

Vitas: "Hey, Gus, everybody taking care of you OK?"

Gus: "Great, V, and how are you —"

Vitas: "Here, take some tickets, and here's some players' passes — I insist. What kind of guitar you playing these days?"

Gus: "Ovation, Fender Strat, and Gibson semi-hollow —"

Vitas: "Great, then I'll get them. Look, I can't hang now, but have my dad bring you out to the house."

On at least three occasions I sat courtside at Vitas's home practice court as he and Bjorn played ferocious sets for hours on end, running like gazelles. (Vitas was so intent on winning his hometown major tournament that whenever the Open changed surfaces, he'd have the same contractors re-do his court with the exact same material.) In these sessions, unlike in the tournaments, Vitas and Bjorn played to a draw on most days. Incredibly, long after Bjorn, me, and other friends left the property, Vitas drove his yellow Rolls into Manhattan, where he partied in the VIP room of Studio 54 until the wee hours.

On a couple of hours sleep at most, he'd return to the Open for a match. He would soon reach Number Three in the world, but could never beat Bjorn and Jimmy in any match of significance.§§§§ Of course they were playing having slept the night before their matches, a decided advantage. Vitas might have easily been the top player in the world if he could have restrained his party side. We were all frustrated and a good bit saddened that our big-hearted friend seemed to be spinning out of control. Everybody tried to talk to him about it, to no avail. It wasn't until the mid-eighties, after an intervention in his Florida condo by his buddy Jimmy Connors, fiancé Janet Jones, and others, that Vitas finally kicked the demons.

Durango never landed a major label record deal, although we came squeaky close on a couple of occasions. Every band has a finite lifespan, and some of the best are the shortest-lived — like that saying about the brightest flame. By 1977, despite having great fun and

---

§§§§ In a famous, but typical, Vitas quip, the Lion remarked to the press in 1979, after ending a 16-match losing streak to Connors, and being asked how he pulled it off: "Nobody beats Vitas Gerulaitis seventeen times in a row!"

developing a strong regional following, we decided it was time to move on; Will felt the pull back to architecture and Arcosanti, and I wanted to pursue songwriting and composing; my skills had accelerated rapidly in Ithaca and I was receiving accolades for both my original songs and my vocal arrangements (I frankly can't recall what Ak's plans were at the time). I had also spent a lot of time in Sleepy Hollow and felt much at home in the recording studio. An additional consideration was that the Unicorn Club was having financial difficulties and would eventually close in 1978.[*****] And with Orleans and other bands moving out, Serling gone, and our recording deal over, it just seemed like an era was coming to a natural end. But we were lucky to have been there while it was in full swing.

By now, I had made so many friends in Lake George — not the least of which was the gorgeous daughter of a resort owner — that it felt like a good place to plant roots for a while. After Durango played a bittersweet farewell show at the Unicorn, we went our separate ways. We had been singing together since 1969, so no one could say we didn't give it the college try.

[*****] Today the Unicorn space is fittingly occupied by the Community School of Music and Arts.

Chapter Twelve

Blue Water, Pt. 2

SINCE IT WAS the off-season when I arrived up north, the new owners of Blue Water Manor gave me a sweetheart deal (i.e. free) for a temporary apartment on the lake, while I looked for a permanent home and established myself in the area as a solo musician, guitar and tennis instructor. But the dominant game plan was always to continue improving my songwriting/arranging skills and attempt to sell my creations in the Big Apple.

Surprisingly, in the nearby towns of Bolton, Lake George Village, Hudson Falls, Glens Falls, and Saratoga Springs, there was a pretty vibrant music scene, and many opportunities for work. I was especially fortunate in that I read music, could double on bass, and loved the "standards," thus I was able to partake in the weekend double-scale jobs (weddings, bar mitzvahs, corporate events, etc.) and the occasional studio date at the small local recording facility. This also meant that I could work with the Dixieland bands on the lake's cruise boats in the summer. One of my regular bandmates on those boat jobs was bassist John Wilcox, the father of Todd Rundgren's drummer, Willie Wilcox, whom I had met in Ithaca. I also booked work with a longtime Bolton jamming pals such as jazz flugelhornist Matt Finley (Rio Jazz) and renowned alto sax jazzman Andy Haigh, with whom I indulged my love of Bossa Nova.

I found a wonderful living arrangement with a couple of the hospital psychiatric staff that came to our gigs. Gary Loke and his girlfriend had a great old house on Diamond Point Road, just up the hill from Blue Lagoon, where so much skinny-dipping had transpired over the years. Our house, with a huge back yard and two giant oak trees out front, sat at the foot of a mountain from which a long and winding road descended right past our front porch. The steep two-lane pass was known for cars losing control of their speed as they hit the flats, where our house was the first they encountered, and it provided me with a major life-altering experience.

All professional entertainers share the experience: having to perform under trying circumstances, such as being ill, or depressed because your girlfriend dumped you an hour before going onstage, or for one of a thousand other reasons. It was at the Diamond Point Road house that I experienced one of the worst such occurrences. It was a beautiful summer evening with the sun setting on the mountaintop, and I just had loaded up my car for a nearby hotel solo gig and made a quick retreat back into the house to see if I had forgotten anything. Just as I got inside the door, I heard the unmistakable sounds of screeching brakes, followed by a deafening explosion — the obvious after-effect of a major car crash. Before I turned around, I already concluded that someone had careened down the mountain and destroyed not only my car, but also every piece of uninsured musical gear I owned.

Being the only person in the house, it was left to me to be the first on the scene, walking quickly — yet feeling like slow motion — back onto the porch and towards my car. Shockingly, my car was untouched, but turning to my right, I saw another vehicle just fifteen feet away, on its side, demolished, and smoking. I raced to the wreck, which had obviously rolled over after having banged off of the giant trees that lined the steep descent. Now I have always been a bit squeamish at all things bloody (hospital emergency rooms are among my least favorite places), so there was a good chance I'd faint if I saw some horrific injuries. I timidly approached the driver's side and peered inside, sort of squinting to shield my optic nerve from what was sure to be gruesome. That brought shock number two.

The car was empty! OK, I lucked out. Obviously some drunk had gotten lucky and was probably wobbling down the road. I turned to go back towards our house and look for him, and as I got near my car I saw shock number three, a detail I had my back turned to when I first checked my jalopy for damage. It was a sight that is seared into my memory: the bloodied body of a young man was literally wrapped around one of our oak trees, obviously thrown from the car. The body was twisted backward around the oak, his back clearly broken, with an array of bloody injuries that my brain has thankfully erased. When I got to him he was unconscious, but convulsing slightly before taking a final breath. I was frozen for an instant, not just because this was the first person I ever saw expire, but also because he looked a bit like me: early thirties, slim, with long dark hair.

Running into the house, I called the police and emergency rescue, and they were there within minutes, confirming the fact that the victim was deceased. As for me, I still had to go to the hotel, tell jokes, and sing to a rowdy crowd of vacationers. Trooper that I was, I somehow got through the night, but for weeks thereafter I had nightmares wherein it was I who was wrapped around that tree. It was an experience that only reaffirmed my general credo to not waste a single day, because it could be your last.

As it had been in Ithaca, one of my first concerns upon arriving in Warren County was how to play free indoor tennis during those long and brutal Lake George winters — even longer and brutal-er than those in Ithaca. Fate stepped in when I got to chatting with an audience member during a break at one of my gigs. Pat LaHaise was the head pro at the closest indoor club, located in Glens Falls, and, after hitting with him there a few times, he made me one of those offers you can't refuse: I could run the club's pro shop a couple days a week and spell him on his teaching for little pay, but play all the free tennis I liked. Additionally, I could share the small ramshackle house he rented next to the club, literally 20 feet away. After spending a year on Diamond Point Road, I accepted Pat's offer, making the Queensbury Racquet Club my home base for the next couple of years.

These years were a time of transition for we Boomers; the liberating energy generated by the Sixties was slowly beginning to dissipate (for most) as we approached our thirties. We were a huge segment of the population, and with many of us now earning real money — making us the newest prey for the vultures of Madison Avenue — consumerism and commercialism exploded almost out of nowhere. Thus, by the late Seventies there was a noticeable shift in the zeitgeist. I began to notice it in my most passionate pursuits, tennis and music, as exponential economic growth became the all-important mantra, obliterating the previous exponential gains in quality.

In 1978 the USTA moved the Open from its perfect, tree-lined village home at the West Side Tennis Club to an enormous, broiling concrete slab in Flushing Meadow, Queens, three-and-a-half miles to the north, where formerly sat the 1964 New York World's Fair. Instead of the large shade trees covering the quiet lanes of Forest Hills, the only shadows cast here were those made by the jumbo jets taking off from nearby La Guardia that made the area quake every two minutes. Players half-joked that the planes were so close that you could lob over them. Instead of the village grocery stores where we stocked up on $3 turkey sandwiches, we now were stranded in the middle of nowhere, with only sanctioned vendors offering ridiculously over-priced hot-dogs and soda.

The stated reason for the relocation was that the tennis association wanted to build a bigger facility, thereby to bring the game to more people. Really? The way to get the game to more people is to build inner city tennis courts and make lessons affordable. I had no trouble finding the game without Flushing. Of course, the unstated reason was the desire to cash in on the exciting talent that had emerged in the last few years. One of the ironic byproducts of human nature is its destruction-by-greed of its own wonderful creations. This disquieting trait had an out-of-control proliferation in late seventies America, and we haven't looked back. The almighty dollar quest was very soon to ruin the professional tennis game. Those who disagree, I can only assume, didn't attend any matches at West Side.

Until this point, it was all so simple: for shoes, you either wore Jack Purcell canvass, or Stan Smith Adidas leather; for racquets, it was Dunlop Maxply, Wilson Jack Kramer, or that goofy T-2000 aluminum that a few pros tried, but only Jimmy Connors embraced (hence his horrible serve and wimpy volley.) Your strings were either VS Gut or nylon. That was it. No one gave a second thought to your choice of shirts, shorts, and other ephemera, thus freeing you to concentrate on just improving your game. But when the Boomers became targeted by the manufacturers, the tennis world — and all other worlds — changed overnight.

In what seemed the blink of an eye, there appeared a glut of new choices, all endorsed by the pros, who now looked like walking billboards with all the logos sewn to their pricey new foreign clothes: Fila, Tacchini, Diadora, Adidas, Puma, Ellesse — it was as though we were learning a new tennis language overnight, supplanting the one that had served the tennis world just fine for hundreds of years. For the "new fans" of Flushing, largely Wall Street tycoons and New York corporate and Real Estate magnates who now commandeered all the good seats, how you dressed became more important than how you played. Being seen was more important than actually watching. For the true fans that had migrated from West Side, where we ate bag lunches in our blue jeans and $10 sneakers, the change was revolting. But we were torn, because the new talent on the scene — Bjorn, Jimmy, Mac, Ilie, and Vitas — were so compelling that we couldn't not go to the matches. Besides, it was always great to hang with Mr. G, who was the head pro at the new facility, and his 23-year-old son, now ranked Number Four in the world. At the shiny new facility, Mr. G gave lessons to one and all, including Vitas's celeb pals like Carlos Santana and Meatloaf. Over the next few years, I would bring promising young players down from upstate to hit with Mr. G, who held his own with these young lions, despite being in his seventies and having had both hips replaced.

I, predictably, rebelled against the crass commercialization, and, along with a couple of fellow employees of the racquet club where I worked part time, did my bit to advertise my disgust. Richie, the club racquet-stringer, managed to get his hands on a batch of FILA logo patches from a salesman, and we promptly applied them to all sorts of objects that would mock the whole status thing: prophylactic machines, the "sanitary napkin" dispenser in the women's locker room, dumpsters, rat poison, etc. We even sewed some of them on our jockstraps and our girlfriends' panties.

I stripped all the decals off of my Bancroft Borg model racquets (still made of wood, thank you) and replaced them with my surname. I figured that since Bancroft didn't advertise for me, why should I advertise for them? When I showed up to play in amateur tournaments, I had an immediate psychological advantage over the guys who thought *I* had an endorsement deal.

When we attended the Open, usually on Guest passes, my friends and I smuggled in our food, refusing to buy the vendor swill. We were under no illusion that we were stemming the tide of consumerism, but we were satisfied that we contributed as little to it as we could while still being technically Americans. Thanks to Bjorn, Vitas, or to their expired passes from West Side, which were easy to cosmetically update, I spent those first years at Flushing in the Players Box. Even the ushers got to know me. Years later, someone approached me saying they saw my photo in a European coffee table autobiography by Bjorn. I wasn't surprised, since I was a regular in the players' lounge and front row guest box. After much pre-Amazon searching, I tracked down the book and ordered a copy from the UK. It was called *Borg By Borg*, and was crammed with beautiful color prints of Bjorn, Vitas and other friends. Lo and behold, on page 56 there I sat in the guest box at that first (1978) Open at Flushing with Bjorn's coach Lennart, his fiancé, Marianna, and perhaps the greatest soccer player of all time, Franz Beckenbauer, a pal of Bjorn's.

But trumping the clothing alteration was the racquet upheaval, and the avatar of the coming revolution was none other than the Orchard Racquet Club's Pammy Shriver, who showed up at Flushing in 1978 armed with her eye-popping 110-square inch Howard Head Prince aluminum beast and former Baltimore Banners coach, Don Candy. When this virtual unknown made it to the final, the masses assumed that the racquet had a lot to do with it. Overnight, everyone (almost) craved a gigantic racquet made of anything but wood.

At the time, and for about eight hundred previous years, the rule governing tennis racquet design was simple to the point of not even being a rule: "*The Frame.* The frame may be of any material, weight, size or shape." (ITF rule as of 1978 [*]). When corporate dweebs realized that a lot more profit could be made from selling mold-stamped synthetic racquets for over $100 than from the traditional labor-intensive, laminated wood frames costing around $30 each, Pandora's Box was exploded open. Players could now be told that they could swing as hard as they wanted without fear of breaking the new contraptions — never mind that these beasts had no feel or control, or that when the ball *did* go in it was going so fast that rushing the net against someone who used one of these cannons felt like driving north in the southbound lane of I-95.

Seizing on the non-rule, companies with no previous interest in the game began marketing tennis "bats" made of aluminum and fiberglass. When the public gobbled up these designs at $100 a pop, the manufacturers upped the ante to see just how crazy these nouveau tennis fans were and how deep their pockets went. Uber-expensive materials such as magnesium, titanium boron, ceramics, graphite, and composites were introduced. Each material had its own allegedly desirable qualities, but ceramics and graphite were the best picks for being very stiff as well as being very good with vibration reduction. Howard Head introduced a smaller framed "red head" aluminum, then

---

[*] http://www.itftennis.com/technical/rules/history/racket.asp

added Arthur Ashe's boron/aluminum "bottle-opener" to his product line. By 1980, racquets could pretty much be divided into two classes: inexpensive racquets made of aluminum and expensive ones made of graphite or a composite. Except for a few holdouts like Bjorn, Vitas, and Mac, wood practically disappeared. Bizarre shapes, designed by rocket surgeons who promised larger sweet spots, were also introduced.[†]

The tennis czars had sanctioned the equivalent of lowering basketball rims to six feet, or arming baseball sluggers with titanium bats, all in the name of "growth." Ironically, the ill-advised decision would hasten the career descents of the very stars that created the boom: Laver, Bjorn, Vitas, Ilie, Vilas, Evert, and McEnroe, all of whom preferred the touch and versatility of wood frames.[‡] As a sort of sour icing on a bad cake, the color of tennis balls was changed in the seventies from white to yellow to make them more visible on television, where the real money lay. However, this change was in vain due to the fact that power tennis was so boring to watch that the boom would soon be over and television tennis ratings would plunge.

In music, the technological revolution destroyed tens of thousands of careers in the late seventies. Many of my peers point to the appearance of Disco music as the watershed, but in fact, Disco was only made possible by the recent advances in technology. The progression went something like this: thanks to improvements in recording decks, as many as 64 tracks became available for Disco's multi-layered wall of sound, which is characterized by massive horn, string and woodwind sections placed over more traditional rock instrumentation and a robotic "four on the floor" kick drum beat. To bring this sound to a club audience would have been impossible had it not been for the concurrent electronic instrument breakthroughs.

The vinyl-spinning Disco sound had been popular in select New York City gay and black clubs for years, but after the Bee Gees released the soundtrack to the monster hit movie *Saturday Night Fever* in 1977, Disco clubs spread like a plague throughout suburbia, where most of us musicians made our livings. The clubgoers, told by the brothers Gibb that, "They should be dancing," demanded the full wall-of-sound to get their boogie on, a logistical and financial impossibility

---

[†] See some here: http://www.80s-tennis.com/pages/oddities.html
[‡] As to the future of racquet evolution, Head has designed a racquet that uses piezoelectric technology, which converts vibration or motion to and from electrical energy. Head's new racquet will allegedly take the vibration resulting from impact with the ball and convert it to electrical energy, which serves to dampen that vibration. A circuit board in the racquet's handle will then amplify that electrical energy and send it back to the piezoelectric ceramic composites in the frame, causing those materials to stiffen.

that required an army of musicians. Thus, live bands were replaced by DJs who merely played the over-produced disks though massive sound systems, as local players became increasingly invisible and devalued.

The musicians who survived were the keyboardists, who, shunted to the background for the two-decade-old electric guitar era, got their revenge due the nascent synth music revolution pioneered by Trumansburg's Bob Moog. After Sequential Circuits released the Prophet 5 keyboard in 1977, a polyphonic version of the Minimoog, keyboard players became the only musicians capable of layering replicas of those horn and string-heavy 64 tracks in a club setting, despite the fact that these synthetic replications sounded horrible to a real musician's ears. The sad fact was that the boogie crowd could have cared less, their bombarded eardrums rendered incapable of distinguishing an overtone-rich Stradivarius from a shrill, oscillator-induced audio algorithm.

Not only were the club dates wiped out, but so too were the lucrative weekend wedding, Bar Mitzvah, and corporate gigs, which often defined our profit margins. In Lake George Village, many music clubs were converted overnight into Discos, as musicians who had honed their craft for decades began to consider other options. Perhaps the first to be hit by the musical depression were the drummers. In 1978, Roland introduced the $200 CR-78 programmable drum machine, capable of reproducing Disco's 120-beats-per-minute hypnotic pulse for the boogie-ers. Combined with the new synths, with which the drum machines could communicate thanks to another new invention (MIDI), a well-armed keyboardist could charge a club for one player, whilst sounding like a horde.

In this new Discoworld, buckskin and blue jean sales plummeted, replaced by see-through blouses, micro-miniskirts, and 5-inch platform ankle-breakers. If the parents of the Boomer first wave were dismayed by their Patchouli-soaked Hippie Chick daughters, I can only imagine a father's shock at seeing his 18-year-old princess walk out the door in 1978 looking like she was auditioning for the Bunny Ranch, while rabid boys in full testosterone overdose, who could care less about dancing, salivated in wait for them at the Disco.

It was hard to believe that I was just one year removed from the musical dreamland known as Ithaca.

But there was more. In 1979, the first compact discs appeared. Combined with synthesizers, CDs further eroded listeners' aural discernment with harsh digital samples of music. Sadly, the public would begin to think of these crude imitations as the norm, and within a short time span completely forget how harmonically rich music is supposed to sound. Additionally, the convenience of CDs and other soon-to-come digital contraptions would herald a generation that demanded instant gratification to go along with its collective microscopic attention span.

Within one year (1975-76), both Microsoft and Apple released their software and computers, and, combined with the new "internet," which initiated access via telephone "dial-up" in seven US cities in 1975, the concepts of sitting and staring would soon be turned into a quasi-religious rite. §

Of course, some took a break from staring at the computer to stare at the newly developed cable television fare. When we first heard about "pay TV" in the mid-seventies, we thought it was a joke. "Who in the world would pay for television?" we asked. It turns out that almost everyone would: by 1978 nearly 16 American million households had cable. As might be expected, waistlines exploded.**

But the seventies still weren't through with us! With the recent passing of many of the original movie moguls, stockholders and Young Turk directors descended on the once family-owned businesses. Like the USTA and the music world, the movie industry now demanded exponential growth, and they got it with "the blockbuster." As so thoroughly chronicled by Peter Biskind in *Easy Riders, Raging Bulls*, the world now lined up for popcorn movies driven by special effects and volume. *Jaws,* the *Star Wars* trilogy, *Close Encounters of the Third Kind, King Kong*, and *Superman* were just the beginning of the quest for $100 million grossing movies. In this new climate, the Harper Lees, Budd Schulbergs, and Herman Wouks of the world would have been laughed out of a big studio pitch meeting.††

---

§ The word "internet" was coined in 1974 by computer scientist Vinton "Father of the Internet" Cerf, and a year later the first internet service, Telenet (later Sprintnet), began as a largely privately funded national computer network.
** Pay television was launched in November 1972 when Service Electric offered Home Box Office (HBO) over its satellite-cable system of a few hundred subscribers in Wilkes-Barre, Pennsylvania. This represented the first successful pay cable service in the nation. The second service to use the satellite was a local television station in Atlanta that broadcast primarily sports and classic movies. WTBS, owned by R.E. "Ted" Turner, was distributed by satellite to cable systems nationwide in 1976, becoming known as the first "superstation."
†† A similar "blockbuster effect" was simultaneously affecting the literary world. In 1974, Mary Higgins Clark saw her first woman-in-jeopardy, by-the-numbers, potboiler, *Where Are the Children?*, sell half a million books. Higgins Clark, who at 83, still cranks out a book a year, has sold 100-million books in the US alone. Much as Coppola (*The Godfather*, 1972) begat Spielberg (*Jaws*, 1975), who begat Lucas (*Star Wars*, 1977), Clark paved the way for similar formula blockbuster authors like James Patterson, who releases a staggering nine books a year (220 million sold), and Nora Roberts, who churns out a paltry six books a year (400 million copies in print.) Don't hold your breath for a *War and Peace* or *The Sound and the Fury* from this crowd.

Many of these blockbuster deals were closed in the LA traffic via another new invention, the cell phone. Created in 1966 by the Swedish electrical engineer Östen Mäkitalo, cell phones were first unleashed on the Tokyo citizenry in 1979, where 20 million citizens had access to the original "cell network." Four years later, America's introductory connection, owned by Ameritech, debuted in Chicago. Of all the technical advances of the seventies, the cell phone might just be the most drug-like; over the next decades, young digital natives would find it almost traumatic to be separated even momentarily from their little radioactive lifelines.

Hollywood's new blockbuster mentality was accompanied by a spate of new media that turned movie actors — of almost any talent level — into super celebrities whose every move had to memorialized. Boomers grew up in an age where movie magazines such as *Modern Screen, Photoplay,* and *Silver Screen* were the provenance of blue-haired women who wanted something to stare at while under the hair dryer at the beauty shop. But starting with *People Magazine* (1974) and *Us Weekly* (1977) the media began targeting younger readers while fostering a near-religious obsession with people who play make-believe for a living. Within a couple of years, *Entertainment Tonight,* followed by *Access Hollywood* and *Extra,* would debut daily on television with glitzy "breaking news" updates on actors, their shopping, jogging, dining, and mating habits. These new media were hugely profitable, not in the least because no journalism was required — the studio publicists happily delivered the scripts and movie clips for free in this perfectly symbiotic enterprise. But there was a downside: children coming up in this world often concluded that celebrity was the most important asset to achieve in life, and mere attention seeking was a way to earn big money with which to purchase the newest digital heroin.

With Disco eating into my gigging opportunities, I had to juggle a variety of styles to keep working: in addition to solo singer/songwriter gigs at places like The Frame in Hudson Falls and Saratoga's venerable Caffé Lena[‡‡], I continued to play standards in weekend wedding bands (when DJs didn't get the gig), and had a

---

[‡‡] Among the countless talents that played in Lena Spencer's tiny second floor coffee house were: Bob Dylan, Arlo Guthrie, Don McLean, Pete Seeger, Odetta, Dave Van Ronk and Oscar Brand, David Wilcox, Jonathan Edwards, Hedy West, David Bromberg, Tom Paxton, Bucky & John Pizzarelli, Commander Cody, Kenny Rankin, Mose Allison, Maria Muldaur, Al Stewart, The Roches, Paul Stookey, Happy and Arty Traum, Emmylou Harris, Carolyn Hester, Jesse Colin Young, Josh White, Emmylou Harris, Carolyn Hester, John Stewart, Arlo Guthrie, Nanci Griffith, Chip Taylor, John Stewart, Nanci Griffith, Loudon Wainwright, lll, Eric Anderson, John Sebastian, and Chip Taylor.

pretty good run in a duo called "Garvin and Burns." For that act, I teamed with Dave "Blotto" Maswick (bass and vocals), as we attempted to pull off virtually impossible songs for duos (Steely Dan, Todd Rundgren, etc) along with twisted comedy routines. I took my name from Dan Ackroyd's inane SNL character "Fred Garvin, Male Prostitute," while Dave became "Chevrolet Burns," from the terrific 1965 movie *A Thousand Clowns*, in which "Nick," a 12-year-old adoptee, is allowed to try out different names before locking one in permanently. One of his temporary monikers was Chevrolet Burns.[§§]

I supplemented my gigging income in various ways. First, one of my tennis partners was the principal of Bolton High School, and he kindly hired me as a teaching sub for band and music classes (I didn't mention the "male prostitute" thing on my teacher bio form.) Eventually, I set up a guitar instruction studio in nearby Glens Falls and found that I had a knack for teaching, which I took very seriously. Word got around, and before too long my lesson calendar was full, with forty to fifty private students per week.

[§§] Other names Nick tried out, on such things as library cards, were "Dr. Morris Fishbine" and author Raphael Sabatini. The lead character, Nick's uncle Murray Burns, was based on the brilliant radio raconteur Jean Shepherd, whose shows I listened to religiously in the seventies.

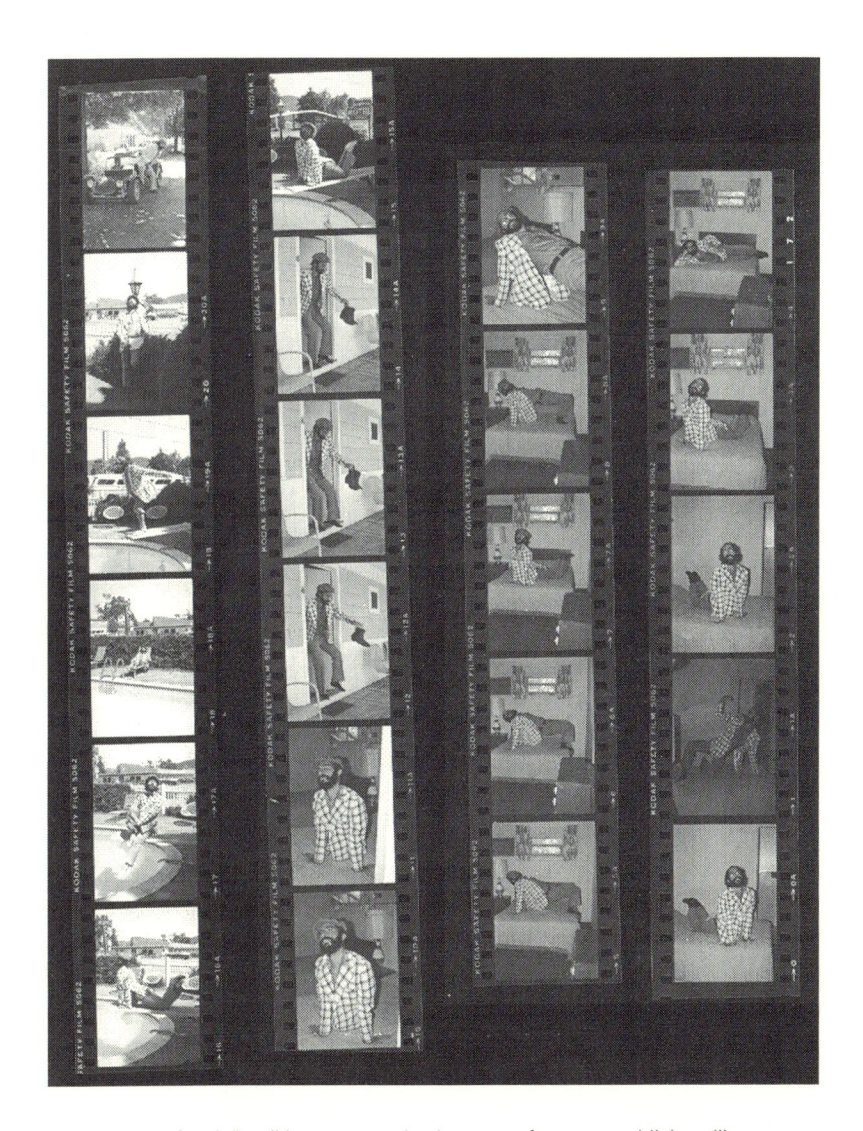

"Fred Garvin" striking some seductive poses for some publicity stills

But I was still writing music regularly and longed for a financial outlet for this vocation. I had dutifully been sending demo reels of my songs to New York publishers, and received so many form rejections that it was becoming something of an existential joke — at one point I wallpapered my instruction room with them. It was then that I realized how similar the wording was on each rejection, and, in a fit of lunacy, I launched my own rejection campaign. I decided to write back to each rejector and decline their rejection in the same impersonal way they dealt with yours truly:

> *From the Office of Gus Russo, songwriter, VP:*
> *Dear Warner Brothers,*
> *Thanks for thinking of us with your rejection submission of 3-20-79. After much consideration, we are sorry to have to pass on your rejection. Although we felt that the letter was well written, it doesn't seem to be a good fit for us at this time. But please feel free to consider us in the future with other rejections you might think we are looking for.*
> *Kind Regards,*
> *Gus Russo / Vice President, A & R (Assholes and Rejections) Dept.*

At least a half-dozen corporate secretaries called me in hysterics, one of whom said she made a hundred photocopies and circulated them throughout her label. But I still didn't get a sale.

Luckily, a girl I was seeing at the time worked for a local radio station and suggested I write commercial jingles for some of their frequent advertisers, who had no way to spruce up their spots. My friend secreted out a list of the station's top buyers and I was off to the races. At the time I owned a four-track Teac reel-to-reel machine that I figured could be used to record said jingles, with me doing all the singing and instrumentation. With my list in hand, I literally went on cold calls and met with the owners of the businesses that used radio most heavily.

To land my first sale, I made the local sporting goods megastore owner an offer that was so low-ball that he couldn't refuse. My modus operandi has always been to work the first time for free or cheap in order to get my foot in the door – musicians are used to auditioning anyway. I had such confidence in my abilities that I knew that finances would quickly take care of themselves if I delivered the goods. Long story short, my first jingle, heavily laden with Beach Boys-style harmonies, was a local smash, and led to a couple of dozen other clients, many of whom were repeat customers who updated their jingles every few months. Soon I was able to afford to hire great local players and book a 24-track recording studio in Saratoga for the higher-budgeted productions. One thing led to another and I was soon producing demos for local bands.

Of course I maintained my part time job at the racquet club, where I played indoor tennis for free most nights after the members left. With keys to the facility, I could literally open it up at any time for workouts, or to bring the occasional girl in for a late night sauna. Like Lake George, it was a pretty hedonistic atmosphere. I not only shared the pro shop duties with stringer extraordinaire Richie,[***] but also more than a few bizarre road trips. Throughout the seventies, I continued to be a ringleader in convincing friends to jump in the car for a day or a week — we thought nothing about driving 300 miles to see a James Brown show. On a recent getaway to Florida, I visited NASA before continuing on to Homestead, where I was in awe at the stonework of Latvian eccentric Edward Leedskalnin in his mind-blowing Coral Castle, which the 100-lb. tuberculosis sufferer built single-handedly by somehow maneuvering about one hundred fourteen-ton slabs of coral.[†††] (He claimed to have mastered the same anti-gravity techniques as the pyramid builders.) We laughed at the fact that while others were visiting Disney World, we were paying reverence to a true eccentric. The castle was just one more proof that human imagination and potential should never be stifled. In a strange way, I revered Mr. Leedskalnin.

On that same trip we crashed at Miami Beach's famous Fountainebleu Hotel with a pal who was the hotel's tennis pro. This was at the height of the "Scarface" cocaine wars. I'll never forget hearing the sounds of automatic gunfire at night on Collins Avenue. My tennis pro friend said we'd be crazy to venture out after sundown.

[***] Richie and I were both fond of trying experimental strings in our racquets. When one of our club members who ran a company that made cardiac catheters offered to give us spools of super thin gauge, high tension catheters, we jumped at the chance to string our racquets up with the super-thin material (the thinner the string, the more spin can be imparted; traditional strings range from 15 to 17 gauge. Our catheter was 19 and higher). I used it for years, and to this day it is the best and most unbreakable "string" I have put in my racquets.
[†††] See: http://en.wikipedia.org/wiki/Coral_Castle

Getting back to the Richie trip…

One night in the racquet club, Richie and I were discussing the upcoming 1978 Halloween night and wondered if there might be a way to do something original. Coincidentally, I had recently read about the Annual Salem Witches Ball, in which hundreds of witches from around the country journey to Salem, Mass. to party. Salem, of course, was the site where nineteen girls were hanged, one pressed to death, and 200 jailed by religious fanatics in the 17th century.

This fifth annual event was hosted by the Official Witch of Salem, Laurie Cabot, a sort of Ann Wilson look-alike, and her two hot "Wiccan" daughters, Jodi and Penny. Laurie was something of a local personality who loved to preach that witches weren't evil, but merely "enlightened," and how they only did good work for the communities in which they lived.‡‡‡ Two years earlier, Cabot had been conscripted by the Boston Red Sox to put spells on their bats when they were suffering through a ten-game losing streak (it worked.)

Richie and the others agreed that there could be no better way to spend All Hallows Eve than with hundreds of pagan girls who thought they were witches. So, on October 31st, along with a couple of other wacky tennis bums, we made the 225-mile drive to Salem in beautiful fall weather, checking in at the historic Hawthorne Inn on historic Essex Street on the historic Salem Commons. Logistically, the hotel was perfect, located just one block from Laurie's Crow Haven Corner Witch Shop, and four blocks from the site of the ball; we figured we would be able to get as hammered as we liked before stumbling back to our rooms.

Hitting the historic streets, we knew immediately that the trip would be memorable: the sidewalks were filled with the visiting witches, strolling along in their finest black capes, black gowns, and black boots — not a Fila logo in sight. Richie had packed a cape for the Ball, and I brought my authentic Groucho Marx "morning coat."

---

‡‡‡ Indeed, Cabot had received awards for working with dyslexic children, and Massachusetts Governor Michael Dukakis bestowed upon her the state's Patriot Award, known as the 'Paul Revere' citation. The award, signed by the Governor and the Treasurer of the Commonwealth of Massachusetts, read: "I proclaim Laurie Cabot the Official Witch of Salem for her work with children of special needs."

We quickly got the tourist thing out of the way, checking out the House of the Seven Gables (where a family of non-fanatics hid persecuted girls in a secret room), Nathanial Hawthorne's home, and the Witch House, where the poor girls were sentenced. Then it was on to the Crow Haven, where we met a warlock named Edzu, who informed us that the Wiccans refer to Halloween as "Samhain," and it was their most sacred day, commemorating the executions of their ancestors. The shop sold all sorts of potions and paraphernalia, and I think we all bought the same thing: a powder that when burnt, makes any girl you're focusing on succumb to you.

After we purchased our love potions from Edzu, I pulled him aside described our real quest:

"We drove for five hours, and we kind of assumed that, with all the Wiccans in town, there might be some other gatherings, you know, like séances. Can you clue us in?"

The black-hooded Edzu hesitated, then responded *sotto voce*:

"OK, I shouldn't tell you this, and you definitely didn't hear it from me. If you should happen to be in The Old Burying Point at two a.m. you might see something interesting." That was it.

The Burying Point turned out to be a 17th century cemetery, the oldest in the US, established in 1637 near the center of town, and we would certainly be there at 2 a.m., hammered or not.

At the Witches Ball we boogied with the Laurie and her daughters (who turned out to be a tad too young) to the sounds of the James Montgomery Blues Band. At 1:45 a.m. our quartet broke away and headed for the old cemetery, and upon arrival saw that we were alone. We shuffled about for a few minutes and just as we reached the conclusion that we had been scammed by Edzu the Warlock, we noticed a spooky procession of over a dozen black-hooded and black-caped figures making their way by individually held candles down Charter Street towards the cemetery, where our trio waited by the gate.

"Holy shit!" more than one of us whispered. "Yeah, this is what we came for!"

The ghoulish parade, made up of half female witches and half male warlocks, walked past us in silence, however each one gave us dirty looks as they opened the gate and proceeded inside the hallowed grounds. The last person in the lineup was a large warlock, who stopped to confront us as the others marched on.

"You don't belong here," he advised in threatening tones.

Richie, who was more in the bag than the rest of us, got right in his face and said something to the effect of: "Fuck you, you broom-riding asshole. What are you going to do, put a curse on us?"

Which is exactly what he did. After speaking some sort of twisted Latin and making wild hand gestures at us, the warlock joined the rest as we laughed in his wake. We followed from a distance, stopping behind a large rectangular tomb to eavesdrop on the coven, which was now about twenty yards away and forming a circle around a gravestone. On command, they put down their candles and withdrew some sharp stones form a bag that one of them had carried. Up until this point, there had been dead quiet in the cemetery. But suddenly, this benevolent group, which for years had been espousing how peaceful, kindly, and misunderstood they really were, began screaming at the grave in the same Latin-esque gobbledygook, and an occasional recognizable English curse word like "Motherfucker!" The looks on their faces were frightful as they next approached the grave, and with the sharp stones and charcoal proceeded to desecrate it. At one point they noticed us behind the tomb and screamed the same curses in our direction, adding, "You don't belong here!" and "Go home before it's too late!"

Ritchie and I, ready for action in Salem

Now, normal people would have been long gone by now, but for some reason — likely single-malt Scotch — we didn't budge. For the next half-hour or so, we watched as the witches moved on to many other markers and repeated the same ritual. When it seemed they were winding down, we decided to make our way back to the Hawthorne, high-five-ing each other on the way and saying, "Now that was the way to spend Halloween!"

The next morning, checking out of the Hawthorne while more than a little hung over, we all asked the same question: Did that really happen last night, or were we that drunk? We decided to visit the cemetery again in our way out of town. When we made our way to the victimized gravesites, indeed they had been horribly marked with random scars and witch hieroglyphics.

We were shocked to see that the names on the graves were "Judge" this, and "Judge" that. I wrote down the names that appeared on a few of the stone slabs: Judge Benjamin Lynde, Judge Jonathan Corwin, Judge John Hawthorne, Peter Webb, Abigail and John Archer. Before hitting the road, we had to make one last stop: we visited the Crow Haven to both thank Edzu for a splendid evening and to ask him what the hell we had witnessed. He was stunned and couldn't believe we actually showed up at the Burying Point. After some prodding, he informed us that every Hallow's Eve, for over four hundred years, witches enter the cemetery to place a curse on both the judges and those who falsely testified against their historical brethren. They believe their spell keeps the accursed from proceeding into the afterlife, condemned to spend eternity in Limbo. We wondered what Governor Dukakis would think of that.

We sleep it off in the Burying Point. (Note the "Shoe-Goo" on my sneaker toes. At the time, the goo was a popular way for tennis players to save their shoes from toe-drag holes.)

Throughout the period my interest in the Kennedy assassination continued, fueled in part by the fact that the US House of Representatives was undertaking full-scale hearings into both JFK's and Martin Luther King's murders. I was making more frequent road trips back to Baltimore and DC, where I continued my dialogue with Bud Fensterwald and others trying to influence the new House Select Committee on Assassinations (HSCA, 1977-1979). I attended a number of the public hearings, and learned that just before the Committee was set to go out of business in early 1979 there would be a public hearing that would make history: a Dallas police recording discovered at the

Committee's 11th hour recorded the sounds of four or more gunshots in the plaza where Kennedy was killed, and Lee Harvey Oswald only had time for three. At that hearing, the committee would also run a first generation copy of the Zapruder film, something never before seen in public. Of course, I would be there to judge for my own eyes.

On the appointed day, December 29, 1978, I went to Capitol Hill with my two younger brothers Tony and Bob, whom I had convinced that they would want to say they were there when history was rewritten. When we entered the large hearing room we were directed to the far rear "public viewing" seats. For me, this was just not going to do. Having driven all the way from Lake George, and having sat front row at the US Open for the last decade, I was not about to sit forty rows back where I couldn't get a good view of the original Zapruder footage. I thus put my well-honed gatecrashing skills into action, and somehow (I forget exactly) convinced a House page that we were witnesses. We were promptly escorted to one of the many unused "witness" seats in the third row, just twenty feet from the projection screen. Seated to my left was a tall, friendly man, wearing a beige "leisure suit," and who spoke with a Texas accent. Before I could learn what he had witnessed, and before I had to concoct a story of why *I* was in the witness section along with my 16-year-old brother, who was two months old when Kennedy was killed, the hearing was called to order.

The Russo Brothers crash the hearings while on national television. (see arrows)

Acoustics experts James Barger of *Bolt, Beranek & Newman*, and Mark Weiss and Ernest Ashkenasy of Queens College had been studying the static-filled tape that displayed no audible gunshots for three months when they came to testify. After some dizzying mathematical testimony from the experts, they announced their conclusion of "a probability of 95 percent or better [that] there was indeed a shot fired from the grassy knoll." hey added that they knew that the grassy knoll weapon had fired a supersonic bullet, since a shock wave had preceded the sound of the muzzle blast (they could detect both phenomena on the tape). They were, they said, also able to place the shooter within a five-foot "circumference." Lastly, they could pinpoint the location of the open Dallas Police microphone — likely on a motorcycle — that accidentally recorded the sounds to within an 18-foot diameter circle, 120 feet behind the President's limousine.

Although we didn't know it then, these renowned experts were wrong about everything, as proven by numerous scientific panels. Coincidentally, one expert, Mark Weiss, had testified five years earlier about another historical tape recording, the "18-and-½ minute gap" tape of Watergate fame. And just like he did with the Dallas tape, he got it wrong, in that case by not catching that the various erasure buzzes were made in different offices and by different people. Thus, in the Watergate case he missed the real conspiracy, while in the Kennedy case he created a false one. It would not be my last experience with the failings of prestigious "highly regarded experts."

Then the star witness was called to testify, and it just so happened to be the tall man in the beige leisure suit seated to my left. Twenty-six year Dallas police veteran H.B. McLain was determined by the committee to have been the riding the motorcycle that was in the 18-foot circle, and which captured the audio on a stuck open microphone. Regrettably, McLain was interrogated as if a hostile witness, with long strings of hypothetical "Is it possible?" questions. Had the questioners merely asked what had happened he would have told them that it was practically inconceivable that he had recorded the tape, or that he was even in the circle that he had to be in to make the mathematics work. Most disturbingly, McLain was not even allowed to listen to the recording he allegedly made. When he finally heard it four months later in the Dallas Sheriff's office, he was incensed.

"If they'd have let me listen to the tapes before I went up there," McLain said later, "I could have told them right quick that it wasn't my [two-wheel] motorcycle but that it was a three-wheeler [*NOTE: The three-wheelers had a distinctively different engine sound*]. In fact, that three-wheeler was three miles away at the Trade Mart, thus they didn't hear any shots on the tapes and their theory was not valid. The noise they heard was the radio popping. Those old radios popped all the time."

But McLain didn't get the chance to say this on this day, and the next day's papers ran bold headlines proclaiming the historic fourth-shot conspiracy.

When McLain finished testifying, the lights were dimmed and, at long last, the famous pristine print of the Zapruder film was shown for the first time. And just as in Geraldo's studio four years earlier, the audience gasped at the carnage wreaked by the destructive shot to Kennedy's head. Only now, the scene was much clearer and focused. In this clear version it was now apparent, especially when the film was played in slow motion, that the President's head jerked forward before going backwards — he had indeed been shot from the rear and the backwards motion was a misleading recoil. When the committee filed its scientific and forensics reports that summer, it also agreed that the alleged "grassy knoll shooter" must have missed – from twenty yards away!

We rode down the House elevator with Weiss and Ashkenasy, peppering them with questions: How could you be so sure that the sub-sonic shockwaves were gunshots? Did you test other wave generating noises? How could a hired mob assassin miss the entire limo from 20 yards? But they weren't interested in answering the questions. They still aren't.

Experts Say That Second Gunman Almost Certainly Shot at Kennedy

By MARJORIE HUNTER
Special to The New York Times

WASHINGTON, Dec. 29 — Acoustics experts said today that tests showed "a probability of 95 percent or better" that a shot was fired from a grassy knoll in Dallas when President Kennedy was assassinated.

The findings would appear to contradict the conclusion of the Warren Commission in 1964 that Lee Harvey Oswald, shooting from a window of the Texas School Book Depository building, acted alone in assassinating the President on Nov. 22, 1963.

The testimony of Mark Weiss and Ernest Aschkenasy, professors at Queens College of the City University of New York, came as the House Select Committee on Assassinations prepared to end a $5.8 million, two-year inquiry into circumstances surrounding the assassinations of President Kennedy and the Rev. Dr. Martin Luther King Jr. The committee goes out of business Wednesday.

In evaluating the Weiss and Aschkenasy findings, the committee's staff concluded that while the new evidence strongly indicated a possible conspiracy and the presence of a second gunman on the grassy knoll, the shots that killed President Kennedy and injured Gov. John Connally of Texas were fired by Oswald. The shot from the knoll, the staff concluded, struck no one and did not strike the Kennedy limousine.

Recording From Motorcycle

The professors' public testimony paralleled reports published last week based on information obtained from committee sources about the Weiss-Aschkenasy analysis of a Dictabelt recording of sounds picked up by a microphone on a police motorcycle. That recording was compared with others made of shooting tests conducted in Dallas last summer.

The professors' findings were corroborated by Dr. James Barger, chief scientist and head of acoustics analysis for Bolt, Beranek and Newman of Cambridge, Mass., who conducted the series of shooting tests.

Dr. Barger had testified in September that there was only a 50-50 probability of a shot from the grassy knoll. But he said that the further analysis by the Queens College professors had convinced him that there was a probability of "95 percent or more" that a shot was fired from the knoll.

Committee photographic experts said in September that a special "enhancement" of a photograph of the Kennedy shooting showed a figure that might be a man near the corner of a wall on the grassy knoll.

Concern Over Findings

Committee members were clearly concerned by the new acoustical evidence, coming so late in the long inquiry. The evidence, said Representative Louis Stokes, the committee chairman, could have an enormous impact on history because it raises "a legal assumption of the possibility of a conspiracy."

The Ohio Democrat noted that the committee had "developed evidence of the outlines of a likely conspiracy" in the death of Dr. King. The evidence heard today, if accepted as valid, "could point to a conspiracy in the assassination of President Kennedy," he said.

Mr. Stokes said the committee inquiry had served to show that "never again should our society respond as it did in the aftermath of the deaths of these two leaders. We did not give these men the types of investigation in depth which were commensurate with the dignity of their lives."

The committee has found no evidence that Dr. King, the civil rights leader, was not shot by his convicted killer, James Earl Ray, who is now in prison in Tennessee. However, the committee has heard evidence that Mr. Ray may have had assistance and that he was prompted to kill by an an offer of money for Dr. King's death.

The second-ranking member of the panel, Richardson Preyer, Democrat of North Carolina, said tonight that the committee's conclusions and recommendations would be issued tomorrow for publication in Sunday newspapers.

Mr. Preyer, who said he found today's witnesses "persuasive," said the panel was trying to decide how the testimony should be pursued — whether, for example, it should be referred to the Justice Department. The committee itself, its long months of hearings completed, goes out of existence next Wednesday.

Mr. Weiss and Mr. Aschkenasy said that they reached their conclusions by taking the Dictabelt and test recordings and comparing bursts of gunfire and echoes at a series of points as the motorcycle moved down the street behind the Kennedy limousine.

Other Explanations Rejected

The professors rejected committee members' suggestions that the sounds on the Dictabelt recording might have been backfire from moving vehicles, exploding firecrackers or perhaps just "acoustical mirages."

They said that while they could not state positively that the noises were made by rifle fire, the noise pattern and reverberating echoes were certain to have been made by something as loud as a rifle.

All three of the acoustics experts testifying today served on panels that examined the White House tape recordings in connection with the Watergate case. Dr. Barger helped analyze the celebrated 18½-minute gap in one White House tape.

Also testifying today was H.B.B. McLain, a Dallas police officer who is believed to have been riding the motorcycle whose microphone apparently stuck in the open position and carried the sounds of the shooting. Mr. McLain said he was not aware that his microphone was on but that "it had stuck before."

Although two years of work had been leading the panel to announce no conspiracy, this last-minute acoustics snafu left them scrambling for an explanation. Thus, forced into a corner by seriously flawed science, they conjectured, with no hard evidence whatsoever, that the mob must have killed Kennedy. Huh?

For me, I came to believe that I had not witnessed history at all, but I had learned a valuable lesson about experts, Congressional hearings, and the importance of using first-generation film footage as evidence.

Chapter Thirteen

Manhattan Madness

ALL THE KNOWLEDGE I had acquired in the jingle business in Glens Falls and at Sleepy Hollow in Ithaca made me ready in 1979 when I received a call from my Latvian fiddle player friend, Edgar Ievins. I hadn't seen Edgar at a gig in some months and he informed me that was because he had moved to Manhattan to be with his girlfriend, Ilze Balodis, an actress in low-budget cult horror flicks such as *Slash of the Knife (The Unkindest Cut of All.)* By day, Ilze was the registrar at the Academy of Dramatic Arts and regularly funneled students into film work. When *Slash*'s writer/director, 28-year old graphic artist Frank Henenlotter, approached her with an idea for a horror movie (actually he prefers to call his works "exploitation movies") with an actual budget, she recommended Edgar, who had majored in accounting, to be the producer of Frank's twisted masterwork, a charming little ditty entitled *Basket Case*. Frank accepted, and with Ilze as casting director, Edgar began the spade work, including finding a composer – hence his call to me. Now, if I passed muster with Henenlotter, I could land the gig, which came without a paycheck.

To say I was thrilled to possibly write a full-length movie score would be an understatement. Since childhood, I had been keenly aware of the music in the background of my favorite movies and television shows — for me it was often the foreground. From James Bernard's thrilling work on the Hammer Horror films to the music of Jerry Goldsmith, Max Steiner, Ennio Morricone, John Barry, and Henry Mancini, I was regularly transported by movie music from my Baltimore neighborhood to the outer reaches of the planet and the imagination. On television, Nelson Riddle's theme for *Route 66* was permanently burned into my cortex – especially after I got to meet the cast when they filmed just six blocks from my home — which, paradoxically, is nowhere near Route 66 — I assume they took a wrong turn. The TV theme that most captivated was the stunning Polynesian melody written by Dorcas Cochran and Lionel Newman (uncle of composers Randy, Alfred, and Thomas Newman) for *Adventures in Paradise* (1959-1962), possibly the favorite TV show of my childhood, and most certainly a key bad influence on my wanderlust. The hour-long weekly series, produced by Dominick Dunne (who decades later became a friend), celebrated the South Seas adventures of a charter schooner boat operator, as fictionalized by James A. Michener. Thanks to that show and the Michener novels, adventures in the South Pacific paradise always remained a goal.

But the prolific composer who was most consistently brilliant was the iconic Bernard Herrmann, who not only terrified us in the Hitchcock movies, but also enthralled us in the great fantasy flickers of my youth, such as *Jason and the Argonauts* and the *Seventh Voyage of Sinbad*. On television he regaled in countless episodes of *The Twilight Zone, Have Gun — Will Travel, Rawhide*, and the *Alfred Hitchcock Hour*, among many others. Amazingly, he composed my two favorite scores, *Journey to the Center of the Earth* and *North by Northwest* in the same year that he wrote two *other* scores (1959.) One year later, he created the sonic masterpiece at the limbic core of *Psycho*. Simply amazing.

Soon after getting the call I was taking a Greyhound down to Port Authority Bus Terminal in midtown. I then transferred to the subway for the short hop to Edgar's East Village neighborhood, an area I had never explored but that was soon to become my second home. I was pretty comfy in the gentrified West Village, thanks to numerous trips to see "Brel" at the Village Gate or jazz at the Blue Note and the Village Vanguard, but the eastern quadrant, which recalled the hardscrabble beatnik West Village of the fifties, was a new experience altogether.

Exiting the Astor Place station near Cooper Union College, I was in another universe, completely unlike midtown: here were street vendors selling used everything on blankets laid out on the sidewalk, struggling young artists busking and jamming on the corners, and hotels with hourly rates (the St. Mark's Hotel still has them.) The aromas of pot, patchouli, petrol, and piss fought for supremacy. Edgar lived four blocks from the station at 110 St. Mark's Place, arguably the hippest three-block street in New York. Here was where Thelonius Monk, Andy Warhol, Lenny Bruce, and Yoko Ono spent their salad days. Abbie Hoffman founded the Yippies one block from Edgar's at #30, while #80 St. Mark's Place housed a legendary speakeasy, where a callow boy named Frank Sinatra was a singing waiter, where Leon Trotsky lived in 1917, and where Lord Buckley gave his final performance before his death in 1960.

Living on those three blocks in 1980 were struggling up-and-comers like Cyndi Lauper, the Ramones, Joe Jackson, and Jeff Buckley.

Just one block from the infamous St. Mark's Bar & Grill, Edgar had the first floor of a tiny storefront that was literally a pile of rubble when he leased it a year earlier. It wasn't much better in 1980 when Edgar showed me in: a tiny cluttered front room, maybe 8 by 10 feet, connected to a small hallway that led to a barely enclosed toilet.

Edgar's former home at 110 St. Mark's Place, where *Basket Case* was produced.

This was where he lived?

"Where do you sleep?" I asked. Or more importantly, where was I going to sleep?

Then Edgar reached up to the ridiculously low ceiling and pulled on a hidden latch, whereupon a secret staircase descended. He explained that his microscopic space was only zoned for commercial use, so he had to be covert about its actual intent as his home.

"You have the master bedroom," Edgar said, pointing upward. "I'll crash at Ilze's." At the top of the stairs was a hidden loft (aha, that's why the ceiling was so low) about six-foot square with about two feet of headspace — and no windows. That first night I tried to illegally sleep there, I felt like Michael Collins alone in his cramped capsule above the far side of the moon, while Armstrong and Aldrin were walking on the surface. It's a good thing I wasn't claustrophobic, but I can't tell you how many times I woke up and banged my head against a wall, or the ceiling. On the plus side, it was very inspirational for someone about to write a horror movie score.

After the thorough 10-second tour of the mad Latvian's sardine can pad, we hit the streets for the one-mile walk over to Frank's place in the upscale West Village.

As soon as we started west we passed 98 St. Mark's Place, which was featured on the cover of Led Zeppelin's *Physical Graffiti* album a few years earlier. A few seconds later, we passed the St. Mark's Bar and Grill, where notables like Keith Richards of the Rolling Stones occasionally dropped in to play some blues. At Astor Place, Edgar suggested that I "turn the cube," the giant metal sculpture ("Alamo") that, with some effort, could be turned on its axis. It became something of a ritual. The streets were alive with young artists, dopers, and castaways, all trying to exist on the fringy outer skin of the Big Apple.

With each westward block we traversed, another layer of grime disappeared — on both the storefronts and the people — until we arrived in the natty West Village, then populated by lots of men holding hands. I had been unaware that this was the center of the gay universe, so named due to the street named "Gay" that was the culture's epicenter.* Moving on, we arrived at Frank's place, a pristine second floor apartment, with an actual kitchen, bathroom, and even wall-to-wall carpet. The walls were adorned with framed movie posters and hundreds of neatly arranged VHS tapes on shelves. But the neatness, upon closer inspection, was misleading: the movie posters were all of gore movies, and every single VHS tape was a low budget, blood-drenched, gore-fest. On one table were placed two flesh-colored latex cones. I guessed, and was correct, that they were from *Saturday Night Live*'s "Conehead" characters. I asked Frank how they ended up in his living room, and he explained that two of SNL's makeup men were going to create the creature and the other latex prosthetic special effects for the forthcoming movie. I was soon meeting with SNL's Kevin Haney and John Caglione, both protégés of the legendary Academy Award winner Dick Smith (*Little Big Man*, *The Godfather*, and *The Exorcist*, to that point.) Both Haney and Caglione would eventually earn their own Oscars, but not for *Basket Case*.

Inside Frank's meticulous refrigerator were fake food, latex body parts, and bottles of movie blood, the secret formula of which had been donated by Dick Smith. Not one ounce of actual food. (I, on the other had, had at least two ounces in mine, mostly ketchup and long-expired salad dressing.)

OK, then. This was going to be an adventure!

Frank was outgoing, in a hyper bizarro way, but we got along great. When we got around to discussing music, he asked me if I had ever heard of Bernard Hermann. I was home free. We fell into a breathless discussion of the minutiae of Hermann's instrumentation, themes, etc. It turned out that we shared a common history with the kinds of music, movies, and TV shows we liked growing up. Suffice it

---

* These men were just fortunate that their scene didn't cluster around Flatbush Ave. in Queens.

to say, I got the gig, although there were certainly more qualified composers within walking distance of Frank's abode. If talent were more important than luck and perseverance, I'd still be making gas masks in that Baltimore sweatshop.

Back upstate, I began to go to school on the great composers. First, I devoured Henry Mancini's seminal book, *Sounds and Scores*. And I watched movies – lots of movies. In the days when VHS tape movies cost as much as $90, most of us owned very few. Thus I did my listening research in movie theaters or watching late night reruns of classic films. In the theaters, I'd sit there taking notes in the dark, noting which instruments made the best combinations, which tempos worked best for different scenes, etc. I had plenty of time to do my homework because Edgar had to raise money for production expenses, almost all of which would go toward the purchase of 16-mm film stock and processing — the actors and crew (including myself) agreed to work in exchange for net profit points. My share was .5%. When, and if, monies became available, $1500 would be devoted to music expenses. I was told that the total budget of the film was slightly south of $20,000, 95% of which went to color film stock and processing.

Returning back upstate on Cloud Nine, I got back to work with my band while Edgar looked for investors. At the time, I was going through an obsession with Big Band music, and especially the singers that fronted the bands, like the Modernaires and the Pied Pipers. The harmonies and arrangements of the Manhattan Transfer also were becoming a huge influence.

For years, to wind down from gigs I would put the all-night radio on,

The great Les Paul and me at Jazzbeaux's picnic.

listening to Al "Jazzbeaux" Collins, who broadcast from the fictional "Purple Grotto" in the bowels of New York's WNEW. When summer came I went to a couple of his picnics held on Staten Island, where I first got to hang with the great Les Paul.

As a result of these influences, I had put together bands — Swing Fever (1980-2) and Swing Shift (1982-3) — that could perform this great material. There were no local club bands like this, so it was a real gamble; this was a good ten years before the swing renaissance led by the likes of Brian Setzer and Kid Creole. Just as when I put together country rock and surf bands in 1960s urban Baltimore, I had to follow my muse, with no regard to the monetary consequences. Surprisingly, we developed quite a loyal following. Our summer gig at a new Lake George club was a highlight: every weekend the club was mobbed, and at 2 a.m. there was still a line to get in. We'd finish around three, and often I'd be up by nine to play in a tennis tournament, or to run the Bolton Open, which I had recently inherited.

Swing Shift

I was making frequent bus trips down to Manhattan, hanging with Edgar and Frank, as they cobbled the production together. I was crashing in Edgar's secret micro-loft during the US Open, an event that was rapidly losing its allure for me thanks to the explosion of commercialism and pre-sold corporate seats. When Edgar informed me that John Lennon showed up almost every day at Nathan's Hot Dogs in Times Square, I started eating there. Sure enough, one day John showed up at the eatery, just a block or so from where he and his fellow Beatles made history on Ed Sullivan's stage, to pick up a couple of malted milks to go. I was amazed at how tiny he was, and I made a point of shaking his hand. He was very gracious as I blubbered something about digging his singing on "Twist and Shout," a vocal no one I knew could duplicate. He laughed and said, "My voice was shredded for weeks after that one. Cheers." I saw John one more time as he and Yoko exited an art house movie theater in the Village. He seemed to love the streets of New York, where locals gave him his space after exchanging polite greetings.

Edgar also came upstate to visit his pals and to get a breather from his Big Apple producer responsibilities. We were hanging on the night of Monday, December 8, 1980, when, as we and two other friends pulled up to my rental house, one of my housemates came running out in the bitter cold, frantic.

"Did you hear? Did you hear what happened?" she implored. "Turn on the radio!"

We sat in the car and listened as we learned that John Lennon had been shot to death outside his midtown apartment building, The Dakota, which overlooked Central Park on the west side. The news of the death of the 40-year-old icon was an emotional jolt comparable to the murders of JFK, MLK, and RFK. But John was a musician, not a politician. What madman would do such a thing? The timing was horrific; after years as drug-addled recluse, Lennon had just recently emerged from the shadows and only three weeks earlier had released his stunning comeback album, *Double Fantasy*, the number one album in the country. He had finally learned to become a good father, doting on his five-year old son, Sean. The murder at the Dakota had a special meaning for Edgar, since one member of our *Basket Case* coterie had been John and Yoko's pot connection. Once we accompanied him as he made a drop-off. John's apartment door cracked open just a couple inches as Yoko reached out for the bag. That was it.

We had gone over a decade since the wave of assassinations of the sixties — Malcolm, JFK, MLK, and RFK — and we had just begun to naively think that era was over. I had hoped that we had somehow gained ground over the gun-promulgating NRA, and it's Second Amendment-distorting sycophants. I was sadly wrong.

As with America's other assassinations, most of us stayed glued to the television to learn the sordid details of the killer and his motive. The news showed thousands of New Yorkers gathering outside John and Yoko's apartment building, trying to console the widow. However, the crowds disrupted the flow of others who lived in the building, prompting Yoko to ask the fans to show their love for her husband on Sunday in one of his favorite places, Central Park. She further requested that people everywhere observe ten minutes of silence and prayer at 2 pm on that day. At the end of the week, Edgar and I made our way down to Manhattan, and on Sunday trekked up to the park's Naumburg Bandshell area in the grey, bitter cold. It would be a day of eerie occurrences.

Walking along Central Park South on West 59th Street, we joined up with a mass of young people headed into the park. Before entering the footpath, I heard a voice from across the wide boulevard yelling: "Hey, Fred!" I ignored it, until he persisted with "Fred! Fred Garvin!" I looked to the other side of 59th and saw another upstater waving at me, a guy I had only met a couple of times, and only knew by *his* stage name, "Sarge Blotto." He was a founder of the band, Blotto, with whom my duo partner, Chevrolet Burns, occasionally played.

I yelled back, "Hey, Sarge!"

That's when I was struck by the absurdity of the moment.

What were the odds that two guys from upstate New York (four hours away) would bump into each other in a city of seven million, *and* only know each other by stage names?

As we all blended in with the huge, teary-eyed crowd, estimated at 150,000 to 200,000, there were people with guitars singing John's songs with choked up voices, and groups handing out "peace" buttons and bumper stickers. Other than the melodies, there was precious little sound — no one seemed to need to speak. We just hugged a lot. Set on an easel on the bandshell was a photo of John in his beloved "New York City" shirt.

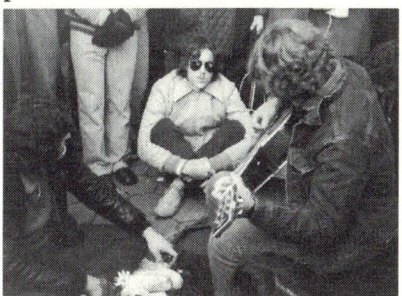

To the side of the shell was a makeshift scaffold on which rested a single speaker column that blasted John's music out to the crowd. There were no speeches or garish displays, just people standing around, hugging, and quietly singing John's songs amidst the barren trees. "Give Peace a Chance" was played many times that day. The only announcement came just before two o'clock, when a male voice emanated from the speaker, saying. "We will now observe ten minutes of silence for John." Thus, exactly at two, we joined people all around the world to honor Yoko's request and John Lennon's memory.

When the music stopped, you could have heard a pin drop amongst the huge throng. The only sounds were birds, some quiet sobbing, and the muted sounds of the city far off in the distance. That's when it happened.

Until now, we had been shivering in the windy, thirty-degree cold, but just seconds after the music stopped, I began to feel a warmth starting at my frozen feet, then working its way up my legs, torso, then face. It was so warm that I took my coat off, and noticed that all of us were turning to strangers, asking in whispers, "Did you feel that?" and "Holy shit!" It seemed to be a group experience, and we all felt it was John's spirit checking in.

As I now stood there in the warmth, I saw a man who released about thirty or more white helium filled balloons into the grey sky. For some reason, my eyes followed those balloons into the heavens. Together, those inflatables lofted westward, above the huge trees, towards the Central Park West border of the huge green oasis. Oh, my God, I thought — I know where they're heading. In the silence I elbowed the person next to me and we watched in astonishment as the balloons made their way to John's top floor apartment in the Dakota on Central Park West and 72nd, about a half a mile away, but in full view on this clear day. The day before, Yoko had been standing at the very window now grazed by the balloons, acknowledging the fans. I couldn't tell from this distance, but I wondered if Yoko was there at about 2:10, when the balloons made their voyage. When the ten minutes of silence concluded, the temperature tumbled back down to the low 30's, and it was over. Many of us walked over to the Dakota, where Yoko came to the window to wave and thank us.

Two weeks later I was back in Manhattan, where I got my first insight into producing "no budget" feature movies. On a cold December night, I accompanied Edgar on his regular after-midnight Upper East Side trolling, the point of which was to gather discarded raw material, including furniture, before the trash men showed up. The Upper East Side trash was the best, Edgar informed me, and we dragged end tables, chests of drawers, and large pieces of plywood and canvas back to St. Mark's Place (as if there was room). These objects found were to become the set dressing and the sets themselves for *Basket Case*. If you should ever see the movie, please know that virtually nothing you see was paid for, and much had been previously owned by Manhattan Blue Bloods who would never know that their discarded sofas, armoires, and beds were immortalized, and blood-stained, in what was to become a cult classic. On one late night scavenge safari it occurred to me how privileged I was to have hung out with both John Waters' Dreamlanders in the Charles Street Village, and now with New York's "John Waters" (Frank Henenlotter) here in Greenwich Village. I frankly don't know how my brain survived.

It was on this December trip that I had a rare drag from a joint (my last ever) when we attended the premiere of a movie that our prosthetic makeup guys, Caglione and Haney, had worked on with the iconic Dick Smith. The movie was entitled *Altered States*, a frenetic, eye-popping journey into cosmic consciousness, hallucinogens, and sensory deprivation tanks. As we entered the massive Loew's Astor Plaza in mid-town, we were informed that the entire audience was getting in for free. Edgar then raced to his favorite seats, 8th row center, pulled out a doobie and passed it down the aisle to our crew. It was a perfect way to see the depicted drug trips as they played out explosively on the massive screen, searing our corneas from just a few feet away.

It was years later that I learned that the movie's plot was "borrowed" from the writings and experiments of visionary scientist Dr. John Lilly, inventor of the sensory deprivation tank, which was featured in the movie. Lilly did much of his work in the late Sixties at Baltimore's Spring Grove State Mental Hospital, which bordered the campus of my alma mater, UMBC. It turned out that as I cut through the hospital grounds every day on my way to class, Lilly was there jumping in the tank. (One day I hope to retrieve that tank from the bowels of the hospital's abandoned buildings — I am told it is still there.)

The next year was a whirlwind of New York City adventures, as I visited as often as possible — I swear that I could have navigated the Port Authority Bus Terminal blindfolded. In addition to hanging with Edgar and visiting the film set, I often sat around with the crew in Frank's apartment discussing the production while wearing Caglione's SNL cones. When I heard that Woody Allen played clarinet every Monday without fail at Michael's Pub[†], I began going there whenever I was in town on that night of the week. I was in way over my head at this pricey club, but I could care less. I was there to listen to Woody, so "big deal" if I had to nurse a coke for two hours. I actually met Woody briefly at the bar one night during his break, where I was sitting

---

[†] Woody even skipped the 1977 Oscar ceremony, in which he won Best Picture, Best Director, and Best Screenplay for *Annie Hall*, because it occurred on Monday, when he had his Michael's gig. Now that's a musician!

chatting with comic Soupy Sales, a fan of Woody and his New Orleans funeral band.

It was at Michael's that I became friends with the great jazz duo Jackie & Roy. Over the years, I saw them often, and they were always kind to send me surprise gifts of autographed albums.

"Here's another one I found in the attic," Jackie would write. "I thought you'd like it." She even took the time to compose handwritten letters to me. What a class act. I remember sitting at their table with my favorite Broadway composer Stephen Sondheim at Michael's when they recorded their live Sondheim tribute album, *A Stephen Sondheim Collection* (1982). That was the night I was introduced to the rare Sondheim movie theme, the mesmerizing melody "Stavisky," which the composer gave to the duo for it's first ever cover recording. These inventors of "vocalese" singing, with over thirty amazing albums to their credit, were among the nicest, and most talented, people I have ever met in show business. It's funny, but initially I had been going to Michael's on a shoestring, but eventually I was there as the guest of two of the greatest singers of my generation.

One day in the summer of 1981 there was a crowd gathered a few doors down from Edgar's on St. Mark's Place, at the very same stoop immortalized by Led Zeppelin. This time, Mick Jagger was sitting there with Peter Tosh, pretending to be waiting for Keith Richards in the video filming of "Waiting on a Friend." The band hung around most of the day, finishing up filming at the St. Mark's Bar & Grill, a favorite of the *Basket Case* team. What a hip neighborhood.

Scenes from one hip neighborhood

It was a pretty amazing period, especially considering what a good run I had in Ithaca: my swing band was enjoying great success in Lake George, Saratoga Springs, and elsewhere; I was spending time in the city hanging with a bunch of rogue filmmakers; my guitar studio in my tiny apartment saw 40 or more private students coming and going each week; I was landing the occasional radio jingle; and I was playing tennis practically every sunny day at the gorgeous lakeside courts of Bolton Landing.

Additionally, every August I was running the "Bolton Open Tennis Tournament," which was now attracting some of the top amateurs in a 100-mile radius. One of my frequent tennis partners was Joe

DeSantis, whose father owned a number of Howard Johnson Restaurant franchises around the lake. Often, after a match or a gig, we'd end up at the Lake George Village "HoJo's," where a cute young Italian waitress named Rachael, whose mother had been hired as food supervisor by Mr. DeSantis, began working in the eighties. I'd like to think that we musicians and tennis bums, with our refined palettes and huge tips, encouraged little Rachael Ray to pursue a career in the food business — but I doubt it.

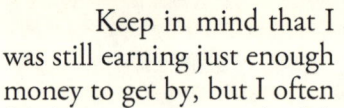

Keep in mind that I was still earning just enough money to get by, but I often felt like I was living the life of a millionaire. I was experiencing life on dozens of levels all at once — and loving it. Great music, tennis, girls, and countless afternoons tube-floating in the crystal clear waters of Paradise Bay with a Margarita in my hand — considering all the deprivations in the rest of the world, I occasionally had pangs of guilt. But I knew I was only able to live like this because I had so little overhead. Here I was thirty years-old and still driving junkers — and proud of it. My "Jungle Cruiser" (held together with gallons of Bondo™ like my previous two bright orange AMC Gremlins) gained its moniker after I coated it with flat green wall paint, applied with a roller, of course. Other great features of the Cruiser included a button placed under the middle section of the one-piece front "bench" seat, which, when sat on or pounded with your fist, engaged the horn. It was great for venting frustration at a bad driver, but if a girl sat on it un-warned, she usually bashed her head into the roof when she got an unexpected horn blast as she tried to get cozy (and, yes, I had an "off" switch.)

I used to shoot arrows through The Cruiser's Bondo-ed body and drive through Glens Falls with them sticking out, as though I had just barely escaped an Apache ambush on Route 9. Now that I think about it, I was (am?) living a performance art piece as a way of life. A regular car game that my bandmates played after a gig at 3 a.m. was racing around the empty parking lot of the Grand Union mega-grocery seeing how many shopping carts we could bang into each other. I used to store all

Me handing out another absurdly oversize check for a "skillion dollars."

my dead tennis balls in the well behind the driver's seat, so that, when I saw a friend walking down the sidewalk, I could reach back and then loft one towards them. I got quite adept at judging speed and distance in knowing how early to release those flaccid Dunlops. I must have littered Warren County with hundreds of the yellow critters over the years.

I was crashing at Chez Edgar during the two weeks of the 1981 US Open, which cemented the changes brought on by the move from Forest Hills.

Nasty & Born — my view at the US Open for 15 years.

Celebrities were everywhere, hogging up the seats formerly used by die-hard tennis fans in the old stadium. At a few matches I sat with comedian, and pal of Vitas's, Alan King in his royal box behind the baseline. A regular celeb attendee was country singer Kenny Rogers, hot off his successes with the songs "Lucille" and "The Gambler." We both preferred smaller grandstand venue and often sat together in the VIP section and discussed music and tennis. I remember that Kenny was flattered that I was impressed with his band The First Edition's rendition of the Mel Tillis classic, "Ruby, Don't Take Your Love to Town." But he was completely blown away when I told him how I met his *earlier* band, The New Christy Minstrels, during one of my pre-teen gatecrashing forays on Atlantic City's Steel Pier.

By this time, I was so accustomed to seeing pop stars at the Open that I always came prepared with demo cassettes of my original songs, hoping to make a sale. ("Carpe Diem" was still my mantra.) When Kenny agreed to give a listen, I went back to Chez Edgar and retrieved a cassette of some country rock originals I had written for Durango and gave them to Kenny the next day in the bleachers. Kenny was very thankful and seemingly earnest when he promised he'd give a good listen when he got home to Nashville and let me know what he thought. I never heard back. I'm certain that the quality of the demos wasn't a turn-off; the songs were pretty strong. I can only assume that for contractual reasons, he couldn't listen to non-union material. Or he was just a jerk. I never found out.

What seats the celebrity entertainers didn't commandeer were pre-sold to the Gordon Gekkos of the world, who only showed up for the finals and semis, as the great unwashed, sitting up in the clouds, coveted those empty courtside seats during the early rounds. At least Alan King and Kenny Rogers, true fans, were there religiously.

Illie Nastase and Vitas at Bjorn's wedding

As usual, Vitas was practicing every day at his Long Island mansion with his best pal, Bjorn Borg. The previous year, Vitas and Romanian wild man Ilie Năstase had served as co-masters of ceremony at the reception following Bjorn's marriage to women's pro Marianna Simionescu in her hometown, Bucharest. After the reception, Vitas and Ilie danced with a harem of beautiful Romanian girls from sundown to sunup, manically entertaining anyone who was still there. "Vitas and I danced together," Ilie wrote, "and I remember he was so full of energy he ended up leaping into my arms." Marianna called the duo, "The most entertaining couple of the evening." Sadly, Borg's marriage to the lovely Marianna lasted only four years, as Bjorn increasingly fell under the sway of his hard-partying pal.

By this time, Vitas, who had broken up with starlet Jennifer O'Neill and was engaged to starlet Janet Jones (later Mrs. Wayne Gretzky), was astonishingly still the number four-ranked player in the world, despite what had become a serious addiction to cocaine. Just two years earlier, we all held our breaths when Vitas made it to the 1979 Open final against McEnroe, only to see him lose in straight sets. We wondered if he had stayed out too late the previous night. Ilie told how Vitas won the prestigious Italian Open in 1977 after an all-nighter of drug bingeing and without ever

Janet and Vitas

going to sleep before the match. Ilie said there were numerous times that Vitas played a match on no sleep. If I heard it once I heard it a hundred times: "My God, if Vitas were clean, he'd be number one." His former teacher Harry Hopman famously remarked, "Nobody has more talent than Vitas." His childhood tennis pal, and now fellow pro, Mary Carillo, said years later, "I certainly do not consider cocaine to be a performance-enhancing drug. The tragedy of Vitas Gerulaitis's career will never leave me."

Among the many horrors of cocaine addiction are paranoia, anxiety, irritability, depression, and anti-social behavior. For the last few years, Vitas had taken turns dancing with all these demons. His old pals were shocked to see him at the Open wearing his gold coke-cutter razor blade around his neck during matches. After matches at the Open, instead of mugging non-stop for fans and pals like before, this Pied Piper-turned-Icarus would race off to his yellow Rolls Royce and head out alone. On court, he was petulant and sullen, often cursing at linesman while incurring fines on a regular basis. On at least a couple of occasions, Vitas stormed off the court when he became enraged at a bad call. He constantly skipped the required post-match pressroom visits. He was soon to receive record fines and suspensions for his rotten demeanor, but they were puny compared to what he was earning in winnings and endorsements. "I'll take the fine every time," he told reporter John Feinstein in 1981. "I don't need the money and I don't need the press either. If I win a tournament I'll take the $60,000 and give it to a bum on the street or something. I'm beyond doing this for money. I'm doing this now for the prestige, that's all. They can fine me all they want." The tennis authorities only got his attention when they came within a whisker of barring from entering Wimbledon one year.

At the depths of it all, I remember sitting in the stands with his dad, who just shook his head in sadness as he watched his now insufferable son's slow implosion. Mrs. G couldn't even bring herself to come to the matches. During one foul-mouthed rant, Vitas's coach, the great Aussie Fred Stolle, actually ran down to the edge of the court, leaned over the railing and scolded his charge, yelling out something like, "Stop acting like a baby and play the damn game!" It actually worked, but only temporarily. Things got so bad that this former hometown hero, whose "G-Men" fan club had previously gushed over him like a rock star, was now often booed at the US Open venue, just minutes from where he grew up.

At this 1981 Open, the men's semi-final was like a private party on Vitas's home court: Vitas and his three best tennis pals, Mac, Jimmy, and Bjorn, all made it to the penultimate round.

On their side of the draw, Borg wiped out Jimmy in straight sets, while McEnroe bested his Port Washington idol in a five set semifinal match, in which both players acted like peevish children. The contest ended, appropriately, on a disputed call that saw Vitas cursing loudly at the umpire. Another fine.

Bjorn vs Jimmy:
The view from Alan King's box.

Within two years, Vitas would undergo treatment for cocaine abuse and be named, but luckily not charged, in a massive cocaine trafficking prosecution.[‡] He retired not long after, having won the Australian Open Singles and Wimbledon Doubles, among his twenty-seven singles and nine doubles championships. And he played, arguably, the greatest match ever, against his best tennis friend, Bjorn Borg, at Wimbledon. But now without the grueling pro schedule to give any structure to his life, those of us who cared for him worried that his life would spiral even further out of control.

It was because of Vitas that I never even tried cocaine, which was now flooding the US, thanks to the legions of "Tony Montanas" that had recently set up shop in Miami and other US points of entry. In Vitas I saw one of the nicest, and most talented people (in tennis *and* music) come completely unhinged thanks to the insidious coca plant extract. His poor immigrant parents seemed in an endless state of melancholy over their beloved only son. I, and the rest of his friends, always blamed the drug, never Vitas, who, through it all, remained (off-court at least) one of the most caring, kind-hearted people alive. Neil Amdur of the *New York Times* wrote that Vitas's "greatest source of satisfaction was pleasing his friends, on and off the court." A more accurate reportage has never been written.

For the rest of the tennis world, Vitas's slide was overshadowed

---

[‡] Had the prosecutors known Vitas, they would have understood why he bought so much of the drug: he just wanted to give it away to all his friends, just like he shared everything. The investigators naturally assumed that anyone who bought so much *must* be a trafficker. Additionally, he was so rich he didn't need to become a drug dealer.

by that of his best friend, Bjorn Borg, who lost to McEnroe in the four-set final. I watched from the stands after the match, as Borg uncharacteristically raced off the court, skipping both the trophy presentations and the press interviews. After a one-minute shower, he ran to his waiting car. The next year, he played only one tournament, in his home neighborhood of Monte Carlo, until finally retiring in 1983, at the young age of twenty-six. The prevailing wisdom was that he was so dispirited by McEnroe's punishing lefty serve that he just gave up (1981 was the eighth year in a row that a lefty won the Open). But insiders knew that was not the real reason for his departure; there were much more serious considerations Borg had been wrestling with, and one had to do with the reason he ran off the court.

It all started in his home country of Sweden a few months earlier, where the Danish spin-off of the radical Italian Red Brigade had "sentenced him [Borg] to death." The Brigade was a violent phenomenon of the Seventies, and the group's 1975 manifesto stated that its goal was a "concentrated strike against the heart of the State, because the state is an imperialist collection of multinational corporations." Bank robberies, kidnappings, assassinations, and drugs and arms trafficking were its major crimes, and in 1978, the Brigade kidnapped and murdered Christian Democrat Aldo Moro, killing five of his bodyguards in the process. For some unknown reason, these revolutionaries now saw Borg as the enemy. Perhaps his exile residency in the tax haven of Monte Carlo had something to do with it.

Borg thus canceled all his scheduled matches in Sweden and returned to his Mediterranean villa, prompting the Gothensburg Tennis Association to fine him $46,511. According to Vitas, Borg's coach, and others with whom I spoke, these threats were never far from Bjorn's mind as he left for the 1981 Open, where he'd be a sitting duck in front of 20,000 rowdy New Yorkers. Keep in mind it was still the season of the assassin in America: six months earlier Reagan was gunned down, and just a few months before that Lennon had been murdered right here in New York.

Bjorn's fears were borne out when, ninety minutes before his semi match against Jimmy, the National Tennis Center received a call from an anonymous man who said he was going to shoot Bjorn on the court. Borg played that match with over 100 New York police officers roaming the stands searching for a man with a rifle. Borg's coach, Lennert, periodically throughout the match gave Borg "all clear" update signals on the changeovers to calm down his boy. Things would get worse on Sunday at the Finals.

After Borg took the first set from Mac on Sunday, another death threat came into the center, but this time there was no gaggle of police to provide security. Lennert signaled to Bjorn from the stands; apparently they had worked out a code in advance. By perhaps symbolically slicing a finger against his throat, Lennert alerted Bjorn that he was in trouble. He then called for more security. It was said that Borg wanted out altogether, and Mac won the next three sets easily, as cops finally arrived to escort the vanquished Swede from center court. "It seemed like he didn't play his game," an unknowing McEnroe later said.

While Mac was left alone on the victory stand outside, Borg was in the locker room, making firewood of about ten racquets in a storm of splinters, in front of Marianna, his parents, and Lennert. He then showered quickly, while four cops stood just outside the stall. Still dripping wet, Borg left the center through a dark back stairwell, through puddles of kitchen grease, led by a dozen security men and Lennert. That was where he quit the game of tennis.

For Borg, the death threats merely sealed a deal that had been in the works for about two years. By 1981, Borg had been on the grueling pro tour for ten years, ever since he dropped out of school at age 14. A reserved, simple man who could usually be seen off in a corner of the players' lounge reading comic books, the Swede was completely burnt out by the late seventies. At Wimbledon he came close to being suffocated by the fans, and in the 1978 final he could hardly hold his racquet with his blistered and bandaged thumb, which was never given time to heal. He told Marianna that he wanted to "quit the business and start to really live a life far from the insane routine."

Borg therefore asked the year-old men's Association of Tennis Professionals (ATP), which oversaw the majors, if he could take a leave from the tour without being penalized, much as the Women's Tennis Association (WTA) had done for Chris Evert the previous year. At the time, Evert was a newlywed, was having trouble beating the more talented newcomer Martina Navratilova, and needed a break. She was allowed to take it; Borg was not.

Unlike the un-challenged WTA, the ATP was at that time worried that rival men's tours like the Texas-based World Championship Tennis (WCT) would lure players to its tour and not the events favored by the ATP. The ATP thus informed Borg that if he took any time off the ATP tour, he would have to qualify for the majors, by basically playing against lowly ranked newcomers in pre-tournament events. And this was a man who had given everything to the sport in the winning of six French Opens and five Wimbledons, and doing so with a great decorum while the McEnroes of the world were taking petulance to a new level. It was an unconscionable humiliation that I believe had more to do with Borg's locker room meltdown than the death threats. The smashing of his work tools symbolized his feeling about the sport. One friend paraphrased what Borg had said to him: "After what I've done for the game, this is the way they treat me. Well, fuck them."

Over the next few months, McEnroe tried unsuccessfully to persuade his friend to reconsider, to no avail. It was the end of an era, and with my friend Vitas and his buddy Bjorn leaving, Laver retiring in 1979, the abandoning of Forest Hills, and the death of the wood racquet, it wasn't long before I stopped going to the Open. I believe my last one was in 1982 or 1983. I still watch all the majors on television, hoping to catch that increasingly rare all-court talent like Pete Sampras and Roger Federer, but I don't feel the draw to attend to see just one or two "complete" players. After spending the Golden Age of Tennis in the player's box, watching a litany of dazzling shot-makers (and entertainers), I just couldn't get excited about the new state of the game.

After the '81 Open, it was back upstate, where I became a complete *Basket Case*, as I dove into the work of writing the score for Frank and Edgar's little blood-feast.

Chapter Fourteen

Basket Cases

FILMING *BASKET CASE* WAS A REAL stop-start affair, as Edgar had to halt production at least a half-dozen times, essentially whenever the bank account was drained. The shoot thus dragged on for much longer than planned, something like six months for what should have taken one.

I suppose it's now time to describe the plot of the crazy movie I was committed to scoring. The story revolves around the murderous adventures of Siamese twins from Glens Falls, one of whom ("Duane") is perfectly normal, while the other ("Belial") is a mutant twisted mass of flesh dangling from his brother's side. When the boys turned twelve, their parents decided to give Duane a normal life, and thus hired a group of crooked veterinarians from Greenwich Village to sever Belial (real MD's wouldn't perform the deadly deed) and throw his dying carcass into a Hefty trash bag for the garbage collectors.

The vets wrestled a resistant Duane onto the operating table, where they performed the murder/amputation. But Belial survived his trash bag and telepathically called out to his awakening beloved twin, who rescued him. After murdering their parents, they were raised to adulthood — Belial in seclusion — by their kindly grandmother. After Granny died, and with the legless Belial being toted around in a wicker basket (get it?), the now grown twenty-somethings journeyed to Manhattan, where they made appointments with the villainous vets, and one-by-one, ripped them to shreds. Frank proudly referred to it as "The first right-to-life movie," and actually tried to get the endorsement of a national anti-abortion group.

The back-story, among the first scenes shot, was filmed just a few blocks from my Glens Falls apartment, and it was a major blast helping the crew squeeze plastic ketchup bottles loaded with Dick Smith's secret movie blood formula all over the set during the ridiculously over-the-top murder scenes.[*] The lighting rig, concocted by the great Bruce Torbet, was a four-by-six plank to which four car headlights were fixed, powered by car batteries. (Bruce intentionally over lit the set in order that the 16-mm film would look normal when blown up to 35.) We filmed one scene at the diner that me and my

---

[*] The movie was appropriately dedicated to the Wizard of Gore, Herschell Gordon Lewis.

fellow musicians frequented almost every morning, and I managed to get myself typecast as a patron in the scene, which was ultimately left on the cutting room floor.

At the New York location (a loft owned by a crew member), painted canvas tarps that we had scavenged on the Upper East Side were painted with housepaint, draped, and turned into "hotel" hallways and "apartment" walls. Caglione and Haney had created three horrific latex/foam Belial creatures, similar to some of those they had recently molded for William Hurt's acid-fueled doppelgänger in *Altered States*. However, unlike Hurt's movie with an actual budget, we had no money for the all-important remote-controlled armatures that could animate the hideous rubber lump. Thus, many of Belial's scenes were shot in such a way that he could be worked like a puppet from just outside the frame.

Yours truly, waiting to be served after "Duane" (Kevin Van Hentenryck) in the Country Diner.

Frank Henenlotter, puppeteer, getting ready to shove Belial into a plate glass window. We couldn't afford safety glass, so Frank wore the shades to save his eyes.

The well-conceived final shot was a disaster. In the climactic scene, Duane flies out of a seedy hotel's third floor window, but Belial grabs him before he can fall to the ground, then he uses his other rubber arm to cling to the hotel's neon sign. As the hookers gather below to watch the drama unfold, the sign breaks and the two brothers fall (seemingly) to their deaths, Belial landing up against his brother's side in the very spot he had been attached for his first twelve years. The problem was that

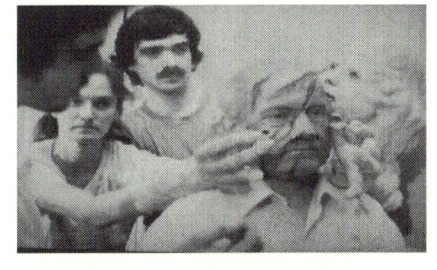

John Caglione, Ilze, and Edgar help Belial give a reverse facelift to Robert Clarke.

Edgar had spent a huge part of our remaining microscopic bank account

on the hotel's neon sign, which read "Hotel Broslin." The whole point of this was for the sign to break during the fall with only four letters remaining lit, so that when the camera pans up from the bodies, the final shot would say "Bros," as in "brothers." However, the neon completely short-circuited, and since we couldn't afford another sign, the scene never included the intended poignancy.

As Frank began editing scenes, I would visit the editing room with a stopwatch and notebook, as the auteur showed me his edits on the Steenbeck and described what he wanted. In the pre-digital, pre-internet, days, scoring a 16-mm movie with no money was a major challenge. Essentially, Frank would describe very specifically the music he needed for each clip, then, with my stopwatch started, he'd roll the film, pointing out specific "hits" that had to be accented within the scene. Unlike many modern movies with a pop music soundtrack, Frank was old school, and wanted a "score" that was perfectly timed to the action. Thus, a typical notation looked like this:

0.0 secs — Duane enters room
3.5 secs — Duane and Belial start to argue
5.0 secs — Belial grabs Duane's balls
5.5 secs — Belial hoists Duane up by his balls
6.0 secs — Close up of Duane as he screams in pain
9.0 secs — Duane breaks free
12.5 secs — Duane and Belial fall backward out the window
Etc…

Some scenes might have twenty or more such hits that had to be perfectly timed to the music. In retrospect, the notes I took are hysterical: "Belial removed from Hefty bag dripping blood," "guest's face gets ripped off," "Belial fondles tits," "father's torso sawed in half," "Belial sniffs dead hooker's panties," etc. *To Kill a Mockingbird* this wasn't. I wondered if Elmer Bernstein started this way.

My challenge was to write the relevant music – hmm, what melody just screams out "father's torso sawed in half"? — back in my Glens Falls living room without having access to the actual movie, using only the scribbled notes I made in New York. I had to just hope that I had been accurate with the Wal-Mart timepiece, and that my memory of the feel and pace of each scene was equally clear. There would be no second chances.

By the time the summer of 1981 rolled around, I had plenty of ideas for musical themes and tape-splicing sound effects for Frank and Edgar's *Basket Case*, but the restraints I endured were typical of anyone who worked on a no-budget movie. The chief downside of this heartwarming project was that the score could contain no guitar or electric bass (per Frank's orders), the only instruments I played with any fluidity.† For compositional and harmonic reasons, I had dabbled at the piano for years, but was not a piano "player" by any stretch. Another slight encumbrance was the fact that there was no money to hire musicians for the instruments Frank desired. Now a normal person would have backed out at this point, but, as you might guess, I had long ago defined "normal" as a dirty word. I usually lived by an old credo of the Kingston Trio: "When in doubt, go ahead!"

Thus began a period of begging and borrowing from every musician I knew. Pretty soon my living room was crammed with a rudimentary — and shrill — Arp String Ensemble synthesizer, a Mini Moog, a kettle drum, vibes, an Echoplex tape looping machine, and my Teac four-track, quarter-inch recorder. Against the wall was my out-of-tune upright piano, which would be used for plucked string melodies ala *Pet Sounds*. I also had a sax-playing pal contribute some "stripper music" lines. With my friend Clutch Reiser on the vibes and kettle drum, I recorded over an hour of *Basket Case* music and sound effects, complete with individual yet contrapuntal themes for the key characters.

The process was not without drama — I can't begin to calculate the number of good takes that were ruined by a neighbor's barking dog, a police siren, or my housemates bounding in when I forgot to tape the "QUIET!" sign on the front door. But without doubt, the best example of dramatics occurred during the frenetic delivery of the master tape to New York. The editing and sound mixing in New York were done after-hours, at the graveyard shifts of studios where friendly employees would allow Frank to work for free or for drastically reduced rates. The project was at the mercy of these enablers' schedules. I was warned well in advance that a particular Sunday had been set aside at a mixing studio, and if the tape didn't arrive by that date, we couldn't get in again for weeks, a catastrophe that would throw all the marketing, duplicating, and film festival plans into chaos.

I was sent a train ticket — Albany to Manhattan — for Sunday morning's ten a.m. Amtrak. If I missed that train, the next one

---

† The only exception being the nightclub scene, where we needed to emulate the sound of a generic band in the background. For this scene, my old partner, Chevrolet Burns, contributed an original rock track he had on the shelf.

wouldn't get me to New York in time for the session. If that happened, Frank and Edgar would make Belial's antics seem tame by comparison. At least that's what I feared. I used every possible moment to tweak the recordings, finishing late on Saturday night.

The next morning, tape in my clutches, I jumped into the dilapidated Jungle Cruiser for the one hour drive to Albany. About fifteen minutes down the I-87 Northway, I hit a bump — a bump that most cars would never have even felt. But for the rusted out Cruiser, it spelled disaster: the frame literally broke in two. I pulled off at the next exit, sparks flying from the undercarriage, and deposited the car on a dirt road. I grabbed the tape and my train ticket and ran back to the Northway, where I stood, jumping up and down hysterically waving at cars to pull over. In a short time, I was given a lift to the train station, where I made the southbound local with literally seconds to spare. *Basket Case* came *that* close to never happening.

Sweating profusely, I took a seat and clutched the tape to my chest all the way down to the city, where Edgar met me at the Port Authority. The guys loved the music, and the mixing session seemed to go fine. Late that night I was back in Albany, where a friend picked me up at the station. Sadly, the next morning I had to put the Cruiser out of its misery. The nearest junkyard was about ten miles from where the broken Chevy sat, thus I drove around Albany, my roommate following, for about a half-hour, with the car scraping the roadway like fingernails on a chalkboard, sparks flying from below. Other cars pulled up along side with passengers holding their ears and screaming at me. I rolled down the window and yelled back, "We're making a movie!" Which we were, sort of —

Now, not only had I not gotten a dime for *Basket Case*, but it cost me the Cruiser! So much for the glamour of movie making.

A few weeks later, when I met with Edgar and Frank to see a rough cut, Edgar warned, "Now, you might not be too happy, but give it a chance to sink in." Whaaa?

In his twisted brilliance, Frank decided to take some of the sections I had so meticulously composed and timed to match the action, and laid them into different, and completely dissimilar scenes. So, for instance, when Belial is raping Duane's girlfriend, Frank used the tender romantic music I had envisioned for one of the flick's rare love scenes. I was, as Edgar predicted, initially pissed, but the more I thought about it, I realized that the effect was so jarring that it actually worked. One of the rules of composing for thrillers is that the music should occasionally set the audience up to be surprised by what actually occurs in the big screen. There are many other such tricks at the composer's disposal.

The only negative that stayed with me was the final quality of the master music track, which had been greatly diminished by a horrible EQ setting at the time of transfer. With all the dynamic range sucked out of it, the result was a shrill musical score that we couldn't afford to re-transfer. I would have been crestfallen had it not been for the huge paychecks I had cashed. Yeah, right.

Thanks to the good folks at *Fangoria Magazine*, who became major pre-release boosters of the movie, producing many colorful multi-page spreads and cover shots, a buzz was starting to grow. Finally, after a preview party at The Underground Club (at which guests dressed in veterinarian smocks and carried wicker baskets) on April 7, 1982, *Basket Case* opened at the sort-of prestigious Waverly Theater in Greenwich Village on April 9. At the time, the Waverly, with its legendary midnight screenings, was arguably the hippest cult movie theater in the country; it's where *Eraserhead* held court before the *Rocky Horror Picture Show* played for a record 95 weeks at the Friday and Saturday midnight shows.

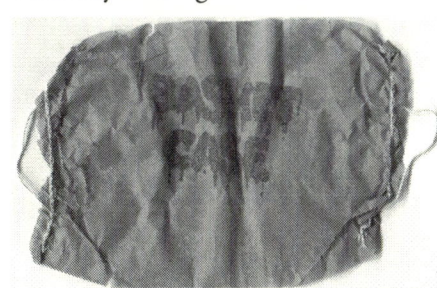

Basket Case followed *Rocky* into the Waverly, where, at some showings, free surgical masks were distributed in order to protect patrons from the flying blood splatters.

Word about this unique little movie spread quickly, as Frank and Edgar prepared to take the celluloid shocker over to the Cannes Film Festival in May. That's right, the same prestigious competition that had previously honored cinematic achievements such as *Apocalypse Now, Taxi Driver, The Conversation, The Birds,* and *Black Orpheus* was now going to regale its audiences with blood drenched psychotic debauchery — but all in the name of brotherly love, of course. To no one's surprise, they couldn't get this freak show into the main competition, so they rented a back-alley theater and spread the Gospel of Belial. It was there that they recruited two completely diverse allies from the Lone Star State in their quest to launch the movie.

At the time, 43-year-old former Texan Rex Reed was one of America's most widely quoted movie critics. Covering Cannes for the *New York Observer*, Reed later described how he discovered *Basket Case*. "Occasionally you get tired of seeing all these Algerian films about people trying to raise enough money to buy a tractor," Reed said at the time. Thus he trolled the village's backstreets in search of "some good old American trash." Be careful what you wish for, as they say; Reed found more than he hoped for when he took a wrong turn into the den that was unspooling *Basket Case*.

Somehow, Frank and Edgar learned that Reed was in attendance, and decided to ambush him as he exited the theater. Without knowing to whom he was speaking, Reed had the following exchange with Frank:

Frank: "Oh, Mr. Reed, what did you think of the movie?"

Reed: "This is the sickest movie I've ever seen."[‡]

An ecstatic Frank had just the quote he hoped for, and the perfect blurb for the movie's one-sheets.

When the resultant posters began popping up all over Manhattan, Reed was incensed that his quote was actually used to promote the movie, but he had no recourse because the quote was not used in a misleading way. Frank *wanted* people to know how sick the movie was. That was his goal all along. Reed later calmed down and had to admit, "I mean, I had never seen a movie quite like it. It was so bad that it was (*pause*) really quite wonderful for its type." Of his "blurb" he said, "I hope nobody thinks it's an endorsement," but then added somewhat paradoxically, "but if you really like sick horror movies, this one is very special." The poster campaign, and the unequivocal embrace of the movie by an outlandish reviewer from Dallas, who also happened to be at the same Cannes screening, helped propel our twisted little lark into a cult movie phenomenon.

[‡] Reed said the exact same thing about *Blue Velvet* four years later, but we were the first.

Twenty-nine-year-old John Bloom, aka "Joe Bob Briggs," was the Drive-In Movie critic for the *Dallas Times Herald*, and enjoyed his own cult following for his quirky reviews of sub-B movies, which he graded by the amount of blood, breasts, crashes, monsters, and, most importantly, Kung-Fu, they contained. His favorites were nominated for the annual Drive Inn Oscars, which took place at the Drive-In Film Festival on Highway 183 Drive-In in scenic Irving, Texas, a virtual clone of Cannes. (I've been there. I know.)

Joe Bob was completely besotted with *Basket Case* ("We're talking classic cinema here one of the top ten movies of the decade."), and immediately gave it eight Drive-In Oscar nominations (Best Director, Best Actor, Actress, Supporting Actor, Supporting Actress, Monster, Gross-Out Scene, and, of course, Best Picture.) The coveted award took the form of a Chevy hubcap, and was referred to as a "Hubby." Briggs soon brought our flick to the Highway 183 Drive-In for its pre-voting review, where it set the attendance record (212 cars). On the hallowed night, *Basket Case* took home the awards for Best Actor, Best Monster, Best Director, Best Gross-Out Scene, and (drum roll) Best Picture. We might not have received a Palme d'Or in France, but we had a Hubby! In the following awards seasons, Joe Bob often complimented the quality of the winning movies, but usually added, "They still ain't no *Basket Case*."

The "legitimate" reviews were starting to come in, and they couldn't have been better if we had written them ourselves:

"The best of the year." —*The East Village Eye*.

"It's like E.T. as written and directed by a psychopath." —*Detroit Free Press*.

"The Midnight Classic of the Year." —*Heavy Metal* magazine.

The *Case* obtained fair distribution, at least playing most of the country's cult movie theaters, but the Waverly would always be the center of its universe. It consistently sold out to rabid fans who came dressed as blood-spattered doctors, nurses, or just kids with wicker baskets. One night I received a call from Edgar, who ordered me to come down to the city.

"You've got to see what's happening at the Waverly," Edgar explained.

"What's that?" I asked.

"First off, they're doing the *Rocky Horror* audience participation thing, but there's more," Edgar said. "And no one will appreciate it more than you."

Intrigued, I was back on the Trailways to the Big Apple for the Friday midnight show — I had too many Fridays open now that the DJs were taking all the gigs. Indeed, as Edgar had described, the Waverly audience was primed (or was that stoned?) and ready to party when the lights went down. To understand what happened next, and why Edgar demanded I check it out, you have to know the opening scene of the movie: with ominous music playing, a man (later identified as a vet named "Dr. Lifflander") is searching the property around his house late at night with a flashlight. Meanwhile, the credits are scrolling by with the names of the cast, director of photography, etc. Suddenly, Lifflander hears a noise in the bushes. He turns quickly and yells, "Who's that?"

It just so happened that, immediately after he uttered the question, the flowing credit appeared: "MUSIC: GUS RUSSO." That prompted the sellout house to answer Lifflander, in the first audience response of the movie, "It's Gus Russo!" To which I responded by yelling, "Its me!," prompting a nice ovation from the crowd, just as Lifflander was having his facial features rearranged to the sound of an Arp synthesizer and Clutch's Tympani drum.

I stayed around for the weekend to visit with Diane M., who used to live in Glens Falls, where she occasionally managed my duo, Garvin & Burns. Diane had wanted to move up in the music industry (there was really no other direction from G & B), so she came down to Manhattan and landed a job as receptionist at Phil Ramone's A & R Studios on 52nd Street. One of the top studios in the world, A & R pioneered digital recording, and released the first commercial compact disk, Billy Joel's aptly named *52nd Street*. Literally anyone who was anyone recorded at A & R, from Sinatra on down, so Diane was not only a friend, but also a nice link to the top level of the music biz. Red-haired Diane was a bit of a bombshell, but without the hardened edges of lifelong city girls, so all the musicians at A & R loved her.

Diane had become great friends with Steely Dan's producer Elliott Scheiner, Paul Simon, jingle queen Florence Warner, Billy Joel's band, and many others. She would soon be dating Billy's guitarist, David Brown. In fact, Billy had always been hanging around Lake George and Glens Falls in the old days — one of my bass players sold Billy a motorcycle. I think Billy and Christy Brinkley later had a place on the lake's East Side. The bottom line was that Billy, David, and the rest of the band were huge *Basket Case* fans, and according to Diane, Billy had a BC poster hanging in his music room.

Before heading back upstate, Diane and I visited with some of her pals from A & R, A-list studio musicians Paul Shaffer and Will Lee. The guys had just began working on the new show, *Late Night with David Letterman*, and we went over to Rockefeller Center and had lunch with them, and stayed to watch the show tape. Paul had previously worked at SNL as musical director, so he also knew Caglione and Haney, who had worked with him there. Shaffer was all jazzed up because he had just signed on to act in an upcoming comedy about a rock band called "Spinal Tap." I kept the name in my memory bank until the movie debuted in 1984, becoming a huge fan — as were most working musicians. A bus trip well worth it.

Basket Case broke *Rocky Horror*'s record at the Waverly, playing there for almost three years. It benefited greatly from the timing of its release, which coincided with the VHS tape revolution; prices had been drastically reduced, and our movie would have a long life on video tape and, later, DVD — although I still didn't see a penny from it. Many years later I would find out why.

I would score one more flicker for Frank and Edgar[§] in a few years, but in the meantime, it was temporarily back to the guitar teaching grind in Glens Falls, as the high-paying gigs continued to dry up.

[§] Today, Frank continues to make renegade movies, his most recent being *Bad Biology* (2008). As for Edgar, he lives near Boston, where he teaches, of all things, cooking. I assume his recipes weren't inspired by the contents of Frank's refrigerator. See: http://www.chefedgar.com

Chapter Fifteen

"This is your brain on the Eighties."

THE EARLY NINETEEN-EIGHTIES had the feeling of impending doom. After a two-year probe, the House Select Committee on Assassinations had just concluded (wrongfully, it turned out) that multiple conspirators had shot at President Kennedy, and that Martin Luther King was also the victim of a conspiracy — and hardly anyone seemed to care. They were too busy consuming.

The corporatization of America was now in complete overdrive, perfectly symbolized by the election of a B-actor as President, a man who, after years of Red-baiting, built his shallow Hollywood "career" by doing the bidding of Tinseltown's mobbed-up studio bosses and becoming a corporate spokesman for General Electric.* Soon, in a nod to his benefactors in the corporate world, he would thrust the country into a debt spiral, prop up the Soviet hardliners through his absurdly vitriolic, vote-grabbing rhetoric, and emasculate the country's Organized Crime Strike Force that had become so bothersome to his puppetmasters — all while never losing his camera-ready smile. He would go on to become a Christ-like figure for his once admirable political party, incredibly the party of Lincoln.

The actor-prez had a lot of help sabotaging the country's better angels. Who can forget the impact of the money-printing machine called MTV, which sarcastically hinted at its agenda with the very first video it ran: "Video Killed the Radio Star," by the Buggles? Simultaneously, personal computers, cell phones, and other forms of digital dope were weaning humans of non-essentials such as books, musicianship, art, family conversations over dinner, long road trips, science, philosophy, quiet contemplation — you name it — anything that didn't run on batteries or alternating current became passé almost overnight.

It seemed like everywhere you turned, money was the new God: Mafia-fronting pornographers were told that the Department of Justice would look the other way while they raped drug-addled young runaways and made lucrative partnerships with beyond reproach

---

* Think that's exaggeration? Kindly read Dennis McDougal's *The Last Mogul*, Dan Moldea's *Dark Victory*, William Kleinknecht's *The Man Who Sold the World*, Will Bunch's *Tear Down This Myth*, or my own *Supermob*. If you're feeling especially inquisitive, get your mitts on Reagan's FBI file. Then get back to me.

companies like General Motors and Time Warner[†] to distribute the filth; most of the major US banks perfected "willful blindness" in laundering the illicit lucre of billionaire South American drug cartels, while New York homeless men caught with joints went to the slammer for a decade under the Governor's harsh new "one-strike" drug laws; the President's pals on the House Ways and Means Committee showed Al Capone how it was done by enacting thousands of tax-"avoiding" loopholes for millionaire sleazebags who didn't want to be bothered with "dodging" taxes in offshore banks or in Switzerland (too inconvenient); formerly family-owned farms were swallowed whole by horrific commercial factory farms that were nothing less than mass torture machines for animals, while the apoplectic population that gorged on its products saw its collective waistline explode and its savings accounts dwindle; indoor shopping malls spread like the Ebola virus, destroying tens of thousands of locally owned businesses. Speaking of viruses, the "Village People" cheerfully told homosexual men that it was great fun to have sex with strangers in bathhouses or the YMCA, even as AIDS was obliterating the gay population.

Just down the road from the Village, Wall Street became a legal casino, where "greed was good," and its gamblers wanted nothing more out of life than McMansions and gargantuan, phallic symbol gas-guzzlers. Perhaps our genetic wisdom sensed that the planet and its Homo sapien visitors were in their last throes, so we'd better gorge ourselves before taking that last great chromosomal trip back into the stars from whence we came. The current generation was in desperate need of its own Joni Mitchell to advise: "We've got to get ourselves back to the garden." But none appeared.

I could go on, but it's too depressing — welcome to the eighties, dear reader.

From the Boomers' perspective, previous cultural epochs seemed to be neatly book-ended by timeframes that lasted approximately a decade: the Cold War/Rock n' Roll Fifties, the Youth Dominance of the Sixties, and the Conspiracy theory/Disco Seventies. But the Technology/Convenience-worshipping born in the early Eighties would prove to have the greatest hold of all — a seismic shift not unlike the invention of the printing press or the mass production of oil-sucking internal combustion transportation. New research shows

---

[†] The Time Warner Cable relationship with pornographers (with its 2010 addition of eight porn cable channels) is perhaps the most insidious, since it got into the smut game in order to finance its relationship with The Disney Channel!

that, unlike the fraudulent LSD scares of the Sixties, this technology, which insidiously eroded young people's attention spans, actually permanently re-wires the brain's neural connections with hits of data that flows through the cerebral cortex like heroin shots.

High tech was more than world changing, it was people-changing. Years later, when techno-addicts were sent off to unplugged detox camps, they experienced the same symptoms as junkies gone cold turkey: dizziness, shakes, depression, sleeplessness, even suicidal tendencies. The icing on the cake was the simultaneous explosion in cases of autism and Attention Deficit Hyperactivity Disorder (ADHD), both likely exacerbated by some still undiscovered environmental culprit.

The second most worshipped new deity was speed: the speed of computers, the speed of making profit, the speed of producing movies and music, even the speed of guitar solos. Everything had to be acquired, and instantly, as the ranks of meditative monks shriveled to near invisibility.

I was noticing the effect in my guitar students. Back when I was a teen guitar student, I followed a methodical course that taught me to read notation, learn scales and improvisation, and understand chord construction theory. This agenda was accomplished through regular assignments that encompassed learning countless styles of music; we started with nursery rhymes, then simple classical melodies, duets, and finally standards such as "As Time Goes By." Much like at Mt. St. Joe, I was rarely was in a position to tell the teacher what I wanted. He simply knew what rudiments were needed, and I could take it from there in any direction I desired. He was right, of course. Folk, Rock, and Folk-Rock would be a piece of cake for anyone who could play Bach and read a chart for "Stardust."

Of my forty plus guitar students per week in the eighties, perhaps three or four would tolerate such a regimen, and I looked forward to their lessons like a dehydrated Bedouin craves an oasis. Many of these serious students became accepted in college music programs and schools like the Berklee School of Music in Boston, but the majority demanded instant gratification via speed licks and other attention-getting effects. At the time, guitarist Eddie Van Halen was all the rage, with his robotic, hyper-fast guitar solos — solos that usually said nothing except that he could generate random tones almost as fast as his computer. More than one attention impaired 13-year-old student asked me to teach him Van Halen's gymnastic "Panama" on his first lesson. I was in no position to argue, since a "junkie" denied simply moved on to another "dealer." And I needed to pay my rent. So I had to learn a litany of mind-numbing, testosterone-fueled, forgettable guitar riffs and show them to these youngsters who would never become actual musicians. It was starting to become like actual work, which I despised.

In the face of all this, a minority of us put on our collective blinders, kept the faith, marched, rallied, read books, lived within our means, and practiced our art. But I, for one, had the feeling that the momentum for entropy was unstoppable. We were just outnumbered and outspent. It was my feeling that Richard Dawkins had actually underestimated *The Selfish Gene*.

Trying to exist in an oasis of sanity in Glens Falls, I fell in with a small, but robust group of counter-culture hipsters that loved nothing more than all-night jams (at least once a week) and having dinner parties that turned into watching movies on video until we were all asleep on couches or the floor. We were all well aware that we were existing outside the mainstream, so these get-togethers served as a mutually reinforcing motivation rally, long before Tony Robbins began charging for it.

The ringleader of this East Coast version of the Electric Kool-Aid Acid Test was "Ray J," a cherubic hippie who struck it rich with a string of head shops that catered to the Deadhead crowd throughout upstate New York; I had written a number of outlandish radio jingles for Ray's stores. Ray also had a house and shop in Key West, where we were all invited to vacation for free. Ray's sole goal in life was to share the wealth with his friends and employees, who worshipped him. He did so in many ways, but his key contribution was the purchase of a secluded party house (with an indoor pool), where he hosted the weekly parties on Sunday nights.

Every Sunday without fail, between two and three-dozen musicians, hippie chicks, and other sundry artists and n'er-do-wells showed up around six o'clock o start cooking the feast. Ray purchased enough food to feed this army, and while he and the girls got it going in the kitchen, the guys tuned up the guitars, chopped wood for the late night campfire, and rolled joints. I was still a tennis addict and never partook of the wacky weed, in my effort to preserve my lungs. But, looking back, between all the second hand pot and cigarette smoke I inhaled in the clubs and at Ray's, I might as well have been a smoker. In those days, it was just inescapable, and when I finally got out of the gigging business, it was one of the key reasons for that decision.

After gorging ourselves, we would start jamming before pairing off with a cutie and heading to the swimming pool, which was a major rush, considering it was often below zero just outside the glass walls. Years later, I would get to interview Hugh Hefner at his Playboy Mansion in LA, and told him of our East Coast version of his debauchery, which also included an indoor pool ("The Grotto"). Hef said, "I always thought about having an East Coast Playboy Mansion. Sounds like you guys beat me to it."‡

As someone allergic to cooking, I can only say that Ray's Sunday bacchanals were a Godsend: I would hardly have to eat the next day, and the leftovers that he made us take home lasted another two. (Throughout my life, most of my kitchen ovens and cupboards have been used for book storage, or dust.) The timing couldn't have been better: combined with the recent popularity of Percy Spencer's microwave oven invention, Ray's take-home goodies could now be re-heated with just the push of a button.§ Way to go, Percy!

Ray Jett and friends

This is not to say that I don't enjoy a great meal – I just don't like to take the time to cook it and clean up afterwards; I am just too obsessed with feeding my brain, as opposed to my stomach. The hours it takes to shop for food, prepare it, and clean up after it, could be spent reading a book, or writing a song, or working on my overhead smash. I know that all this prattle sounds a tad un-American, but I have always believed Americans are food obsessive, and consequently,

---

‡ I was there to interview him for an ABC special on Marilyn Monroe and the Kennedys. Hef was very friendly, but refused to go on the record.
§ By the early eighties, Spencer's 1945 invention was finally brought down to an affordable price, and they spread like wildfire.

overfed. "Three squares a day" is virtually unknown to most of the world, and for good reason.

Ray and I were also ringleaders of great summer concert whirlwind. A few years earlier, I had enlisted Ray in my gatecrashing hobby, and with him as a partner, the game had reached new heights. In Saratoga, just south of Lake George and Glens Falls, there exists a beautiful, half-enclosed "summer shed" concert venue called the Saratoga Performing Arts Center, or SPAC.** I began seeing shows there during my days at Blue Water Manor, and later, with Durango, during our summer hiatus on the lake. I was fortunate to have been at SPAC on August 18, 1973, for a concert by the Benny Goodman Quintet, in what turned out to be the band's last official gig with drumming genius Gene Krupa (also on board were Teddy Wilson, Slam Stewart, and Lionel Hampton.) Gene was dying from leukemia, and his solos were short and weak, but he received standing ovations for each one from the tearful crowd. He died two months later.

From June through September, hundreds of top performers played to sold-out houses at SPAC, and, unless you were wealthy, you sat in the back, or on the lawn. As you might guess, that just wasn't good enough for myself, Ray, or for the rest of our gang. It so happened that one of my Bolton Landing tennis partners was a Whitney trust fund kid, who inadvertently told me the trick to getting great seats at SPAC: the only way to get into the first three rows was to be a SPAC "Member," contributing about $2,000 per year to the Foundation. Until this point, almost all members were Blue Bloods like the Whitneys, Mellons, and Rockefellers, who also had homes on Lake George's Millionaire's Row, and were more interested in SPAC's ballet and symphony tickets. These members were then given advance notice about concert bookings, a ticket discount, and invitations to private Balls at the Saratoga Spa.†† Ray's deep pockets, combined with my chutzpah left us only one thing to do: we joined the well-heeled set for three months every year. Ray would pay for the membership, and together we split the price of tickets, often maxing out my one credit card.

Thus, in late April, on the day we'd get our advance member notice of the summer schedule, Ray and I would race to the Saratoga box office on the Spa grounds, beating the Whitney kids, who were probably boating drunk in Paradise Bay, and go berserk the minute it opened. The exchange at the ticket window went something like this:

** Opened in 1964, SPAC seats 5,200 in the enclosed section, and 20,000 on the lawn.
†† Ray and I actually attended one such Ball, where we stood out like sore thumbs. But we had a great time coaxing a couple of rich "Skiddies" (Skidmore girls) back to the Lake for a dip.

Me: "I'd like eight seats each for Jackson Browne, Billy Joel, the Everly Brothers, the Beach Boys, Joe Jackson, Chicago, Paul Simon, James Taylor, Manhattan Transfer, Fleetwood Mac, The Four Tops, Stevie Wonder, CSNY, Kenny Loggins, Asleep at the Wheel, and twenty for the Grateful Dead."
Cashier, who looked stunned: "Nothing for the New York Symphony?"
Me: "No thanks."
Cashier: "That will be $4,300."
Me: "Fine. We'll pay half in cash and half on this credit card."

A couple of weeks later, our massive envelope of tickets arrived, almost all front row, center— we were set for the summer. Saving a few for ourselves, we would then distribute the ducats among our friends for face value, plus an extra ten dollars to pay for Ray's membership fee (and our tickets, of course); with the discount, the tickets were still cheaper than those sold to the public — and they were front row. Any tickets that went unsold were advertised in the *Glens Falls Post Star* classified section. To get around bothersome scalping laws, we placed the following typical ad: "Kenny Loggins poster for sale, $50 — free bonus: TWO GREAT SEATS TO HIS SPAC CONCERT NEXT WEEK!"

Thus, for a couple of days of hard work, we essentially had front row seats to every show for years — for free! The icing on this cake was my ability to get us backstage after the concerts, using my tried-and-true SNL technique (see Ch. 11). And just like at NBC, there would always be a great buffet waiting backstage, so we also saved on the overpriced SPAC vendor junk. Consider, dear reader, the irony: while the Whitneys were standing in line for hot dogs and popcorn, we were loading up on lobster and New York State wine with Carly Simon. Sometimes, we got backstage *before* the show, made friends with the band, and found ourselves sitting in the wings for the entire night. Such was the case the first time I met my musical hero, Brian Wilson.

During this period, Brian, who had been in drug-induced seclusion for years, tried to make a comeback with the Beach Boys, but he would often just get up in the middle of a song, bored, and wander off. Knowing this, I took a folding chair in the wings, closest to his piano setup. As expected, when he wandered off, he slumped into the chair next to me, as his shrink, Eugene Landy, raced over and gave him a deep scalp massage while I attempted to engage the big guy in chit-chat about the tracking of *Pet Sounds*. When Landy thought Brian had enough, he sent him back out, as if back into a football game after an injury timeout. His brother, Dennis, astoundingly drunk, also took walkabouts during the show, but had a different body part massaged.

At the time, Dennis was dating Karen Lamm, the ex-wife of the band Chicago's leader (and good pal of my friend Bill Gable), Bobby Lamm. On his breaks, Dennis sat himself behind the drum riser, whereupon Karen wrapped herself around him and they proceeded to commence one of the most furious public makeout sessions I have ever seen — while Brian was having his scalp rearranged twenty feet away, and the rest of the "Boys," held together by brother Carl, sang about "California Girls." Strange days.

Karen Lamm and Dennis Wilson

Since Ray and I were so carefree and outgoing — and Ray had the best pot in Warren County — we had no trouble hanging with many of the bands until the wee hours back at their hotel bars, usually either the Gideon Putnam Spa Hotel (on the Park grounds), or the Sagamore, on Lake George, where we knew all the staff. The day after the Beach Boys show, I hung with them at the Sagamore in Bolton, and showed them around the small town, taking a couple of the forty-something "Boys" to the local Laundromat, and going to Happy Hour while their clothes dried.

Some of my favorite memories were getting to hang with the Four Tops, the Temptations, and the Manhattan Transfer. One night we were closing down the Holiday Inn bar with the Temps and the Tops, who had just performed at SPAC. It was a great scene — just a couple of plastered insurance salesmen in Albany on business, the incognito Motown stars, myself, Ray, and a couple of our pals discussing our mutual love for *a cappella* jazz singing. The Tops were especially fond of the style, as I recall. Up on the tiny bandstand, a lounge trio was doing their lethargic take on *The Girl From Ipanema*, unaware of the identities of the members of their audience. When they asked for a last request, I asked if my friends could do a number. Happy to end their night, the band leader said, "Be our guest."

With that, the Four Tops, along with Ali Woodson from the Temps humbly stood in front of the platform in the near empty lounge (after playing before 10,000 at SPAC), and sang a stunning *a cappella* version of "Misty." The poor lounge trio stood by the bar with their mouths agape. When the guys returned to the bar, one of the inebriated salesmen placed himself a couple inches from the Tops' Duke Fakir's face and suggested, "You guys should start a band." To which Duke politely replied, "Thanks, maybe we will." It was all we could do to keep from bursting out laughing. We never let on to the trio, who looked like they wanted to throw their gear in the dumpster, or the salesmen who their serenaders had been.

We traded addresses, and I stayed in touch with Duke, Levi Stubbs, and Ali for years, and linked up backstage with them at a few more future shows. Duke told great tales of Diane "Diana" Ross, his former girlfriend, Stevie Wonder, Martha Reeves, and the rest of the Motor City minstrels. He described how the Tops had been each other's best friends since they were grade-schoolers, playing together intact for a record forty-three years, and they truly loved each other like the best of brothers. At one meeting, Levi inscribed a press photo to me: "To the Fifth Top, Gus." It's something I'll always treasure. As I write this, of the nine guys we hung with that night, only Duke of the Tops, and Otis Williams and Richard Street of the Temps remain.

Over the course of six or seven years, we were backstage so frequently that the security guards at the stage door entrance got to know us and waved us in without even asking. For a couple of seasons, I didn't even have to use any gimmicks to get in because I had noticed where the guard kept rolls of the peel-off, stick-on backstage passes. On two occasions I lifted a roll or two — probably a hundred passes — that lasted me until they changed the design. I still have a few.

I remember one rainy night, as my date and I made our way backstage, I asked the gatekeeper if we could leave our umbrellas with him so we didn't have to lug them around all night while we dined at the buffet with the members of Heart. His response almost caused us to implode with stifled laughter.

> *Guard*: "Pal, you can leave anything with me here, because this place is as secure as a Fort Knox. Nobody gets back here who isn't authorized."

We left him the umbrellas before racing off to explode with laughter behind Nancy Wilson's amplifier stack; by this time, I had been getting into "Fort Knox" unauthorized hundreds of times for years. The only cautionary element of this long-running giggle was how to explain who we were in case a security guard got overly curious — it actually happened a couple of times. Essentially, for the Saratoga guards, we were with the band. In case the band asked, we were with Saratoga. The trick was to make sure we were never with both entities at the same time. Most bands were happy to play along and cover for us, once we told them we were just crashing. The only time I was momentarily speechless was when, after a couple dozen backstage forays, one rent-a-cop asked: "How do you guys know so many bands?" After an awkward pause at the long overdue question, I came up with something along the lines of: "My brother is the promoter." Whatever…it worked.

Only one time did we miscalculate the ticket buying fans. During the Seventies, the Grateful Dead were all the rage, setting attendance records everywhere they played, especially at SPAC. Thus, when I received my order of a couple dozen front and second row seats, I thought the profit would alone finance the rest of the summer's shows. Not the case. It seems that Deadheads didn't care about actually seeing the grungy minstrels, they just want to hear them, and preferably where there was some room to do their Deadhead mazurka dance, or whatever they called it. More than once, after I informed a Patchouli reeking stoner about my front row seats for sale, did I hear, to my astonishment, "That's way cool, dude, but do you have anything back on the lawn?"‡‡

---

‡‡ Funny Deadhead story: for a time I shared my apartment with a beautiful Irish Deadhead named Kelly. It was through her that I learned of a favorite Deadhead practice whenever the band was at SPAC. On the night after a concert she came home with a horrible cuts and bruises on her forehead. She explained that she fell down and hit her head on a rock after inhaling too much nitrous oxide, and in Saratoga, the hippies had a unique way of obtaining the laughing gas: At various spots in

With *Basket Case* behind me, it was back to summer partying on Lake George, teaching guitar during the eternal upstate New York winter season, and playing whatever gigs we could steal from the DJs for my swing bands or any other combination. Although the gray, brutally cold, and snowy winters were a horror, the summers on the lake were so perfect that I rationalized the trade-off.

Between performing with the top band in Bolton Landing, running the Bolton Open Tennis Tournament, rafting in nearby Paradise Bay, and playing concerts at the open stage in Rogers Memorial Park, people started referring to me as the town's summertime Mayor. But there was a slight discontent brewing. Not only were the light-deprived winters taking their toll (they had seemed less painful when I was in my twenties), but there was also this gnawing feeling that I was having too much fun, a topic regularly bolstered by a voice from a distant land. A recurring life theme were the long-distance phone conversations with my Italian mother back in Baltimore, who asked me at least six times a year, "When are you going to come home and get a job?" To which I'd respond, "As soon as I stop having fun and the adventure is over." I'm still saying that to her in 2011.

Although getting a "job" would never be a consideration, there was a subtlety in mom's entreaties that had some weight — the idea of maturity. Although my idea was far different from hers, it was a fact that I was now in my early thirties and I had inadvertently allowed life's potential as a personal joyride to blind me to my responsibilities as a human and as a brief tenant of the planet Earth, along with billions of other sapiens and trillions (?) of animals. I had not been a bad person by any stretch, but I had certainly been diverted from my days as a political activist who always kept the big picture near the front of my brain. Of course, the idea of a "mature human" is almost an oxymoron, given our absurdly destructive genetic mandate, but I believe we should at least make an attempt at rising above the selfishness imprinted on our chromosomes.

Since I possessed no discretionary income with which to donate to charity, I once again devoted my spare time to political candidates (mostly at the local level), environmental groups, and animal rights organizations. Many were the night I spent in the cold outside the

---

Saratoga Park, the Spa's famous sulphur-laced water flowed naturally up to free drinking fountains, where the elderly lined up to fill their plastic cups. Of course, a byproduct of the water was nitrous oxide, which was vented on the other side of the rock from the fountain. Thus the impetuous Deadheads lined up on one side of the fountain, while the health-seeking Bluebloods up from Manhattan lined up on the other. I checked out the scene one day — absolutely hysterical. Kelly had just taken too big of a hit and passed out, falling down the rock face.

Glens Falls Civic Center protesting the circus, or gathering signatures on petitions aimed at controlling the pollution created in the Hudson River by the ubiquitous paper mills in Warren County. We tried desperately to prevent the Pyramid Company from building a mall in town at the cost of dozens of locally owned businesses. As usual, and just as they had in Ithaca, Pyramid won, got their mall, and sent many longtime mom-and-pop store owners to the unemployment line.

I also ramped up my interest in the JFK assassination, making regular trips to DC to slog through the microfilm at the old National Archives building before walking the few blocks to Bud Fensterwald's immense, but poorly organized, document trove on F Street. While in DC, I also nurtured my relationships with HSCA investigators and consultants I had met years earlier — gumshoes like William Scott Malone, Kevin Walsh, Bud Fensterwald, and Mark Allen. It was on one of these research trips that I conjured a way to combine my ability to gain access to off-limits places with my interest in the Kennedy investigation. At the time, the only records for review at the Archives were the Warren Commission and FBI investigative files, perhaps hundreds of thousands of pages, all stored on unwieldy microfilm. But what I really wanted to get my mitts on were the four million plus documents and recorded interviews generated by the HSCA, but which were still classified. Committee investigators had, off the record, made it known that they had interviewed people who made confessions to the committee, but were summarily disregarded by the panel's honchos. After five or six years had passed since the HSCA's work, we began to feel that these records would never see the light of day. What made this all the more certain was the stand taken by the Congressional Black Caucus, which had instigated the hearings in the first place. A senior investigator told me that the committee's files on Martin Luther King contained the FBI surveillance of his private life and were so incendiary that they couldn't be divulged.

One day at the Archives, as I rested my bleary eyes from their painful microfilm-scanning task, I walked to a far removed alcove and noticed a binder in the Finding Aids area. It was merely marked "Record Group 233," which I knew to be the federal number allocated to the HSCA. I took the binder to my desk, and there, read page after page of titles of the files that I and other researchers so coveted — like the one that read: "Thomas Beckham Confession." And stamped across every page in bold red was the word "EMBARGOED." When I noticed that all the files had unique number designations an idea started to germinate.

For months I had noticed that during certain hours, especially lunch, college interns or other inexperienced staff covered the reference desk assignment. Also, on certain days of the week there were a couple of staff that were — how do I put this? — a tad slow on the uptake. I decided to try something at once crazy, but at the same time so crazy that it might work (and no, I didn't use my SPAC passes): I would show up on the days and hours when certain young people were behind the desk, and hand them request forms that only noted the record group and file code, careful never to mention the words "Kennedy" or "assassination," or especially "EMBARGOED." I made a photocopy of the finding aid and took it home along with a fistful of blank request forms, which I filled out with the codes for the HSCA interviews I most wanted to hear. There were literally hundreds of 60-minute cassette tapes, so I envisioned this being an ongoing operation for quite some time. I would ask for just a few at a time, given that there were only so many that could be screened in a day.

A few days later I returned to the Archives, which I had come to regard as another "Ft. Knox" (like SPAC's backstage) that was just waiting for a new visitor. I inserted the furtive requests within a stack of benign record groups that I had no real interest in, walked up to the collegiate desk assistant and handed them over. I went back to my chair, where I vacillated between holding my breath and wondering if I might learn what the inside of a federal prison looked like by the end of the day.

After what seemed like a lifetime, but was probably only thirty minutes, a comely young assistant wheeled over a cart loaded with document boxes and cassette tapes labeled "Record Group 233." I struggled hard to keep my eyebrows and facial muscles frozen, while I was literally screaming on the inside. "Thank you," I uttered very academically and unemotionally.

There they were, about a dozen priceless field interviews conducted for the Committee — and now for me. I would be the first person outside of the investigators to hear the material. Sy Hersh and Bob Woodward, eat your hearts out! I put on earphones and began playing the tapes, taking extensive notes.

THIS IS YOUR BRAIN ON THE EIGHTIES 291

After a few days of this I raced over to Bud Fensterwald, swearing him to secrecy, and described the gambit. Bud was practically speechless. "This is the mother lode!" he said — as though I didn't know it. My chutzpah impressed the former Senate investigator, and would take our collegiality to a higher level; from that point on, Bud, a millionaire, would always be willing to buy me an airline ticket and a hotel room if I found someone in some far flung locale who needed to be interviewed.

Bud Fensterwald being questioned by Carl Bernstein and other press during the trial of the Watergate burglars.

I made a copy of the RG 233 finding aid, and handed the project over to Bud, since I was due back in New York, and it was agreed that Bud would take over the covert op until I could return in a couple months. On my next visit I noticed that some researchers, listening to interviews on unclassified topics, had brought blank tapes and were actually making copies to another deck; the next day I arrived with blanks and did the same with the HSCA material. I didn't know it at the time, but the taping process would lead to the downfall of the whole operation.

When I mentioned the taping to Bud, he suggested we rent some sort of machine to dub the tapes at high speed. After some research, I found an audio facility that rented me a "tape stamper" which would run and print out duplicates at six times normal speed. With Bud funding the operation, I rented the expensive — and bulky — gadget, purchased about fifty blanks, and trundled into the Archives. It was a rare misstep in my gate crashing strategies.

As usual, I asked for, and received the HSCA cassettes, this time many more than usual to accommodate my high-speed duping machine. There I sat, with this enormous machine and stacks of cassettes piled a foot high. Standing out like a sore thumb, I attracted the attention of an archivist who raced over and interrupted me just as I was about to make my first copy.

"What are you doing?" he asked incredulously.

"I just thought I'd speed up the process with this machine. One of the staff told me last week that I could do it." (They actually had.)

"Whoever told you that is mistaken. You can only use our machines to copy tapes, and they *cannot* be sped up — the tapes could break," he explained.

The archivist started to turn away, then did a double-take.

"Wait a minute," he said staring at the HSCA recordings. "Where the hell did you get these?"

"I just requested them on the forms."

"You can't have these, they're classified!"

He immediately gathered up the tapes and spirited them back to the employee's area, where I heard the unmistakable sound of employees being reamed out in very loud tones. I grabbed my tape stamper and blanks and headed out onto Pennsylvania Avenue, then quickly back to Baltimore to gather my things at my mom's house, alert Fensterwald, and then back to Glens Falls, where I fully expected the FBI to be waiting for me.

The G-men never showed, but I was later told that the incident prompted a Congressional investigation and a battery of new training protocols for Archives employees. But by this time, Bud and I had hundreds of pages of notes and transcripts to digest and to give more direction to our research.

Back upstate, I was at the breaking point with the long, bitter winters, and thus began formulating a plan of escape. Combined with the huge drop-off in gigs for working musicians, and the general free-fall of the New York State economy, the harsh climate sealed the deal. I had lived in The Empire State since the early seventies, and spent tourist seasons there since the sixties. My relocation there was due in part to my seduction by the stunning summers in Adirondack Park, without giving any thought to the Snow Belt's legendary winters. A typical Glens Falls nine-month "off-season" consisted of regular snowfalls every few days, often causing gigs to be cancelled at the last minute. The extreme cold (one February saw eighteen days flirting with twenty-below-zero) and unending depressing gray skies are hard to imagine without living through them. The annual deep freezes were so unrelenting that cars froze solid, their rubber belts and plastic parts morphing into brittle black chunks that lay in pieces on the ice-covered driveway in the morning; most inhabitants kept electrical engine warmers going all night so the oil wouldn't turn to hardened shellac by morning. Why do locals put up with it? Because the summers are just that gorgeous. But most transplants, including myself, eventually cry

"Uncle!" Other pals were plotting the same getaway, and I agreed with my Lake George Village friend Jim, who said he was going to strap a snow shovel to the front fender of his Volvo, head south, and not stop until the locals had no idea what the strange ornament was. (He ended up in Tennessee.)

     I figured that, if worse came to worst, I could finally put my poli-sci degree to use by working with a forward thinking Southern politician — that is, if I could find one. But before I could pull that trigger, I decided it was worth giving the James A. Michener thing a try. I managed to save enough for a two-week exploratory junket to a place I had never seen in person. Who knows, perhaps tennis-playing musicians were still appreciated in the South Pacific?

Chapter Sixteen

Adventures in Paradise

FEBRUARY 1986 SAW me take my first thirteen-hour flight to Hawaii, and, having just escaped the frozen wasteland of upstate New York, seeing the approaching beauty of Diamond Head from our 4,000-foot approach vector was — pardon the cliché — a religious experience.

Our 747 had just passed through the most beautiful white cumulus clouds when the first vision of Hawaii broke through, and I immediately understood Captain Cook's obsession with these "Sandwich Islands" and the inspiration for Fletcher Christian's Tahitian mutineers — the apparition was probably no less dreamlike from their sailing ships 4,000 feet offshore from Polynesia. Michener had conjured such a vision to represent a not-so-distant, yet always unattainable place of innocence and happiness. My quest was to prove Michener wrong — I was going to attain it.

For the next ten minutes of the descent, my brain was alternating between the melodic music themes of *Adventures in Paradise* and *Bali Ha'i*. I hadn't even landed and I was already so mesmerized that I actually contemplated reaching into my bag and tearing up my return ticket. Who could leave this magical place?

The typical air route from the US mainland to Honolulu first circles around the iconic extinct volcano, past Waikiki Beach, Ala Moana Beach Park, Pearl Harbor, and finally on to the Honolulu International Airport. For someone accustomed to the murky oceanic shores of Atlantic City where diving horses quickly disappeared from their Steel Pier perch, seeing the clear turquoise sea of the southern Pacific, beneath which you could actually observe the coral reefs, made me recalibrate my notion of beauty.

I had arm-twisted my 22-year-old brother Bob, a handsome kid with a great sense of humor, who, unlike me, had zero wanderlust, and seemed content to live out his life in the old neighborhood, to join me in the trek. We had booked a package deal that included one week each on Honolulu and Maui, with rental cars and hotels inclusive. Exiting the jetway, we were greeted by beautiful moo-moo clad Hawaiian *wahines* who adorned us with flower leis, and when we felt our first Pacific breezes outside the terminal we became intoxicated by the scent of plumeria that drifts down from the mountains when the trade winds are right. I had never been in a place that smelled so good. The drive to our Waikiki hotel began in an unremarkable industrial area before we reached Ala Moana ("path to the sea") Boulevard, which borders the park of the same name. There I drove by packed tennis courts and countless joggers circling the park; everyone was slim and tanned, and the Hawaiian girls, with their exotic genetic mix were positively stunning. The contrast with the pallid residents of Glens Falls, covered head-to-toe in Michelin Man style goose-down clothing, and packing on ten pounds every winter was jarring. In just these first few moments, this enchanting place felt more like "home" than any place I had ever been.

After checking in at our Waikiki hotel, we threw our bags into the room, turned on our heels, and headed directly to the legendary beach three blocks away. Even though it was nearing sunset, I had to get to that coastline pronto.

Standing on that expanse in the shadow of Diamond Head, a view I had seen in countless movies and television shows of the Sixties, was infinitely more picturesque and breath taking than can be portrayed on celluloid or postcards. Even though the sun was low, there was a large crowd, mostly Japanese – this was at the height of the booming Japanese economy, and they couldn't spend enough time in Honolulu shopping — there to witness the legendary sunset over the western Pacific Ocean. There was also a film crew down by the shoreline, a regular occurrence I would learn, where models were often shot in the glow of the diffuse "golden hour" light. But this film crew was much larger than for a typical shoot, so we ambled down to check it out.

Thus, in addition to a large gaggle of stunning bikini models and a breathtaking Waikiki sunset, my first minutes on a Hawaiian beach were spent admiring what I estimated to be an 18-inch waist that belonged to actress Heather Locklear, as she cavorted with William "Captain Kirk" Shatner on the shoreline. It turned out that they were there filming an episode ("Bloodsport") of the television series "TJ Hooker."

Bob and I spoke briefly with the actors; Heather's sister and some of the crew let on that Heather was always exhausted during the shoot because she stayed up all night yakking on the phone with her new boyfriend, Tommy Lee, who was on tour in Europe with his band Mötley Crüe. They would soon marry. During the course of our stay we ran into them occasionally over the next few days as they continued working in Waikiki.

As seen on TV...    ...and what we saw

The surreal experience only served to underscore the contrast between life in hard-frozen Glens Falls and what existed beyond the New York State horizon. In just my first hour in Waikiki, I learned some valuable lessons: it is just human nature to lose perspective, be forgetful, get lazy, or just get caught up in ruts. For the last few years, the music biz in upstate New York had landed me in a comfortable rut, and I needed this tropical jolt to bring me back to my senses. I vowed then and there to get back in the game.

Over the next few days, we did the predictable touring around, seeing sights such as Pearl Harbor, Diamond Head, Hanauma Bay, the "Toilet Bowl" blowhole, the pineapple fields, and the North Shore surf culture.

I was especially stoked to snorkel at Hanauma, the site of Elvis Presley's shack in *Blue Hawaii*, whereas Bob was, understandably, drawn back to Waikiki Beach. On the road to Haunama we made a quick stop at an iconic piece of property that was being featured on millions of American TV sets every week.

At the time, the TV series *Magnum PI* was a network juggernaut, and it seemed that every couple of days you'd run into the crew filming a scene, squeezing the lumbering actor Tom Selleck ("Magnum") into his tiny red Ferrari; it's a small island, after all, and the producers seemed to favor the same half-dozen locations. On off-days, stars Selleck, Larry Manetti, and Roger Mosley were often seen playing pick-up basketball on the public courts at Kapiolani Park, just down the street from the Diamond Head Tennis Club. But I was more interested in the gorgeous estate used for the exterior scenes of Magnum's seaside compound known as "Robin's Nest," so we hopped in our rental and headed out of Waikiki. Located on the Makai (eastern) side of Oahu, the property was actually the Anderson Estate, owned by the wealthiest resident on the island, and had also served as an occasional backdrop for shows such as *Hawaii-Five-O* and later, *MacGuyver*. From the Kalanianaole Highway it borders, nothing can be seen due to the eight-ft wall that encloses the two-acre parcel. Thus we decamped at the nearby Waimanalo Beach Park and made our way to Robin's Nest along the public beach (all beachfront in Honolulu is public.) The view was/is amazing, with a tidal pool created by the Andersons at the shoreline and a bird sanctuary Manana Island

The view from "Robin's Nest"

("Rabbit Island") just offshore. Of course, we swam in the pool for a while, pretending it was our private slice of Paradise. In future years, I would take many a date to the scenic location.

We visited the 1000-ft. Nu'uanu Pali Cliffs that overlook the Makai side. This was the site of the famous 1795 battle that saw the Big Island's King Kamehameha cast some 400 hundred enemy Oahu warriors over the cliffs, thus uniting all the islands under one government. The overlook, said to be haunted by the goddess Pele and sundry warrior-ghosts, makes for a great tourist photos. On the day we stopped by, a large cluster of Japanese tourists was posing for their obligatory group photo, and I coaxed Bob into sneaking into the party, so as to confuse them when they arrived back in Tokyo and developed their memento. I took out one of the many disposable cameras we bought and made our own copy.[*]

---

[*] I'm sure that the idea to crash the photo was inspired by the antics of *Mad Magazine's* gonzo artist, Sergio Aragones. Every year, *Mad*'s publisher William M. Gaines took his entire editorial staff on a men-only "madtrip" to some far-flung locale for two weeks. *In Mad: The World of William M.*

After the requisite touring, it was time to check out the local tennis talent, a decision that quickly validated the great maxim Mr. G imparted on son Vitas: "All you need is a tennis racquet and you'll make friends all over the world." I immediately fell in with great groups of local players at the Ala Moana Beach Park public tennis courts and the clay courts of the Diamond Head Tennis Club. Many would become friends for life.

I wonder which one is the interloper from Baltimore?

For me, Ala Moana became like a second home. The ten courts bordered my favorite beach strand on Oahu, so the regimen became two hours of tennis, followed by an hour of swimming – repeated over and over until it was time to grab some dinner. Then it was back to the park at sundown, where the local tennis bums usually made a campfire on the beach, and broke out the "Greenies" (Heinekens), guitars, and ukes; it seemed that I shared these two great passions with the Hawaiians: tennis and music. Knowing literally thousands of pop hits, I was soon leading sing-alongs, feeling like one of Elvis's characters in one of his Hawaiian epics. Hawaiians live for music, and we'd often grab dinner at a nearby Sushi Restaurant that featured Karaoke singing. They also revere the environment and all the animals that inhabit it. Whereas the Judeo-Christian God is an otherworldly deity, Pele, the Hawaiian goddess, is embodied in nature you can see, feel, and smell. To worship Pele, one must worship nature. It took almost 5,000 miles, but I had finally located a community of kindred spirits.

With my new friends, I checked out the annual Carnival held at the prestigious Punahou School at the foot of the Manoa highlands. On the beautiful grounds where a young Barack Obama had matriculated seven years earlier and where Kingston Trio founders Bobby Shane and Dave Guard met three decades prior, my taste buds were sated by the sumptuous, coconut-filled, sugar-topped, malasada

---

Gaines (Frank Jacobs, 1973), the story is told how one of Aragone's hobbies on these trips was to infiltrate the group photos of foreign tourists. As a loyal reader of all things *Mad* in those days, I'm certain Aragone's idea settled in my subconscious.

pastries — a welcome counterbalance to the glue-like poi I was only able to sample for a micro-second before passing it back to a local. After other nights spent in the Waikiki nightclubs, we attended the Honolulu Film festival held at the University of Hawaii.

We spent a couple of days on Maui, where we did the 3 a.m. drive up to the top of the 10,000-foot extinct volcano, Haleakala, whose summit temperature dips fifty degrees below what it is on the beautiful Maui beaches. Even in the dead of night, Haleakala provides a great payoff, thanks to its wondrous window on the cosmos. Here in the cleanest air on earth, the starlight is borderline overwhelming; the celestial bodies seem enormous and infinitely closer. My second *Hawaiian Religious Experience*. Communications satellites were plainly visible passing overhead, as was the Soviet Soyuz space station. But by far the most memorable sight was the slowly moving speck known as Halley's Comet, making its once-every-75-year appearance. Although the image was small, no one on earth that winter saw it better than those of us who were lucky enough to stand on a 10,000-ft. peak in the middle of the Pacific Ocean. If nothing else, I've been blessed with good timing.

But all of the above was but the prequel to the main event: sunrise. On the long, chilly drive up in the middle of the night, Bob had worried that a "nice sunrise" was going to be a tad anti-climactic. Even though I had the same doubt, I assured him that this was supposed to be the greatest sunrise on earth. Now, as dawn approached and with the stars now invisible in the morning light, we looked at each other shivering, but hoping for the best. That's when *Hawaiian Religious Experience Number Three* occurred. As the sun's light slowly took stage in the eastern sky, we realized that we were far above the cloud line, and that's what makes it so spectacular: seeing the sun appear, first over the clouds, exploding in hues of blue, purple, and orange (thanks to the ever-present volcanic dust), then above the mountaintops.[†] (For photo evidence, see: www.gusrusso.com)

[†] Of course, these are "guy color" descriptions, for those of us whose hue vocabulary is limited to that first set of primary color "Crayolas" we were given as toddlers — you know, red, blue, green, etc. I'm sure someone who works for *Land's End* or *J. Crew* could draw on a more precise lexicon, however, none of said employees were with us on Haleakala that night. I have often wondered if what we were seeing was actually a mix of mauve, turquoise, cyan, burgundy, azure, teal, lavender, puce, slate (as opposed to light slate), umber, magenta, chartreuse, sage,

After a few days in Maui it was back to Honolulu, where I again connected up with my new local friends on the tennis courts of Ala Moana and Diamond Head. By this time, both Bob and I had our eyes on a couple of stunning *wahines* we had met on our very first day in Waikiki. Here's where I have to proffer a warning to female readers: You are advised to skip over the following politically incorrect, borderline sexist pages.

So, guys, let's talk about the girls of Hawaii. First, their appearance: despite the fact that idealized standards of female beauty varies with the observer, I'd wager that 95% of humans with eyesight would agree that the exotic genetic blend known as "Hawaiian" is unsurpassed. (Again, for photo evidence, see www.gusrusso.com.)

At this stage of evolution, many Hawaiians carry chromosomes from Polynesia and Asia, with a soupçon of Europe, Africa, and South America thrown in for good measure. Their outdoor lifestyles and natural diets keep them healthy, toned, and happy. To this day, the most beautiful girl I ever conned into going out with me was a local girl, one quarter Hawaiian, one quarter Tahitian, one quarter Irish, and one quarter German — naturally stunning, but without the attitude that usually accompanies such beauty. Whether playing tennis, snorkeling, or just walking down the street to get a newspaper, you encounter a non-stop parade of dark-haired loveliness. Bob and I joked about getting whiplash from the constant neck-turning as the *wahines* traversed in all directions, an inconceivable affliction where I lived.

Now here's the kicker: for the most part, these ladies are overwhelmingly friendly and extremely approachable. Girls with a fraction of this refinement in Glens Falls (if you could find one) were usually standoffish when approached. Here, where such beauty is commonplace, they were more than happy to dance, accept a drink, play tennis, or join you for a swim out to the reef. In fact, I don't recall any of them saying "No thanks." The most average looking local guys all had gorgeous girlfriends or wives — something rarely seen on the mainland, unless, of course, you frequented Beverly Hills.

A typical bachelor day in Honolulu: stroll along the small retaining wall that borders the sand at the mile-long Ala Moana beach, surveying the

---

aquamarine, sienna, Goldenrod, stone, jonquil, olive, cognac, cinder, seashell, burberry, brulée, ash, burlywood, saddle, thistle, lime, oyster, wheat, khaki, pepper, ochre, rust, salsa, heather, Patagonia, capeline, peach, ivory, cornsilk, salmon, coral, plum, orchid, tomato, and, my personal favorite, olive drab.

girls working on their tans, while strains of the Beach Boys' "Girls on the Beach" play in your head. After picking your favorite lovely, throw your blanket down nearby, say "Aloha," and you're off.‡ Often that simple greeting would lead to a discussion of what book she is reading, the recently posted jellyfish warning, and from there to an informal "rice bowl" lunch or "shave ice." That might progress to dinner and a movie that same night. It's all very civilized, even romantic, especially when you end up strolling Waikiki Beach by moonlight, or getting out your guitar. Being a tennis player made the adventure even less contrived than asking about the jellies; there were always solo girls hitting against the wall or sitting on the bleachers, just waiting to hit with someone. Every day and night (the courts were lit)!

However, things usually come to a screeching halt when the male tourist tries to "close the deal," so to speak. That's where most Hawaiian girls typically draw the line — and for good reason; they are constantly bombarded by male tourists who either break their hearts by never returning, or lie about their marital status. So the Hawaiians treat the date as a pleasant night out, nothing more. Now the Japanese girls on vacation were another story altogether. In the eighties, the yen was on the top of the currency heap, and many Japanese saw Hawaii as either a weekend shopping spree, or an orgy of real estate investment. The shoppers, who carried pocketbooks stuffed with hundred dollar bills, cruised Kalakaua Avenue with a vengeance, and the shop owners stayed open until the last Asian tourist had dropped his/her last C-note (by contrast, if only inexpensive trinket-buying mainlanders were in the shops, they were escorted out promptly at closing time.)

Braving the hordes of after-dark prostitutes that pounded the pavement in relentless pursuit of their deep-pocketed Japanese male relatives, the females saw Hawaii as a reprieve from their rigid second-class citizen lives back in Yokohama or Roppongi. I was stunned to see how the Japanese men, seemingly stuck in medieval chauvinism, treated their women, many of whom still walked three feet behind their male superiors. Everywhere, it seemed, the women were bowing in subservience to the demands of their men. Thus, when the men were off doing their thing, their women staged a once-a-year mini-rebellion, and they had

---

‡ On the occasion that I saw a great girl on an otherwise deserted beach, I'd open up with one of my favorite movie ice-breaker lines. A young Cybil Shepherd used it in her second movie, *The Heartbreak Kid* (1972). Upon encountering Charles Grodin's character, whom she had never met, sunning himself on a deserted hotel beach in Miami, she uttered the brilliant entrée, "You're in my spot!" If the person on the blanket has a sense of humor, the line works every time.

no time for small talk. I had no inkling that these timid looking beauties could be capable of sexual abandon until Thurlow, one of my Hawaiian tennis buddies, educated me about the seeming incongruity.

"They're so used to being ignored," Thurlow advised, "that if you just treat them with any respect, you won't know what hit you."

"But what if they don't speak English?" I asked.

"Doesn't matter, bra," came the response.

That evening I approached an Asian lovely that was hitting against the wall, and inquired if she'd like to share a court with me. She smiled, nodded, and meekly whispered "Hai (yes)." After an hour on the court, which consisted mostly of me giving her a lesson — despite me knowing no Japanese and her knowing about ten words of English — she walked to the net, shook my hand and proceeded to blow my mind.

"Sex — you like?" she whispered.

After hoisting my jaw from the Deco-Turf, I uttered my first-ever Japanese word: "Hai??"

Then my little singles partner pointed to the reef — this little minx had either done this before, or had planned it out in advance. We threw our gear on the beach and swam out to the reef about twenty yards offshore. The sun having long since set, we were alone in the fading light as I sat on a smooth section of coral, the water up to my shoulders. My new best friend sat on my lap and we proceeded to churn our love butter. She was momentarily confused when she heard me whisper to myself, "God bless you, Thurlow!"

When we had finished, she bowed to me on the shore and disappeared. I called after her:

"Tomorrow?"

"Tomorrow, home," she answered. "*Domo*."

I was crestfallen, but at the same time I was heartened to know that there were always beautiful Japanese and local girls practicing against that wall. And my brother Bob, it turned out, was having his own assignation with a local girl he had met on the beach at Waikiki. Best vacation I ever had.

Before we knew what hit us, our 12-day reverie came to a crushing end. After trying to convince me to stay (as, apparently, so many vacationers had done), my new Hawaiian tennis pals threw me a going away barbecue on the beach at Ala Moana.

It was explained to me that most tourists are kept at a polite distance, seen as "Ugly American" style despoilers. However, occasionally, exceptions are made. I was one of the lucky ones, progressing from *haole* ("soulless foreigner") to *kama'aina* ("child of the island".) Having already checked out of the hotel, it was all I could do to tear myself away from this idyll and head to the airport, but I promised them I'd return soon (I would) and that I would take the spirit of "Aloha" with me back to the Ticonderoga tundra I called home. They asked the time of our flight, and I assumed they were just curious, but I later learned that they had a reason for their inquiry.

My Ala Moana tennis pals bid me "Aloha"

Making our way back to the Honolulu International Airport in a deep funk, Bob and I felt like we were in a funeral procession. Returning to the dark, frozen north after having seen Paradise seemed like a prison sentence. And I was an innocent man! On the plane, which I imagined was piloted by Captain Bligh, I recalled sitting on a bench in Kapiolani Park with a 75-year-old Hawaiian tennis player named Roland. "Think about where you want to retire and just go there now, while you're young enough to enjoy it. I see so many seniors who retire here, but are too infirm to swim or surf or play tennis or hike to the waterfalls. It frustrates them to no end. I even heard of a mainland woman that saved her whole life to retire in Hawaii, but she died just a month before retirement. She never even got to see it."

Thus I resolved to return to Honolulu quicker than you can say Humuhumunukunukuapua'a (the state fish.) I could live in Glens Falls for a thousand years and never come close to the sense of tranquility I had just experienced in two weeks. Thus my new master plan was to return for an extended stay, and if this land was really what it seemed, to find a way to live there full-time.

As we began our ascent, I looked out the window and saw that our vector took us right over Ala Moana Beach Park, where, I later learned, my new friends were giving me their own local version of a goodbye wave, raising a Greenie with one hand and a "shaka" sign with the other.

Chapter Seventeen

Brain Damage

RETURNING TO THE Great Off-White North, I settled back into my familiar rhythm, teaching guitar by day, playing gigs in the ever-diminishing number of venues on the weekends, and tennis non-stop. The club crumbs left us by the DJs were actually accompanied by a lower pay scale than we received before the Great Disco Revolution — and that had been nothing to write home about. Talk about rubbing salt in the wound. It is a sad fact that journeymen musicians are the only segment of the workforce that doesn't merit a cost of living pay increase. (I recently played a band gig, as I write this in 2011, for $500, the same fee paid to my group Durango in 1974, and countless CYO dance bands in the Sixties.) Now in the late Eighties, we were, with no help from corrupt musicians' unions, forced to accept a pay scale that our predecessors had received in the Fifties! Unlike most of the American workforce, we were going backwards, full speed ahead.

Although that summer on idyllic Lake George was still euphoric, with its temporary up-tick in gigs, it had finally occurred to me that an LG summer was only eight weeks in duration. Duh. With the live music scene in steep decline, those few weeks no longer seemed worth the forty-four weeks of waiting; as Sondheim noted, "Perpetual Anticipation" is an unhealthy lifestyle, all things considered. To make matters worse, the non-stop parade of guitar students had taken on some disturbing new traits: laziness, lack of focus, and monumental impatience.

WARNING: RANT ALERT

I concluded that the combined effects of MTV, *Entertainment Tonight*, and mind-numbing video games had turned the "Me Generation" into automatons that demanded not only instant gratification, as previously ranted, but also celebrity for celebrity's sake. With the seductive visual power of "videos" being unchallenged by the transcendent power of live music (since there were now so few places to hear it), actual music and musicianship were sadly becoming irrelevant— at a time, ironically, when, thanks to recent advances in overseas child labor exploitation, good quality musical gear was much more affordable. It was not uncommon in the Sixties to save for years to purchase a Fender or Gibson guitar. Now, a reasonable facsimile could be had for a fraction of the price. Who'd have ever dreamt that "Les Paul" or "Leo Fender" style guitars, the very essence of American Pop, would have "Made in Malaysia" stamped on the back and a $150 price tag on the front? However, no one could seem to afford the time to master these newly affordable instruments.

It was about this time that guitar transcription magazines began to proliferate, and their shorthand language for teaching rock songs only added to the musical misery created by the digital onslaught. In order to sell more copies to the new hordes of illiterate, zero-attention span guitarists, and these publications displayed representations of a fingerboard with marks where one should drop his fingers to replicate a particular melody or chord. Thanks to this prehistoric "tablature," or TAB, most young players were now recreating music lines without the slightest idea of what they were playing, the names of the notes, or the theoretical underpinnings for why the notes worked. Worst of all, they now had no musical language with which to instantly communicate with other musicians — they had to show each other pictures of what to do. This time wasting sign language would, of course, render them impotent in a studio setting, an orchestra, a pick-up wedding gig, and the countless other ways musicians made music and earned a living. TAB had created armies of circus monkeys, mindlessly performing by rote. But in this new world of instant gratification, it caught on like wildfire, and since I had no interest in animal husbandry, I refused to use TAB, and thus began seeing more dropouts by kids unable to cope with learning even the most rudimentary musical language or theory.

Oh, did I mention that there was now little to no respect for the glorious musical history that got us here in the first place? Whereas previous generations of musicians, including rockers, were well-versed in all the pop music that came before them, this new crop could care less about classics by the Erroll Garners, George Gershwins, and Cole Porters of the world, the very icons whose influence gave nuance to the music of the Beatles, the Beach Boys, the Doors, the Mamas and Papas, and the rest. It was Glenn Miller who inspired the Liverpudlian "mop tops" to give "She Loves You" a Big Band "Major Sixth" chord harmonic cadence, Gershwin that gave young Brian Wilson the orchestral palette that made *Pet Sounds* possible, Bach that showed Ray Manzarek how to open the Doors' "Light My Fire" with baroque organ arpeggios, and the classically trained jazzers The Hi-Los and The Four Freshmen who taught the Beach Boys, the Mamas and the Papas and the Association how to blend human voices. I doubt that today you could find a 16-year-old rocker who has even heard of "Misty," let alone knows how to play it.

Simultaneously, I was seeing a similar disdain for nuance among young tennis players. The game was quickly being reduced to an endless, coma inducing series of looping forehands and backhands combined with power serves. That was it— the game had been reduced to three shots. Gone were the topspin lob, the "chip and charge" approach, the stab volley, the drop volley, the half volley, the slice forehand, the slice backhand, the flat forehand, the flat backhand, the drop shot, the backspin drop, the twist serve, and the reverse spin serve, to name a few. These were the shots we used to drill endlessly, and which made the strategic aspect of the game so appealing to all who came before. Watching a Rod Laver or a Ken Rosewall execute each one of these shots with the precision of Mayo Clinic surgeons was what drew my generation to the game in the first place. As a result of this sea change (and the lack of compelling personalities), tennis television ratings fell off a cliff, as they deserved to. Unthinkably, the greatest sport had become boring. Even I was having trouble watching: whereas I used to be glued to every televised event, for the first time I was switching off tennis matches in favor of a good movie, or The Gong Show.

On a big week in 1986, I taught 45 guitar lessons, approximately five of which to kids who actually had a chance of being real musicians — a total ratio reversal from when I had started teaching just a few years previous. As depressing as it was, the late Eighties zeitgeist was positively Renaissance-like compared to the one that was to follow in the wake of the unleashing of "digital heroin" on the unsuspecting populace in the nineties.[*] The intellectual downturn was startling and was being simultaneously noticed by all my teaching colleagues. Let me state emphatically that this narrative is in no way a criticism of the 80's kids; it was just horrible timing to be a young human at this juncture of de-evolution. My peers and me would have likely suffocated in the same cultural quicksand had we have been born twenty or more years later than we were. Believe me, I thank my lucky stars every day that I arrived on the scene when I did, and I feel terrible for those growing up today with the smothering, addictive challenges they face.

---

[*] Teenage attention spans of the Eighties were practically interminable compared to those of today's permanently distracted digital natives, for whom a long musical practice session might last all of seven minutes, during which a couple dozen incoming momentous text messages have to be addressed. Today's music instructors must fight the temptation to blow their brains out on a daily basis.

OK— this teaching thing was beginning to feel like an actual job, something that obviously went against the very core of my being. I thus began to formulate a long-range master plan: I would spend much of the next two years scouting my eventual retirement in Honolulu, in advance of moving back to the MD/DC area temporarily, where I would utilize my contacts at Jack Anderson's office and with friends who worked with the HSCA to start breaking into investigative reporting, screenwriting, and documentary producing. Additionally, the close proximity to the National Archives, FBI, NSA, and CIA headquarters would give me access to information mother loads, which I had a gift for exploiting. Siddhartha Jr. was ready to ascend another branch in the tree of knowledge. As a bonus, if all went as planned, I would bank just enough money by retirement time to fade into a Hawaiian sunset while strumming "Aloha Oe" on a koa wood 'ukulele.

To keep my resolve firm, I plastered my expansive apartment (pardon the inside joke) with posters from Hawaii (obviously leaving a bit of space for the ever-present Kate Bush image), and plotted my escape from the desolate nether regions known collectively as "Upstate." I stayed in regular contact with my Ala Moana tennis buddies and told them to keep their antennae out for sublets in the fall of 1986. Apart from the regular hedonism that occurred during a Lake George summer, the weekly twenty-four hour parties at Chez Ray Jett, and the nightly front row seats at SPAC, there were a few more notable adventures to be had before making my getaway to Hawaii.

By this time, our little epic *Basket Case* had developed a strong cult following, earned rave reviews in the fan press, won a number of zero-prestige horror awards, and performed well in the nascent consumer video market. Consequently, Frank and Edgar were able to secure an actual budget from an actual film financier, Andre Blay of Embassy Films, for their next feel-good effort. I was delighted when they called and asked me to compose the score. Over the years, I had read a number of Frank's scripts, one more outlandish than the next, and Blay chose Frank's most tame script to produce, the tale of an ancient eel-like parasite that needs to ingest fresh human brains to survive. The creature, Aylmer, coaxes a succession of human supplicants to secure the sustenance in exchange for injecting them with his own blue blood, the greatest and most addictive opiate in the universe. Just as Frank had described *Basket Case* as the "first right to life movie," he now rationalized this latest gorefest, christened *Brain Damage*, as "a cautionary tale-slash-metaphor for crack addiction." Personally, I think it was just an excuse to use up the leftover bottles of Dick Smith movie blood left over in Frank's refrigerator from his earlier effort. Waste not, want not.

The best part of this project was that I would have an actual salary, an expense account to hire actual musicians, and a production budget to book actual recording studios. Since *Damage* would not go into production for another year, I could compose basic themes at my leisure. And I couldn't imagine a more appropriately inspirational place Mai Tai from a coconut shell, while the sun disappears quietly on the Pacific Ocean's Western horizon. I had already heard from Diamond Head tennis pals Hank and Laura May that Hank's brother had an unused guest room in Manoa Heights that I was welcome to inhabit for little more than cost (I think I paid $65 a month.) Thus, at summer's end I closed a deal with two of Ray Jett's coterie to sublet my pad until the spring of 1987. Then I sold a collectible Fender Strat for $5,000,[†] and, combined with my savings and *Brain Damage* advance, I headed off to a new home in late September with far more in my pocket than when I first moved to Ithaca. Looking back, it is clear that I was (am) merely trying to extend the era of Boomer bliss seeking by finding new places, a shrinking list to be sure, where such a vocation is still appreciated.

In addition to packing my guitar, tennis and snorkel gear, I tossed copies of the seminal composition books "Arranged By Nelson Riddle" and "Henry Mancini's Sounds and Scores" into my suitcase. Arriving late in Honolulu, and with a touch of the flu, I felt like I just wanted to crash upon arrival, so I spent the first night at the same Waikiki hotel as I had last year. When I learned that the pool and Jacuzzi were still open, I thought I'd order a Blue Hawaii from the bar, wander down to the Jacuzzi, and relax a bit before packing it in — I'd make my way up to rainbow saturated Manoa in the morning.[‡] Imagine my delight when I approached the hot tub, cocktail in hand, and saw that the bubbling bowl only had room for one more soaker;

[†] A lot more to this story: This was a 1954 Sunburst Strat (first year made) in near mint condition (one minor ding only.) I had acquired the guitar from a young guitar student a few years earlier for the absurd price of $200 (he was anxious to buy an Eddie Van Halen Kramer!) When offered $5K by an Albany vintage broker, who assured me that the collectible guitar market had peaked, I sold it to him, bought a beautiful new $800 1986 Strat Plus, which I still own, and placed the rest in my Hawaii fund. But here's the punch line: ten years later I was in LA, and made my requisite viewing of the vintage wall at the LA Guitar Center on Sunset. What I saw hanging there must have made me go pale, because a salesperson approached and asked if anything was wrong. I explained that I had owned and sold a similar, yet much more pristine, 1954 sunburst than the one hanging on the wall. He asked how much I got for it. "Oh, just $120,000 less than you're asking for it." But I still wouldn't trade my Hawaiian winter for that guitar.

[‡] Manoa is the home of the University of Hawaii, whose sports teams bear the fitting name, The Rainbows.

the other eight seats were occupied by a flock of touring, bikini-clad Japanese coeds, who all smiled, raised their champagne flutes, and beckoned me in. Squeezing into my spot, one of the girls meandered behind us giving us backrubs. Gazing up at the moon through the palm trees as my shoulders were being massaged by a lovely Asian absolute stranger, my thoughts drifted not to Siddhartha, but to another former Ithacan, Ulysses (or was it Steely Dan, or Cream?): "Could it be that I have found my home at last? Home at Last?"

I won't bore the reader with tales of Hedonism Hawaiian Style, which are endless, but the most important aspects of the seven-month odyssey, those involving the Boomer learning curve, cannot be overlooked. Since I chose to associate almost exclusively with local Hawaiians, I slowly became immersed in Polynesian culture and its polytheistic religious beliefs — they see gods in every part of nature. Hawaiians see themselves as part of, not separate from, the natural world. Because the early Hawaiians depended on nature for everything, the *kapu* system of Tahitian laws was intimately connected with reverence and respect for mother Earth. Hawaiians adopted a system of laws and rituals that revered and protected the *mana* (spiritual power or energy), which exists in all living things, including animals, many of which were believed to be gods who watched over the family. Many of the songs I heard on the beach at Ala Moana were inspired by the traditional Hawaiian reverence for the natural beauty of Hawaii's forests, volcanic mountains, oceans, birds, and animals.

This *Aloha Aina* (love of the land) was one of the earliest examples of environmental protectionism and placed the Hawaiians a millennia ahead of the 21st century "green movement." The Hawaiians consider forests as *wao akua*, the realm of the gods, and their *ahupua'a* system of water and land management protects the upland water sources that sustained human life in the lowlands. "To maintain our own beauty, we must maintain the beauty of the forest," said Hawaiian historian Pua Kanahele. "If we cut down the forest, we cut down ourselves." Before the US overthrow, the Hawaiians had instituted a system of land management in which no one took from the land more than what was needed. The land was the *'a-ina*, or "that which feeds," and its rich diversity helped shape and inspire the native culture. Likewise, water is also gift from the gods, and Hawaiians historically took an active part in its use and conservation.

BRAIN DAMAGE 311

Like the Native Americans, who also lived in balance with nature, the Hawaiians saw their world turned upside-down with the arrival of the white man in the late 18th century, culminating in the 1893 overthrow of the Hawaiian monarchy by corrupt "missionaries" who were supported by US marines. One hundred years later, President Bill Clinton signed Public Law 103-150, otherwise known as "The Apology Resolution," in which America formally apologized for the U.S. Government's role in supporting the overthrow of the Kingdom of Hawaii. By the time this Boomer arrived on their shores, most, but not all, Hawaiians had been seduced by the capitalist vixen.

Yet it was not difficult to see that just below the surface the ancient philosophies were still a part of their DNA.

Many were the times that a friend and I hiked to the interior, searching for tourist-proof waterfalls in order to make offerings to Pele of leaf-wrapped shells and shiny stones. I found my awareness and love of animals growing during this time; snorkeling with the beautiful marine life, watching whales breach off Rabbit Island, or just hand feeding the sea birds on the North Shore made me reconsider my relationship with these innocent creatures that are treated so horribly by my species.

The locals I chose to associate with were among many who eschewed the corporatization of their islands, to they extent that they backed political candidates who demanded secession from the US. Their refreshing abhorrence of status symbols reminded me of the gang at Chez Ray J, except with much better tans. All that was needed in our Honolulu gang was a pair of shorts, sneakers, rackets, a guitar, food, and a roof over your head. Taking the place of the Fila and Tacchini logos that engulfed the US Open were simple T-shirts emblazoned with Hawaiian references — that was real status. No one cared who made the few necessities you owned, especially when you were escorting a beautiful Asian girl to a movie or to that coral reef at sunset. The only thing that seemed to matter was how friendly you were. What a concept!

The days all blurred together in a vision of low-rent, victimless hedonism and reverence for the wonder of nature, but in mid-winter I would make one quick trip back East to attend to meetings for our upcoming movie, see if my apartment was still standing, etc. After the visit, I was returning to Hawaii and decided to make my first side trip to the city of JFK's assassination to meet some of the witnesses I had been speaking with by phone for so many years. As luck would have it, the family of one of my guitar students had just relocated to Dallas and invited me to stay with them while I checked out the scene of the crime.

Since I had been convinced by the ballistics and trajectory work of the 1979 HSCA that Oswald alone had shot the President, and then by the National Academy of Sciences that no other shooters fired from the bushes, the witnesses I spoke with were only of mild interest — I focused my research efforts on Oswald's motive and whether others might have been aware of it in advance, to me the only question still worth answering. Thus, what was most powerful about Dallas was just standing in the spaces where the seminal events had occurred. Of course, first up were Dealey Plaza and the Texas School Book Depository. It would be an understatement to say I was stunned by the smallness of the plaza; everything was so close that a former military man like Oswald couldn't possibly miss.

At the time of my first visit, the Depository functioned as the Dallas County Administration Building, although the sixth floor was left spookily empty and unused. Through my new friend, former Dallas Detective and Pearl Harbor attack survivor Jim Leavelle — who was famously handcuffed to the assassin on the day he was killed by Jack Ruby — I gained access to the sixth floor "sniper's perch."[§]

As Jim and I squatted down in Oswald's window and watched the cars pass six floors below, I was again stunned by how easy it all seemed. Why hadn't conspiracy writers such as Mark Lane written about *this*? I felt lied to by Lane and the legion of "conspirati" who had

---

[§] Jim says he felt the same helpless feeling aboard the USS Whitney in 1941 watching the USS Arizona blow up and watching Ruby shoot Oswald: "In both cases, I couldn't do anything."

fanned the flames of multiple shooters for years — they had to know about this vest-pocket shooting gallery. My rumination was interrupted when Jim spoke up.

"Gus, have you ever fired a rifle?" Jim asked.

"The last thing I fired was a BB gun when I was about eight," I said.

"Well, then it might take me a half an hour to teach you how to do what Oswald did. It's like shooting fish in a barrel."

One of the more interesting witnesses I interviewed on this trip was Buell Frazier, Oswald's co-employee and only friend at the Depository. It was Frazier who drove Oswald to work, long package in hand, on the fateful morning. Frazier, who had become reclusive since the murder, had always been of interest to me because of a number of FBI reports that hinted that he was much closer to Oswald than he admitted in his testimony.

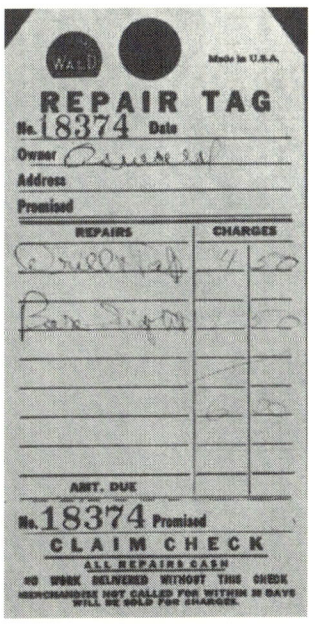

Among the tantalizing bits was a local gun shop receipt for an "Oswald," who had come in three weeks before the murders in order to have a scope mounted on a rifle that, according to the shop repairman, "could only have been a .303 British Enfield," the very model owned by Oswald's 19-year-old friend Buell, who according to another un-validated report, had allegedly accompanied Oswald to a shooting range in the weeks prior to the killings of the President and Officer J.D. Tippit. The Dallas PD, certain there was more to the relationship, subjected Buell to a harsh interrogation well into the night of the murders. Since then, Frazier had only given one or two interviews.

I, too, wondered if Frazier had even a hint of his friend's murderous plan, and I convinced my host, who had developed an interest in the case since his relocation from New York, that we should go knock on Buell's apartment door and try to chat him up.

It was a blistering hot Dallas day when we found Buell's place and knocked for a few minutes before the door cracked open an inch. Behind a chain security lock, Frazier spoke in a whisper, saying he didn't want to speak or even open the door. I remember staying on that sun-drenched porch for what seemed like a half hour trying to engage this guy and get him to at least open the door. My skin, even though it had been tested in Hawaii, was beginning to burn up when Frazier took mercy and came out to speak to us. I quickly suggested we might sit on a bench under a nearby tree to relieve my burning flesh. Frazier laughed and agreed.

After spending that first hour of many with Buell, I came to the conclusion that this was one scared, but innocent, rabbit— twenty-four years after the assassination. He seemed so traumatized by the events of November 22, 1963 that he lived in constant fear that someone would dredge up his innocent youthful friendship with a hated assassin-to-be, and ruin the life he had painstakingly rebuilt in the ensuing years. Frazier, who adamantly denied to me that he had driven Oswald to the shooting range or lent him the Enfield, had in fact lost many jobs and friendships when his brief Oswaldian history became known. But it was also clear to me that he was still hiding the extent of that odd friendship because, I believed, he feared that some might mistakenly conclude that he had foreknowledge of the killer's intent, just like the Dallas interrogators had done. If it were true that he had indeed innocently leant Oswald his Enfield .303 and driven him to the shooting range, such conclusions would quickly be reached by many— but not by me. Buell was one of the good guys, who, in trying to befriend a lonely new fellow employee, got caught up in the great American tragedy. We would stay in touch for years.

Castro's lover/would-be assassin Marita Lorenz with Detective Jim Leavelle and me.

I take a fall where Oswald was shot.

Relaxing in Oswald's prison cell.

Before leaving Dallas, I convinced a friend to drive me to Rose Hill cemetery in Ft. Worth, the site of Oswald's final resting place. Due to previous vandalism and theft, the facility historically refused to direct people to the flat stone that signifies the reviled assassin's grave, and most, including my friend on previous visits, had been unable to locate it on the large parcel. Within minutes of driving through the winding paths, I got this strange feeling as we passed by a large oak tree. "Stop here," I said. I walked just a few steps from the path, looked down, and there it was: a reddish stone, and the only one I saw inscribed with just one chilling word: "OSWALD."

After a few days in Dallas I took my connecting flight back to Honolulu, where I spent the next four delicious months. In the spring I returned to "Upstate," where I began the serious work of scoring Frank and Edgar's new horror flick. I concluded that the way to get the most bang for the producers' bucks was to push the technical envelope, as it then existed. Recent advances in computer interfaces made it possible to daisy-chain any number of synthesizers, drum machines, samplers — whatever — to one controlling computer, thus creating the illusion of a large orchestra, albeit digital. A cue could sound like thirty musicians were playing, and had we hired that many actual players, we would have been way over budget. Additionally, keys and tempos could be changed with a keystroke, massaged to exactly fit the action on screen, without having to be painstakingly re-written while studio players on the clock twiddled their thumbs. Luckily, the producers agreed.

Since I knew my way around the piano (I had an old upright in my living room), I purchased an E-Max sampling synth keyboard, and began the painful process of writing out charts for violins, woodwinds, horn sections, harps — you name it. The decision was not an easy one; computers were putting working musicians like me out of business at a frightening speed, and here I was contributing to the problem. I think that the undertaking was my symbolic way of crying "Uncle" to the new digital overlords who had in fact all but won the music wars. The game was up, as I and countless of my musical colleagues had decided to move on to new careers. For hundreds of years, it had been possible to earn a middle-class income as a "musician," but for the vast majority of us, that vocation would soon be over. It was a realization that was, and remains, sad beyond description. Furthermore, I knew that Frank and Edgar wanted this soundtrack to rival those of bigger budgeted horror flicks such as *Re-Animator*, which employed a genuine symphony orchestra, thus I really had no choice. I was able, however, to hire at least a couple of live musicians for every cue; properly blended, a real violinist can boost the illusion created by the digital ones. Frank hired percussionist Clutch Reiser, who had helped out on our earlier effort, to create a live palette of vibes and other percussive sounds. What made the whole thing possible was the inclusion of Glens Falls keyboardist and computer geek Matt Donnelly, who linked all these new gadgets together, and helped me upload the score in "step-time" keystrokes, one laborious dotted eighth note at a time.

Today, computer generated scores are ubiquitous, not only on the big screen, but especially on television, as many traditional recording studios have long since been shuttered, and countless playing careers extinguished. But back in 1987, this was Promethean, and hardly anyone north of New York City knew how to pull it off other than Matt. It was an amazing thing to hear, when, after working out endless glitches in the nascent technology, Matt finally pressed the "play button" and the dozen or so synths that clogged my tiny apartment all played in harmony. It was a great leap forward from the soundscape we were able to create for *Basket Case*, however the convenience came at a great price for those of us who really cared: the carefully designed ambience and the engineering talent utilized in the great recording studios were nowhere to be found, and the sound suffered. We were in the early years of the "convenience epidemic," which, as I write this, has claimed quality as its victim almost totally.

Apart from that pressed button, my second favorite memory

from the gig was the opening line of a profile piece done in the local paper: "When you think of *Brain Damage*," the article announced, "think of Glens Falls musicians Gus Russo and Clutch Reiser, plus South Glens Falls musician/computer whiz Matt Donnelly." I couldn't agree more.

Our newest effort looked and sounded infinitely better than our first, and when it debuted in 1988 garnered terrific reviews. Like *Basket Case, Brain Damage* developed a strong cult following and had a lucrative afterlife in the commercial video market. But I had no illusions that a new career awaited me as a film composer; at that time, the good jobs were infrequent, and they were usually given to synth players who could commandeer both the computers and the notes. The big-paying studio film work was controlled by a very tight clique of composers that had devoted a lifetime to getting in that position, and they rarely cracked open the door to let in a newcomer. Thus I maintained my plan to come in from the cold by moving closer to Washington, and forge a new career in the only other skill I had left apart from tennis and music: investigating the Kennedy story. There was never any doubt that I would follow my passions, as I had done with tennis and music; the challenge now was to find someone to pay me for researching the assassination. Outside of the staffers for the government's two investigations years ago, no one I knew of had such a gig. But then again, no one else I knew had Players' Box seats at the US Open for fifteen years running, or had done the other umpteen crazy things I had managed to pull off since high school. This was no time to abandon Siddhartha and Joseph Campbell.

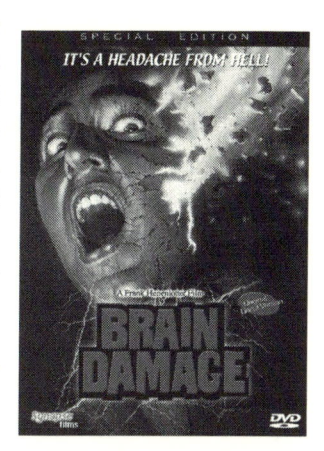

While others wasted time deciding if Oswald was even involved, I had devoted my energies to trying to ascertain his motive, and whether he was the weaponized tool of one of JFK's many enemies, and why so many documents were still classified. I was unconvinced that this politically hyper-charged man committed the ultimate political crime for no discernable reason, as officialdom was trying to proselytize. Thus, I had been scouring all the available resources to try to nail down the issue. Slowly, most of the popular scenarios fell by the wayside when scrutinized, but there remained two compelling possibilities that actually grew stronger upon closer inspection: the CIA's Mexico City Station and its Cuban adversary in that city were at the heart of many still-withheld secret documents and countless unpursued leads. Why? Additionally, the blasé way officialdom dealt with the South of the Border episode in its reports, while simultaneously burying its Mexico City leads in deep storage, convinced me that the heart of the story lay there. For it was into this murky espionage capital that Oswald had practically dissolved for almost a week, two months before shooting the President. It would take me fifteen more years to determine if rogue or sanctioned agents from the CIA or Cuba's murderous G-2 had done some business with the killer, business that provoked four countries (the US, Cuba, Mexico, and the USSR) into suppressing their files on the episode.

As it turned out, one of America's most dogged investigative reporters, a man with whom I had some contact years earlier, was also drawn to the Cuban/Mexico City angle: syndicated columnist Jack Anderson. Upon learning that Jack was beginning research for a 25th anniversary documentary (*Who Murdered JFK? An American Exposé*, 1988), I reached out to him and was quickly employed on a part-time basis to coalesce all my Cuban files and funnel them to his Washington producers. It was my first paid investigative work, and the reception my work received from Jack strengthened my resolve to move back down to the DC area. By 1989, after two more winters in Hawaii and one more Lake George summer, I would be back in my Mid-Atlantic roots, crafting proposals to any media that would listen.

Just as I had headed for Ithaca with a clear strategy for forging a new career in music, I would do the same in moving back to my Baltimore homeland. After some library research, and knowing that the thirtieth anniversary of Kennedy's death was approaching, I decided on five targets for pitches on Kennedy projects: Don Hewitt, creator and producer of *60 Minutes*; Jennifer Lawson, head of national programming for the Corporation for Public Broadcasting in Arlington, VA; CBS News anchor Dan Rather, who was a local reporter in Dallas on the day of the Kennedy killing; through my HSCA pal William Scott Malone, who was now the lead investigative reporter for PBS's *Frontline* series, I would craft a proposal to send to his bosses in Boston; and lastly, as a long shot, I would write a fictional screenplay *roman à clef* thriller that might start a controversy over the secrecy surrounding the killing. I devoured how-to-write-screenplay books by the likes of Syd Field, bought a used Macintosh SE with a gargantuan one megabyte of RAM, and got to work. By mid-1988, without knowing anyone in Hollywood, I sent that rather amateurish feature script to the Santa Monica office of the only power player who seemed to relish tackling political controversies, Hollywood's *bête noir* wunderkind, Oliver Stone, fresh from *Salvador, Platoon,* and *Wall Street.*

I worked on all of these strategies while slowly closing down my apartment. But before the relocation, there was at least one more musical adventure worth noting. Although the computers and their DJ co-conspirators were winning the club wars, there were a few battle victories worth savoring for the lowly real musician. Those of us who could solo still had the coffee houses to fall back on, and it was at one of those venues that the next crazy adventure commenced. One of my favorite hangouts, and occasional performance venue, was Caffé Lena[**], in nearby Saratoga Springs, a second-floor java joint with iconic stature. Lena Spencer opened the tiny second floor venue in 1960, and (as detailed in Chapter 12) was the acoustic home of countless legends, including Bob Dylan and Arlo Guthrie. It was at the Caffé that I formed lifelong friendships with the likes of jazzers John and Bucky Pizzarelli, and former Kingston Trio member John Stewart.

Dylan, girlfriend/muse/artiist Suze Rotolo, Lena, and Pasha the Cat.   Caffé entrance   Don Mclean on stage

When I saw that one of my top youthful musical inspirations, John Phillips, was scheduled at the Caffé for two nights, I bought my tickets immediately. I had been aware of John since his days with The Journeymen, a group formed by Kingston Trio manager Frank Werber in 1961, when Werber was among the few who knew that Trio founder Dave Guard would soon be leaving the group due to financial and other disputes — this new group with Phillips was planned as Werber's

---

[**] Still open today, the Caffé is the longest running coffee house in the US. Lena passed away in 1989.

fallback. But the Trio reformed with John Stewart taking Guard's spot, the Journeymen foundered, and Phillips survived for a time by co-writing with Stewart some of the Trio's best new songs. As a Trio fanatic, I was well aware of these great tunes ("Chilly Winds," "Oh, Miss Mary," "Goin' Away for to Leave You."), and had played them in my early CYO folk groups.

Phillips next surfaced in late 1965, when his mind blowing composition "California Dreamin,'" sung by his new group, first emanated from car radios, causing many a teen driver to pull over lest they crash from the exhilaration the song produced. It wasn't until I saw this new group, *The Mamas and the Papas*, on the Ed Sullivan Show that I realized its leader was the same guy who had written for the Trio. Formed with brilliant Canadian tenor Denny Doherty, ex-Baltimorean Cass Elliott (ne Ellen Cohen), and recently expelled high school beauty from California Michelle "Michie" Gilliam (soon-to-be Mrs. Phillips), the group created a sumptuous blend of folk, rock, Brian Wilson, Four Freshmen, and Kingston Trio. Naturally, Phillips immediately entered my pantheon of greats.††

Also, as noted in Chapter Four, Phillips, at the height of his popularity organized with producer Lou Adler the first, and arguably best, outdoor rock festival, Monterey Pop, in 1967.‡‡ But by sheer chance, John had in recent years become a fixture in Bolton Landing— my town!—where he had supposedly come to dry out after a drug trafficking conviction in Manhattan in 1981. I had met him

Papa John as I knew him in the Eighties

---

†† Some examples of Phillips's songs: Monday, Monday, Go Where You Wanna Go, California Dreamin', Creeque Alley, Look Through My Window, Twelve-Thirty: Young Girls Are Coming To The Canyon, Words of Love, I Saw Her Again Last Night, San Francisco (Be Sure To Wear Some Flowers In Your Hair) (for Scott McKenzie), Kokomo (for the Beach Boys).
‡‡ Some of the other performers: Laura Nyro, The Association, Lou Rawls, Johnny Rivers, The Animals, Simon & Garfunkel, The Byrds, Country Joe & The Fish, Al Kooper, Paul Butterfield Blues Band, Steve Miller, Jefferson Airplane, Booker T, The Grateful Dead, Scott McKenzie, and the Mamas & the Papas.

barside a couple of times at clubs that my band had worked, especially The Landing and The Algonquin. John was usually plastered on screwdrivers, so not much came of it, however I was not about to miss a rare performance of the master at Lena's.

On opening night of the two-night stand, I went with a few friends and guitar students and listened as John attacked his classics with a couple of back-up musicians, and no soundman. Always the best of raconteurs, John was very entertaining, but his playing was beyond sloppy: out of tune, forgetful, poorly balanced, and painful to the ears of musicians. John jokingly brushed off his inability to remember the intros to some of his songs, saying he was lucky to remember his name after living through the sixties.

"Anybody out there remember the Sixties?" John asked. "Well, if you do then you couldn't have been there."[§§] Funny line, but most of us didn't come to hear stand-up. I felt I had to rescue a member of the pantheon. Thus, during his break, I re-introduced myself, and suggested ever so politely that, being familiar with the room, I could quickly re-set the PA (although I was a good teacher, I couldn't do anything about his musicianship in a mere thirty minutes). "Have at it," John said with his ubiquitous broad smile. I made my adjustments, and after John played the first song he was so impressed with the improvement that he thanked me from the stage, and even audience members applauded the improvement.

At the end of the show, I asked John if I could try out his 12-string — the instrument that had been there at the creation of so many wonderful songs — and he put it in my hands without hesitation.

"Have a blast," John said. When I gripped the first chord, I knew that the instrument was one, but not the only, reason things had sounded so sour that night. If it were possible, that poor guitar was in worse shape than its owner— old strings, bowed neck, high bridge, etc. By my measure, it was unplayable. When I remarked to John that he was playing at huge disadvantage with this set-up, he wasn't surprised, noting how it had been abused on the road.

"Is it fixable?" he asked.

[§§] John was so talented, and so simultaneously out of it, that he is the only person I've ever known who could write a hit song and never even know it until the royalty statements came in. John wrote "Me and My Uncle," a Grateful Dead staple, in a 1963 haze of Tequilas, while Judy Collins had a tape recorder running. The next day John forgot the whole incident, but Judy later released the song, as did the Dead. When the checks arrived at John's house, he called Judy saying there must be some mistake: "I never wrote this!" Then Judy played him the cassette.

"Definitely, in fact, even I could make these adjustments," I explained.

"Would you mind? The only thing is I need it back for tomorrow's show," John said.

Knowing it would be an honor for me to adjust the guitar of the great John Phillips, I readily agreed to do the fix gratis. Well, I did make one demand for my services.

"John, I'll fix the guitar if you let me finish out the gig with you," I offered. "The icing on the cake is I know all the intros." I assured him I remembered them note-for-note from when I pulled them off the vinyl twenty years ago. I actually did.

"See you tomorrow at eight," he smiled. "And feel free to sing a harmony."

When the night ended, I headed home and immediately proceeded to try and get that guitar off of life support. It would be an all night affair with the curvy lady, just not the kind where you're searching for that spare toothbrush in the morning. I cut the strings off, planed and polished the frets, dressed the fingerboard, re-set the neck curve, and re-slotted the nut. Midway through my labors, I recall taking a break, standing back and looking at the instrument on my sofa.

"That's freaking John Phillips' guitar!" I thought to myself. He just gave it to a guy he barely knew, totally trusting of a stranger. Amazing. I would learn over the next year hanging with John that he was like that, seemingly only interested in having fun with his friends, and with no obvious interest in possessions other than those he could share— including drugs. I then thought of all the great songs that had been played, and possibly written, on that instrument, shook my head in amazement and got back to work. The next morning, after a couple hours sleep, I bought a new set of strings at the local music store, strung that lady up, and tried to "play in" the strings during the afternoon.

I handed John his guitar that night, and he gave it one strum and smiled that famous smile.

"Where have you been all my life?" he asked the guitar. "C'mon, let's go out and make some music," he said to me. Thus, with a giant of the era, I walked onto the tiny stage that Dylan had commanded years before. Our enthusiasm was infectious that night, as John hit his stride and I had trouble wiping the silly grin off my face, not only because of whom I was backing up, but because I happened to be playing my butt off that night. When I played both simultaneous guitar lines from the iconic intro to "California Dreamin'" John looked back at me in amazement, and after I tore through the solo to "Creeque

Alley" he "slapped me five," as one of my students, Liz Woodbury, released the shutter on her camera. Great timing, Lizzo. ***

I was in musician heaven, playing with one of my songwriting heroes, and earning his respect to boot. But jamming with Papa John that first night was bittersweet, not only because of the sadness at seeing what had become of one of the great talents (he looked fifteen years older than his actual age of fifty-three), but also because it reminded me of the good old days at the Unicorn in Ithaca, and the amazing concert experiences that used to be had on a nightly basis, but that were now becoming increasingly infrequent for all musicians. And it made me think of my long-lost troubled Lithuanian tennis pal: another brilliant, self-destructive Pied Piper with a fun-loving heart and an addictive brain.

After the gig, we went to a bar next door where John bought all the rounds, and proceeded to regale me with great tales of Lennon, McCartney, Monterey Pop, Roman Polanski, Brian Wilson, Sharon Tate, and countless other household names with whom had had played and partied. Many of these stories are recounted in his autobio (and the greatest rock autobio ever), *Papa John*. We waxed on about our mutual love of the Four Freshmen and the Hi-Los, and I wondered aloud if it was because we shared the same August 30 birthday. At some point I told John I was working on a movie called *Brain Damage*, to which he replied, "I didn't know they were making a movie of my life!"

Over the next year, I jammed with John occasionally in his cabin at the Colonial Court Motel in Bolton, which he shared with his on-again-off-again wife, South African actress Genevieve Waite, his two toddlers, Bijou and Tamerlane, with occasional visits from daughters

---

*** Lizzo was and is an amazing creative talent, and is now one of the premier chamber music composers in New York. Check her out here: http://www.heardmusic.net/
Incidentally, her nickname comes from the secret club name were all given by Paul "Pee-Wee Herman" Reubens. I used to see him perform at Caroline's Comedy Club in Chelsea before he broke it big. We all joined his fan club and were given our "secret" names, which consisted of just adding an "o" sound to your name. Somehow my code name leaked out and for years my best friends called me "Gusso." To this day, I am certain that "Danno" from *Hawaii Five-O* was also a member of our secret club.

Chynna, a stunning teen sired with Michelle, and daughter from his first wife, Mack (born Laura MacKenzie), then a hot young Hollywood actress, who shared her dad's drug dependency issues as well as his drugs.[†††]

Eventually I got to meet and play with members of the New Mamas and Papas: John, Elaine "Spanky" McFarlane (formerly of Spanky and Our Gang, singing Cass's parts), Scott McKenzie, and Mack, who filled in for her step-mom Michelle. Original Papa Denny Doherty even rolled through from time to time. Mack moved to Bolton with her husband, Lone Justice guitarist Mick Barakan (who went by the name "Shane Fontayne") and their baby boy Shane. They were set up by an old Bolton acquaintance, a lawyer and boat enthusiast with the most appropriate middle name ever, and his own massive drug problems, Rolf Ondeck Ronning. I had known Rolf, Bolton's most high-profile (read: *infamous*) attorney and Real Estate agent since the late sixties, and he was a regular at my band's Bolton gigs. We often joined him afterwards for a trippy late-night wooden boat ride up to the Narrows, as we drunkenly announced "Rolf's on deck!" which would of course be true even if he wasn't on a boat. Rolf, who had just lost his law license after serving three years for cocaine trafficking, welcomed Mack and Mick to town, found them a cabin and gave them his extra pickup truck in order to get around. The Phillips tribe was a magnet for druggies like Rolf, and the concept of them getting clean in Bolton was a running town joke. I decided to keep a safe distance from the madness.

I doubt anyone, least of all me, knows how such a dysfunctional life begins. But, for what it's worth, I have a theory, based on many talks with John, about what was one huge contributor to his decent into the abyss: he never got over losing Michelle. The pair divorced in 1970 after her serial infidelities with John's friends, fellow musicians, celebrities, and even fellow Papa, Denny Doherty. John told me how much it crushed him to know what she was doing— she didn't even try to be discreet. As Michelle later wrote in her autobiography *California Dreamin'*, "I was a terrible person, I really was…Had I been a reliable, monogamous woman, this wouldn't have been such a rocky

---

[†††] Mack, using her full middle name MacKenzie (which inspired John's early singing partner Phil Blondheim to change his name to "Scott McKenzie"), had recently starred in the hit sitcom, *One Day at a Time*. After John's death many years later, Mack recounted a long-term incestuous relationship with her father. Given both their purple-haze existences, anything was possible, including, as John joked that night at Lena's, totally damaged, undependable memories. The fog was that thick in their world. But I never saw a hint of it, nor do I believe that John would ever intentionally hurt any of his children, whom he adored.

tale... I was not stable." Many of John's most poignant hits were about Michelle's cheating ways.

The worst thing about having a rare beauty like Michelle as a mate (especially if you're an average looking guy like John) is that if it ever ends, it's all the more painful knowing that landing a goddess like that twice in one's life is almost impossible. It can eat at you until it's downright debilitating. Given that "Michie" was one of the most physically perfect human specimens ever (or as Denny called her, "The Slurp of the Century"— and he ought to know because he slurped her), John entered, in my opinion, a lifelong depression. Hell, *I've* got a schoolboy crush on Michelle and I've never even met her!

*   *   *

Moving back to Maryland was a pretty emotional affair, with decade long pals hosting going-away parties and jam sessions. With many of my friends also planning to escape from New York, we were all pretty realistic about the fact that we didn't know where our crazy journeys would take us, and had no idea if or when we'd see each other again. It was obvious that an era was coming to a close.

Logistically, the move was, typically for me, atypical. Over a period of six months, I'd leisurely boxed up my books (many hundreds) and music and delivered them to a commercial trucking company, who loaded them on palettes before delivering them to my mother's garage in Baltimore. I junked my car and furniture before loading what was left (clothes, research files, amps, speaker, guitars and other musical gear) into a Ryder truck and set out for the eight-hour drive, accompanied by a friend from Maryland, while charting the new course.

I financed the interregnum by following the advice of Papa John, who advised that I should just do what he did when he organized the Mamas and the Papas in St. Thomas by running up a $30,000 American Express Card tab (about $200,000 today), which he never paid off. It worked for him, he said. "I still can't get a credit card," John told me, "but I can buy a mansion in Beverly Hills with cash, so go figure."

Thus, upon arrival in Catonsville, I headed straight for the ATM, and proceeded to withdraw the first of many $500 cash advances from Visa (I didn't qualify for AmEx), ending up a couple of years later with a bill totaling less than half of John's, while making minimum monthly payments. Much as John went to the Virgin Islands to forge his new band, I took off for Hawaii for the next few months, staying with friends, but unlike John Phillips, cleared my head of professional music for the first time in twenty years. Between tennis matches in Hawaii, I crafted the proposals for PBS and Frontline, and waited for a reply from Stone.

Once again, Hawaii was perfect. In addition to the normal joys of Paradise, other highlights included meeting another Beatle (my third[‡‡‡]) on Maui and running into, of all people, John Phillips in Honolulu. I was on one of many side trips to Maui with a friend when we stopped at a shave ice stand near Wailua on the Hana Road, which meanders along the north shore to the sleepy village of Hana on the east coast. As we approached the stand, the customer in front of us was just paying for his rainbow-colored treat, and when he turned around I instantly recognized George "the quiet Beatle" Harrison, there with a local friend who turned out to be a caretaker at George's 63-acre estate in Nahiku, not far from Wailua. I introduced myself and we chitchatted for a few minutes at a picnic bench.

George Harrison with his wife Olivia in Hawaii

Although he was initially very reserved — I suspect because since John's murder he had to be wary of "fans" — he soon loosened up when I told him of my own "Beatle band" days in high school. He smiled when I told him how many years I struggled with his guitar riff to "Help!" when the singers say "Won't you *pleeaasse, please* help me?" George said that he thought he nicked it from a rockabilly record, maybe Carl Perkins. "Funny," he said. "You wanted to sound like us, and all we wanted to do was sound like your Elvis." He spoke of his

---

[‡‡‡] In addition to the previously mentioned encounters with John Lennon, in the early seventies, I managed to crash a Paul McCartney recording session at New York's A & R Studios, thanks to an engineer friend who worked there. I sat in the booth and eavesdropped as Paul spent an hour or so laying down a piano track for the *Ram* album. Paul was most gracious when I met him at the end of the session. Three down, Ringo to go.

love for the ukulele and the tranquil Maui east coast, which I also loved. The encounter inspired me to write a new song, "Hawaii," which included a tribute to Hana. Soon George was flashing us a shaka sign as he jumped into his Jeep and bid us a smiling "Aloha," albeit with a Liverpool accent.

A far more coincidental Hawaiian brush with celebrity took place when I opened the *Honolulu Advertiser* and saw that my Bolton Landing pals, John Phillips and the New Mamas and Papas were playing a gig at Gussie L'Amour's nightclub out near the Honolulu International Airport. Opened for about five years at the time, Gussie's was a locals' hangout, far from the tourist areas of the island. It was a low-rent "sports bar," with a large pool room and a performance area that featured everything from female oil wrestling to closed circuit sporting events to the occasional big name concert with performers as varied as The Stray Cats and Nancy Sinatra. On the night of John's show, I took a date whom I'm certain thought many of my crazy tales were the product of a vivid fantasy life. Sometimes even I thought so.

Thus when she went off to the ladies room, I made my way backstage and got hugs all around from the band. I returned to our table, and a few songs into the set, John addressed the crowd of about 200 Hawaiians.

"Ladies and gentlemen, we have an old friend in the crowd tonight. Let's have a big hand for one of the best guitarists in New York, Gus Russo!" With that, the crowd of befuddled locals politely applauded someone they had never even heard of. Towards the end of the show, John invited me to sing along the group on his newest composition, "Kokomo," then a hit for the Beach Boys, and the ultimate show closer, "California Dreamin'." For both tunes I shared a mic with John's troubled daughter Mack.[§§§]

1988-89 represented my last extended stay in Hawaii, although I would continue to vacation there whenever possible, never losing sight of my goal to return with a vengeance when it was Social Security time. In the meantime, I returned to Maryland to see if my various proposals would ignite the next series of adventures. Not in my wildest dreams could I have predicted what was waiting for me on the Mainland.

[§§§] Sadly, Gussie's closed in 2004.

Chapter Eighteen

Beginnings and Endings

AMONG THE MESSAGES waiting for me upon arrival in Maryland was one from ASCAP, the American Society of Composers, Authors and Publishers. This organization protects the copyrights of composers and handles the disbursement of performance royalties for their works. I could only guess that they were trying to persuade me to join their ranks, since I had written a slew of commercial jingles years before. I recalled receiving what appeared to be form letters from ASCAP when I lived in Glens Falls, and I had routinely tossed them unopened into the circular file. Never being much of a joiner, my trashcan was always clogged with anything I perceived to be a "come-on" for membership. But this ASCAP gang was more persistent than most, so when they called again I took the call and began to tell them I wasn't interested, when the voice on the other end interrupted, saying, "Well, you should be, unless you want me to tear up this check."

"Come again?"

"This is the same 'Gus Russo' who composed *Basket Case* and *Brain Damage*?" the ASCAP rep asked.

"It depends," I said. "Is that 'Gus Russo' being sued for plagiarism?" I suddenly worried that my Bernard Herrmann inspirations might have crossed the legal line.

"Not at all," the rep said. "That 'Gus Russo' has had a large royalty check sitting here for three years, and we're about to give up trying to find him. Too bad for him."

"Don't give up just yet," I said. "I'm him." I gave ASCAP my mother's address, and one week later I received a check, with a statement showing all the bank interest that had accrued over the years of my being unreachable. Grand total: $21,000 (about $35,000 in today's money), a virtual pot of gold for a musician about to insanely embark on another low-paying vocation, writing. The bounty afforded me the wherewithal to rent a nice suburban three-story townhouse, pay off my credit card debt, buy a chocolate lab puppy (Scout), a tortoise shell kitten (Mrs. Teasedale), some furniture for them to destroy, and most importantly, the CD of *Pet Sounds*, which finally got released after seven years of delays.

It would be the beginning of an almost simultaneous run of good fortune that convinced me that I must be pretty adept at writing proposals: in rapid succession, I heard from PBS' Jennifer Lawson, *60 Minutes*' Don Hewitt, CBS's Dan Rather, *Frontline*'s Mike Sullivan, and Hollywood's Oliver Stone (hence the first chapter of this book). Amazingly, all wanted to work with me in some capacity— was Pele thanking me for those gifts? I enlisted a group of friends as house sitters, bought some luggage, and proceeded to rack up so many frequent flier miles that my next four round trips to Hawaii and one to Spain were free.

The inertia and synergy from these associations would propel the next twenty years of my life, in which I would write, research, or produce sixteen documentaries for major networks in four countries, write seven books[*] (including this), and have countless more bizarre encounters and adventures, as I investigated, often in tandem with the world's most talented investigative icons, the mysteries of my youth: the JFK assassination, the shadow world of organized crime, the death of Marilyn Monroe, UFOs, the CIA's real "X-Files," among them. The profits, of course, went to buying new guitars and various animal charities.

The crazy stories and anecdotes have continued to pile up as I have chased down and interviewed over 8,000 people (according to my computerized address book) since that first paid foray with Jack Anderson, but those tales are for another book. Should there be sufficient interest in this first volume, I'll take a deep breath and jump into the second, in which I track down legendary gangsters, alleged and actual assassins, spies from at least five countries, Lee Harvey Oswald's daughters, not to mention his widow, and most importantly, skinny dip in the waters of Ibiza with a Swedish flight attendant.[†] Actually, now that I think about it, the truly most important part of the whirlwind has been the countless new friends I have made in far-flung corners of the world. But then again, that Swede...

Along the way, there have been the losses of relatives, girlfriends, pets, and library books— all the expected events that are a part of a natural plan, and therefore are eventually comprehendible.

---

[*] Hollywood has optioned two of my books, bought one outright, and two of my feature scripts are under strong consideration at this writing.
[†] Personal highlights included getting thanked for my assistance by the lawyers who crushed OJ Simpson in his civil trial, acknowledged from the dais of the National Press Club by Oliver Stone, from the Grammy stage by the Kingston Trio, from the Beverly Hills Friars Club podium by Steve Allen, and becoming instrumental in securing the release of over five million secret government documents.

Then there's that first personal tragedy that makes no sense and catapults you into a new, more sanguine take on life. One such shocking loss carried a special symbolism for me and the time I have grown up in that it merits mention before I hit the "save" command one last time. I wouldn't mention it except for the fact that it felt to me like a fitting exclamation point on the end of a pretty happy-go-lucky era. The passing of tennis's youthful Pied Piper was all the more searing given the irony that his name meant "life," yet in 1994 he gave new meaning to the tennis term "sudden death."

Like me, my old Lake George buddy, Vitas Gerulaitis, who was now 40-years old, was also happily at the beginning of a promising new stage in his life. We were two Baby Boomers in our forties just trying to marry our bliss to some sort of profession— almost like grown-ups. Although my friend had attained heights I never would, part of the reason we felt connected was because we were both guys from humble roots, with families who worked their way up from nothing. And despite setbacks, we had done pretty well with what we were bequeathed— racquets, guitars, and the love of a family.

Vitas appeared in Seattle on September 16, 1994, where he participated in a seniors doubles match/exhibition with four of his best friends, Jimmy Connors, Bjorn Borg, and John Lloyd. In addition to embracing the game again after his descent in the eighties, Vitas, now a phoenix, had recently broken new ground as television's first full-time color tennis analyst. Working the US Open for CBS the previous two weeks, he was a natural, providing great insight and humor in the booth during the matches, and engaging the players who loved him down on the court for post-match interviews. He set the standard for all the player/analysts that were to follow. Watching him for those two weeks had actually convinced me to start going back to the Open the next year now that Vitas was back on the scene. The party had returned after a fourteen-year hiatus.

Those who were there in Seattle on the 16th described the doubles match as more like a comedy concert than a tennis match, with all eyes on Vitas the Ringmaster, who had the crowd in stitches with every piece of *schtick* he grabbed from his vast comedy arsenal; he obviously brought out his "A" material for this gig. The other players didn't have a chance, with icons Borg and Connors, two of the most exciting champions in history, becoming practically invisible, as they joined the audience cracking up at their pal's antics.

"You should have seen Vitas in Seattle," Lloyd later recalled. "You should have *heard* him. After the first set, I said to Jimmy, 'The other three of us might as well not even be here. This is Vitas' room.' And Jimmy said, 'Aren't they all?'"

"From all the signs of what I saw in Seattle," Connors added, "he was back to being the old Vitas in the way he played and had fun. He brought the house down."

After the match, Vitas approached Jimmy, who was also the tour creator, and begged off from the next day's match in order to play in a charity event run by Jack Whitaker and his wife, former tennis star Nancy Chaffee Whitaker, that same day all the way back in New York. Connors wasn't happy to lose his crowd pleaser, but he relented, knowing how much charity work meant to the Lion. Two days later — and for the rest of his life — Jimmy would regret that he had ever allowed Vitas to leave the "Emerald City." Vitas lived for his friends and charities— and Jimmy knew it. Just eleven days earlier at the Open, Vitas had performed another act of mercy for the number one player in the world, an introvert who bonded with few in the tennis world, but he was absolutely helpless when confronted with the charm of the Lithuanian Lion.

"I couldn't tell you I had any close friends in high school," Pete Sampras said. "You need them. Vitas is someone I can talk to." To Pete, he had become "Uncle Vitas," the mentor who gave him priceless pointers for free before he made it to the top of the heap. Thus Pete joined our happy fraternity, the one that called Vitas a "brother," and the friendship that began on a driving range in Florida a few years ago became a rock of strength for Sampras.

At that 1994 Open, Sampras, out of shape because of an injury early in the summer, lost his legs against Peruvian Jaime Yzaga in the fourth round, nearly ruined his feet, the bottoms raw by the end. He never even got to a fifth-set tie-breaker— Yzaga, a tough baseliner ranked No. 23 in the world that day, beat him 7-5 in the last set.

"I hit the wall," Sampras said. "After I lost that match to Yzaga I collapsed on the floor in the trainer's room, and there were all these doctors hovering around," Sampras recalled. "When the IV kicked in for me, the first thing I saw was the familiar face of Vitas Gerulaitis. And I told everyone to leave but him. Vitas unlaced my shoes, put a dry shirt on me, packed up my bag, and told me he understood just how bad I was feeling." Vitas then carried Sampras's racquets back to the locker room, then later out to his car, and when the reporters began to encircle Pete, Vitas put him in the car and took the time to give the reporters some quotes, running the gauntlet for his friend who was too weak to speak.

"There were days when I needed someone to carry my racquets, and I was just a contender," Vitas told Mike Lupica that night. "Today I carried the champion's rackets."

"He was just there to get me better, and that's the memory I have of him. That's the sort of friend he was," said Sampras, who had golfed with Gerulaitis in Portland, just before Seattle, and had planned to take a vacation with him "to golf school" in December (in recent years, Vitas had become obsessed with the game).

It was just typical Vitas. Three years earlier, he had helped his pal Connors off of the court after a stunning, and draining, 5-set quarterfinal US Open victory by the 39-year-old over 24-year-old upstart Aaron Krickstein. So I suppose Jimmy felt he owed Vitas one when he asked to be relieved of his duties in Seattle.

Taking the Friday night red-eye back to his stomping grounds, Vitas dropped his bags off the next morning in a pool cottage at the 4.5-acre Southampton estate of real estate tycoon and friend Marty Raynes, located at 170 Meadow Lane, near Shinnecock Bay. Bleary eyed, he then, as promised, went to play in the charity event before coming back to the estate for a well-deserved late afternoon nap in the cottage.

As was his fashion, he played himself to sleep with his trusty old Strat, a model instrument that I recall recommending to him when he was a 15-year-old kid playing a cheap Les Paul knock-off. This would be the last time he played it. They found him the next day, fully clothed, his guitar and tennis racquets by his side along with an uneaten sandwich.

I was back in Maryland when the news came across CNN. Having just watched Vitas for two weeks on CBS, I had been elated that he was back, and now this. It was a cruel twist of fate and a jarring personal shock, to say the least. My first reaction was the same as everyone who knew him: he must have relapsed. Either that, or his heart, weakened from years of coke abuse, just gave out. Maybe he wasn't a phoenix after all, but still an Icarus. At least that would be an ending we could understand and live with, but the one we got in the coming days made the tragedy all the more senseless and harder to accept.

It turned out that my friend had succumbed to carbon monoxide poisoning, the result of a swimming pool heater that had leaked into the air conditioning system of the pool cottage where he napped. An autopsy showed the gas had displaced 75% of the oxygen in Vitas's blood. I thought instantly of how another 40-year-old guitarist who, 14 years earlier, had also just turned his life around, only to see it end for no reason. Vitas became tennis's John Lennon, except that Vitas spent more time in Harlem with the poor.

Vitas's wake was held at St. Dominic's Church in Oyster Bay, near the home he shared with his now inconsolable mother and sister; they had just lost the family patriarch, "Mr. G," three years earlier, but they never expected this. Tennis tournaments around the world were canceled, as the top players flocked to the North Shore for the funeral of tennis's most beloved ambassador. I was so shaken that I couldn't bring myself to go. I absolutely dread funerals, and try to avoid them whenever possible, preferring to give my condolences to the family privately. It just seems to me that those closest to the deceased suffer horribly at these affairs, and I couldn't bear to see Mrs. G go through it. I'm sure there are studies that show that funerals help the healing process, but I never bought it. Seeing the waxen figure of someone you wish to remember in life just seems to compound the loss, and having all those eyes staring at you while you're trying to cope just seems to ratchet up the pressure. I was later told that Ruta and Mrs. G collapsed into each other's arms at the wake. "My boy had plans again," Mrs. G had cried. "My boy had plans."

On the other hand, I believe that carrying a friend to his final rest is an honor, and had I have been asked, I would have done so without hesitation. Instead, I called Ruta and her mom to offer my condolences and explained why I wouldn't be there, but I would prefer to make a large contribution to Vitas's Youth Foundation. Hearing my cracking voice, they were very understanding. I sent them a long letter of condolence, and Ruta sent me a beautiful reply, together with the Mass Cards. In the letter, Ruta wrote, "I must tell you how touched we were by your words. We laughed and cried at the same time. I even made copies of your letter, because it can be enjoyed by so many people who loved Vitas. You are really a very special friend." The letter meant so much to me that I saved it. It was possibly the first time I realized that I might possess a gift for writing, or at least for affecting people with my writing. That boost was very likely one of the factors that led me to pursue a writing career — a posthumous gift from my old Howard Beach pal.

Poignantly, the number one, two, and three players from 1979 (Borg, McEnroe, and Connors) were among Vitas's pallbearers, while that year's number four was in the coffin they now carried. They were also carrying Vitas's favorite #5 iron, placed inside the coffin by his sister. Waiting inside the church were a *Who's Who* of tennis history: Billie Jean King, Chris Evert, Tony Trabert, John Lloyd, Fred Stolle, and Cliff Drysdale, among them. Also there were celebs like comedian Alan King, actress Janet Jones and her husband Wayne Gretsky. Everyone there heard eulogies fit for a king.

"I remember this big blond streak," fellow pro and analyst Mary Carillo said, remembering the first time she saw Vitas when they were both teen-agers at the Port Washington Tennis Academy. "He was the most dazzling thing I'd ever seen." She made the church laugh with her stories because Vitas was still in the room and he was all about laughter. She recalled the infamous pajama party he threw in his Pittsburgh hotel room on his 21st birthday, the one where he invited everyone in attendance at that night's WTT match to come— a thousand showed up, much to the uninformed hotel manager's dismay. Then Jimmy Connors was up, telling about a time when a fan in Huntsville, Alabama mistook Vitas for Bjorn, even with Bjorn in the same elevator. Vitas signed his buddy's name and when Connors asked him why later, he replied, "Always give them something to make them happy." Tough guy Connors barely held it together as

Mrs. G and Ruta

Johnny Mac in shock

he finished by saying, "He was my friend and I loved him and I'm going to miss him." Then Connors lost it. The other tough guy in the room, Johnny Mac, had been asked to speak, but he was so distraught that he had to decline, unable to stop crying. Everyone cried that day at

St. Dominic's. It was Vitas's room again, and he controlled the situation, as usual.

The mourners then followed Vitas's hearse to St. Charles Cemetery in Farmingdale. All the top players were there, most in tears. Janet Jones later remarked that it seemed as though these giants had all "lost their heart." The wound would remain raw for all of us who were lucky to know Vitas. Sixteen years later, when a long overdue documentary on Vitas was produced, most of these icons choked up or cried, and Jones practically sobbed. It was as though Vitas had died yesterday, the injury was still that fresh. It was all that Jimmy Connors could do to not break down again, his chin twitching with emotion. When Thanksgiving arrived a few weeks later, Jimmy took care of all the Gerulaitis family's expenses when he flew them out to his California home to spend that first difficult holiday without their boy.

Mac, Connors, and Borg carry their pal to his final rest.

At the graveside, Msgr. Charles Ribaudo said "Telling Vitas Gerulaitis stories, that's what's going to live on." And indeed they did. In the coming days and weeks, the testimonials poured in:
• For John McEnroe, Vitas was "an inspiration," a kid from the old neighborhood who conquered the big time, a kid he "looked up to."
• Pat O'Brien: "When you sat with Vitas you had the best seat in the house...Simply put, to know Vitas was to love him."
• Janet Jones: "His game plan was always to give, never to take."
• Chris Evert: "Vitas put friends and family before money and career."
• Mike Lupica: "He loved all the charity work with all of his great heart."
• John Lloyd: "He was a great bloke. You never picked up a tab with Vitas. It didn't matter if you went out with him and 10 other people he didn't even know. He would have his credit card out before anybody. He had a very generous spirit. Someone told me that one year he had the third highest American Express bill for an individual in the world. He would use it to fly everywhere with ladies in private jets."
• Brad Gilbert: "I only saw his good side, never saw him mistreat anybody, and no matter if any of the scars from his past show up in his heart, what matters was that he was a guy with a great heart."
• Bob Binns, college classmate: "I'll remember Vitas as a guy who wanted to be liked by everyone and pretty much was. At Columbia, Vitas could be counted on to stick his head in the dorm room and say:

'Enough studying. Let's go out.'"

•Guillermo Vilas: "Vitas always loved kids. He always referred to himself as a fighter, and he always liked to help kids overcome whatever was happening to them. He was from New York, where it's hard to play tennis, and if kids said they couldn't play tennis, he would tell them: 'I got a racquet. I played. I hustled my way in.' He was teaching them how to survive. He'd tell them to play against the wall, hang out, get friendly and ask people to play with them."

•Alan King: "He was bigger than life, a great figure, and a pretty good tennis player. He was a very New York type of figure, not unlike Joe Namath."

Ruta thinks her brother's death accelerated their mother's decline and eventual death from Alzheimer's, although she also believes the disease was a blessing in disguise "because eventually she was able to forget he died or ever had a son." Ruta, meanwhile, cherishes the memories, and the walls of her home bear her favorite photos of her always-smiling big brother. "I carry a pocket-size photo of him in my purse," she adds.

Although many friends were frustrated that Vitas never achieved the number one ranking, the fact is that he pulled off something infinitely more difficult. All Vitas really wanted, he told one interviewer, was for the world to love him. He certainly achieved that lofty goal. "Everyone loves Vitas," was a common phrase heard in the men's locker room during his years on the tour. If you introduced yourself in the players' lounge, as I so often did, as a friend of Vitas's, you were "in." As *New York Times* sports columnist Neil Amdur wrote in memoriam, "To those closest to Gerulaitis, his friendship was a source of strength. For Gerulaitis, pleasing his friends, on and off the court, was perhaps his greatest source of satisfaction."

Not a US Open goes by without one of the commentators (usually Mac, or Jimmy, or Drysdale) invoking Vitas's name when something funny occurs on the court. Usually they say something like, "Vitas did that first," or "Vitas would have loved that." These quips are usually followed by an awkward silence before someone, often McEnroe, says, "We miss you, Vitas."

Vitas, a true pioneer in giving back to the community, and perhaps the most admired tennis star of his time, lives on through the Vitas Gerulaitis Youth Foundation, founded many years before his death, which in turn supports the Vitas Gerulaitis Youth Tennis Center in Queens, New York. The foundation promotes the greatest sport to inner city kids of today, and continues Vitas's unselfish devotion to the game. The Vitas Gerulaitis "For the Love of Tennis" Award is presented yearly by the USTA (United States Tennis Association)/Eastern Long Island Region. New York City bestows a Community Service Award in his name, and the "Ready, Set, Racquet!" program, inspired by Vitas, has distributed more than 150,000 junior tennis racquets at WTT matches and other events. In Vilnius, the capital of Lithuania, a homeland he never even got to visit, there is now the Vitas Gerulaitis Memorial Tennis Centre.

Another legacy: many credit Vitas's death for the launch of the carbon monoxide detector industry. First Alert detector sales skyrocketed after the tragedy on Long Island. Chicago began requiring them in most homes in 1994. Soon New York joined Rhode Island, West Virginia, New Jersey, and about two-dozen cities and counties in requiring homebuilders to install carbon monoxide detectors in every new house. As a result, untold hundreds of lives have been saved.

THE PIED PIPER

I have no idea what comes after this crazy life, but there are many of us who hope that whatever it is it includes hanging with Vitas again, only this time we pick up the check.

*   *   *

OK, we're getting close. I can feel it. As we approach the finish line, allow me a few paragraphs to convey my intentions in writing *Boomer Days*. My fondest hope is that I've provided some moments of pleasant nostalgia for all my fellow Boomers who lived through this insane time. But my more-fondest hope is that those of you who arrived later on the scene will now get some idea of what this "Sixties thing" was all about, and why old people prattle on about it *ad nauseum*. And my even-more-fondest hope is that you will "get it," and take a step back from the joyless digital brink on which you so precariously cling. I know that speed is the thing today, but those of us who have seen both the IGY world and the 4G world can tell you uncategorically that the slower speed was infinitely more enlightening, rewarding, and just plain fun.

A word to the "digital natives": For those of my generation who created much of this over-populated, polluted, celebrity obsessed, techno world, I sincerely apologize. We American Boomers were the most fortunate of all the post-industrial revolution generations: we arrived after the horrific global conflicts of the twentieth century, but before the coming twenty first century global collapse of the environment, and the civilizations that depend on it. Yet we squandered the opportunity. But, with luck, it's still not too late to cast off the past and carpe diem. I am convinced that your generation is the last best hope for humankind to avoid the terrifying world envisioned by philosophers like Craig Dilworth (*Too Smart For Our Own Good*, 2010), leading scientists and environmentalists like Lester Brown in his *Plan B* book series, or even that cultural wasteland depicted by filmmaker Mike Judge in his 2006 black comedy *Idiocracy*. So, become involved while there is still just a remote chance that this beautiful world and *all* the creatures that inhabit it can still be salvaged. There is almost no time left. Seriously.

We hippie "tree-huggers," "peaceniks," and "vegans" actually had a pretty good idea, now you have the challenge to realize it. If you figure out a way to save this curious grain of sand on the universal beach and return to a more humane way of life, you'll put all of us "peace and love" types to shame. But it won't be easy; the vast majority of humankind seems completely unable — or unwilling — to see what's so obviously coming, and they'll fight you at every turn in order to blindly preserve the bloated, self-destructive, status quo. But I'm rooting for you.

And, while you're at it, take a deep breath, and when you exhale try whistling a great melody (have you noticed that young

people don't whistle anymore?). Music may be the greatest contribution of our supremely flawed species to the cosmological soup, so embrace it. Then unplug, adopt a dog, pick up a guitar or tennis racquet, and stick out your thumb. The real world and the beautiful animals that inhabit it put the virtual one to shame, and we're losing it fast. The experience of actually seeing it might provide you the needed motivation to do what's urgently needed. Good Luck!
Mahalo and Aloha,

    Gus Russo
    May 2011

FADE OUT: MUSIC UP— As CREDITS ROLL a CHORUS sings:
    "Row, row, row your boat gently down the stream.
    Merrily, merrily, merrily, merrily — life is but a dream

Epilogue

SOON AFTER VITAS'S PASSING, I found myself in Hawaii on vacation. A friend and I drove along the Kalanianaole Highway one morning and ended up near Koko Head watching a pod of dolphins frolicking about a quarter mile offshore. My friend Joanie pointed out a solitary white-haired kayaker near the shoreline.

"You know who that is?" she asked.

"No idea."

"Well, it's Captain Adam Troy," she explained. "He's down here almost every day."

Indeed it was. Gardner McKay, who inspired me so much as a youth watching him portray Captain Troy every week as he sailed the South Pacific in search of adventure on the television series *Adventures in Paradise*, had in fact traded in his schooner for a kayak and was living in Hawaii.

"Aloha, Captain Troy!" we yelled to him. He just looked up, smiled, and flashed a shaka back at us. I knew his TV character was a hero, but I had no idea that the man behind the image might also be admirable. But after he died in seven short years, his widow published his memoir, entitled *Journey Without a Map* (I wish I had thought of that), and it gave me a new respect for the man behind the illusion. It turns out that we had more in common than James A. Michener. Like me, Gard had spent great years in Ithaca, where he attended Cornell, and like me he had rejected a conventional life in favor of following his bliss. After walking out on his stardom at its height, he traveled the world endlessly in search of peace and wisdom, and, like me, he came to love animals more than most humans. Among the many tasty epigrams he left behind were: "We are all circling the drain; some of us are better swimmers," and the last words of the book: "We began with simplicity, we worked, traveled, fought, lived a lifetime, and if we've been lucky, we've attained simplicity."

Thus, in the spirit of Captain Troy, I feel it incumbent upon me to share with readers like you, who gave me so much of their precious time, a few more *bon mots*, ideas that I have plastered to the wall above my computer in an effort to keep balanced in an unbalanced world. I hope that some of them resonate with you.

"The struggle itself towards the heights is enough to fill a man's heart. One must imagine Sisyphus happy."
— Camus, in his essay *The Myth of Sisyphus*

"Write from the heart."
— John Stewart

"Things Change."
— Batman

"Reject rejection."
— Yours truly

"Be kind to the animals, the true custodians of the planet, for they are helpless against humans, who kill and mistreat trillions of them a year."
— Yours truly

"Chance favors the prepared mind."
— Pasteur

"The earth is a depot, where wingless angels pass the time waiting for the long ride home. Seeing a small boy smiling in the corner I said: 'You must be anxious to go home.' 'I am home,' he replied. 'I just come here to play the games.'"
— Oliver Makin, 1903

"Sometimes nothing can be a real cool hand."
—"Lucas Jackson"

And some anonymous quotes I wish I had invented:

"If you dare, keep investing in yourself. In fact, double down."

"You can't stay young forever, but you can act immature your whole life."

"The more I see of man, the more I like dogs."

"Don't fight for land, fight for perspective."

"Stuff is the enemy of freedom."

"I want to be the person my dog thinks I am."

"Only you can prevent narcissism"

*　　　*　　　*

Acknowledgements and Mea Culpas

As you might imagine, it is impossible to individually acknowledge all of the enabling earthly, and possibly divine, creatures that contributed to a lifelong roller coaster ride. Thus, a blanket "Thank You" goes out to all of you — you know who you are — who in any way contributed to the experiences and memories contained herein.

But this physical depiction you now hold in your hands owes its specific existence to a handful of friends who convinced/coerced me to type it up, and others who then aided in its production. For years, I have been goaded into writing down these anecdotes, but I was able to successfully parry my friends' exhortations with my own counter-arguments: I'm too busy; no one would publish it; it's too egotistical, etc., etc. It wasn't until neighbor and University of Maryland Baltimore County (UMBC) writing instructor Mitzi Mabe introduced me to her esteemed retired colleague, Professor Wally Shugg, that I ran out of excuses. Over many a dinner conversation they argued that my journey was more than a tad interesting, informative, and as so it should be passed on to a new generation curious about "The Sixties," and to my Boomer peers who are now retiring and might be looking for something nostalgic to read.

I was nonetheless doing just fine in my refusal stance until Wally said ever so forcefully: "There's no argument. You have to do it. Just write one page a day before you start your other work, and in a year or so you'll have a book." It was a brilliant dialectic for which I had no good retort. A page a day is not that much work (I thought), and I had nothing better to do at 6 a.m.— except sleep! Mitzi and Wally even offered to read and critique chapters as they were created and to listen once a month as I read them aloud. Lastly, Mitzi even volunteered her college students to read the pages-in-progress. One evening, too tired to argue anymore, I gave up, went home and set my alarm. And here we are, three hundred-plus pages later.

Thanks also go to Mitzi's writing students at UMBC who took valuable time from their studies (not to mention the onslaught of pressing text messages and tweets) to read and respond so enthusiastically to the early pages.

Next up comes neighbor Brendan Kennedy, photographer and graphic designer for his company BK Design, who volunteered his down time to shoot the covers and perform the labor-intensive interior design and layout, proofing as he went along. This little account never would have happened without Brendan's talents and selfless friendship.

Out of nowhere, writer, comedian, and fellow Bad Movie connaisseur Pat Storck volunteered to set up a website and assist with the book's needed online presence.

The collegial support of Dan Moldea's seventy-plus member "DC Author's Dinner Group" is a constant source of incredible encouragement, sharing, and endless "inside the beltway" yarns, barbs, and info. I don't know of a similar troop anywhere, and I am lucky to be part of it.

Lastly, I apologize for any factual errors. As an investigative author and documentarian for the last few life chapters, I have learned all too well about the fallibility of human memory. Memory merge, in which true memories are blurred together with what one has been told, and event compression, are almost impossible to completely overcome. Perhaps the most disturbing example of such mnemonic muddles can be seen in the groundbreaking findings of Joseph Le Doux at NYU's Center for Neural Science, which determined that memories are damaged *every time the brain retrieves them—* pretty scary stuff for those of us interested in history. All that said, much time was spent interviewing family, friends and colleagues mentioned in each chapter to make certain my recollections (and theirs) are as accurate as possible. Thanks to the nature of digital print-on-demand publishing, I can correct any errors as they come up, and will do so. So, nitpickers, have at it and pick those nits.

I predict more similar errors can be found at: www.gusrusso.com

About the Author

You want more? Geesh. Oh, alright.

For over twenty years, Gus Russo has been an investigative reporter, author of six non-fiction books, and writer and/or producer of many national and international documentaries for major networks. His books have received Book of the Month Club and History Book Club Featured Selections, three have been optioned for films, and one, *The Outfit*, was a Pulitzer nominee. His most recent book, *Brothers in Arms: The Kennedys, the Castros, and the Politics of Murder* (October 2008), was named Winner of the 2008 History Prize by the New York Book Festival.

Russo has worked an investigative reporter for PBS' Frontline series, as well as ABC News Special Reports with Peter Jennings (*Dangerous World: The Kennedy Years*, and *JFK: Beyond Conspiracy*), Dan Rather's *CBS Reports*, and Jack Anderson Specials; he has been a consultant for programs such as *Sixty Minutes, Sixty Minutes II*, and *Eye To Eye with Connie Chung*; as well as documentary productions based in England, France, Germany, Japan, and Mexico. Russo has appeared on countless radio and TV programs, including NPR's *Wait, Wait...Don't Tell Me!*, The History Channel (numerous shows), A&E's *Biography* (Jack Ruby), *Hardball with Chris Matthews*, MSNBC's *Nachman*, and Dan Rather's 1993 special *Who Killed JFK?* Russo has been a research consultant to numerous writers, including Seymour Hersh, Michael Gross, Anthony Summers, and Laurence Leamer, and has written for *The Baltimore Sun, The Nation, The Washington Post, Book Forum, American Heritage, The Huffington Post*, and for two years was a regular contributor to the health-related website Healthlynx.com. Russo recently co-produced and co-wrote the documentary feature film *Generation 9-11* for Academy Award-winning director Nigel Nobel.

In another life, Russo was a professional musician, composer, bandleader, and private instructor. In that incarnation, he played with, or in tandem with, many well-known acts including John Phillips, The New Mamas and Papas, Phoebe Snow, Michael Murphy, The Byrds, Livingston Taylor, Poco, Mary Travers (Peter, Paul and Mary), Commander Cody, and Firefall (w/ Rick Roberts). Russo the musician also wrote commercial jingles and low-budget film scores (*Basket Case, Brain Damage*, etc.)

"Oh — Hi, Mark."

Made in the USA
Lexington, KY
31 May 2011